A Guidebook for Teaching
UNITED STATES HISTORY

Earliest Times to the Civil War

A Guidebook for Teaching
UNITED STATES HISTORY

Earliest Times to the Civil War

TEDD LEVY

DONNA COLLINS KRASNOW

Allyn and Bacon, Inc.   **Boston • London • Sydney**

This book is part of A GUIDEBOOK FOR TEACHING Series

Copyright © 1979 by Allyn and Bacon, Inc., 470 Atlantic Avenue, Boston, Massachusetts 02210.

Library of Congress Cataloging in Publication Data

Levy, Tedd.
  A guidebook for teaching United States history.

  (A Guidebook for teaching series)
  Includes bibliographies.
    1. United States—History—Colonial period, ca. 1600-1775—Study and teaching.   2. United States—History—Revolution, 1775-1783—Study and teaching.   3. United States—History—1783-1865—Study and teaching.   I. Krasnow, Donna Collins, 1948- joint author.   II. Title.   III. Series.
E188.L48   973'.07   78-31805
ISBN 0-205-06503-1

Production Editor: Sandy Stanewick
Manufacturing Buyer: Linda Card

Printed in the United States of America

Dedication

To our parents
Reuben Levy and Gertrude Joseph Levy
Carroll Jeremiah Collins, Jr. and Elaine George Collins
and to our children
Janel and Jennifer Levy
Stephanie Krasnow

About the authors

Tedd Levy is currently a social studies teacher in the Norwalk, Connecticut, Public Schools. He has taught on the middle and high school levels, has authored numerous articles, and has conducted in-service workshops. He received his M.S. from the University of Bridgeport.

Donna Collins Krasnow is a United States History teacher in Norwalk, Connecticut. She has participated in the National Science Foundation sponsored program for implementing new social studies programs, has made presentations on new methods for teaching social studies, and is a graduate of the University of California, Berkeley.

Gene Stanford, Consulting Editor for the *Guidebook for Teaching Series*, received his Ph.D. and his M.A. from the University of Colorado. Among his numerous professional affiliations are Associate Professor of Education and Director of Teacher Education Programs at Utica College of Syracuse University, member of the National Council of Teachers of English, and member of the International Council on Education for Teaching. Dr. Stanford is the author of several books, among them, *A Guidebook for Teaching Composition, A Guidebook for Teaching Creative Writing, A Guidebook for Teaching about the English Language,* and *Human Interaction in Education,* all published by Allyn and Bacon, Inc.

Contents

Preface

A Guidebook for Teaching U.S. History is designed to provide practical ideas and resources for developing student understanding of significant historical events and processes. The hundreds of classroom activities are intended to reflect a variety of teaching strategies. The classroom teacher could not and would not want to use all of them.

Among the activities you will find are suggestions and forms for developing basic history and social science skills, ideas for oral and visual history projects, valuing exercises, role playing, information for brief teacher presentations, small-group activities, discussion questions, individual student investigations, class assignments, and evaluation activities for assessing student achievements.

There are many books telling teachers how to teach, but this is not meant to be one of them. This book does not suggest strict adherence to a specific instructional approach or the use of particular instructional materials. You can select those activities and materials that best suit your curriculum, textbooks, and style of instruction. We hope the variety of activities presented here tempts you to try new strategies as well.

The selections in each volume of the *Guidebook* unavoidably reflect our own preference regarding the teaching of U.S. history. We believe, for example, that students learn most effectively when they are actively participating in the learning experience. There is a time and a need for individual, small-group, and entire class work. Group activities facilitate the exchange of ideas and provide meaningful socializing experiences. And finally, we believe that the U.S. history class is an excellent forum for examining the continuing needs and concerns of human beings and for analyzing the changing times and conditions in which the human experience takes place.

We have divided our subject into two parts: volume one, *Earliest Times to the Civil War,* and volume two, *Mid-nineteenth Century to the Present.* Since our introductory comments include observations and activities that apply equally well to either volume, the first chapter for each volume is identical. Both volumes are arranged in roughly chronological order, although themes and major ideas are used as subtopics within each chapter. We think the chapter arrangement parallels most U.S. history textbooks, and the subtopic arrangement offers flexibility for other types of organization. Needless to say, we encourage you to use and adapt whatever activities are appropriate for your own needs, regardless of our placement in these volumes.

Each chapter includes five sections:

1. An introduction provides an overview of important themes and ideas for instruction;

2. A list of performance objectives for measuring student achievements is based on the methods and materials in the chapter, saving you the tedium of writing objectives for lesson plans;

3. Most of the chapter deals with the ideas and materials for student learning experiences. Designed to stimulate interest and develop insight, they may be modified to enhance almost any curriculum. And, most important, they include Reproduction Pages that can be duplicated for student use. Located in the back of each volume, these perforated pages will save you hours of preparation time;

4. A list of suggestions or additional activities is included for assessing student learning experiences. These include traditional evaluation methods as well as other approaches suitable for additional teaching activities; and

5. An annotated list of resources, books, filmstrips, photographs, slides, tapes, simulations, professional organizations, and other resources that can help the teacher. A separate appendix lists the addresses of the producers of materials.

Many of the activities and approaches included in this book were developed for, and used successfully with, our own classes. We feel confident, therefore, that many other teachers will find them useful and practical. But we have no way of knowing without feedback from those people who try them. We invite you to write us your comments about the book and have included a Feedback Form that appears at the end of each volume. Your comments will help us make improvements and will help determine the kinds of activities to include in future books in the *Guidebook for Teaching Series*.

Although much of the material in this book is derived from our own experience, we wish to acknowledge the contributions of a number of our colleagues: Karen Wiley for originally suggesting we do this book; Morris Gall for reading early drafts and making helpful suggestions; and to Carl Bauer, Alison Carter, Tom Collins, Henry Hicks, Jim McLaughlin, David Victor, and Jack Winters, who contributed ideas and parts of various chapters, improving the quality of the book and making our task easier. And our thanks go as well to the reviewers who also read the book in early stages and provided helpful suggestions—Professors Jan L. Tucker of Florida International University, Robert B. Pratt of the University of Northern Iowa, and R. Jerrald Shive of Cleveland State University; Ron Savage, Director of Secondary Social Studies in the Fairfax, Virginia, County School District; Charles L. Mistakos, Social Studies Coordinator in the Chelmsford, Massachusetts, Public Schools; and Robert Kuklis of Weston, Connecticut, High School.

Our thanks also to Gene Stanford, editor of this series, and Bob Roen, managing editor at Allyn and Bacon, for their support and encouragement during the many months we worked on this publication, and to Judith Gimple who put our final draft into publishable form.

And, for permission to reprint materials previously published, we wish to thank the Center for Global Perspectives, the Center for Teaching International Relations at the University of Denver, the American Numismatic Association, Orbis Books, The Society for History Education, Allyn and Bacon, and the National Council for the Social Studies for excerpts from several of their important publications.

First, foremost, and finally, our thanks to our spouses—Carol and Gary—who edited, criticized, tolerated late-night typing, and very much shared the drudgery as well as the excitement of writing this book.

Tedd Levy
Donna Collins Krasnow

1

Teaching U.S. History

WHAT HAPPENED?

Just as surely as a condemned man scratches lines upon the wall of his cell or a six-year-old chases the flames from the candles on her birthday cake, we all have a sense of history. It may take the form of keeping a diary or checking the calendar; it may be saving trinkets or treasured landmarks; or it may be immortalizing oneself by painting one's initials on the school wall or having them on special license plates. It may be donating a library or a library book. Or, lastly, it may be erecting a gravestone.

Our personal history records where we have been and influences where we are going. Take this case, for instance. On the second day of school, a new student came into my room with a blue laundry bag slung over his shoulder. It made him look like Santa Claus, except he wasn't very jolly. Opening his pack, he held the bottom and shook its contents onto my desk. "Here," he said, "my summer vacation." He rolled the bag into a ball and threw it with apparent disgust into the corner and left without another word.

The remains of his summer included:

- several photographs of a girl his age
- a calendar with dates circled in July and August
- an envelope without contents and dated September 1
- an inexpensive ring
- a record entitled *Time in a Bottle*
- ticket stubs
- matches from a fancy restaurant
- an empty checkbook

The reconstruction of his summer adventure is a task for a detective—or a historian. Given this evidence, how could we find out *what happened?* What additional information or evidence would we need? Where could it be obtained? How accurate and applicable is the information? What is the most plausible explanation? What remains unknown?

Historians work with insufficient or vastly overwhelming evidence. They select, organize, and seek meaning from this limited or imperfect accumulation of data. Their work is open to varying interpretations and subject to personal biases and assumptions. The method of the historian, perhaps more than the detective, is imprecise and individualistic. The detective eventually receives a verdict on his work before a court of law, or at least at some point he is able to say the case is closed. The historian, on the other hand, presents his case to the public where it becomes grist for the mills of continual reevaluation and reinterpretation.

In this *Guidebook,* we view history as the continuous and interrelated past and present. It is what we know about everything that has happened. It is what we remember about what has been said and done. It is the accumulation of past experiences for today's use. However imperfect, the study of the past is essential for understanding the way we are today.

The purpose of this book is to provide practical ways of involving students in examining *what happened.* We want to encourage learning from the experiences of others and from the ideas and actions of the past. If successful, we will help students understand that they share similar concerns with earlier individuals and that current issues have historical roots. We hope the study of history provides students with the competencies needed to shape and control their own future in a complex and changing world. In short, we want our summertime Santa to use his experiences to have a better next year.

HISTORY IN SCHOOL TODAY

Over five million students in twenty-five thousand secondary schools are studying U.S. history or taking courses in American studies. But historians say that interest in history is declining. The situation has become so alarming that they have called it a "crisis."[1]

In addition to declining interest in U.S. history, recent surveys show there is a corresponding decline in knowledge. One survey given to college freshmen found that students knew remarkably little history. They knew highlight events such as the Declaration of Independence but little of the context in which these events took place. In fact, they lacked the kind of information historians thought they needed to understand both the present and the past.[2]

While declining student interest and increasing professional concern swirl around the school scene, the teacher faces the difficult task of deciding what should be taught and how it should be done.[3] There are many approaches to investigating the past, unlimited interpretations of what has been said and done, and little agreement on what constitutes the essentials of knowledge of history. When one considers the infinite number of human interactions that occur in a single day, the artifacts created, the records written, the thoughts expressed, the actions taken, it is obvious that the raw materials of history require selectivity and organization. Only a small portion of the past can ever be known, and it is subject to

1. Richard S. Kirkendall, "The Status of History in the Schools," *Journal of American History* (September 1975), p. 569.

2. "Times Test of College Freshmen Shows Knowledge of American History Limited," *New York Times,* May 2, 1976. Also see follow-up articles in the *Times:* "High Schools Cut Priority for Teaching U.S. History," May 3, 1976; "Students Stress the Positive in History," May 4, 1976; and "History Means Little to 'Now' Generation," May 9, 1976.

3. For an insightful view of the "crisis" in history with proposals for improving conditions, see: Peter N. Stearns, "Cleo Contra Cassandra," *The History Teacher* (November 1977), pp. 7-28.

various explanations. In a sense, all history is interpretation. The task of deciding how to organize instruction in U.S. history is, in a word, difficult.

The problem of content has been handled in several ways, each with strengths and weaknesses. History has been organized chronologically, thematically, or topically, by social issues or persisting problems, by comparative approaches, and by various combinations. These approaches are all artificial arrangements that define time and place in an effort to afford insight into the human condition. The activities and observations in this *Guidebook* are applicable to any of these approaches.

A *chronological* approach to U.S. history emphasizes a sequence of development. The linear progression highlights continuity as well as change. Since there are few limitations in deciding what to study, this approach can become unwieldy and excessively concerned with *coverage* at the expense of understanding. This criticism has best been expressed as "one damn thing after another." There is little agreement among historians and educators over the value of studying history within a time-line frame of reference. Many say this approach develops a needed sense of perspective and provides a basis for historical comparisons. The chronological approach usually emphasizes large-scale national events such as wars and elections or great transformations such as the industrial revolution or the westward movement. This approach sacrifices the more intensive examination of events. However, it is the most commonly used organizational arrangement for the study of history and forms the chapter outline for this *Guidebook*.

Topical or thematic approaches to history have become increasingly popular during the past several years. An issue, event, or idea becomes the focus for defining the program, and this allows for a more intensive examination than would be possible with a chronological study. There is often an emphasis on causes and consequences and on developing a sense of perspective within the topic limitations. Concern has often been expressed that this method sacrifices the study of other important historical matters and that greater understanding of one topic does not transfer to others. Questions have been raised about the criteria for selecting particular topics. But the topical approach is often favored as the basis of mini-courses and for individual units with textbooks.

A *problems*, or *persisting issues*, approach centers on difficulties within, between, and among individuals and groups. Issues are usually selected on the basis of their value for today and are used to examine problems and the ways in which they are handled. Problems involve such matters as individual rights versus government authority; free press versus a fair trial; and other political, economic, and social issues.

The *comparative* approach is an effort to focus on similarities and differences in two or more societies. Comparisons can be made on the basis of common origins, order of occurrence, place, or some other identified characteristic. The objective is to provide students with an expanded understanding of their past and an enlarged social perspective. Increased time and trouble for preparation, often without a corresponding increase in student interest, is an initial difficulty. Also, care needs to be taken in noting that similarities can be misleading and that differences can be instructive. A favorable consideration for this approach is the time-and-place flexibility that allows for updating and globalizing U.S. history.

The difficulty of selecting and organizing history content has been recognized for many years. Paul Ward, Executive Secretary of the American Historical Association, observed some time ago that history was in trouble with accumulated facts. It will not move forward in the schools, he said, "until it decides to be radically selective and use fresh approaches. What should shape these approaches are the key issues of the mid-twentieth century." Ward went on to say: "They must be translated into specific and well-structured questions that can get satisfying answers from the historical evidence, while still remaining questions that the children know about or are likely to run into outside their history courses."[4]

A similar assertion for reorganizing history came from Richard Kirkendall, Executive Secretary of the Organization of American Historians. He said that historians can demonstrate the value of historical perspective and comparisons and the importance of a sense of time and place. Historians can work more effectively, he suggested, "to demonstrate the importance for present problems of the understanding that history supplies. The situation calls for imagination and innovation among historians and a willingness and ability to tap other disciplines. It also calls for respect for the traditions and the unique features of history itself."[5]

Realizing that history is imperfect interpretation and that only a small part of the past can be known, the selection and organization of content realistically rests with what the teacher thinks is interesting, informative, and important.[6] Based on students' needs, and probably limited by available materials and local requirements, your approach has probably been varied and reasonably successful. We encourage you to select and adapt the activities in this *Guidebook* that achieve your objectives and allow you to try new approaches.

ORGANIZING FOR INSTRUCTION: GOALS AND STUDENTS

Many claims have been made for U.S. history that sound glorious and are unquestionably accepted as important goals. A realistic appraisal often suggests that the chances of actually accomplishing many of these goals requires more than the effort of one teacher in one U.S. history classroom. Some goals are such large concerns that they deserve the attention of the entire school and community. The study of history alone cannot guarantee healthy democratic attitudes, fairness, acceptance of the dignity of human beings, honesty, appreciation for "the American way of life," true patriotism, or sound moral values. There are, of course, wide differences of opinion over what these ideals mean and uncertainty in determining when one has them.

The study of history cannot provide a means of solving present problems or predict the future or insure that we will not repeat the mistakes of the past. It may be able to show the willing learner some possibilities, but the accumulation of facts does not provide a *lesson* without interpretation and there is an abundance of competing interpretations for any important event. When history is analytical, instead of only descriptive, it can offer a useful

4. Paul Ward, "The Awkward Social Science: History," in *Social Science in the Schools*, eds. Irving Morrissett and W. Williams Stevens, Jr. (New York: Holt, Rinehart & Winston, 1971) p. 29.

5. Kirkendall, *Journal of American History*, pp. 569–70.

6. In a very limited survey of self-selected individuals, and admittedly subject to distortion, history materials reported to have worked best with students were: Larry Cuban and Philip Roden, *Promise of America* (Glenview, Ill.: Scott, Foresman, 1971); Corinne Hoextner, Ira Peck, et al., *American Adventures Program* (New York: Scholastic Book Services, 1970); Martin W. Sandler, Edwin C. Rozwenc, and Edward C. Martin, *The People Make a Nation* (Boston: Allyn & Bacon, 1975); and Edwin Fenton (ed.), *The American: A History of the U.S.* (New York: Holt, Rinehart & Winston, 1970). Irving Morrissett, "Fifth Report: Ratings of 21 Social Studies Materials," *Social Education* (November–December 1975), pp. 510–13. It should also be noted that some materials were not on the original list for responses and others have been published since the survey was taken. Even though this survey is somewhat incomplete and dated, the materials that worked *best* with students have reorganized history content, there is a high student interest factor, many personalized or social history accounts, a limited selection of content, emphasis on student inquiry, easy reading, and an attractive overall design and format.

framework to use for looking to the future. But it is not an unbiased prophet nor an objective forecaster.

The study of history cannot automatically lead to clear thinking, critical analysis, suspended judgments, weighing of evidence, sound decision making, problem solving, or other desirable learning traits. But the use of a rational approach of study is a basic objective; without it, the student is likely to accomplish less than is desirable and function less effectively as a person.

Students arrive in class with considerable historical background that can be used in working toward teaching objectives. Even though students form their own subculture with an emphasis on the here and now, their life is permeated with historical referent points. In the *home*, an exasperated parent rebukes his offending offspring—without realizing the historical analysis—by saying, "When I was your age. . . ." And what youngster has not defended his or her actions with the historical justification that "times have changed"?

Students constantly seek historical data for making *personal decisions.* A sophomore beginning his first job asks his friends about working; a girl going on a blind date wants to know what the boy looks or acts like; or a teacher is absent and students want to know about the substitute. A friend gets hurt and the first question is "What happened?" An unexpectedly high score on an exam and the question is "How'd you do it?" Greeting a friend is "How've you been?" or "What's new?"—all everyday history questions and unconscious referent points.

In addition to these everyday history concerns, there are *social-cultural influences* that provide historical images. These are the mental pictures that have developed from personal experiences, and they serve practical or emotional needs. For example, everyone's personal history includes notable *firsts:* the first day of school, the first date, the first airplane flight. Images of *important people* provide another aspect of individual histories: a favorite teacher, a friendly neighbor, the autograph of a film star, a visit to a congressman's office. Emotional *public events* also add to our collection of historic images: Super Bowl playoffs, the assassination of a popular leader, the start of a war, a riot in city streets. Some historical images have become so commonplace that they are symbolic or stereotyped representations for national values: the Spirit of '76, Washington crossing the Delaware, the signing of the Declaration of Independence, immigrants arriving at Ellis Island, or the raising of the flag at Iwo Jima.

Students are constantly processing information about the past, which is used for shaping their thoughts and actions. In short, history is the interaction of the past with the present. We are all walking historians.

GUIDELINES FOR SOCIAL STUDIES PROGRAMS*

1. The social studies program should be directly related to the concerns of students.
2. The social studies program should deal with the real world.
3. The social studies program should draw from currently valid knowledge representative of man's experience, culture, and beliefs.
4. Objectives should be thoughtfully selected and clearly stated in such form as to furnish direction to the program.
5. Learning activities should engage the student directly and actively in the learning process.
6. Strategies of instruction and learning activities should rely on a broad range of learning resources.
7. The social studies program must facilitate the organization of experience.
8. Evaluation should be useful, systematic, comprehensive, and valid for the objectives of the program.
9. Social studies education should receive vigorous support as a vital and responsible part of the school program.

ORGANIZING FOR INSTRUCTION: METHODS AND STUDENTS

The commonly accepted framework for identifying important aspects of the learning process—knowledge, abilities, values, social participation—is also a convenient way for developing instructional activities. But, in school or out, students respond to a combination of intellect and emotion in a total environment of many variables.

Several social science and history methods are especially useful for helping students develop responsibility for their own learning—an often stated but elusive instructional goal. The following examples are methods for achieving knowledge objectives, but, as is easily evident, other aspects of the learning process are also involved.

- *Observation survey:* This usually includes a checklist of items that provide the specifics for the study. It is useful in strengthening the reliability of eyewitness accounts and in gathering and organizing great amounts of data.

- *Questionnaire:* This is often structured with specific questions for polling a sample of the population. There are various types, including forced choice, priority ranking, and opinion continuums. Open-ended questions can provide new insights but are difficult and time-consuming to use.

- *Interview:* This is used to detect areas for further probing in an effort to uncover information or seek patterns. Students sometimes mistakenly view interviews as conversations. Having objectives, an outline, and sufficient background information before the interview takes place can help overcome this problem and make this an important data-gathering method.

- *Examination of primary sources:* Artifacts, realia, diaries, letters, photographs, tape recordings, and other primary sources provide the basic materials for history re-

Social Studies Curriculum Guidelines (Washington, D.C.: National Council for the Social Studies, 1971), pp. 15-28.

search. Student experience in asking questions, analyzing, and making warranted conclusions is the anticipated outcome.

- *Research into secondary sources:* This is the most common approach to history and most other school subjects.

The method of study or the way of working in each of these examples is an investigatory approach which requires a systematic asking and answering of significant questions. Each includes gathering and examining evidence to determine its appropriateness and meaning. Students must evaluate evidence to determine if it is accurate, reliable, and applicable to the specific issue being investigated. They must use criteria to judge its validity and be alert to distortions and biases.

Interpretations are directly tied to the evidence. Is there sufficient evidence for drawing reasonable hypotheses? Are facts and concepts used to support generalizations? Are student thoughts arranged in an orderly manner for providing insight into past events or ideas? Are the findings subject to independent verification?

A second aspect of the learning process has to do with *abilities*. These can be grouped around intellectual or thinking skills, data-processing skills, and human relations skills.

- *Thinking skills:* These include the ability to ask significant questions, analyze social problems, make appropriate decisions, and examine one's own values.

- *Data-processing skills:* These include locating and compiling information, interpreting data, organizing and assessing source material, identifying hypotheses, making warranted inferences, and reading critically.

- *Human relations skills:* These are related to empathy; sensitivity to the ideas, interests, and feelings of others; and effective communication skills.

You may have heard someone say that "It's tough enough teaching what you're supposed to, without having to worry about 'values,' " or someone else say that "It is none of the school's business." But it is obvious to the most casual observer that students learn many values in school. A clock in every room says that time is important. Add a bell between classes and a punishment system for tardiness or unauthorized absences, and students are learning values in a very powerful way.

Values are used as standards for judging right and wrong, beauty and ugliness, good and bad. They help evaluate ideas, actions, and people. Values are based on learning experiences and act as emotional commitments that guide events in our lives. Individual or community values shape actions and have consequences. Community values have led to the observance of certain holidays, the inclusion of U.S. history in the curriculum, and the level of support for the school program. Your values have helped determine the methods and materials you use for instruction. Student values will influence their efforts and ultimate accomplishments.

Opportunities to examine values in school or society are available in many everyday situations. These might include such time-honored topics as hard work, desire to get ahead, "keeping up with the Joneses," pursuing "the almighty dollar," or worshiping heroes. A conscious examination of these and other value-laden topics is useful in understanding much of what is said and done, both today and in the past. History is filled with cases in which an individual or group is faced with a choice between alternatives. Students need to determine not only the facts of the situation but the values that went into making the decision.

Jack R. Fraenkel, a noted social studies educator, has suggested that the values of an event be examined by using a simple three-question framework: (1) What happened? (facts). (2) Why did it happen? (reasons). (3) What does the person or group consider important? (values).[7]

Value issues are judged on the basis of some criteria. The alternatives and their consequences can be analyzed from several points of view. Fraenkel noted the following:

- Moral: Does it enhance the lives and dignity of human beings?

- Legal: Are the laws of the society improved?

- Ecological: Is the natural environment helped?

- Economic: Are funds sufficient for costs?

- Health and safety: Are the lives of human beings protected?

Another way to analyze responses is to use the outline suggested by Lawrence Kohlberg for judging moral behavior. He has identified six stages of progressively sophisticated moral development and suggests that practice in working with dilemmas may help a person move to higher levels.[8]

The practice frequently suggested for helping students develop their moral reasoning involves four steps: (1) Confront the student with a dilemma; for example: Should law-abiding citizens rebel against the established government in England? Should Truman drop the atomic bomb? Should Wilson maintain neutrality? (2) Encourage the student to take a position. (3) Explore and test student reasoning. (4) Reflect on reasoning for maintaining or changing a position on the issue.[9]

The fourth category that deserves deliberate attention as part of the learning process is *social participation.* This is simply providing opportunities for students to work with others in the classroom, school, and community. The type and extent of the participation depends on your goals and the needs, abilities, and maturity of the student.

Activities providing for social participation help bring previously learned knowledge, abilities, and values together in a meaningful new learning experience. Classroom opportunities for social participation include working with a partner, student tutoring, small-group work, role playing, games/simulations. Other experiences within a school setting include cooperative or competitive activities with other classes, surveys and interviews, dramatic presentations, student conferences and programs, student government activities, and various helping or service-type projects.

Student participation in the community calls for some judgment in selecting students and activities. It is better, of course, if responsible students work to meet genuine needs of the community and the results are respected and valued. A number of projects have been undertaken in various communities. A living history center was popular in one eastern high school for its slide-tape presentation about its town's heritage; collecting and preserving local artifacts, memorabilia, and even historic sites has gained considerable attention; students have established or contributed to museums and historical societies; oral history

7. Carl Ubbelohde and Jack R. Fraenkel, eds., *Values of the American Heritage: Challenges, Case Studies, and Teaching Strategies* (Washington, D.C.: National Council for the Social Studies, 1976), pp. 146–213.

8. Lawrence Kohlberg, "Moral Development and the New Social Studies," *Social Education* (May 1975), pp. 369–375.

9. Ronald E. Galbraith and Thomas M. Jones, "Teaching Strategies for Moral Dilemmas," *Social Education* (January 1975), pp. 16–22.

projects involving local customs, folklore, occupations, family life, and so on have become the focus of student projects in some communities; and junior historians; archaeological helpers; and work with government officials, professionals, and tradespeople have become popular. Perhaps the best-known student project work in recent years has been the research about Appalachian life published as the *Foxfire* books.[10]

Social participation activities under the auspices of the school provide students with a semiprotected setting in which they can make decisions and be held accountable for the consequences. It provides an opportunity to learn from other students and adults and often helps correct distorted views of *the real world*. Classroom discussions of social participation activities can provide additional learning experiences as students review their observations and actions and evaluate the intellectual and emotional components of the experience. Social participation activities are basic to the social studies and history and help provide learning that encourages competent citizenship.

INQUIRY AND DOING HISTORY

Inquiry, like history, is a systematic process of asking questions and examining answers. It is a rational, step-by-step process, generally starting with some situation or problem to which the inquirer seeks explanations, solutions, or some other objective. Most important, inquiry is finding out for oneself.

It has often been suggested that an approach to teaching history is to have the student act as historian. While this idea may sound agreeable and logical, it may not be practical or even desirable to organize an entire secondary school program on this method. But, while there are many ways of inquiring into the past as a historian, they all deal with similar basic processes that are adaptable to your class, particularly for independent study, special projects, and small-group work.

A Process of Doing History

1. *Question:* State the problem or issue for which you are seeking information. The more specific the question, the more precise the research. Define the search by stating your purpose. What do you want to find out? What time, place, people, situation, and relationships relate to your purpose?

2. *Investigate:* Suggest a possible answer to your question—a hypothesis. Where can the facts, ideas, and evidence be found? What do you have to observe? Record? Read?

3. *Select and interpret:* Analyze and evaluate the available data. Are they relevant for

---

10. Eliot Wigginton, *The Foxfire Book* (Garden City, N.Y.: Doubleday, 1972). The first and most popular of these books is about "hog dressing, log cabin building, mountain crafts and foods, planting by the signs, snake lore, hunting tales, faith healing, moonshining and other affairs of plain living."

For a carefully reasoned statement with numerous practical suggestions regarding youth participation in the community, see: Dan Conrad and Diane Hedin, "Learning and Earning Citizenship Through Participation," in James P. Shaver, ed., *Building Rationales for Citizenship Education* (Arlington, Va.: National Council for the Social Studies, 1977), pp. 48–73.

For additional information about youth projects in general, a free quarterly newsletter promoting and reporting activities in which youth assume responsible roles is available from *Resources for Youth*. See Appendix A for address.

answering your question, solving your problem, reaching your objective? Are different or additional data needed? Are they accurate? Authentic? Reliable? Appropriate? Is your interpretation warranted by the evidence? Biased or distorted? What changes are needed to improve the original hypothesis?

4. *Communicate:* As a result of your investigation, what is your reasoned explanation, solution, intepretation, generalization, conclusion, or recommended action? What is your revised hypothesis? How is the hypothesis supported by evidence? What is its meaning, importance, or value?

An assumption generally found among students is that the only significant historical events and individuals are those they read about in their textbooks. Historians and textbook authors, for various reasons, have concentrated on great national events, great national figures, and other national circumstances for many years. This national perspective provides the framework for studying the past. A strict adherence to only this perspective, though, would be a disservice to students. It would be unreal to teach the history of the United States in a manner that is unconnected with the lives of ordinary people or with other nations.

Global connections have always existed and form a continuing theme throughout U.S. history starting with the first Asian settlers and the later European invaders. The technology, trade, communication, and political interactions of the past have increased many times through the years, and a realistic view of most national events requires a global perspective.

Correspondingly, views of the local community and ordinary individuals also provide essential realism and insight that would otherwise be missing. Local history or community studies—including anything from a family, a neighborhood, or a region—are especially meaningful for students, since they allow them to work within a familiar setting and with easily available resources. The opportunity to examine primary sources and physical remains; to interview observers or participants; and perhaps to be recognized for making an important or interesting local contribution can make history an exciting, involving, and worthwhile endeavor.

Some have criticized local history as being too limited to serve useful purposes. It may also suffer from simply being *boosterism.* But it can provide insight into such diverse and important topics as social structure, mobility, class, political behavior, economic changes, demography, and family life. All communities interact with the larger historical issues within a national and international setting. The interpretation of issues from the viewpoint of ordinary people provides a perspective that more fully develops the national focus and the activities of extraordinary citizens.[11]

Carefully developed local studies can serve as case studies for examining issues in depth, making comparisons with other communities, and for relating local events to national developments. Local studies provide opportunities for increased understanding of the lives of the vast majority of people. Since it is probably the only area in which students can interact to any great degree with their historical environment, it provides the experience for inquiring into history; for questioning, investigating, selecting and interpreting, and communicating about past events.

One easy starting point for studying local history is a field study of a historic house or building. The staff at Old Sturbridge Village in Massachusetts, a re-created early-nineteenth-

---

11. A leading authority of this social history approach, Jack P. Greene, has written that new historians concentrate on three areas: the basic conditions of life, the structure of economic and social life, and the belief systems of ordinary people. "The 'New History': From Top to Bottom," *New York Times,* January 8, 1975.

century New England community, has suggested ways in which historic houses can be used to engage students in the lives of people in the past.[12]

The first step in using local historic sites is to become familiar with available materials and personnel. Assuming this is satisfactory, decide what you want students to get from the experience and outline a method of investigating the topic. Students should know very specifically what information they are seeking before visiting a site.

A meaningful approach for involving the entire class is to establish small groups and have each assume the role of a family member or other individual who would have used or lived in the building. Another approach is to have the study organized around themes of leisure, economy, religion, home life, and anything else that would be significant for people in the historic setting.

Comparisons can be made with contemporary family life and homes. How does each view everyday life, economic matters, the effects of change and technology, and so on. A simple chart can help students organize their comparison.

Questions	Colonial Home	Victorian Home	Today
What are the rights and responsibilities of children?			
What sections of the house *belonged* to family members?			

Communitywide topics for research and study might include those that have to do with issues or events that have changed the community or those that exist and influence the community; or the topic could be a general examination of how the community or some part of it came to be the way it is.

A creative Colorado teacher has had students work on independent projects that have included the development of ranching and the life-styles associated with it, the evolution of farming techniques, a comparative study of the image of the western bad man with the career of an outlaw buried in a local cemetery, and a study that traced the ethnic composition of the community through various stages of its growth.[13]

Other topics that can be formulated into questions for research include: changing occupations; working conditions; the impact of the railroad or automobile, machines and technology, water supply, the factory system, the first railroad; the first television broadcast; the Roaring Twenties, the Great Depression, World War I or II; abolitionists; suffragists, Prohibition; architectural styles; and education.

Information can be obtained from many places: libraries, government offices, newspaper office files, historical societies, industries, real estate offices, cemeteries, museums, historic markers, and local *experts* wherever one can find them. Published or written sources

12. A number of publications are available for purchase that emphasize ways of actively involving students in field study experiences and in historic analysis. Write Museum Education Center, Old Sturbridge Village. See Appendix A for address.

13. For a practical explanation of how one teacher organized and conducted a local history study, see: Fay D. Metcalf, "Grass Roots History," in Glenn M. Linden and Mathew T. Downey, eds., *Teaching American History* (Boulder, Colo.: Social Science Education Consortium, 1975), pp. 69–86.

of local information include local or state history books; anniversary publications; newspapers; genealogical records; school yearbooks; annual business reports; reports of public agencies; and public records, including tax records, census data, minutes of meetings, school records, deeds, construction data, and so on.

Additional help is often available from *old-timers,* museum curators, history buffs, authors, teachers, lawyers, and friends or family members who might have photographs, tools, letters, diaries, or other artifacts and records.

The availability of resources in the community makes local history exciting and realistic for students. The chance to do something with the results of their work provides an extra reward and recognition. And the finished product can serve other useful purposes by having it placed in the school and community libraries, exhibiting it at local historical sites, presenting copies to those who helped, and exchanging it with other schools for similar products.

Oral and/or visual methods of studying or presenting local history have been popular for many years. Easily portable and inexpensive recording equipment and cameras have been widely used as student research tools and for making presentations. Oral history and visual history offer heightened human interest and interaction. When seriously pursued, they have an emotional impact on the learning attitudes of students that is difficult to surpass with any other method.[14]

USING EVALUATION FOR INSTRUCTION

One of the continuing tasks of instruction is to gather data to find out what students know, can do, or feel about a topic. With this information, judgments can be made about individual achievements, and instruction can be revised or repeated to make learning more effective.

Classroom interactions provide a great amount of information about the efficiency of instruction and the progress of students. But it is often unorganized *feelings* that are absorbed by sensitive teachers. These feelings can be more clearly identified and supported by reserving class time to have students indicate what they thought were the most important parts of the lesson, or those parts that were unclear. This serves as a review, of course, but also provides usable information for judging the effectiveness of the lesson. Depending on one's style, this can be done as a regular part of each class or at the end of a major unit of work. There may be times when one wants to have a student conduct this discussion. Such times will increase the flow of comments and help promote a nonthreatening atmosphere.

Another approach to obtain student feedback is to divide the class into small groups to answer a series of questions. The questions can be reproduced and one copy given to each group. What was the most important thing we learned? What remains confusing? What do

14. Publications that are particularly helpful for community studies include: Clifford L. Lord, *Teaching History with Community Resources,* 2d ed. (New York: Teachers College Press, Columbia University, 1967); David Weitzman, *My Backyard History Book* (Boston: Little, Brown, 1975); Jeffrey Griffith et al., *Classroom Projects Using Photography: For the Secondary School Level* (Rochester, N.Y.: Eastman Kodak, 1975); Vincent L. Jones et al., *Family History for Fun and Profit* (Salt Lake City, Utah: The Genealogical Institute, 1972); and several publications from the American Association for State and Local History, Nashville, Tenn. (see Appendix A for address). See especially: Willa K. Baum, *Oral History for the Local Historical Society,* 1974; Richard W. Hale, Jr., *Methods of Research for the Amateur Historian,* 1969; John J. Newman, *Cemetery Transcribing: Preparation and Procedures,* 1971; William G. Tyrrell, *Tape-Recording Local History,* 1973; and Sam B. Warner, Jr., *Writing Local History,* 1973.

we want to know more about? After each group answers the questions, one person from each group reports the group's responses. This method provides the safety-in-anonymity factor that some students seem to need. In some cases it will serve the teacher's purposes just as well simply to collect the group reports.

Questionnaires and scales provide relatively easy ways of obtaining information before and during the course of instruction. They can also serve as a baseline for measuring changes at the end of a lesson or unit of work. These devices are useful for measuring attitudes and help develop student interest, since they are normally personalized. It is always worthwhile to emphasize that there are no "right" or "wrong" answers, although there may be "better" or "worse" answers depending on student reasoning. There are a few basic approaches to use with these questionnaires and many variations.

One way is to identify the topic for which information is sought and then develop a list of matched pairs. These *semantic differentials* are usually separated by five or seven spaces where the student indicates with a checkmark his or her thoughts on the topic. For example:

The study of history is:

difficult	___	___	✓	___	___	easy
important	✓	___	___	___	___	trivial
interesting	✓	___	___	___	___	boring
useful	✓	___	___	___	___	useless

People who left England to colonize North America were:

smart	___	___	___	___	___	dumb
hardworking	___	___	___	___	___	lazy
loyal	___	___	___	___	___	traitors
generous	___	___	___	___	___	greedy
serious	___	___	___	___	___	fun-loving

The listing and use of matched pairs can be very flexible. The same set of matched pairs can be used with other topics and comparisons made. English settlers could be compared, for instance, with the French, the Spanish, or native American inhabitants.

Another popular use for this instrument is to measure changes that occur after instruction. Have students complete the survey either before or very early in a unit of work and then again after instruction. They can compare their original attitudes with their views after studying the topic and discuss the reasons for the changes.

The views of the class can be tabulated by recording the number of student responses for each blank. A class profile can be obtained by vertically connecting the most frequently marked blank for each item. When used as a preliminary survey and then again after instruction, the profile provides a graphic representation of changes in student views. Some teachers place all *desirable* descriptors on one side when they plan to develop a class profile that allows everyone easily to see and compare the movement that takes place between the preliminary survey and the second one.

Another common device provides for responses of differing intensity. Called the *Likert* scale after its developer, it lists an attitudinal statement to which the student must respond by indicating the extent of agreement or disagreement.

	Strongly Agree	Agree	Disagree	Strongly Disagree
The study of history is essential for survival.	____	____	____	____
Since you can't know for certain what happened in the past, it is a waste to try to find out.	____	____	____	____
History is of no use to me.	____	____	____	____
There is no progress without conflict.	____	____	____	____
Life was simpler 300 years ago.	____	____	____	____

An *uncertain* column may be added, although some people normally gravitate toward the middle rather than take a position. A large number of responses in an *uncertain* column may also indicate that the statement needs to be reworded.

A similar approach for determining the intensity of student attitudes is to indicate that *strongly agree* represents the numerical value of 10, and *strongly disagree* represents 1. Then have students respond by placing a number from 1 to 10 in a single blank space. If desirable, class averages can then be developed for each item.

How strongly do you feel about each of these items? Rate them anywhere from 1 for *strongly disagree*, to 10 for *strongly agree*. If you were neutral, for instance, you would rate the item 5.

People explore to gain fame and fortune. ____

Nations explore for wealth and power. ____

Exploration is as important today as it was in the past. ____

Europeans brought more harm than good to North America. ____

The most common classroom evaluation, other than so-called quizzes, is probably the test given at the end of a lesson, chapter, or semester. This evaluation or grading at the end of a section of work or period of time is normally used to measure, or sum up, student achievements in reaching the objectives. When objectives are clearly stated in terms of what students are able to do after instruction, they know in advance what is expected, and teaching procedures and materials can be directed toward that end. The evaluation is a way of finding out the amount and quality of student knowledge or abilities.

In stating the *goals* of instruction, statements that indicate students will "understand" or "appreciate" or "know" a particular topic are perfectly fine. But in stating the *objectives* of instruction they are not very useful. The objectives of instruction indicate specifically *what will be done*, the *situation* under which it will occur, and the *level of acceptable performance*. A few examples:

action: define, label, list, outline, paraphrase, summarize, predict, apply, diagram, classify, design, locate, generalize, prove, hypothesize

situation: from a list, after reading a paragraph, when given two statements, after viewing a film, as a result of a discussion

level of acceptance: seven out of ten, in every case, within ten minutes

These tests often require the factual recall of information. They are easy to construct and correct and are therefore popular. They have limited use in determining what students understand or can do. These are very real limitations even though there may be times when you want information about what students remember. A quick and easy method for giving and correcting these papers is to ask the questions orally and have each student complete two answer sheets while taking the test. Collect one answer sheet immediately after the test is completed. Then review the questions and answers with students scoring their own papers. When this is completed, the student-corrected papers can be collected.

The considerable amount of time needed for constructing tests can be gradually overcome by maintaining a file of good questions, or at least keeping old tests—not to use again, but to eliminate the misleading or inappropriate items and note the better ones. Exchanging tests with other teachers, establishing a department file, or using publications with test items can also be useful.

Questions for essay tests can be developed with deceptive ease. However, they should relate to the instructional objectives and require more than evidence that the student remembered some facts. Avoid questions that begin with "who," "what," "when," or "list," since they basically test for memory. Avoid questions that are so open and vague that they do not measure what has been taught—for example, "What do you think?" or "Write all you know." Avoid double meanings or imprecise words: "great," "many," "usually," "often." Particularly avoid using "always," "all," and "never."

Questions on better essay tests often require the student to apply generalizations to new situations, analyze relationships, solve problems, or make judgments according to some criteria. Here are four steps for improving test questions:[15]

1. *Know what your objectives are and use them exclusively as the basis for test questions.* Every test question measures some objective, and students quickly analyze what to study when they see the first test or quiz of the year. What *you* say is important is not nearly as impressive as what your *tests* say is important.

2. *Base each question on a single, specific idea, concept, or piece of information derived from one of your objectives.*

3. *Determine what students would be able to do if they were able to use each idea, concept, or piece of information rather than merely know it.* The simple but significant key to this guideline is the difference between two words: "use" versus "know." There are many ways that people use information, ideas, and concepts. In preparing questions, ask yourself what students would do if they could: (a) predict, (b) judge, or (c) interpret events using the information, ideas, and concepts you have derived from your objectives.

4. *Write your test questions based on these uses of information and ask the questions so that students must make judgments, predictions, or interpretations.* If you have stated your objectives; identified specific ideas or concepts that have been derived from the objectives; and indicated the judgments, predictions, or interpretations you want students to use, the task of actually writing the questions will be simple.

GRADING TESTS

The decision regarding the type of test to use is often based on practical personal considerations rather than an educational idealism. A test that takes five minutes to evaluate for each

---

15. These guidelines are based on Clair M. Bowman, Sr., "Improving Your Test Questions: Four Easy Steps," *W.E.S. Bulletin* (March 1976).

of 125 or more students equals three or four very full nights of tedious work. A thorough search for alternatives is a reasonable reaction.

One way to save time—and also to help students who are having difficulty with essay tests—is to provide specific directions for structuring answers. This can be done by having students write the first paragraph as a general description or explanation, with the remaining paragraphs providing details. Similarly, you may wish to emphasize the importance of a topic sentence or important generalizations for each paragraph, followed by the facts and concepts supporting that one idea. When students are asked to underline generalizations, for instance, this includes another means of evaluation while also helping them organize their thoughts.

Developing workable ways in which students can judge other student papers can also provide valuable learning experiences.[16] Using a coding system instead of student names helps make this feasible. Birthdates, parts of a telephone number or social security numbers, or simply distributing a paper to have students write their names alongside consecutive numbers allows sufficient anonymity. A coding system also reduces your unconscious influences when reviewing papers. Your disposition when working on the paper, student personalities, past accomplishments, and the order in which tests are corrected can each affect your evaluation.

Another approach in having students review other student papers is to divide the class into small groups and distribute the papers. Each member of the group reads each paper and notes its strengths and weaknesses on a small piece of paper, which is then attached to the test paper. Each person in the group does this, and after each test paper has been read and circulated it receives several evaluative observations. This approach recognizes the better papers and provides a considerable amount of critical, nonthreatening feedback for the student. Groups can select the best paper and read it to the class. Grades can be assigned by the group at your discretion. By using a numerical scoring system, A=4, B=3, C=2, D=1, a group average for each paper can be obtained.

Another, similar approach also divides the class into groups and students are informed that their task is to help each other improve their papers.[17] Explain that each person will be given a grade for his or her own paper and, if you wish, a grade for the average of the papers in the group. Focus the attention of the group on specific aspects of the topic to be improved; it may be supporting facts, concepts, major ideas, generalizations, specific content, and so on. All students in the group can offer suggestions for improving all papers, or the group can have each person function as the expert in a specific area: one for content, one for English usage, one for generalizations, and so on.

This latter procedure identifies students with particular talents, and they can be used as tutors to work directly with other students. When this procedure is used, both the tutor and the person being helped often seem to learn a great deal of subject matter and how to work with others. Tutors are more effective when they offer explanations and are friendly than if they tell what should be done or use ridicule. Giving suggestions and reminders is more helpful than doing the work for someone. Develop and post a class list of tutors with their specialties, and the system can function as the need arises and be initiated by those who want the help. Put your own name on the list.

---

16. Many of the following procedures are more fully developed in Gene Stanford and Marie N. Smith, *A Guidebook for Teaching Composition* (Boston: Allyn & Bacon, 1977), pp. 17-36.

17. Ibid., pp. 31-33.

SELECTED LEARNING EXPERIENCES

These activities are included to illustrate the comments made in this chapter. While many are particularly useful at the beginning or end of instruction, most can be easily adapted for various topics throughout the course.

Reproduction Pages are found at the end of the book. Use these to make duplicating masters or overhead transparencies. Most of all, use the ideas and activities as working materials: add to, subtract from, multiply, or divide them as they serve your purposes.

1. Ask one student to complete the statement: The history of the United States is . . . Have that student select another student to add to the statement. Continue until a large number of responses have been obtained. A variation is to put the statement on the board without any explanation. Give the chalk to one student and motion him or her to write a response, then allow the student to give the chalk to any other student to write another response; and so on.

2. Have students select pictures from their textbooks that they think best represent the United States. Form small groups and have each group select the five best pictures. Place descriptions of the pictures on the board. Have each group explain the reasons for their selection. It is not necessary, nor even desirable, to work toward consensus. Discuss selectivity of data, interpretations, biases.

3. Show headlines from the front page of a newspaper. Ask students which headlines they think will be in the history books one hundred years from now. What makes an event historically important? What events not reported on a daily basis in the newspaper are important? (These could include hunger, technology, resource allocation, population increase, and so on.) Have students develop a set of standards for including events in history books. This activity may be pursued at greater length by applying student-developed standards to recent or past events.

4. Myths and legends contribute to the common background for a culture. They are often perpetuated as fact. Have students attempt to discover the stories behind any of the following incidents:

    • The life of John Smith is saved by Pocahontas.

    • George Washington admits to chopping down the cherry tree.

    • Ethan Allen demands the surrender of Fort Ticonderoga "in the name of the Great Jehovah and the Continental Congress."

    There are many other events that have been questioned and are worthy topics for student investigators:

    • Queen Isabella I pawns her jewels for Columbus.

    • Betsy Ross sews the first American flag.

    • Stories surrounding the names of Davy Crockett, Daniel Boone, Buffalo Bill, Johnny Appleseed.

    To organize the investigation, have students attempt to answer the following questions:

    • How did the story start?

- What evidence is available?

- What is the *time lag* between the event and the reporting of it?

- What is the possible motivation of the reporter?

- What appear to be the actual facts?

- What have been the consequences of the story?

Discuss bias, lack of sources, reliability of evidence, oversimplification, folklore, cultural values.

5. Using Reproduction Page 1, "Map of United States," have students fill in the names of as many states as possible. Have students then group state names into categories. What conclusions can be drawn about states' names? About the history of the United States? (State capitals, rivers, and other political or geographic features can be used.) Students should recognize names of notable individuals and the widespread use of native and English names for states.

REPRODUCTION PAGE 1

MAP OF THE UNITED STATES

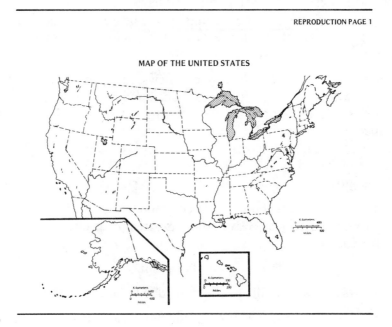

---

6. Present a series of pictures or slides showing people, buildings, or other man-made objects. Ask students to determine the locations. Ask what clues were used. What, if any, evidence is there that the people or objects are located in the United States? What features are convincing proof of being American? Discuss drawing warranted conclusions, cultural bias, examining evidence. There will be obvious differences of opinion among students based on a single, simple picture. Consider the multitude of differences possible for interpreting and writing history.

7. Have students bring from home an object or objects that represent their life. When the objects are available, form small groups for the purpose of asking questions about the objects that would help determine their importance. Use Reproduction Page 2, "Analyzing Artifacts," to help examine the objects and draw conclusions about them (chalk, key, rabbit's foot, coin).

ANALYZING ARTIFACTS

One of the first tasks of a historian is to ask questions. These are often based on objects that people have had and used. From these artifacts the historian attempts to find clues to help answer his questions about people's ways of living and thinking. If your only evidence was an unfamiliar object, what questions could you ask that might provide important information?

Question	*Possible answer*	*Importance*
1. _____	1. _____	1. _____
2. _____	2. _____	2. _____
3. _____	3. _____	3. _____

Use the following questions as a guide for analyzing the artifact you have in class. Write a possible answer to the question and tell why it might be important for understanding the artifact and the people who created it.

1. What is the physical evidence? Size? Shape? Color? Texture? Parts? Etc.

2. What might be reasonably said about the object? Origin? Construction? Function? Etc.

3. What conclusions might be made about its meaning or value to its owner? What might be said about the society or culture?

4. What more needs to be known before making positive statements?

---

8. History research. Find people in the past with your first (and/or last) name. Find events that occurred on your birthday throughout history. Prepare a list of people who made great contributions before they were twenty-five years old.

9. Interpretations. What do you consider to be the most important event in this century? (World War II, the Great Depression, dropping the atomic bomb, space travel, creation of United Nations, the Russian Revolution, the development of Communist China, and so on.) Have students select one event and write what they think is important about it. Then have them find how it is treated in their textbook. Make a comparison with other history books. Develop an outline that can be used in making comparisons. For example:

(Quantified information)

• How many times is the event mentioned?

• What is the length of treatment of the topic (in lines or paragraphs or pages)?

- How many pictures are included about the event? How large are they?
- How many questions relate to the topic? How many suggested readings?

(Qualified information)

- How has the event affected human beings? (Use quotes from texts being compared.)
- What conditions caused the event to develop?
- What have been the consequences of the event?
- What is its relationship with other events of the time?
- Why does it seem to be included in the text?
- What type of events do you think the author(s) feel are important?

10. Reliability of evidence. Using Reproduction Page 3, "Sources of Information," have students determine what affects the reliability of evidence—time, distance from event, emotions, knowledge, motivations of reporter, and so on.

REPRODUCTION PAGE 3

SOURCES OF INFORMATION

Listed below are sources of information that might be used by a historian. Decide which source provides the most *reliable* evidence. Place the number 1 alongside the most reliable source, number 2 alongside the next most reliable, and so on. Then note any particular *biases* or *strengths* for each item.

Reliability		Possible biases	Possible strengths
_____	newspaper report		
_____	diary of person involved		
_____	ballad about the event		
_____	photograph of the event		
_____	novel based on actual events		
_____	letter describing the event by participant		
_____	story told by someone who was there		
_____	description in a history book		
_____	television program about the event		

_____   several tools, weapons,   _____   _____
              objects from the event   _____   _____
                                             _____   _____

1. What affects the reliability of data?

2. Does actual participation in an event provide more or less reliability? Explain.

3. This list includes both *primary* and *secondary* sources of information. Place the
   letter *P* alongside each primary source, the letter *S* alongside each secondary source.

---

11. Meanings of words and symbols. Distribute copies of Reproduction Page 4,
    "Symbols," to students and have them write what each symbol represents. Have
    them share their responses and note the similarity. How is it possible that simple
    pictures result in such similar responses? (If responses are very different, find out
    what they represent and what experiences led to this view.) Discuss cultural
    biases, stereotypes, the dangers of shortcut thinking.

REPRODUCTION PAGE 4

SYMBOLS

There are many signs that represent commonly understood ideas in our society. Some are
widely advertised trademarks that are designed to create feelings of strength, trust, speed,
endurance. A skull and crossbones warns of danger, Cupid is an unmistakable sign of love,
and so on. Can you think of others?

A country also has symbols that represent ideas. Write what each of the following
symbols represent. In the last block list other symbols.

A. A number of groups still suffer from stereotyped thinking. For the purposes of exposing and examining this problem, have students list what they think of when you mention X group. Place responses on the board and discuss where these views came from. What influences our thinking? What can we do about it?

B. Have students survey newspapers and television programs for evidence of stereotypes and report to the class. Another outstanding case of the use of stereotypes is on greeting cards. Have students survey these cards to see how the following are portrayed: old people, Chinese, American Indians, teachers, students, and so on.

12. What could students say about the history of their own lives? Using Reproduction Page 5, "Incomplete History," have students answer the questions of their own history.

REPRODUCTION PAGE 5

INCOMPLETE HISTORY

History is always incomplete. It is never set for all time. New information is discovered, new interpretations made, new theories suggested. This is true for a country or even a single event. It is true even for your own life. To see what we mean, answer the following questions.

1. What historical evidence is available about your life (documents, diaries, people, reports, certificates, and so on)?

2. Once assembled and examined, could these sources of information be used to write the complete history of your life?

3. Could two people use the same information about your life and write different stories? Could both interpretations be different and still be valid? What is meant by interpretation?

4. One way to organize the information about you is to tell which happened first, then next, and so on. What other ways can the information be organized?

5. If someone wrote a history of your life based on the available evidence, what aspects of your life would be most emphasized? What would be left out that you think is important?

6. What conclusions can you make about the writing of history of a country or important event?

---

13. Group interview. A student volunteer is questioned at length about his or her personal history. The volunteer has the option of not answering any question and, to keep things fair, can later ask the interviewers any of the questions asked during the interview. After a sufficient amount of data have been developed, have the class write a report on the life of the person interviewed. These can later be read. Discuss selectivity of data, interpretation, biases, reliability of sources, and organization.

14. History interview. Form groups of three. Two students interview the third about his or her background. This process is repeated, so that each person is interviewed by the other two. Each person is to write the *History* of the other two in the group. Compare the similarities and differences between the histories based on the same information.

15. Divide the class into groups and have each write a history of the first day of school. Assign each group the task of writing from one perspective. Groups may be formed around the following perspectives: (1) chronology; (2) biography; (3) thematic or issue-oriented; (4) identifiable group (ethnic, race, sex, blonds, students, six footers, and so on); (5) place (hall, classroom, lavatory, office, library); (6) comparative (student-teacher-administration, other schools, home, office, other times); (7) problems (conflicts, independence-dependence, power-authority, freedom-responsibility, individual-group).

16. Have students list the five or ten greatest people of America's past. This may be done individually and then shared with others or as a group activity. Have several lists read or placed on the board. Ask students to group the names. Which types are most common? What assumptions are made about "great"? Check the list to determine the number of women, blacks, Chicanos. Also check military and political figures compared with artists and educators, sports figures compared with scientists, and so on. Discuss biases, perceptions, values.

   A. A variation of this activity is to have students list five important events of the past that are most characteristic of the United States. How many are related to war and violence? Technology? Politics?

17. Miscellaneous written or spoken activities that emphasize knowledge and skill development:

letter to editor	speech
editorial	letter of recommendation
news report	imaginary conversation
advice-type column	obituary
script (TV, radio, play)	birth announcement
skit	greeting card
diary	slogan
poem	short story
song	map
headline	floor plan
question	diagram
outline	chart, graph

18. Miscellaneous *doing* activities:

making mobiles	bulletin board
model building	cartoon
photography	illustrated brochure
tape-recording (video, audio)	mural
film	time line (pictorial)
committee	sculpture

collage   exhibit, fair
field study   advertisement
library research   observation and recording

19. Miscellaneous activities for stimulating social participation:

group presentations to other classes

group planning for field study

group planning, conducting, evaluating questionnaire, surveys

a forum in which various groups present different views

a panel presentation followed by small-group discussions

classroom hearings in which experts give testimony, answer questions, with final decision voted by class

guest speaker with class groups responsible for specific topics

role play

games/simulations

clinic where problem is presented and small groups determine best treatment or response

group interview where several people question several others

debating teams

20. Knowledge and research skills. Have students find answers to the following historical questions:

- When was George Washington born? Why are different dates reported?

- When was Thanksgiving first officially celebrated?

- What was the relationship between Abraham Lincoln and Ann Rutledge?

- What was the cause of Warren G. Harding's death?

21. Hall of Fame. The Hall of Fame for Great Americans honors men and women who have made outstanding contributions to the advancement of human welfare. The persons honored represent qualities of leadership, vision, and intellect that may inspire future generations. Divide the class into groups of about five students and have each group consider and nominate one person from each of the five fields of endeavor: (1) arts, (2) sciences, (3) humanities, (4) government, and (5) business and labor. These nominations are to be presented to the Board of Trustees who will hear presentations and select one new member to the Hall of Fame from each of the five categories. The Board of Trustees can be composed of one member from each group. Use Reproduction Page 6, "Hall of Fame," for each group to record its nominations.

Election to the Hall of Fame is commemorated by an inscription and likeness of the individual. Use the following questions to discuss the class selections after they have been made:

- How have the elected individuals demonstrated their greatness?

- What does the "advancement of human welfare" mean?

- What factors seemed to most influence the actual selection?

- What did you (or the Board of Trustees) consider most important in selecting individuals?

- A country honors what it believes in. Do you agree?

- What does the class selection say about the values we consider important?

REPRODUCTION PAGE 6

HALL OF FAME

The Hall of Fame for Great Americans is dedicated to honoring men and women who have made outstanding contributions to the advancement of human welfare. Persons eligible for election must be American citizens and have been dead for at least twenty-five years.

One person from each of the five principal fields listed below shall be elected. Subheadings are intended only to provide suggestions of categories that might be considered. The task of your group is to nominate one person for each of the five fields. Be prepared to explain why the selection was made.

Field of Endeavor	Person Nominated
I. ARTS	_____
1. musicians, composers, singers	
2. theatrical, dance, film performers	
3. producers, directors, dramatists	
4. painters, sculptors, photographers	
5. craftsmen and artisans	
II. SCIENCES	_____
1. health, biological, environmental scientists	
2. inventors	
3. physical scientists, engineers, architects	
4. land, sea, space explorers	
5. social scientists, economists, psychologists, sociologists, political scientists	
III. HUMANITIES	_____
1. authors, historians	
2. educators, philosophers, social welfare leaders	
3. religious leaders	
4. social, political reformers	
5. journalists, broadcasters, editors	
IV. GOVERNMENT	_____
1. statesmen	
2. lawyers, judges	
3. armed forces	
4. diplomats, ambassadors	
5. public administrators	
V. BUSINESS AND LABOR	_____
1. business, financial leaders	
2. labor leaders	
3. farmers	
4. publishers	
5. advertising executives	

---

22. There are a number of activities that directly involve students in local history. A few samples are:

- Locate and mark historical sites. Prepare a brochure with a map and descriptions for a walking or riding tour, perhaps similar to Boston's Freedom Trail.

- Write brief statements about interesting or important aspects of the town's history for use by the radio station or newspaper.

- Develop an inventory of sources of historical information—people and places—and have an index file or booklet available for use by students, teachers, or residents seeking specialized information.

- Develop an oral history library on a particular topic or time period in the community.

- Hold a history conference on the use and abuse of local history. Invite several local experts and include student presentations and projects.

- Hold a family history fair. Have individual students make presentations or displays about their family's past: taped interviews, family tree with photographs, artifacts with explanations, slides, student-prepared family history books, and so on.

23. Several additional, all-purpose reproduction pages have been included for your use as appropriate. They are Reproduction Pages 7–18.

REPRODUCTION PAGE 7

VALUE ANALYSIS FORM

This form is to help you compare the values of different people in similar situations. Write the name of the people or groups you are comparing at the top of the columns on the right side.

A statement of the question or issue: _____

_____

People or Group   1 _____ 2 _____

1. What happened?

2. Why did this happen?

3. What do you think this person values?

4. What makes you think he/she values this?

5. What differences were there in what the people did?

6. What similarities were there in what the people did?

7. Why do you think people act this way in these sorts of situations?

REPRODUCTION PAGE 8

DILEMMA DECISION FORM

Directions: Briefly explain what the situation or event is that you are considering. Then decide what you would do in this situation. After writing what you would do, review the categories listed below and see which one comes closest to describing what you would do. Then write your reasons for making that decision in that block.

1. What the situation is: _____

_____

2. In this case, the action I would take is: _____

_____

3. Which of the categories below comes closest to matching what you would do? List your reasons for taking that action in that block.

1. Follow directions or be punished.

   _____
   _____
   _____
   _____

2. Do it because you'll get a reward or compliment.

   _____
   _____
   _____
   _____

3. It pleases others.

   _____
   _____
   _____
   _____

4. To maintain law and order, it's your responsibility.

   _____
   _____
   _____
   _____

5. Individuals have rights in a society.

   _____
   _____
   _____
   _____

6. Conscience says that all human beings have rights.

   _____
   _____
   _____
   _____

FAMILY CHART

Complete the information for your family. Write names in the appropriate places. Add lines for stepparents if needed. For each letter put the following information: b—born, d—died, place—place of birth.

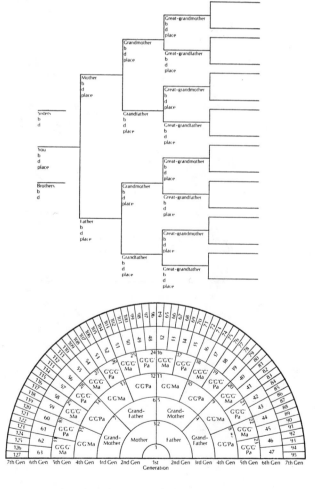

FAN OR BLOOD LINES CHART

FIELD STUDY: HISTORIC HOUSE

History investigation: What was life like in this house?

Family composition: What evidence is there that shows the number, approximate ages, and sex of the residents? Servants? Hired men? Tenants? Relatives? What was the composition of this family?

Family roles and functions: What were the responsibilities of each member of the family? How did each contribute to the family economy? How did the children learn what they were supposed to do? How were they disciplined? What evidence is there of religious beliefs? Political views and participation? Education? Where was each member of the family at dawn? Midday? Early evening?

Family interaction: What evidence is there that family members were alone? Together? What situations might have caused conflicts between them? How might these have been resolved? When would children leave the family?

Economic interdependence: What things did the family produce for itself? What things could not be produced by the family? How did the family get the things that it did not produce? What exchanges were made with others? Whom did the family depend on? Who depended on the family?

Use of technology: What are the sources of heat? Light? What laborsaving devices are there? Automatic machines? Hand tools? What implements were used for cooking? For working in or around the house? Cleaning? Washing?

Communication: How did the family convey messages to others? How did news come to the house? How did the family travel?

Interior design: How many fireplaces are there? Windows? Doors? What does the furniture tell about its owners? How does the arrangement of the furniture tell about family members? What objects are strictly ornamental or artistic?

Land use: How large is the land area around the house? How was the land used? Garden? Farm? Landscaped yard? Animal barns? Toolsheds? Other buildings? Fruit trees? Grape arbors? Streams and ponds? Walls and fences? Paths? Cleared areas? Natural areas?

Comment on the following hypotheses:
1. Human beings have gained increasing control over their environment.
2. Family life was much more cohesive long ago than it is today.
3. Technology provides increasing benefits for human beings.

FIELD STUDY: OLD CEMETERY

Cemeteries provide an obvious source of information about the past. They can provide data about individuals and families, medical and health care, occupations, and life in the community. Here are some questions to help organize your study.

1. Who owns the larger plots? What information is provided about their background? How many generations are there? Are relatives still living in the community?

2. What names are found more commonly than others? What period of time seems to be most common? Are certain ethnic groups common?

3. What is an average or approximate size of most families? What seems to be an average life span? Do men or women seem to live longer? What are causes of death that are noted? From what wars are there soldiers?

4. What occupations seem to be most common? Do these change over a period of time? What are some possible causes for this change? What occupations are given, if any, for women?

5. What epitaphs are especially interesting? What architectural styles seem to be represented by the headstones? Are there any special markings or flags? Are foreign languages used on any headstones?

6. When are the earliest graves? Why was the cemetery located here? Who owns and maintains the cemetery today? Is it still in use? Are there restrictions on who is buried there? What was the community like at the time the cemetery began?

ORAL HISTORY

Guidelines for conducting an oral history interview.

Before the interview:

1. Decide what information you want and who might have it.

2. Contact the person and give a general idea of what you would like to ask.

3. Think of all the questions you can ask and then organize them into major categories. Research your *topic* and *person* as much as possible—the more the better—and then make an outline of the information you want.

4. Practice asking questions with another student to keep the person on the topic.

5. Obtain a tape recorder and tape that you will use and practice working it so that it can be done very easily.

Conducting the interview:

1. Spend the first few minutes in general conversation to "warm up" the person being interviewed and to check the operation of your tape recorder. Have paper and pencil for taking notes.

2. Be an active listener. Find out: Why? How? When? Where?

3. Don't interrupt a good story with questions. Instead write notes so you may ask the questions later.

4. Don't worry about silences; allow the person time to think.

5. Interview only one person at a time. If you work with another person, only one of you should be responsible for asking most of the questions.

6. Be courteous. Don't overstay your welcome. An older person may get tired. A business person may have other appointments. If needed and it is agreeable, return for a second session instead of staying too long.

7. Remember to change the tape at the proper time. Ask the person to wait a moment while you do so.

After the interview:

1. Complete the cataloging form.

2. Determine the best ways to use the information on the tape.

3. Write a thank you letter to the person interviewed.

REPRODUCTION PAGE 13

ORAL HISTORY CATALOGING FORM

General Topic of Interview _____

Date _____ Place _____ Length _____

Person interviewed _____

Qualifications to speak on topic _____
_____

address _____

(If appropriate) Occupation _____ _____

(If appropriate) Birthdate/place _____

Interviewer _____

Purpose of interview _____
_____

School and class _____

Sources and related information _____
_____
_____

Interview: List subjects covered in the interview in approximate order. Include brief comments about what was said and approximate time.

Approximate time   *Subject covered and comments*

REPRODUCTION PAGE 14

EVALUATION OF ORAL HISTORY PROJECT

Give each of the items listed below a score from 1 to 10: 1 would be very unsatisfactory, 5 is about average, 10 is outstanding.

Item	*Score*
Preinterview Preparation	
1. Research of topic and background of individual to be interviewed	____
2. Organization of questions and development of outline	____
Quality of Interview	
3. Organized and prepared	____
4. Smooth performance (personal interaction and technical operation, question-asking style)	____
5. Development of worthwhile information	____
6. Alert, intelligent, courteous listener; follows up unexpected information, keeps interview on topic	____
Postinterview Organization and Presentation	
7. Key ideas identified	____
8. Interpretations and conclusions based on evidence	____
9. Information relates to larger issues; provides insight into human condition	____
10. Cataloging form fully completed	____
TOTAL SCORE	____

REPRODUCTION PAGE 15

GUIDELINES FOR VISUAL HISTORY PROJECT

1. Decide the question you wish to consider.

2. Conduct a preliminary search for information and opportunities for visuals.

3. Refine outline, using dialogue or descriptions for each major idea. Make notes about picture possibilities. (Divide paper into two columns: narration and visuals.)

4. Continue to refine narration and visuals, place each narration and visual combination on a single index card. Sequence cards and, if possible, tack onto a bulletin board.

5. Make arrangements to take pictures (sources might include local sites, museum pieces, students in costume, old photographs, postcards, magazines). Prepare title and credit pictures and other printed materials (these may be typed onto transparent film, cut, and placed in a holder).

6. Tape interviews, music, and other effects to be included with narration.

7. Revise and edit ideas and pictures. Retake visuals, rewrite script, rethink approach. Be critical and aim for perfection.

8. Put it all together again and preview before a small group for their *critical* reactions. Make additional changes as needed.

9. Premier presentation before class.

REPRODUCTION PAGE 16

VISUAL ANALYSIS FORM

Pictures by artists, cartoonists, photographers, and others capture a moment and convey a message. For the historian, a picture is an important source of information. Here are some questions to help analyze visual messages.

1. What, if any, is the title of the picture?

2. Who is the artist? What do you know about his background or views?

3. What is the perspective of the artist; from what position does he view the subject(s) in the picture? How does this affect your opinion of the subject(s) in the picture?

4. Is anybody or anything being criticized or complimented? What features of the person, place, or thing attract attention?

5. What symbols or stereotypes are in the picture? Which are positive signs? Negative?

6. What parts of the picture are drawn out of proportion—either too small or too large—and why are they done that way?

7. What would be a one-sentence description of the message or point of view of this picture?

8. What facts would you need to know to support or disprove this message? What questions would you need to have answered?

9. What, if anything, do you think the artist would like to see happen about this issue?

10. Write a brief paragraph stating why you agree or disagree with the view expressed in this picture. Or find another picture or cartoon that represents another point of view on the same topic.

REPRODUCTION PAGE 17

EVALUATION OF HISTORICAL INQUIRY

Read each question and decide how you would evaluate your historical inquiry. Place a check in the space from 1, weakness, to 5, strength.

	weakness				strength
	1	2	3	4	5

1. Was the question for investigation specific and achievable? Did it involve an important issue?

2. Were you able to locate the needed data?

3. Did you recognize and account for biases? Points of view?

4. Was a plausible hypothesis suggested?

5. Did you use a variety of sources? Primary? Secondary? Nonprint? Is there an indication that some were valued more than others?

6. Do you understand the process of selecting and interpreting data? Multiple causation? Fact versus opinion?

7. Were findings organized in a way that related to the hypothesis? Was the hypothesis refined as a result of research?

8. Are the findings clear to others? Were you able to express a point of view or conviction based on your research?

9. Are the findings interesting or important to others?

10. Can generalizations be made? Was your original question answered? Or was a problem solved? An action recommended? Objectives achieved?

REPRODUCTION PAGE 18

EVALUATION OF WRITTEN AND ORAL PRESENTATIONS

Place a checkmark on one of the five spaces between the two statements. For example, if the report was not too good but not too bad, you would place a checkmark at the middle space:

good report	___ ___ ✓ ___ ___	poor report
well organized	___ ___ ___ ___ ___	disorganized
important information	___ ___ ___ ___ ___	unimportant information
thorough presentation	___ ___ ___ ___ ___	skimpy presentation
helpful visuals, maps, etc.	___ ___ ___ ___ ___	poor or no visuals
interesting	___ ___ ___ ___ ___	boring
person seems to know topic	___ ___ ___ ___ ___	person seems ill informed
person able to answer questions	___ ___ ___ ___ ___	person unable to answer questions
audience learned many new things	___ ___ ___ ___ ___	audience did not learn anything new
overall presentation was excellent	___ ___ ___ ___ ___	overall presentation was poor

Total number of check marks in each column   ___ ___ ___ ___ ___

In each column, multiply check marks by   10   8   6   4   2

and place that number in this space   ___ + ___ + ___ + ___ + ___ = ___

and add the numbers from the spaces to get a total score of ___

RESOURCES FOR TEACHING

Below is a list of materials that have been selected for their *practicality*—they can be easily used by teachers; *availability*—they can be obtained with a minimum of funds; and *quality*—they are thoughtfully developed and appropriate for teacher or student use. Addresses of publishers can be found in the alphabetical list on pages 191–199.

Books, Pamphlets, and Articles

Abramowitz, Jack. *The American Nation: Adventure in Freedom*. Chicago, Ill.: Follett, 1975.
    Eight chronological units divided into basic lessons for daily work by students. Each lesson centers on a reading selection of about one page and includes vocabulary, comprehension, and short exercises. Additional reading sections summarize lessons or provide information about people or events. Highly structured and for students with learning difficulties.

Allen, Jack, and Betts, John L. *History: U.S.A.* New York: American Book, 1976.
    A chronological presentation emphasizing historical methods, problem solving, important ideas, and sequence.

Anderson, Howard R., and Lindquist, E. F. *Selected Test Items in American History*. Washington, D.C.: National Council for the Social Studies (NCSS), 1964.
    Introductory chapter about testing followed by 1,062 multiple-choice questions arranged in 16 traditional categories.

Association of Teachers of Social Studies in the City of New York, The. *Handbook for the Teaching of Social Studies*. Boston: Allyn and Bacon, 1977.
    Practical information on questioning techniques, simulations, independent study, planning new courses, teaching values.

Borg, Kirsten E. A. *USA: Perspectives on Our History*. Evanston, Ill.: McDougal, Littell, 1974.
    Based on seven topical volumes, this combined single text uses case studies, biographical anecdotes, and you-are-there narratives within a broad chronological framework.

Botein, Stephen; Leon, Warren; Novak, Michael; Rosenzweig, Roy; and Warden, G. B. *Experiments in History Teaching*. Cambridge, Mass.: Harvard-Danforth Center for Teaching and Learning, 1977.
    Insights and examples of innovative teaching arranged under topics of cultural artifacts, community history, personality, history from the bottom up, and quantifying the past.

Brady, Marion, and Brady, Howard. *Idea and Action in American History*. Englewood Cliffs, N.J.: Prentice-Hall, 1977.
    Each unit includes narrative sections to provide an orientation and summation. A substantial part of each unit is made up of activities designed to relate key ideas with human behavior.

Bragdon, Henry B.; Cole, Charles W.; and McCutchen, Samuel P. *A Free People: The United States in the Formative Years*, and *A Free People in the Twentieth Century*. New York: Macmillan, 1978.
    Popular, long-standing text that features a chronological approach emphasizing interdisciplinary topics and international settings.

Branson, Margaret Stimmann. *Inquiry Experiences in American History*. Lexington, Mass.: Ginn, 1975.
    A variety of activities to stimulate student thinking. This paperbound text can supplement other texts and various teaching methods.

_____. *Land of Challenge;* and Unger, Irwin, and Johnson, H. Mark. *Land of Progress*. Lexington, Mass.: Ginn, 1975.
    Both volumes are organized chronologically and are a set. *Challenge* presents material from the earliest days to Reconstruction, and *Progress*, after summarizing this material, concludes the story.

Brown, Ralph, and Brown, Marian, eds. *American History Booklist for High Schools*. Washington, D.C.: NCSS, 1969.
    Introductory chapter on basic collections followed by 15 chapters on major historical periods.

Brown, Richard, ed. *The Human Side of American History*. Boston, Mass.: Ginn, 1962.
    Numerous excerpts from firsthand accounts, diaries, journals, news stories that tell about life in America.

_____, and Halsey, Van, eds. *Key Dimensions in American History*. Menlo Park, Calif.: Addison-Wesley, 1970–1974.
    Popularly known as the Amherst series, each paperbound volume explores a historic event. Based on an open-ended question and using many primary sources, these booklets are for the advanced high school student.

Buggey, Joanne; Danzer, Gerald A.; Mitsakos,

Charles L.; and Risinger, C. Frederick. *America! America!* Glenview, Ill.: Scott, Foresman, 1977.

A chronology with numerous primary sources and student activities. Easy reading and attractive visuals highlight this intermediate text that can be used equally well with high school students.

Burns, Robert E.; Boyer, Lee R.; Felton, James R.; Gleason, Philip; Lyon, John J.; O'Neill, James E.; and Tull, Charles J. *Episodes in American History: An Inquiry Approach.* Lexington, Mass.: Ginn, 1973.

Chronological presentation with brief overview of content for each unit followed by numerous primary source excerpts that are designed to provide insight and raise questions.

Cartwright, William H., and Watson, Richard L., Jr., eds. *The Reinterpretation of American History and Culture.* Washington, D.C.: NCSS, 1973.

Each of the 25 topical chapters provides observations about principal developments in American history and culture.

Catalog of United States Government Audiovisual Materials, A. Washington, D.C.: National Archives and Records Service, General Services Administration.

This publication includes a wide range of more than 3,000 items.

Chicago History of American Civilization Series. Culver City, Calif.: Social Studies School Service.

Twenty paperbound volumes, each by a recognized historian, on popular as well as neglected topics.

Clark, James I. *History of the American People.* Evanston, Ill.: McDougal, Littell, 1975.

Easy student reading that emphasizes social history—institutions, people, and their lives— within a general chronology.

_____, and Remini, Robert V. *Freedom's Frontiers: The Story of the American People.* Beverly Hills, Calif.: Benziger, 1975.

Chronology with focus on specific issues within an era. Introductory photo essays for each section.

Cleary, Polly Chase; Madison, Sarah; and Mitsakos, Charles L. *Study America: An Interdisciplinary Approach to American Studies.* New York: Bantam, 1976.

Six self-contained units, each including five or six copies of six to eight different volumes plus duplicating masters, photo aids, and a useful teacher's guide. Each volume is a historically interesting or important comment on America's past. Easily lends itself to work with English teachers.

Cuban, Larry, and Roden, Philip. *Promise of America.* Glenview, Ill.: Scott, Foresman, 1975.

Topical approach within a broad chronological framework. Five paperbound volumes are available individually, each with primary sources, case studies, and other content that encourages student inquiry. A very usable teacher's guide is available for the series.

Eames, E. Ashley, and Martin, Nancy Stone. *Case Studies in American History.* Cambridge, Mass.: Educators Publishing Service, 1964.

Fourteen cases of about four to six pages long on major historical issues.

Fancett, Verna S. *The Endless Chain: Cause and Effect.* New York: Macmillan, 1975.

Case studies, vignettes, cartoons to explain concepts originally developed by the social studies project at Syracuse University. Meant for students but valuable for teachers.

Farmer, Robert A. *1000 Ideas for Term Papers: American History.* New York: Arco, 1969.

Easy-to-use listing of ideas arranged by historical period.

Feder, Bernard. *Viewpoints: U.S.A.* New York: American Book, 1972.

Source material presented as historical problems and followed by student inquiry activities or questions. Units are available separately for supplementary work.

Flanagan, John C.; Mager, Robert F.; and Shanner, William M. *Social Studies Behavioral Objectives.* New York: Westinghouse Learning Corp., 1971.

An extensive listing of social studies objectives by school level and subject area.

Freidel, Frank, and Drewry, Henry N. *America Is.* Columbus, Ohio: Charles E. Merrill, 1978.

A narrative chronology that concentrates on the relationship of people, ideas, and events. Easy reading for intermediate level students.

Gardner, William E.; Beery, Robert W.; Olson, James R.; and Rood, Kenneth A. *Selected Case Studies in American History,* Vols. I and II. Boston: Allyn and Bacon, 1969, 1970.

Concise, well-developed cases reflecting major historical events. Based on the idea that students need to examine evidence and reach their own conclusions.

Goldstein, Eleanor, ed. *Bicentennial: American Issues Forum.* Boca Raton, Fla.: Social Issues Resources Series (SIRS), 1976.

The span of U.S. history represented by reprinted articles and observations of historical interest or importance and organized around themes originally developed to celebrate the Bicentennial. An unusually varied and valuable source of information packaged in a three-ring binder, with teacher's guide, filmstrip, and cassette.

Gordon, Irving L. *American Studies: A Conceptual Approach*. New York: Amsco, 1975.
Similar to history review books but organized with major sections on the American people, government, economic life, civilization in historical perspective, and world affairs.

Graff, Henry F., and Bohannan, Paul. *The Call of Freedom* and *The Promise of Democracy*. Chicago: Rand McNally, 1978.
This set is designed for use at the intermediate level and high school level. The first, and easier title, includes content through the Civil War period. Both use many primary sources and include lively visuals.

Griffith, Jerry. *Classroom Projects Using Photography: For the Secondary School Level*. Rochester, N.Y.: Eastman Kodak, 1975.
Easy-to-use publication with sections on purpose, materials, equipment, procedures, and evaluation.

Gruver, R. B. *An American History*. Reading, Mass.: Addison-Wesley, 1976.
Political, social, economic introduction to U.S. history.

Harnadek, Anita. *Critical Thinking*. Troy, Mich.: Midwest, 1976.
Problems and activities on logic, reasoning errors, propaganda techniques, advertising, and arguments.

Hawley, Robert C., and Hawley, Isabel L. *Developing Human Potential*. Amherst, Mass.: Education Research Associates, 1975.
Over 80 activities, worksheets, and forms to help develop competencies in creativity, motivation, communication, and evaluation.

Historical Statistics of the United States: Colonial Times to 1970 (2 vols.). Washington, D.C.: U.S. Bureau of the Census, 1975.
Everything you've always wanted to know about almost everything: population, health, migration, labor, income, wealth, expenditures, social statistics, land, water, climate, agriculture, forestry, fisheries, minerals, construction, housing, manufactures, transportation, communication, energy, distribution, services, international transactions, businesses, productivity, technology, finances, government, and more.

Hoextner, Corinne, and Peck, Ira. *American Adventures Program*. Englewood Cliffs, N.J.: Scholastic, 1970.
Program includes short, easily read, high-interest events that emphasize people and social history. Designed for intermediate level, it can be used with high school students with reading problems.

Hofstadter, Richard; Miller, William; and Aaron, Daniel, as revised by Jordan, Winthrop D., and Litwack, Leon. *The United States*. Englewood Cliffs, N.J.: Prentice-Hall, 1976.
Standard text for higher-ability high school students. Study guide and workbook available.

Horn, Robert E., ed. *The Guide to Simulations/Games for Education and Training*. Cranford, N.J.: Didactic Systems, 1977.
Descriptions and evaluations of over 1,400 games/simulations, 59 of which are history. Also useful are related topics of community issues, domestic politics, international relations, legal systems, military, practical economics, social studies, urban, and frame games.

Jacobs, William Jay. *Search for Freedom*. Beverly Hills, Calif.: Benziger, 1973.
Biographical approach that presents U.S. history through the lives of the people who helped to make it.

_____. *Women in American History*. Beverly Hills, Calif.: Benziger, 1976.
Women and their hopes and fears through all the years of American history. Good supplement to most traditional books. Provides important and often overlooked information about contributions made by women.

Jensen, Oliver; Kerr, Joan Peterson; and Belsky, Murray, eds. *American Album*. New York: Ballantine, 1970.
Photographs of the time America was growing—the late 1800s through early 1900s.

Johnson, Harry A. *Guide to Media and Materials on Ethnic American Minorities*. New York: Bowker, 1976.
Information on selecting and using media related to groups with accompanying bibliography about ethnic minorities.

Jones, Vincent L. *Family History for Fun and Profit*. Salt Lake City, Utah: Publishers Press, 1972.
A how-to-do-it book with detailed information, suggestions, and forms.

Katz, William Loren. *Eyewitness: The Negro in American History*. New York: Pitman, 1967.
Picks up where many old texts leave off by pro-

viding exciting and essential information about often overlooked aspects of American life.

Kellogg, William O., *How to Prepare for the Advanced Placement Examination in American History*. Woodbury, N.Y.: Barron's Educational Series, 1977.

Help for students and reminders for teachers in developing history skills and other basic skills. The content of the publication can be used for instructional purposes whether or not students are preparing for advanced placement examination.

Kellum, David R. *American History through Conflicting Interpretations*. New York: Teachers College Press, Columbia University, 1969.

Nine basic units for structuring a year's program around basic questions.

Kownslar, Allan, ed. *Teaching American History: The Quest for Relevancy*. Washington, D.C.: NCSS, 1974.

Practical publication that includes several lessons and student materials on the incompleteness of history, inquiry, big ideas, empathy, myths, questioning procedures, and relevancy.

_____ . *Tips for Teaching About the Bicentennial in the Social Studies: Four Lessons*. Boulder, Colo.: ERIC Clearinghouse for Social Studies/Social Science Education (ERIC/ChESS), 1975.

Lesson plans and student materials for recurring themes of dedication, humor, frontier, and loyalty.

_____ , and Frizzle, Donald B. *Discovering American History*. New York: Holt, Rinehart & Winston, 1967.

Emphasizes historical inquiry and uses many primary source materials. Focuses on causation, role of the individual, authority, duties and responsibilities of government, values, frontier, and change.

Leinwand, Gerald. *The Pageant of American History*. Boston: Allyn and Bacon, 1975.

Chronological and topical organization with particular attention to minorities, cities, and day-to-day life. Case studies and inquiry-oriented activities included.

Linden, Glenn M., and Downey, Matthew T., eds. *Teaching American History: Structured Inquiry Approaches*. Boulder, Colo.: ERIC/ChESS, 1975.

Practical lessons and student materials for teaching social, interdisciplinary, comparative, and local history.

Local Community, The: A Handbook for Teachers. New York: Macmillan, 1971.

Developed for the high school geography project, this book includes useful ideas and activities with application to history, particularly for map and graph skills.

Lomax, Alan. *The Folk Songs of North America*. Garden City, N.Y.: Doubleday, 1975.

The story of folk songs in their historical and cultural setting. Words and music about lumberjacks, keelboatmen, wagon trains, and everyone else who ever told a story with a song. Delightful social history.

Lord, Clifford L. *Teaching with Community Resources*. New York: Teachers College Press, Columbia University, 1967.

The guide for getting started in the community— research, field trips, community resources, special activities.

Meltzer, Milton, ed. *In Their Own Words: A History of the American Negro*. New York: Thomas Y. Crowell, 1965.

A chronological collection of primary sources of black life in America.

Metcalf, Fay D., and Downey, Matthew T. *Teaching Local History: Trends, Tips, and Resources*. Boulder, Colo.: ERIC/ChESS and Social Science Education Consortium (SSEC), 1977.

Information, ideas, activities for community studies. Chapters on social, economic, and family history, architecture, folklore, and resources.

National Council for the Social Studies. *Social Studies Curriculum Guidelines*. Washington, D.C.: NCSS, 1971.

Suggests that the advancement of human dignity is the major purpose of social studies education. A basic rationale, the guidelines, and an evaluation checklist for assessment and curriculum development are included.

Newton, Richard R., and Sprague, Peter F. *The Newspaper in the American History Classroom*. Washington, D.C.: American Newspaper Publishers Association Foundation, 1974.

The why and how of using newspapers for teaching key issues in U.S. history. Fourteen illustrative lessons.

O'Connor, John E., and Jackson, Martin A. *Teaching History with Film*. Washington, D.C.: American Historical Association, 1974.

Describes and suggests ways of using films in the history classroom.

100 Events That Shaped America, The. New York: Time, 1975.

Brief narrative and exciting photos or drawings with interesting list of events. Available with a strategy book containing questions and activities for each of the 100 events.

Pulliam, William E.; O'Neil, William L.; and Bowman, Clair M. *America Rediscovered.* Boston: Houghton Mifflin, 1977.

Focus on four disciplines—economics, international relations, political science, sociology—each beginning with a contemporary case and followed by a chronological presentation emphasizing important concepts. Student activities designed for analysis and application of basic ideas.

Ralston, Leonard F., and Negley, Harold H. *The Search for Freedom: Basic American History;* and Wiltz, John Edward. *The Search for Identity: Modern American History.* Philadelphia: Lippincott, 1978.

A two-volume set dividing at Reconstruction. Each volume provides a general overview of the content covered in the other.

Ramos, June E., and Crevling, Barbara. *Selective Bibliography in United States History Resources.* Boulder, Colo.: ERIC/ChESS and SSEC, 1977.

An annotated listing of basic and supplementary materials. Includes information about grade level, reading level, cost, and a descriptive overview.

Reprint Series in American History. Indianapolis, Ind.: Bobbs-Merrill.

This series includes hundreds of articles previously published in scholarly journals on important historical issues. Write for catalog.

Robertson, James, ed. *Old Glory.* New York: Warner, 1973.

Lively paperback with selections on hometown history projects and suggestions for using local resources for researching community history.

Roden, Philip. *The Elusive Truth.* Glenview, Ill.: Scott, Foresman, 1973.

Brightly written little book with many examples and activities on assumptions, influences, symbols, illogic, false issues, statistics, generalizations, and evidence. Great help for clearer thinking.

Sandler, Martin W. *In Search of America.* Lexington, Mass.: Ginn, 1975.

Four paperbound volumes that use photos, paintings, cartoons, advertisements, and other visuals to present the history of the United States. Questions and independent work are designed to have students use their own experiences to interact with the material.

———; Rozwenc, Edwin C.; and Martin, Edward C.

The People Make a Nation. Boston: Allyn & Bacon, 1975.

The evolution of American institutions—government, politics, industry, foreign policy, economics, social organizations—mostly from the perspective of ordinary people. Historical method incorporated within text.

Scott, John Anthony, ed. *The Living History Library.* New York: Random House, 1975.

Several copies of 11 volumes designed to provide a classroom library. In addition, there are 36 skill cards and 56 topic cards and a teacher's guide to help develop student research skills.

Seaberg, Stanley; Stopsky, F.; and Winks, Robin. *The American Experience.* Reading, Mass.: Addison-Wesley, 1975.

Thematic and chronological with primary sources in each chapter.

Sebolt, Alberta P., ed. "Using the Community to Explore 200 Years of History," *Social Education* (November–December 1975).

This special issue includes articles on community education, teaching family history, case study of a New England town, using a diary to re-create the past, and resources for local history. Available from NCSS.

Sellers, Charles G.; Mayer, Henry; Paynter, Edward L.; Saxton, Alexander; Shumsky, Neil L.; and Smith, Kent. *As It Happened: A History of the United States.* New York: McGraw-Hill, 1975.

Organized into eight units of in-depth analyses of key issues. Many primary source materials and a variety of student questions and activities.

Shaftel, Fannie R., and Shaftel, George. *Role-Playing for Social Values: Decision Making in the Social Studies.* Englewood Cliffs, N.J.: Prentice-Hall, 1967.

Helpful and now standard guide for using role playing in the classroom.

Smith, Lew. *The American Dream.* Glenview, Ill.: Scott, Foresman, 1977.

A chronology with key ideas introducing each chapter followed by several readings for student analysis.

Smith, Gary R. *Teaching about U.S. History: A Comparative Approach.* Denver: Center for Teaching International Relations, University of Denver, 1978.

Teacher instructions and student materials for 33 classroom activities for personalizing U.S. history, supplementing major topics, developing basic skills, and incorporating multicultural content and current issues.

Social Studies Curriculum Materials Data Book. Boulder, Colo.: SSEC.

This unique social studies publication includes hundreds of analyses of social studies materials, textbooks, games, supplementary materials, and teacher resources. Each two-page description includes comments about objectives, content, teaching procedures, intended user characteristics, and cost. Lists virtually all quality social studies materials and is periodically updated.

Spectrum Eyewitness Accounts of American History. Culver City, Calif.: Social Studies School Service.

Fifteen paperbacks, each by a recognized historian, using primary sources and about how people lived during key periods in U.S. history.

Stephens, Lester D. *Probing the Past.* Boston: Allyn and Bacon, 1974.

Instructional plans, materials, discussion ideas, and evaluation techniques to help the U.S. history teacher.

Stereotypes, Distortions and Omissions in U.S. History Textbooks. New York: The Council on Interracial Books for Children, The Racism and Sexism Resource Center for Educators, 1977.

A content analysis of more than a dozen popular history texts for their treatment of African Americans, Asian Americans, Chicanos, native Americans, Puerto Ricans, and women. Checklists, bibliography, and other useful information are included.

Suid, Murray, and Suid, Roberta. *Happy Birthday to U.S.* Menlo Park, Calif.: Addison-Wesley, 1975.

Over 100 mostly do-it-yourself activities easily adaptable to the classroom. Focus is on personal interests that are easily related to historical issues.

Todd, Lewis Paul, and Curti, Merle. *Rise of the American Nation.* New York: Harcourt Brace Jovanovich, 1977.

Narrative chronology with numerous reproductions of artwork. This classic text was first published in 1950.

Ubbelohde, Carl, and Fraenkel, Jack R., eds. *Values of the American Heritage: Challenge, Case Studies, and Teaching Strategies.* Washington, D.C.: NCSS, 1976.

An examination of life, liberty, and the pursuit of happiness with cases on the impressment of seamen, the trial of Susan B. Anthony, the Mormon frontier experience, and the Standard Oil Company. Also includes a concise explanation, with practical classroom applications, for teaching about values.

Ver Steeg, Clarence L., and Hofstadter, Richard. *A People and a Nation.* New York: Harper & Row, 1975.

A chronology incorporating many primary sources, contemporary data, and emphasizing the social sciences.

Wade, Richard C., ed. *Life in America Series.* Boston: Houghton Mifflin, 1968–1974.

Several titles by various authors, each using primary sources to relate the development, achievements, and prospects of workingmen, immigrants, women, youth, etc.

Weinstein, Allen, and Wilson, R. Jackson. *Freedom and Crisis: An American History.* New York: Random House, 1974.

A combination narrative and case study seeks to provide coverage and in-depth analysis within a chronological framework. Pairs of chapters provide the format; the first is a narrative episode, and the second is an interpretative chapter.

Weisberger, Bernard A. *The Impact of Our Past.* New York: McGraw-Hill, 1976.

Chronological arrangement. Each chapter begins with conflicting historical interpretations, followed by three or four chapters of historical data, and concluding with issues that relate content to contemporary concerns.

Weitzman, David. *My Backyard History Book.* Boston: Little, Brown, 1975.

Stimulating new way to look at old things—family and home, interviews, photocopying, Main Street, junkyards. Many personal and local history projects suggested.

Why Remember? Corte Madera, Calif.: Chandler & Sharp, 1973.

An interview with Erich Gruen about history, the historian, and education. Good reading about relevance, the process of the historian, and aspects of historiography.

Wood, Leonard C.; Gabriel, Ralph H.; and Biller, Edward. *America: Its People and Values.* New York: Harcourt Brace Jovanovich, 1975.

A chronological narrative that includes inquiry sections, brief biographical sketches, and notable artworks.

Other Resources

American Association for State and Local History. Nashville, Tenn.

Has a large number of publications available, including technical leaflets and books for the historian and teacher. Provides services and publishes *History News,* a monthly.

American Bibliographic Center—Clio Press. Santa Barbara, Calif.

Outstanding single source for bibliographic information for virtually all U.S. history publications. Publishes *The New American: History and Life,* comprehensive and current bibliography including *Part A, Article Abstracts and Citations,* which covers more than 2,000 journals; *Part B, Index to Book Reviews,* drawing on more than 100 key history publications; and *Part C, American History Index (Books, Articles, and Dissertations).*

American Experience, The. Englewood Cliffs, N.J.: Scholastic.

Twenty portfolios of American views developed in cooperation with the Smithsonian Institution. Each contains fifty 11″ x 14″ color prints.

American Heritage. Marion, Ohio.

High-quality, popular publication with informative articles and attractive illustrations. Older issues can sometimes be obtained from former subscribers at bargain prices, an excellent addition to the classroom library.

American Historical Association. Washington, D.C.

A number of booklets providing informed commentary on major historical periods and events is available. Write for brochure. Also publishes *The American Historical Review;* includes scholarly articles and extensive review of books.

American History Illustrated. The National Historical Society. Gettysburg, Pa.

Articles of interest and attractive illustrations. Annual subscription is for ten issues.

American Quarterly. Philadelphia, Pa. American Studies Association, University of Pennsylvania.

Variety of articles on America's past. Annual subscription is for five issues.

Anti-Defamation League of B'nai B'rith. New York, N.Y.

Useful materials available on disadvantaged, ethnic and minority groups, prejudice, extremism, and other topics. Write for publications list.

Caedmon Records. New York, N.Y.

Extensive collection of records on various U.S. history topics. Write for catalog.

Center for Cassette Studies, The. Los Angeles, Calif.

Extensive collection of tapes of actual historical events. Write for free catalog and supplements.

Civil War Times. Boulder, Colo.

Action-packed articles attractively illustrated. Annual subscription is for ten issues.

Critical Thinking Aids. New York: Modern Learning Aids.

A series of 100 inexpensive filmstrips that present information, pose questions, offer alternatives, and then depict what actually happened. Designed for intermediate level classes, they can be used to motivate and challenge reluctant high school learners. Each title includes a teacher's guide.

Current History, Philadelphia, Pa.

Theme-focused issues that provide historical background of current events. Annual subscription is for eleven issues.

Documentary Photo Aids. Mount Dora, Fla.

Photographs and cartoons on heavy-gloss paper stock. Sets available for many U.S. history topics and vary in price. Write for free catalog.

Documents in the National Archives. Washington, D.C.: General Services Administration.

Catalogs listing some of the available resources from the National Archives and Records Service. Available upon request.

Early American Life. Boulder, Colo.

Articles of everyday life attractively illustrated. Annual subscription is for six issues.

Earwitness to History. Princeton, N.J.: Visual Education Corporation.

Oral history recordings, documentary source tapes, folk history, immigrants, national figures. Write for information about their program.

Educational Record Sales. New York, N.Y.

A source for records, cassettes, and transparencies. Materials from various companies. Send for secondary catalog.

8 mm Documents Project, The. Boulder, Colo.: Thorne Films.

Short, silent film segments of original newsreel footage covering more than 100 events during the twentieth century.

ERIC Clearinghouse for Social Studies/Social Science Education. Boulder, Colo.

Provides information about available resources. Publishes a newsletter, bibliographies, state of the art, and other papers. Responds to reasonable inquiries and provides a computer search service to identify materials, articles, and guides. Write for further information, charges, and to be placed on the mailing list.

Folkways Records. New York, N.Y.

Extensive collection of folk and other songs, interviews, and other events. Write for complete listing.

Free Loan Educational Films: School Catalog. New York: Modern Talking Picture Service.

Free films on a variety of subjects. Write for catalog.

History Teacher, The. California State University, Long Beach, Calif.: The Society for History Education.

Articles of historical and education importance, especially for secondary and college teachers. Provides review of teaching materials, books, and other items of interest. Subscribers also receive *Network News Exchange* and have access to no-cost books and low-cost reprints. Annual subscription is for four issues.

Hoffman, Robert M. *News of the Nation: A Newspaper History of the United States.* Englewood Cliffs, N.J.: Prentice-Hall, 1975.

Kit includes copies of 46 four-page newspapers presenting information about key historic events, social news; includes maps and photographs.

Ideas. Washington, D.C.

Publishes bimonthly bulletin to exchange information among producers of *Foxfire*-type publications. Especially appropriate for local and ethnic history, research, writing, and production. Write for sample and subscription rate.

Independent Student Inquiry Packets, Troy, Mich.: Instructional Products Services.

Classroom packets containing forms with questions for student investigations. Packets on colonial era, nationalism, Manifest Destiny, Civil War, industrial era, World War I, and the Great Depression through the 1960s.

Jackdaws. New York: Grossman.

Reproductions of original documents and other materials. Packet includes suggestions for their use. Many topics available. An inexpensive way to provide students with a feel for primary sources.

Journal of American History, The. Bloomington, Ind.: Organization of American Historians.

Scholarly articles and book reviews. Annual subscription of four issues with membership. Write for application and information.

Journal of the Society of Architectural Historians. Philadelphia, Pa.

Articles on historical architecture in the United States and elesewhere. Illustrated with photos, plans, etc. Annual subscription of four issues plus newsletter.

Journal of Southern History, The. New Orleans, La.: Southern Historical Association, History Department, Tulane University.

Scholarly articles and book reviews, professional announcements, news, and notes. Annual subscription of four issues.

Library of Congress. Music Division, Recorded Sound Section, Washington, D.C.

Folk music, blues, ballads, railroad songs, fiddle tunes, spirituals, work songs, game songs, and others available at low cost. Write for free publication, *Folk Recordings.*

Link, The. Boulder, Colo.

Quarterly newsletter having one or more social science articles plus professional announcements, brief reviews, and other timely information.

Listening Library. Old Greenwich, Conn.

Records and filmstrips in all subject areas. Send for catalog.

National Archives and Records Service. Washington, D.C.: General Services Administration.

Has attractive publications, reproductions of historical documents, prints, posters, and other materials at reasonable prices.

Write for free catalog.

Select Audiovisual Records: Pictures of the Civil War

Select List of Sound Recordings: Voices of World War II

Select Picture List: Indians of the United States

Select Picture List: United States Navy, 1775–1941

Select Audiovisual Records: Pictures of the Revolutionary War

Documents from America's Past: Reproductions of Historical Documents In the National Archives

The National Archives also publishes *Prologue,* featuring articles on American history as reflected in the materials preserved in the archives.

National Council for the Social Studies. Washington, D.C.

The professional organization for history and social studies teachers. Has an extensive publications program, conducts regional and national meetings, provides services as resources permit. Publishes *Social Education,* which contains articles of practical interest and professional importance. Members also receive additional publications and a periodic newsletter.

National Gallery of Art. Washington, D.C.
Books, postcards, reproductions, slides, recordings, and sculpture reproductions are available. Also has a free lending program. Write for *Slide Lectures and Films* brochure.

National Trust for Historic Preservation. Washington, D.C.
Its purpose is to preserve historic sites for public use. Members receive publications, admission benefits, merchandise discounts, and other benefits. Write for fact sheet, application, and sample materials.

Negro History Bulletin. Washington, D.C. The Association for the Study of Afro-American Life and History.
Articles of historic and contemporary interest, often aimed to teacher audience. Annual subscription of eight issues.

New England Quarterly, The: A Historical Review of New England Life and Letters. Brunswick, Me.: Hubbard Hall.
Scholarly articles and book reviews. Annual subscription of four issues.

Nicholas Books. Williamstown, Mass.
History books for teachers and students at discount prices. Write for catalog.

Oral History Association. New York: Columbia University.
A depository for nationally significant interviews and recorded reminiscence. Has some publications and is helpful to those seeking to involve students in oral history projects. For *transcribed* oral history in microfilm or microfiche, write for a catalog, See Appendix A listing for the Microfilming Corporation of America.

Pacific Historical Review. Berkeley, Calif.: University of California Press.
Scholarly articles and book reviews on American expansionism and postfrontier developments of the twentieth-century American West. Annual subscription of four issues.

Pacifica Tape Library. Los Angeles, Calif.
Distributes wide variety of mostly post-1945 radio programs. Write for listings on history, politics, women, black studies, and sociology.

Publishers Central Bureau. Avenel, N.J.
One of several such firms selling publisher's overstock and discontinued titles at greatly reduced prices. Usually has a fairly good selection of popular history titles. Write for latest catalog.

Puzzle, Lakeside, Calif.: Interact, 1972.
A simulation that places students in the role of biographer. Resources located throughout the school and student groups must locate, prepare, and then defend a final report.

Smithsonian Institution. Washington, D.C.
Membership privileges and monthly magazine, *Smithsonian,* which reports on the arts, sciences, and history.

Social Science Education Consortium (SSEC). Boulder, Colo.
Provides a variety of educational services and has an extensive publications program. Assists with curriculum analysis and adoption efforts, conducts staff development programs, offers consultations, and generally serves the history and social studies profession. The Boulder office contains an outstanding resource center that provides the base for the ERIC/ChESS Clearinghouse. Visitors are welcome. Send for publications brochure and to be placed on their mailing list. If requesting assistance, state specific needs.

Social Studies School Service. Culver City, Calif.
The most comprehensive single source for materials. Issues a catalog, valuable in itself, and periodic supplements and specific topic catalogs listing all types of materials (except 16-mm film) for teaching history and the social studies. If you do not already receive the catalog, write for one.

State Historical Associations.
Many state, and some local, organizations often have a surprisingly large and general range of services and materials. Most are anxious to help, but are rarely used by most teachers.

State Universities.
Every state university has a film library that is designed to serve teachers of the region. Films that may rent from commercial sources are often available from your state university for the cost of postage. (Many local libraries also have free loan films.)

Teaching Economics in American History. New York: Joint Council on Economic Education, 1977.
Boxed set of 60 spirit masters for classroom activities, 20 color posters, and teacher's manual that examine economic aspects of history topics.

U.S. Government Printing Office. Superintendent of Documents, Washington, D.C.
Distributes free monthly listing of government publications, many on historical topics. Write to be placed on the mailing list. Also ask for free

listings for: *Military History, Historical Handbook Series, U.S. Army in World War II, Civil War,* and any others related to U.S. history.

Value Questionnaires for United States History. Sun Valley, Calif.: Creative Classroom Activities/Edu-Game, 1975.

Ready to reproduce and use, 18 questionnaires on basic history issues.

What is History? New York: Guidance Associates, 1976.

Two-part filmstrip showing problems of gathering and interpreting information and work of historian. Student manuals and teacher's guide included.

2

Exploration and Colonization

This chapter includes activities to develop or review basic social science ideas. If you are starting your course with material from this chapter, it is important to review students' skills and knowledge of chronology; their sense of time and historical perspective; and their ability to use investigative methods, to form hypotheses, and to interpret maps. Many of the activities in this chapter, as well as in other chapters, are easily adapted to other content areas, and you may wish to return to this chapter during the course. Reproduction Pages found at the end of this book may be used as is or modified to serve particular needs.

The period of exploration witnessed intense national competition for power. Life in the American colonies was frequently affected by the rivalry of emerging European nations. At the same time, it was natural that colonists with varied backgrounds and interests would be concerned with their own development. So while colonization implies control, there was also a growth of self-reliance. As the dominance of England in North America increased, so, too, did the independence of the colonies themselves. Finally, after 169 years of growing independence from England and growing interdependence among themselves as Americans, the thirteen colonies unanimously made the momentous decision to declare their independence.

PERFORMANCE OBJECTIVES

As a result of working with the activities in this chapter, students will be able to:
1. Place events in proper historical sequence, understand chronological order, and have a greater awareness of historical perspectives.
2. Use and understand historical methods—questioning, interpreting data, making warranted generalizations, forming and testing hypotheses—to examine the lives and events of the past.
3. Prepare and interpret maps.
4. Arrange man-made and natural features on a map to show an understanding of the relationship between people and their environment.
5. Arrange items from a list on the basis of some stated criteria.
6. Note and explain the essential features of a government.
7. Take a position regarding a moral issue and defend it in a rational way.
8. Find and use evidence from a variety of sources and write a generalization based on these data.
9. Explain the human dimension of important historical events and relate these to contemporary situations.

LEARNING EXPERIENCES

Topic 1:   Establishing a Sense of Time

Over a long period of time the importance of calendars and clocks begins to fade, and time is associated with memorable events or the life spans of significant people. The life and events students have already experienced offer the greatest history capsule the teacher has available. These activities use each student's life to develop a sense of time and chronology.

1. Draw a line across the top of a piece of paper or use the margin line on notebook paper by holding the paper sideways. On the left side, have students place the year of their birth. On the right side, have them place today's date. Then have them place an X on the line for each important event in their life—enter school, win award, break leg, vacation, death of relative, birth of brother, and so on. Each event should be briefly noted with an explanation beneath the lifeline. Students should also include the date and their age when the event took place.
   Discuss: What type events are important to you? Why are they important? Did everyone in the class select similar events? Would the events be similar to those that would be important for the history of a country? If you lived to be one hundred and did this activity, which events would remain on your line? Why are others omitted? How does time influence what we think is important?

2. An alternate strategy would be to draw a line so that one end represents birth, the other death. Place X's where you think important events will take place and briefly describe what they will be. Discuss in a manner similar to the previous activity.

3. The use of previous activities offers many possibilities for encouraging students to

examine their lives and times from a historical perspective. What evidence exists to prove that each event actually happened? What is its reliability? What will be available one hundred or four hundred years from now? What evidence will exist after you are gone to prove you existed and did certain things? What problems would develop in trying to write a history of your life if only the evidence you have listed were available? Can history ever be complete? Given the same evidence, would different people prepare different stories of your life? What ways exist to reconstruct what happened in the past?

4. This activity is to establish connections between today and the past. Placing a sheet of paper in a horizontal position, fold it into four equal columns. At the top on the extreme left side, place the year 1600; on the first fold 1700, on the second fold 1800, on the third fold 1900, and at the extreme right 2000. Depending on the space that is available, add vertical lines representing every ten, twenty-five or fifty years. Draw a line at the top of the paper from the year of your birth to today. Now, your objective is to get to the year 1600 in as few generations as possible. Using any real people, draw a line for their life span. The only requirement is that each person must have been born before the previous one. Place the name, birth date, and death date below each lifeline. Continue doing this until you reach 1600. You can use family records, history textbooks, or any other source.

    This activity might also be undertaken in small groups in class. It can be made easier by allowing a ten-year credit to be divided and used to help make connections between generations. It can be made more challenging by requiring each person to have known the one before him or her. Or it may be limited to specific people: family members, politicians, adventurers, artists and musicians, women, people born in your state.

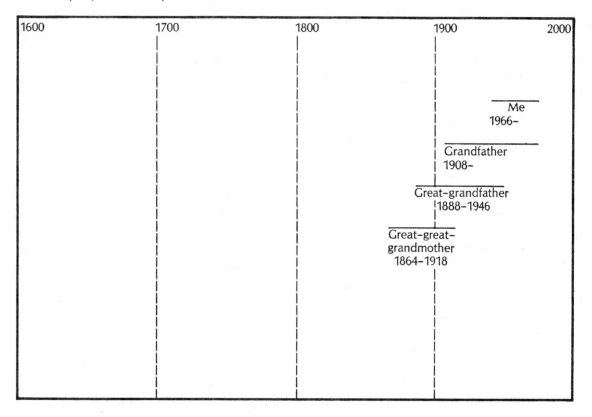

Discuss: What is the average length of a generation? What is an average life span? What changes have taken place through the years? What kinds of people were used to make the ties to the past? What kinds of people do we seem to keep information about? Are the more recently selected people different in any important way from those selected for earlier dates? Were there any discrepancies regarding birth and death dates?

Topic 2:   Early Inhabitants of North America

Archaeological excavations in Illinois are providing a picture of early life in North America. These findings show a rich, agricultural type of existence that is quite different from the generally accepted older views of early inhabitants which presented them as having a marginal life as hunters and gatherers.

The people who inhabited the site seven thousand to eighty-five hundred years ago lived in a village composed of nuclear families, with permanent circular houses of stick walls woven around vertical poles. They hunted deer, fished, preserved food in pits, and used fire.

It is called the Koster site after the farm on which it is located, and more than a dozen layers of periodic habitation have been found since excavations began in 1969. A team of anthropologists from Northwestern University think that the Indians who lived there may have learned to select needed resources from their own environment as early as 10,000 B.C. By A.D. 800 to 1000 the society was agricultural and under pressure from other tribes. They apparently fled eastward, and by A.D. 1200 they disappeared.

The following activity is used to develop an understanding of historical methodology: questioning, interpreting data, generalizing, and hypothesizing and testing.

1. Have students work individually or in small groups. Distribute Reproduction Page 19, "Archaeological Evidence," and have them answer and discuss their responses. Have students use this limited amount of evidence to reconstruct the life of the people.

2. List the objects listed below on the board or reproduce them and distribute them to students. Have students attempt to classify them and then question what remains to be known before making statements about the people. Based on the list of objects, what generalizations can be made about the people who used them?

wooden bowl
curved stick, pointed and notched
   at each end
cylinder of bark, one end covered
   with leather
small curved and hollow wood
   with charred inside
clamshells, several small, smooth
   parts of shells

flat wooden stick
animal sinews
several flat, smooth rocks
several sharp-edged, pointed rocks
tortoise shell
animal bones
large, hollow tree with cutaway side

REPRODUCTION PAGE 19

ARCHAEOLOGICAL EVIDENCE

Archaeologists are people who study the remains of past cultures. They often face problems trying to decipher the meanings of the artifacts they find. To better understand the difficulties of their work, think about your own life. What historical evidence is available about your life? How accurate a picture would it provide 100 or 1,000 years from now? How do we know what happened before written record were kept?

Here is some evidence. Can you reconstruct the lives of the people?

Excavations at an archaeological site in central Illinois have uncovered artifacts, skeletons, plants, and animal remains of people believed to have lived there many years ago. Studies by anthropologists, archaeologists, botanists, and biologists have indicated that the people were not nomads, but lived in villages.

Historical evidence has been found in several layers, called horizons. The oldest dates from 7,000 to 8,500 years ago. In this horizon, several items have been found, including a buried dog, a buried infant, a roasting pit, a thatched house, hickory nuts, and drying deerskin.

Another horizon, from 4,500 to 7,000 years ago, contained fish on racks, a hearth lined with clay, mussel shells, a large roasting pit, and more thatched houses.

The most recent horizon, from 800 to 1,200 years ago, contains evidence of earth ovens with limestone bottoms, pots, planted crops (probably corn), and more thatched houses.

- What statements can you make for sure about these people?

- What statements can you make that are probably true about these people?

- Prepare an archaeological report explaining the questions you believe need to be answered about these people and what you would expect to discover.

Several artifacts and other remains have been discovered. What do you think is the probable meaning of each?

Artifact	*Probable Meaning*
buried human being and animals	_____
thatched houses	_____
animal skin	_____
use of clay and limestone	_____
fireplaces	_____

Based on the evidence, and the meaning you give to it, what can be said about the way people lived in this area and the changes. Use the topics below as the outline for your report.

- Why people first lived here:

- Observations about work, play, family, beliefs, relations with others:

- What eventually happened to them:

Topic 3:   European Discovery and Colonization

The European discovery and settlement of North America is far removed from the daily concerns of most students. But the issues of the sixteenth century remain as basic questions: What makes a discovery important? Is conflict between different groups of people inevitable? Who owns and controls the land? What are the meanings of the terms "civilized," "progress," "primitive," and "basic rights"?

1.   Explore these basic questions by using Reproduction Page 20, "Discovery Questionnaire," or Reproduction Page 21, "Settlement Questionnaire," as introductory activities. Students can complete the questionnaire and discuss their decisions in small groups. You may wish to have groups attempt to reach consensus on as many statements as possible. Representatives from each group can report on how the group functioned and the decisions that were made. Questionnaires can be used again at the end of your formal instruction and students can compare their responses to determine what, if any, changes occurred.

REPRODUCTION PAGE 20

DISCOVERY QUESTIONNAIRE

Directions: Place a check in the column that best expresses your views: SD—*strongly disagree;* D—*disagree;* A—*agree;* SA—*strongly agree.*

	SD	D	A	SA
1. All important discoveries in the world have already been made.	___	___	___	___
2. Exploration of the moon today is as important as exploration of North America was in the sixteenth century.	___	___	___	___
3. Discovery of new lands has always meant progress.	___	___	___	___
4. A discovery is important only if it can be put to some use.	___	___	___	___
5. There would be fewer problems today if North America was never settled by Europeans.	___	___	___	___
6. There would have been few conflicts in North America if Indians had adopted European ways.	___	___	___	___
7. People of different backgrounds will naturally fight with each other.	___	___	___	___
8. The European settlers were more civilized than the native Americans.	___	___	___	___
9. In the long run, primitive people benefit from contact with more advanced people.	___	___	___	___
10. There was nothing unusual about the European discovery and settlement. The same things would happen today.	___	___	___	___

SETTLEMENT QUESTIONNAIRE

Directions: Place a check in the column that best expresses your views: SD—*strongly disagree;* D—*disagree;* A—*agree;* SA—*strongly agree.*

	SD	D	A	SA
1. There was nothing the Indians could have done to prevent the European settlement.	___	___	___	___
2. Indians should be given their land back.	___	___	___	___
3. Explorers have a right to claim land they settle.	___	___	___	___
4. A person who owns land can use it any way he or she pleases.	___	___	___	___
5. No one really owns land. They just use it for a period of time.	___	___	___	___
6. If a person takes your land you have the right to get it back any way you can.	___	___	___	___
7. Land should be taken from a person if it helps others.	___	___	___	___
8. People who live in any area should help new settlers get started.	___	___	___	___
9. Europeans had a right to settle in North America.	___	___	___	___
10. The Indians had (have) a right to force the Europeans from North America.	___	___	___	___

2. The questionnaire can also be used to survey the opinions of other students, native Americans, real estate agents, construction workers, or other groups to compare and analyze results. This information can be presented in graph or chart form.

3. Individual statements from the questionnaires can be used as topics for debate. And do not overlook the opportunity to discuss the meanings of key terms, the uncertainty of some of our opinions, and the difficulty of collecting and interpreting data.

4. What evidence do you need to prove a discovery? Many claims have been made for discovering North America and its native inhabitants. Reproduction Page 22, "Claims of Discovery," lists several individuals and the known evidence supporting their claims of discovery. Distribute this page to students and have them analyze the evidence and draw conclusions about its reliability. What are the strengths and weaknesses of each type of evidence? Several of these, and other, claims can provide topics for additional research.

5. As an individual or group activity, have students find answers to these questions:

    • What did the European explorers seek?

    • What did they find?

    • Of what importance was what they found? To whom?

    • How successful were the explorers?

    After students have prepared answers to these questions, discuss: Are the conclusions based on facts? Why are there differences between student findings? How did you decide to select some facts and not others? Of what importance are your own values in determining the *success* of the explorers? How would you answer the following: In reading history, one should accept statements that . . .

REPRODUCTION PAGE 22

CLAIMS OF DISCOVERY

Group and discovery	Evidence	What you need to know to prove or disprove claim
Explorers from Iberian Peninsula settle in Susquehanna Valley, about 800–600 B.C.	translations from 400 stones found in area	
Norsemen settle in Newfoundland, A.D. 1000	written records, maps, artifacts	
Arab sailors in North or South America	Arabic records from Middle Ages mention plants and animals known only in America	
Chinese group reaches Mexico, about A.D. 450	legend; similarities between Aztec and Chinese language, mythology, coinage	
St. Brendan travels from Ireland to North America, about A.D. 500	archaeological findings in Newfoundland; Irish legends	
Hebrews to Tennessee-Georgia area, 1000 B.C.	similarities between Hebrew and Yuchi, an old Georgia tribe, in customs, language	
Phoenicians to North and South America	translations of inscriptions	
Romans to York, Maine, area, A.D. 200	Latin inscription in rock and discovery of Roman coin	
Welsh to Mobile, Alabama, area, A.D. 1170	Some Welsh words in Indian languages; monument erected by Daughters of American Revolution	

6. A similar activity can be arranged from the perspective of the first Americans. Have students respond to the following questions from the view of the "discovered" inhabitants:

   • When did the European invasion first begin to destroy the native people?

- Where did the Europeans do the most damage?

- How did the Europeans overwhelm the native people?

- In what ways were the Europeans inferior?

7. This activity is basically a map skills exercise in which students determine the components of an *ideal* location for settlement. Some familiarity with basic geographical terminology is helpful. Atlases with both large- and small-scale maps of the East Coast of North America would be helpful. Have students complete Reproduction Page 23, "Ideal Settlement."

   After the "Ideal Settlement" form has been completed and discussed, have students draw a map showing all the features they selected on the form. Remind them to include a legend, scale of miles/kilometers, longitude and latitude, the direction of north, and so on. Discuss and add to the map when appropriate: What buildings would you construct? What activities would you undertake to survive? What types of people would you want to settle the area? What tools and equipment would you use? What effect does the settlement and its population have on the land? How did the land influence the settlement? What were the advantages and disadvantages of the settlements at Jamestown? Plymouth? Of the first settlers in your community?

   To pursue this map activity further, particularly as it relates to the interaction between people and the land, have students describe the occupations and economy that develop. Some suggestions related to occupations include agriculture, manufacturing, handicrafts, mining, construction, trade and commerce, transportation and communication, and services. Suggestions related to economic development include herding, hunting and fishing and collecting, forestry, stock raising, agriculture, manufacturing and commerce, and mining.

REPRODUCTION PAGE 23

IDEAL SETTLEMENT

Imagine you are the leader of a group of settlers sailing from Europe to North America in 1600. You can direct your ship anywhere along the Atlantic coast. Before leaving for the journey, you need to decide on the site you will select. Your objectives are: (1) to find mineral resources; (2) to find a water route to the Pacific; and (3) to develop and control trade.

What do you select?

Land (check one)

_____ flat coastal   Further explanation:
_____ low and hilly
_____ mostly mountainous
_____ combination

Land features

_____ rivers and streams   Further explanation:
_____ rapids
_____ marsh and swamp
_____ lakes and ponds
_____ bays and inlets
_____ shoreline
_____ mountains
_____ rolling hills
_____ plains
_____ plateaus
_____ deltas
_____ peninsulas and capes
_____ islands

· *Elevation* (check one)

_____ 0–305 meters   Further explanation:
_____ 305–610 meters
_____ 610–1525 meters
_____ 1525–3050 meters

Climate

_____ tropical rainy   Further explanation:
_____ dry steppe
_____ humid (with warm or cool summer)
_____ tundra

Temperature (check one)

_____ always cold   Fill in average temperature:
_____ cold winter, cool summer   _____ January
_____ cold winter, mild summer   _____ April
_____ cool winter, mild summer   _____ July
_____ cold winter, hot summer   _____ October
_____ cool winter, hot summer
_____ mild winter, hot summer
_____ always hot

Rainfall (check one)

_____ under 12.5 cm   Further explanation:
_____ 12.5–50 cm
_____ 50–100 cm
_____ 100–150 cm
_____ 150–200 cm
_____ over 200 cm

Natural vegetation (check one)

_____ evergreens   Further explanation:
_____ deciduous
_____ grasslands
_____ mixed
_____ shrubs and dwarf growth
_____ no vegetation

Soil (check one)

_____ alluvial   Further explanation:
_____ tundra
_____ forest
_____ prairie
_____ desert
_____ mountain

Population density (check one)

_____ under one (per square mile/km)   Further explanation:
_____ 1–10
_____ 10–25
_____ 25–50
_____ 50–100
_____ 100–1,000
_____ over 1,000

8. This activity is to encourage students to think about the requirements for survival in any early settlement. It is based on the well-known National Aeronautics and Space Administration (NASA) activity for survival on the moon. Distribute copies of Reproduction Page 24, "Survival and Settlement," and have students arrange the items on this page in order of importance for their survival. This should be followed with small-group discussions to reach consensus. Discuss: What reasons do you have for placing the items in the order you did? Which items are important because they allow you to leave the area? What items would be most important if you were entirely by yourself? If you were with a group of one hundred or more? What items would you want to add to the list (that existed in the 1600s)? What items would you add from today? What materials, supplies, knowledge, and people are most important in beginning a settlement?

SURVIVAL AND SETTLEMENT

Imagine you are one of the first settlers in North America in 1607. Your first task is to stay alive. Place the following items in order of importance to you. In the blank space, write a 1 for the most important item, a 2 for the next most important, and so on for the rest of the list.

_____ seeds

_____ several gold coins

_____ sword

_____ shovel and hoe

_____ 50 feet of cord

_____ 5 gallons fresh water

_____ 6 blankets

_____ small rowboat

_____ compass

_____ best available map of North America

Explain the reasons for your arrangement:

---

9. What skills and abilities are best for establishing a new colony? Jamestown almost failed because of the large number of nonworking gentlemen among the first settlers. This activity is to encourage students to think about the people and occupations that are most useful in establishing a settlement. The list has been developed from a list of original Jamestown settlers. Except for the many gentlemen, there were only one or two individuals holding each of the other occupations on the list. Distribute Reproduction Page 25, "People Make a Difference."

   Another element can be added to this activity by adding such variables as age, physical or mental limitations, social class, or special skills or attitudes that help or endanger the group. For instance, one, some, or all of a group can be very old or very young; others could have chronic coughs, probably tuberculosis; some could have low intelligence, be crippled, deaf, emotionally unstable, or be especially friendly, have language ability, and so on.

   Similar approaches to this activity would be to have students place the occupations in order of importance, or to select the six most important. Students could also be asked to develop their own list of ten people and skills that would be most important in starting a colony in 1600. Discuss: Why did you select the people you did? What difficulties might arise among the people you selected? What kinds of skills do you think were important in starting a new colony in 1600? Would the same be true today? What would happen to your group if they met a hostile group already in the area where you settled? What would happen if some refused to work or obey any rules? Which people would best represent your interests in the group?

   To realize that choices have consequences, and to help bring this activity to a logical and meaningful close, have students write a history of the colony one year, and fifty years, after settlement.

REPRODUCTION PAGE 25

PEOPLE MAKE A DIFFERENCE

You are a London merchant during the early 1600s and have invested in establishing a
colony in North America. You must select people to explore and settle this new land. Since
they are establishing a new colony it is very important that they be chosen with great care.
Your ship is limited to exactly 100 people. You have prepared a list of possible choices and
now must decide who will go. No one else can be taken. Alongside each person, place the
number you will take. You may decide that some are not needed, but the entire list must
total 100.

Person	Number to be taken
gentleman	――――
carpenter	――――
laborer	――――
surgeon	――――
blacksmith	――――
sailor	――――
barber	――――
mason	――――
bricklayer	――――
tailor	――――
drummer	――――
jeweler	――――
goldsmith	――――
druggist	――――
soldier	――――
	100

Why did you select the people you did?

Topic 4:   Organizing and Governing the Colonies

1. The Virginia Company ran into problems raising funds, recruiting a proper labor
    force, and maintaining authority over the settlers. A series of regulations known as
    Dale's Code, after Captain Thomas Dale, was developed to promote the interests
    of the company. This activity examines the economic and political development of
    the first settlement. It has to do with *leaders, laborers, land,* and *laws.* Success
    eventually came to the Virginia Company, it should be noted, because of the
    introduction of tobacco, private property, political freedom, and women.

    Divide the class into groups representing investors, appointed leaders, and
    ordinary settlers, and have them develop responses to the following questions: How
    do you obtain leaders? What religious practices are to be followed? How are laws
    enforced? What punishments are used? What individual rights should exist? How
    should trade be regulated? What conditions exist for workers? What military
    responsibilities do people have?

Distribute copies of Reproduction Page 26, "Governing a Colony," and have students compare their responses with Dale's Code. The questions can be answered individually or in small groups.

A related activity is to role play a discussion of Dale's Code between Dale and a few leaders on one side and the rest of the class as laborers on the other side. Inform the class that the code has just been announced by Dale at a meeting of the colony and he asks if there are any comments.

REPRODUCTION PAGE 26

GOVERNING A COLONY

Rules and Regulations of Virginia Company. Developed by Thomas Dale.

1. There is to be one governor with complete power.
2. Settlers are marched to church twice a day.
3. Men are to be divided into groups under the control of an officer.
4. No one can return to England without permission.

The following are punishable by serving in the ship's galleys or by death:

5. Slander against the company or its officers.
6. Unauthorized trading with the Indians.
7. Theft.
8. Killing any domestic animal without permission of the company.
9. A false accounting by any supply keeper.
10. All men must keep regular hours of work. The first offense is punishable by lying with neck and heels tied together all night, the second offense is punishable by whipping, and the third offense is punishable by serving one year in the ship's galleys.
11. All people shall have a military rank and specific responsibilities.

Your goals are to (a) increase profits, (b) obtain more workers, and (c) keep control of the colony.

1. Which regulations and/or punishments would you change or eliminate?

2. What new regulations would you develop?

3. Develop a program that would best accomplish the company's objectives.

---

2. About thirty-five Separatists and sixty-five other Englishmen sailed for Virginia Colony in 1620 but arrived far to the north. They were beyond the jurisdiction of Virginia and not subject to control by their sponsor, the London Company. They agreed to establish just laws and to obey them and signed an agreement aboard their ship, the *Mayflower.*

Distribute Reproduction Page 27, "Will Separatists Stay Together?," to groups of students divided into church members (Separatists) and nonchurch members (often known as Strangers). Have each group develop a statement about establishing a government. Everyone within the class—Separatists and Strangers—must agree with the final statement. Compare with the Mayflower Compact.

WILL SEPARATISTS STAY TOGETHER?

You are the leader of a religious group moving across an ocean into an unknown wilderness. Your trip has been paid for by an investment company. This company asked you to take several people who were not members of your religious group. There are about twice as many nonchurch members as there are members. The company also wants you to settle on company-owned land to establish your community. Every time your group moved in the past, church members signed an agreement, or covenant, promising to help one another, follow the Bible, support the church, and obey church elders. Now you are about to land and realize that (1) you are not in the territory owned by the company, and (2) several nonchurch members are threatening to go their own way. You want to keep the group together. What kind of covenant can you write that all will sign?

We, the church and nonchurch members of this group,

Signed:

---

3. The Virginia frontier was subject to repeated attacks from the native people. Sir William Berkeley, governor of Virginia, refused to take action to protect small farmers and other frontier settlers. One of them, Nathaniel Bacon, organized a small force and defeated a group of the natives. Later Bacon marched to the capital and forced Berkeley to prepare a campaign against the natives. Bacon and his followers left the capital, and Berkeley labeled them traitors and ordered their arrest. Hearing this, they returned, destroyed the capital, and seized control of the government. Bacon became ill and died. Berkeley returned, subdued the revolt, and was shortly thereafter removed from office because of his actions by King Charles II.

Distribute Reproduction Page 28, "Retreat or Revolt?," and have students decide a course of action, individually or in groups.

RETREAT OR REVOLT?

You and your friends live far inland at the foot of some rolling mountains. The government and wealthy people in your colony live along the fertile coast and are not concerned with the dangers you face from hostile Indians. The taxes you pay are used to pay the salaries of the governor and legislators. The right to vote is restricted to those owning houses. Everyone has to attend *Church of England* services or be fined. The members of the legislature set their own salary. No roads or other improvements have been made. You want the government to build forts and provide protection against attacks of Indians. The governor was told of Indian attacks but has done nothing. Finally, about 500 men join with you in a successful battle against some Indians. Now some of the men are urging you to march toward the capital where the governor and legislature are in session. They want to take over the government. If you return home, you disappoint your followers and perhaps lose any chance for making changes. If you go to the capital, you know it is likely to lead to armed conflict with considerable death and destruction.

In this case, here is what I would do and why I would do it:

4. This activity centers on a paraphrased agreement between the London Company, known as *adventurers,* and the Pilgrims, known as *planters,* prior to sailing for the New World. Divide the class into adventurers and planters and distribute Reproduction Page 29, "Getting What You Want." Each side should decide how they would complete the form to their own advantage. Which items are critical, and which are negotiable? After they have planned their bargaining strategy, have both sides meet to reach agreement on the provisions of this arrangment to finance the new settlement.

The actual agreement for Reproduction Page 29 provided the following:

1. (no change)
2. (no change)
3. 7; is divided among the
   shareholders
4. (no change)
5. 7; equally; equally

6. 7
7. 16; 10; 16
8. 10; 50
9. 7
10. their meat, drink, apparel, and
    all provisions

REPRODUCTION PAGE 29

GETTING WHAT YOU WANT

Agreement Between Adventurers and Planters

1. The adventurers (those remaining in England but venturing their money) and planters do agree that every person that goeth being aged 16 years and upward shall be given a single share of the company.

2. That he that goeth in person, and furnishes himself out in money or other provisions be given a double share of the company.

3. The persons transported, and the adventurers shall continue their partnership for _____ years during which time all profits and benefits that are not got by trade, working, fishing, or any other means shall remain in the common stock of the company until _____.

4. That a number of additional fit persons be taken to work upon the land, building houses, tilling and planting the ground, and making such commodities as shall be most useful for the colony.

5. That at the end of _____ years, the profits, houses, lands, goods be divided _____ for adventurers, _____ for planters; which done, every man shall be free from other of them of any debt concerning this adventure.

6. Whosoever cometh to the colony hereafter or invest in the company shall at the end of _____ years be allowed a proportionate amount of the profit.

7. He that shall take his wife and children, or servants, shall be allowed for every person now aged _____ years and upward, a single share in the division of the company profits or if he provide them necessities, a double share. If they be between _____ years old and _____ years, then two of them shall be reckoned as one person.

8. That such children under the age of _____ years have no other share in the division of company profits but shall receive _____ acres of land.

9. That such persons as die before the _____ years are up, their executors shall have their share, proportionately to the time of their life in the colony.

10. That all such as are of this colony are to have (the following items) _____

out of the common stock and goods of the colony.

Additional provisions:

Topic 5:   Economic Decisions and Social-Cultural Patterns

Economic considerations were a prime motivation for establishing colonies in the New World. Early ideas about economic organization were modified or scrapped as experiences with landownership, labor systems, and production and distribution caused the settlers to reexamine their economic practices.

1. This activity asks students to rank statements about the distribution of a limited amount of food. In this, or any ranking, it is often worthwhile to have students complete the task individually and then see if consensus can be reached in small groups. If you wish to pursue the matter at greater length, each group can present its decisions and rationale and a class consensus can be developed.[1]

REPRODUCTION PAGE 30

DISTRIBUTION OF SCARCE RESOURCES

Imagine you are with the first settlers in the New World. Your food and other resources are in short supply, and you must decide how the remaining amount will be distributed. Put the following items in order; number 1 is your first choice, number 2 your second choice, and so on. Then briefly explain the reasons for your selections.

_____ I would give food to the 10 percent of the group who worked hardest.

_____ I would get some more food and save it all until we had enough for a party.

_____ I would sell the food to the highest bidder.

_____ I would divide the food equally so that everyone would have an equal, although very small, amount.

_____ I would give the food to the three hungriest people.

_____ I would hold an election to select three people to receive the food.

_____ I would just say that it is available and let anyone who wanted it get it.

_____ I would give it to the people who have the best chance of surviving.

_____ I would give it to the weakest.

I decided this way because:

Use Reproduction Page 30, "Distribution of Scarce Resources," for the student ranking. In a general way, the statements are related to the following ideas about economic distribution:

* Puritan ethic (give to those who worked hardest)

* hedonist (save for a party)

* capitalist (sell to highest bidder)

* commune (divide equally)

---

1. This activity is based on an idea originally developed by Bob Clifton, Metropolitan State College, Denver, Colorado, and used by the Center for Teaching International Relations, University of Denver, in an experimental program.

- Marxist (give to the hungriest)

- survival of fittest (let those who can best get it have it)

- triage (give it to those with best chance of surviving)

Another approach with the statements from Reproduction Page 30 is to assign one statement to each person or group and have arguments prepared and presented to the rest of the class. The class, representing early settlers, has to decide which approach is best to follow. A limited amount of food—apples, candy, or something similar—can be used to add realism and extra interest to the proceedings.

Follow-up work greatly enhances this activity. Students should relate the distribution methods to the decisions made by settlers in Jamestown, Plymouth, and elsewhere. Comparisons can be made with the United States today.

The statements can be easily modified to investigate issues of land distribution, tool use, work arrangements, and other basic economic issues. How do the decisions affect other aspects of economic development? How are the settlers affected by their environment? The environment by the settlers? How do economic decisions affect their relations with each other? The social structure?

2. The arrangement of a traditional New England town indicates considerable self-sufficiency on the part of the early inhabitants. Their interaction with others can be seen at the meetinghouse, the village common, and the mill, but they thought of themselves as self-reliant individuals. Reproduction Page 31, "Map of a Colonial Town," allows you to discuss the everyday life of New England colonists. It also provides an opportunity to develop basic map skills. Have students complete the information on the reproduction page and then prepare a map representing a New England community.

REPRODUCTION PAGE 31

MAP OF A COLONIAL TOWN

A New England colonial town had a *village green* or *common* and a *meetinghouse* located in the center of the community. In later years there might have been a *school*.

Each family owned a *house and land* in town, and many people often had a *barn, toolshed, well, outhouse,* and *garden.* Away from the town a family might own a *field* for growing corn and grazing animals. They often shared the *woods* and *pasture.*

A *road* went through the town and was used to get to the outlying areas. Houses were close together for protection, usually along a main road. A river often provided waterpower for the *mill.*

Complete the information below. Then name your town and draw a map showing what it would look like.

Scale of kilometers: one centimeter on the map equals_____meters

The direction north is shown on the map by _____

My town will be called:_____

Draw the symbols for each of these features:

village green	meetinghouse
school	house
barn	toolshed

well	outhouse
garden	field
woods	pasture
road	mill

3. Slavery and the use of indentured servants existed from the days of the earliest settlements. While indentures decided to come to the New World, slaves were captured and brought against their will; while indentures were eventually let go and usually given land, slavery was a permanent condition; while the indentured system is related to apprenticeships and training periods for employment and discrimination based on economic status and skills, the slave system is related to the control of one human being by another and discrimination based on race. Reproduction Page 32, "Slave Ship," is a brief case in which the student is presented with a balanced, but risky, situation aboard a slave ship in which a decision must be made. It can be used individually or in small groups.

REPRODUCTION PAGE 32

SLAVE SHIP

You are a sailor aboard a slave trader heading to the British North American colonies. The ship owner is a wealthy and respected member of a New England community. He, like most everyone else, thinks there is nothing wrong with enslaving non-Christians. You have heard that there have been more than 100 successful slave revolts at sea but know that most are unsuccessful. You feel that slavery is wrong and inhuman but need a job on a ship. Your task is to help sail the ship and inspect below deck each day to make sure the slaves are secured and that no pieces of iron, wood, or knives are hidden. Upon entering the hold, you surprisingly knock over an African and instinctively grab him and hold a knife to his neck. Looking up, you see that all the slaves are out of their chains. Many have knives and are momentarily stunned at what has happened. You can quickly and safely leave by locking the door and trapping everyone below. Or you can lead the revolt and hope to take over the ship. You hear another sailor coming, and the slaves are recovering from their surprise. What do you do?

4. Reproduction Page 33, "Return the Runaway?," is a situation in which the student must decide what to do in the case of a runaway slave.

REPRODUCTION PAGE 33

RETURN THE RUNAWAY?

You have read advertisements in the paper about runaway slaves and servants. Sizable rewards are offered for their capture and return. You are having some pots and pans repaired and recently hired an itinerant tinker to do the work. He fits the description of a runaway. If you turn him in to the courthouse you will receive a reward of five pounds—a sizable amount. But you also know that he will probably be punished severely. You think people should obey the law but don't think that being a runaway is a serious crime. The tinker is bringing your pots and pans back tomorrow morning. Do you obey the law and receive a reward by turning him in, or do you warn him about the advertisement and perhaps help him escape?

5. This activity uses Reproduction Page 34, "Which Way for Witchcraft?," to place students in the difficult position of examining self-interest and community pressures. Like other case studies, it can be used individually or in small groups and provides a common base for the class to further study the strange events associated with the witch hysteria.

An alternate or follow-up strategy is to have students assume roles as jurors in a witchcraft trial that eventually put twenty people to death. Several years have now passed, and you and the community realize that a terrible mistake has been made. A meeting of your church is called, and you are asked to explain what can be done.

REPRODUCTION PAGE 34

WHICH WAY FOR WITCHCRAFT?

The people of your town believe that criminals have to be punished. If they are not, God will cause everyone to suffer from some natural disaster. The way to prevent everyone from being punished is to have the sinner repent—say he or she is sorry for the wrongdoing and change. And if the person does this there is really no reason for the townspeople to punish him or her. A few teenage girls claim that your image pinches them and causes them great pain. They become hysterical in your presence and say that you are a witch. You are brought to trial before the church leaders who, like yourself, believe that Satan can cause these strange happenings. You can escape punishment and probably death by confessing to being a witch, even though you know you are not. If you confess you will be expected to name other townspeople who are also witches. You can confess to something you know is not so and accuse others to save yourself, or you can tell the truth as you know it and face the consequences. The trial ends and you are asked to make a statement in your own behalf. What do you say?

---

6. This activity uses superstitions to examine individual beliefs about the supernatural. There were a number of conditions that led to the Salem witch trials and hysteria. The purpose of this strategy is to have students consider their own rational and nonrational ideas and discuss conditions that make their beliefs harmless or dangerous. Is there a basis of truth? Use Reproduction Page 35, "Do You Believe?," for this strategy.

REPRODUCTION PAGE 35

DO YOU BELIEVE?

Directions: Circle the number indicating how strongly you believe in each of the statements.

DO YOU BELIEVE...	no				yes
• *that these things can bring good luck?*					
1. throwing salt over your left shoulder	1	2	3	4	5
2. rabbit's foot	1	2	3	4	5
3. knocking on wood	1	2	3	4	5
• *that these things can bring bad luck?*					
1. number 13	1	2	3	4	5
2. black cat crosses your path	1	2	3	4	5
3. walking under a ladder	1	2	3	4	5
4. opening an umbrella indoors	1	2	3	4	5
5. breaking a mirror	1	2	3	4	5

- *that these things are so?*

1. that there are supernatural things that can't be scientifically explained	1	2	3	4	5
2. that some people have extrasensory perception (can know things without seeing, hearing, feeling, touching, or smelling them)	1	2	3	4	5
3. that some people can make others act in unusual ways or "cast a spell"	1	2	3	4	5
4. a person's character can be read from the lines on the palm of his or her hands	1	2	3	4	5
5. that some people today can be called witches and do have unusual powers	1	2	3	4	5

Do you think people's beliefs are: Helpful? Harmful? Dangerous? When do the beliefs of one person make a difference to another person? Are there beliefs that everyone should have? What controls, if any, should a community have on the beliefs of citizens?

7. This activity is another case study in which the student is to take the role of a participant in a historical event. It is Andrew Hamilton's defense of John Peter Zenger, which is frequently referred to as establishing the principle of freedom of the press. It can be used as an individual assignment but lends itself to role playing in a courtroom situation. Assign roles for the prosecutor, defense attorney, judge, defendant, governor, and the jury. Prior research into the *Zenger* case will help develop the historical importance of the role play. Use Reproduction Page 36, "Publish or Protect?" for this activity.

REPRODUCTION PAGE 36

PUBLISH OR PROTECT?

You have to defend the publisher of the *New York Weekly Journal* who has printed articles criticizing the governor for establishing special courts without approval from the legislature. The governor has also removed judges from the courts without any cause for doing so. The publisher you are defending wrote that the liberties of the people are in danger and they will be made slaves if the governor can do as he pleases. This angered the governor, of course, and the publisher was arrested and is being tried for libel. The judge in this case wants the jury to make its decision on whether the publisher did or did not publish the critical articles. His instructions to the jury state that no government can exist if people criticize those who are appointed to run its affairs. It is necessary for government that the people have a good opinion of it. To create distrust about the management of the government has always been a crime. No government can be safe without punishing the people who criticize it. It is now your chance to present the case for the defense to the jury. What do you say?

Topic 6:   Growing Independence and Interdependence

Colonial trade indicates the interdependent nature of the economic system that existed during the seventeenth and eighteenth centuries. British policy and colonial interests resulted in a degree of colonial dependence on England. But mutual interests encouraged interdependent relationships among the colonists themselves that slowly evolved to rival and then challenge the dependency on England.

1. Divide the class into small working groups and have each imagine that it is a wealthy, powerful, manufacturing country that has established colonies to provide natural resources and to serve as a market for your finished goods. Your manufactured products are needed in the colonies but you are worried that they are starting their own industries. The colonies have developed a brisk trade for their

own resources and are beginning to compete with, rather than serve, the mother country. Your manufactures and the resources of your colonies are listed below. Your task is to write trade laws that will aid your industries and maintain or expand the market in the colonies. Among the approaches for regulating trade are various types of taxes, control of shipping vessels, restriction of trading places, limitation on colonial manufacturing. Inform students of the products and have them write trade laws to (a) aid their own industries, and (b) maintain or expand the colonial market.

Resources of the Colonies	*English Manufactured Goods*
lumber	cloth
whale oil and bone	nails
codfish	guns
wheat	china
furs	furniture
tobacco	bricks
naval stores	machinery
indigo	glass
rice	

Discuss: What economic or political events would encourage the colonies to deal with each other? What conditions create trade advantages? How can colonists with resources gain advantages over England and its manufactured goods?

2. Use Reproduction Page 37, "A Colonial Sort," and cut the page into separate slips of paper or prepare cards. Give each student or small group a package of all the cards. Have the students group the cards into logical categories and explain the reasoning behind their card sort. Several categories are possible, although you may wish to inform them that they are to develop three groups. If this is done, the items are arranged in categories on the reproduction page as New England, 1–11; Middle Colonies, 12–20; and Southern Colonies, 21–30.

   After the sort has been completed, ask: What is the influence of geography in each area? Which cards are most characteristic of the area? Which are the most significant developments for each area? What conclusions can be drawn about each area? Are the conclusions warranted?

   The relationship between areas can be explored by asking: What similarities exist between the cards for each area? Differences? What cards represent ties to the other areas? Which cards represent possible conflicts with other areas? Which cards represent the growth of democracy in each area?

REPRODUCTION PAGE 37

A COLONIAL SORT

Directions for Teacher: The items on this page are to be cut into individual statements or made into cards. Many sorts are possible. A major sort for this listing is New England (1–11), Middle Colonies (12–20), and Southern Colonies (21–30).

1. hilly and rocky land and many good harbors

2. self-sufficient family farms

16. Zenger trial establishes freedom of the press

17. first circulating library

3. fishing, whaling, and shipbuilding

18. Toleration Act provides religious freedom for Christians

4. triangular trade

19. large patroons granted to wealthy settlers

5. strict "blue laws" forbade Sunday entertainment

20. *Poor Richard's Almanac*

6. first public school system

21. fertile soil and long growing season

7. King Philip's War

22. tobacco, rice, and indigo produced as "cash crops"

8. town meeting determines local affairs

23. main house surrounded by smaller separate buildings

9. Williams establishes principle of separation of church and state

24. private tutors for wealthy children

10. Separatists

25. Bacon's Rebellion

11. Massasoit

26. first representative assembly

12. coastal plains and fertile farmland

27. plantation system of agriculture

13. great wheat and corn production

28. Powhatan

14. Dutch architectural influence

29. slave system

15. King's College

30. colony settled as buffer with Spanish territory

3. The "Colonial Sort" can be used in several other ways.

    • Select one concept or idea—cooperation, power, systems—and have students find items that are related to that idea. Have them explain their selections.

    • Use each item as a small research topic and have students find additional information about their topic.

    • The sort can be used as a pretest or evaluative device by giving students the categories of New England, Middle Colonies, and Southern Colonies and instructing them to match the items with the proper category.

    • The items can also be used as answers and a class session conducted in which students ask appropriate questions to suit the answer.

    • A number of other categories can be developed by students and data obtained to create another card sort. Provide students with duplicating masters and have them develop another set of items.

4. The danger to the colonists from the French and Indians increased during the 1750s until war finally erupted in 1754. Delegates from seven colonies met in Albany for the purpose of uniting all English colonies. It was an important step toward cooperation. The plan, however, was rejected by Parliament for fear that

the colonies would become a threat to English interests; and it was rejected by the colonies, who feared loss of local government control. Reproduction Page 38, "A Plan of Union," is based on a proposal made by Benjamin Franklin, the Pennsylvania delegate.

Divide the class into an equal number of small groups and distribute Reproduction Page 38. Have half the groups list arguments and advantages for having the colonies form a union based on the proposal. Have the others prepare statements against forming a union. After sufficient time has elapsed, the two groups are to meet and attempt to match advantage with disadvantage until as many as possible are equalized. The group must then reach a consensus on forming or not forming a union. Each group is to prepare a statement indicating its position and present its decision and reasons to the class. Can the class reach one conclusion?

An alternate strategy using Reproduction Page 38 is to divide the class into seven groups. Each is to develop a statement accepting or rejecting the plan of union. Exchange this information and attempt to reach a class consensus. The groups represent: (a) Parliament, (b) Massachusetts shipbuilders, (c) New York merchants, (d) Pennsylvania farmers, (e) Virginia planters, (f) Iroquois Indians, and (g) Benjamin Franklin.

Discuss: If accepted, how would this plan of union help or harm the colonists? The English? The Indians? The French?

REPRODUCTION PAGE 38

A PLAN OF UNION

It is during the 1750s and the colonies face increasing danger from their enemies. A meeting is called, and seven colonies send delegates to write a plan of union. They make the following decisions:

1. That there be a president general and a Grand Council

2. That the president general should be appointed by the king of England

3. That the Grand Council have representatives chosen by each colony based on population (Massachusetts and Virginia, for example, the largest, would have seven representatives; Rhode Island would have two; and so on)

4. That the Grand Council should appoint its own Speaker. The Speaker would become president general if the president general died in office

5. That the president general would approve all acts of the grand council

6. That the president general, with the advice of the Grand Council, would have the following powers:

   - make treaties and declare war with the Indian nations
   - regulate trade
   - purchase land
   - regulate new settlements
   - raise and pay for an army and navy
   - make laws
   - levy taxes

---

5. The clash for control of the Ohio River Valley was an important contributing factor leading to the French and Indian War. Divide the class into two groups, English and Colonists, and French and Indians. Provide each with a brief description of their background in North America. Additional research can be assigned to develop resources and advantages for the group the students represent. Each group should be asked to determine its objectives, develop a course of action, and speculate on the likely results.

English and Colonists	*New France*
In 1755, about 1.5 million people in numerous cities along the Atlantic coast.	In 1755, about 65,000 trappers, soldiers, missionaries, and adventurers throughout Canada and North America between the Appalachians and the Mississippi.
Most are self-sufficient in agriculture; there are merchants and craftsmen and the beginnings of manufacturing.	Except for furs for trading, the French are dependent on France.
Colonies are mostly self-governing; colonies are jealous and suspicious of each other; they seek to avoid expenses and gain profits wherever possible.	There is a unity of command; the people know the forest and are friendly with most Indians; European allies are Austria, Russia, and Spain.
British are friendly with the Iroquois Indians.	

After students have considered their relative positions, present them with appropriate information from Reproduction Page 39, "Clash over Colonial Land." The columns on this reproduction page are basically the same except each is written from the perspective of the English or the French. After students respond to the questions at the end of the columns, have them exchange their letters with the other group and continue doing this until the problem is resolved. The Virginian described in the case is Lieutenant Governor Robert Dinwiddie and the officer sent with a warning to the French is George Washington. The French governor general of Canada is Duquesne.

Discuss: What is the basis of the English claim to the land? The French claim? Which country has a better claim? How do nations establish claims to territories that are accepted by other nations? What claims do the Indians have to the land? How could this dispute have been resolved in other ways?

REPRODUCTION PAGE 39

CLASH OVER COLONIAL LAND

British and Colonists	*New France*
Several prominent Englishmen and Virginians have organized the Ohio Company (1748) to establish trading posts and settlements in the Ohio River Valley. A grant of 200,000 acres was obtained from the king with a promise of 300,000 more acres if 100 families settled the area within seven years. You fear encroachment by Pennsylvanians as well as French settlers and have a wagon road cut to the area and send explorers to locate favorable land for settlement.	Last year the governor general of Canada sent about 215 French soldiers and a force of Indians to take control of the Ohio River Valley for France. The group traveled overland and by canoe posting notices on trees and burying lead plates claiming the land for the French king. Word has been received that the British are interested in the fertile lands and have been supporting colonial attempts to establish settlements in the Ohio River Valley.
News has reached you that the French have sent a sizable force to construct a line of forts in the area. An English trading post has been seized and occupied by the French.	You have sent an expedition of 1000 men to build a line of forts in this area to hold it for France. An English trading post was taken and now the English have sent a warning to the commander of one of the forts saying the area belongs to England. A small group of colonists delivered the message demanding that your soldiers withdraw. The soldiers informed the colonists that the Ohio River Valley would be held for France until other orders came from you, as governor general of Canada.
You are alarmed and send a warning to the French accusing them of trespassing on English lands. The officer sent to warn the French to withdraw from the Ohio returns with the message that the French plan to stay until they are told to move by French officials.	

Your objective is to gain the Ohio River Valley.	You are responsible for establishing French policy for North America. Your objective is to gain and hold the Ohio River Valley.
1. What courses of action are available to you?	1. What courses of action are available to you?
2. What are the consequences of each?	2. What are the consequences of each?
3. Which do you select? What do you hope/expect to happen?	3. Which do you select? What do you hope/expect to happen?
—Write a letter to the French governor general regarding the presence of French soldiers in the Ohio River Valley.	—Write a letter to the colonial governor regarding the presence of English settlers in the Ohio River Valley.

6. Have the class brainstorm questions about life in the colonies. After obtaining a number of items, combine and revise the list to eliminate duplication and obviously inappropriate suggestions. Have students or small groups investigate one question and report their findings to the class. Reproduction Page 40, "Student Investigations," can be used at this time and throughout the course.

REPRODUCTION PAGE 40

STUDENT INVESTIGATIONS

Question to be investigated: _____

_____

Hypothesis (your educated guess at the answer)

Evidence (what you found to prove or disprove your hypothesis)

    Explain evidence   *Source of information*

Revised hypothesis and further explanation (based on your evidence, this is the best answer to the original question)

ASSESSING LEARNING EXPERIENCES

Several of the activities from the previous section of this chapter can be used for evaluating student achievements. The questionnaires, in particular, are useful for pretest and posttest purposes. The approaches suggested here can also be used as further teaching activities or for individual student investigations.

1. Each of the following have been given as possible reasons for exploring and colonizing the New World:

    • poor living conditions in home country

    • desire for a new start in life

    • chance to obtain wealth and land

    • love of adventure

    • desire to convert others to your religion

    • desire to escape persecution in home country

    What examples or evidence is there that the Spanish, French, or English came for any of these reasons?

    Find and interview three people who have recently moved into your community. What reasons seem to be most important to them for moving?

    Prepare a report to the class: Based on your research, people today (are) (are not) similar to the European explorers of North America because:

2. Social scientists have identified four ways in which people relate to one another after their first contacts: extermination, accommodation, assimilation, or amalgamation. What does each of these mean? Find examples of each of these showing the interactions between Europeans and Indians, French-English-Spanish, and among various colonies.

    Find recent evidence indicating that people still interact with each other in one of these four ways. On the basis of your findings, report on the way human beings relate with each other today: better, worse, or the same as in the seventeenth and eighteenth centuries.

3. Have individuals select one, or small groups select all, of the following topics and explain how the colonists solved problems of (a) leadership; (b) obtaining food, clothing, and shelter; (c) determining working arrangements; (d) making economic decisions (landownership, property, exchange, production, distribution); (e) questions of crime and punishment; and (f) handling unforeseen emergencies.

4. Open-ended questions can be used for evaluative purposes, but, of course, the responses will vary widely. The information is often revealing and helpful for reviewing or revising instruction. Some questions for this chapter:

    • I learned that . . .

    • The best thing about colonial times . . .

    • The worst thing about colonial times . . .

    • If I lived during this period I would . . .

    • If I were an Indian when the colonists were arriving I would . . .

    • When studying history, one should . . .

RESOURCES FOR TEACHING

Below is a selected list of materials and resources for teaching about the exploration and colonization of North America. These materials—and those that are included in the chapters that follow—are meant to update and supplement the extensive bibliographies that exist in most teacher's guides. We have listed materials and resources that meet our criteria of being especially useful to the teacher, moderately priced, and thoughtfully developed. Addresses of publishers can be found in the alphabetical list on pages 191–199.

Books, Pamphlets, and Articles

Burns, Robert; Boyer, Lee R.; and Felton, James R. *Episodes in American History: Early Americans.* Lexington, Mass.: Ginn, 1973.

> Extensive use of contemporary accounts and observations of early historians provides insight into the life of the first Americans, Euro-Americans, and Afro-Americans during the colonial period.

Kownslar, Allan O., ed. "Inquiring about Early American Indian Life: The Jumanos," *Teaching American History: The Quest for Relevancy.* Washington, D.C.: National Council for the Social Sciences (NCSS), 1974, pp. 20–39.

> A carefully developed activity with teaching strategies and student materials for teaching about an early Indian group in the Southwest. The major focus is on the incompleteness of history.

Other Resources

Adopt. Lakeside, Calif.: Interact.

> Students decide on the most logical location for a hunting and gathering society. This game develops the idea of the importance of environment to society.

American Heritage Series, The: Discovery and Exploration, and *Colonial America.* New York: McGraw-Hill.

> Both of these sets have five color-sound filmstrips with attractive reproductions of paintings, maps, woodcuts, and artifacts of the period. Informative teacher's guide provides information about the visuals and suggests student activities.

American Museum of Natural History. New York, N.Y.

> Has photographic collection and other materials relating to native Americans.

Colonial Era, The. Troy, Mich.: Instructional Products Services.

> This independent student inquiry packet provides forms and materials for student research on any of fifteen questions. Contract proposals, evaluation forms, conferences reports, and other teacher aids are included.

Colonial Williamsburg. Williamsburg, Va.

> The most outstanding example of a restored colonial community and worth every effort to visit. In addition, several inexpensive films, filmstrips, records, slides, and publications are available about everyday colonial life. Write for catalog.

Critical Thinking Aids. New York: Modern Learning Aids.

> These short filmstrips pose leading questions, offer choices in which students consider alternatives and consequences, and then relate what actually occurred. Eight titles have been grouped into *Explorers and Colonies, 1492-1664,* and nine as *Separate Colonies, 1664-1765,* and are available from the publisher or Social Studies School Service.

Culture Contact II. Cambridge, Mass.: Abt.

> A popular game in which a trading expedition lands on an isolated island inhabited by a non-industrial tribe. Simulates intercultural problems.

Decision-Making: Locating a Colony. Fresno, Calif.: Involvement.

> Students use a map and documents to determine the location of a new colony in seventeenth-century America. This simulation is part of a package which also includes activities about Bunker Hill, Dred Scott, Antietam, Pullman, and economic growth.

Digging up America's Past. Washington, D.C.: National Geographic.

> Five color-sound filmstrips of civilization in the Western Hemisphere, the European conquerors, and settlers who followed Columbus.

Early American Life. Boulder, Colo.: The Early American Life Society.

> This attractive journal for historians and the general public has articles on issues and events of colonial times and others on antiques, cooking,

decorations, and collecting. Numerous advertisements for reproductions and resorts with a colonial flavor.

Educational Masterprints Company. Garden City, N.Y.

Packets of duplicating masters on basic history topics. Several relate to exploration and colonization themes. Write for catalog.

Interaction: A Balance of Power in Colonial America. Sun Valley, Calif.: Edu-Game.

This simulation illustrates conflicts of interest prior to the American Revolution with an emphasis on social and economic differences. Competition between groups—frontiersmen, bankers, merchants, small farmers—and the passing of favorable laws and the financial rewards and penalties provide the structure for the game.

Jackdaws. New York: Grossman.

Packets of facsimiles of original documents, letters, maps, newspapers, posters. Background information and teaching suggestions are included. Jackdaws are available on numerous topics. Among those related to exploration and colonization are: *Columbus and the Discovery of America, The Mayflower and the Pilgrim Fathers, Immigration in Colonial Times, Salem Village and the Witch Hysteria.*

John Peter Zenger Trial, The. Wilton, Conn.: Current Affairs.

One filmstrip accompanied by two recordings, one giving arguments of the prosecutor, the other giving the arguments of the defense. Students decide verdict for themselves and compare their decision with what actually happened.

Museum of the American Indian. New York, N.Y.

Has photographic collections and other materials relating to native Americans.

Plimouth Plantation. Plymouth, Mass.

A *living* village that re-creates the Pilgrim settlement as it was in 1627. Several buildings, exhibits, demonstrations, and publications. The ship *Mayflower II* and other points of colonial interest are nearby. Write for educational mail order catalog.

Smithsonian Institution. Washington, D.C.

Has publications and materials suitable for classroom use. Write for the *Introductory Bibliography on the American Indian.* For photographs and additional information ask about the National Anthropological Archives collection.

Social Studies School Service. Culver City, Calif.

Catalog has extensive listing of various materials that relate to exploration and colonization. See the latest issue for new materials.

U.S. Department of the Interior. Bureau of Indian Affairs, Washington, D.C.

Has photographic collections and other materials relating to native Americans.

U.S. History—Colonial Period. Washington, D.C.: Photo Lab.

Sets of color slides, with identifying titles, available on Jamestown, Plymouth, Salem, and Williamsburg.

University Museum. University of Pennsylvania, Philadelphia, Pa.

Has photographic collections and other materials relating to native Americans.

Virtue. Lakeside, Calif.: Interact.

A simulation involving students in roles of members of an idealistic community establishing a society based upon Puritan values: devotion, aspiration, work, knowledge, sacrifice, honesty, modesty, purity.

Walett, Francis G., ed. *Historical Facsimile Packet.* Boston: Allyn & Bacon.

Historical reproduction of 135 documents about events during colonial and revolutionary times. Reproduced from the collection of the American Antiquarian Society.

William and Mary Quarterly—A Magazine of Early American History. Williamsburg, Va.: Institute of Early American History and Culture.

Articles on colonial, revolutionary, and early national periods in American history. The institute also has scholarly publications and bibliography available.

3

The American Revolution

After more than 150 years of developing American customs and institutions, the colonies began to receive considerable royal attention and, within a twenty-year period from 1763 to 1783, dissolved the political bands that had connected them with England. The first of the world's great revolutions has had a profound effect ever since and has been followed by similar upheavals in France, several South American countries, Mexico, Russia, China, many African nations, and several other countries.

This chapter begins with the *idea* of revolution because it is important for understanding world conditions today: great and rapid change, conflict, violence, propaganda, economic insecurity, government insensitivity, internal strife, and the quest for human rights.

The American Revolution was unique in many ways when compared with others, and the remaining topics in this chapter are designed to help you develop this perspective. The colonies were well established with experienced leaders and mature political institutions by the time they revolted. Their standard and style of living surpassed that of the nation they were rebelling against. Large segments of the so-called responsible members of society—the press, religious leaders, merchants, and others—supported the cause. There were differences, it is true. Loyalists were expelled and their property confiscated, but there was never the terror or bloodshed frequently associated with later revolutions. Similarly, the first generation of revolutionary leaders was never deposed by violent, more radical followers. The emphasis was on limited government. Important governing documents were available for public debate and formal ratification.[1]

This chapter, then, is about "the course of human events" that gave birth to the United States and has shaped and influenced the world ever since.

---

1. Crane Brinton, *The Anatomy of Revolution*, rev. ed. (New York: Prentice-Hall, 1952). The English, American, French, and Russian revolutions are analyzed and used to provide guidelines for looking at revolutions. This standard work is a very helpful, nontechnical source for teachers.

PERFORMANCE OBJECTIVES

As a result of the learning experiences in this chapter, the student will be able to:
1. Analyze the causes of revolutions by applying a theoretical framework.
2. Make judgments concerning legal principles.
3. Differentiate propaganda from other information.
4. Gather and interpret data from several people.
5. Read and interpret simple maps.
6. Identify and analyze stereotyped views of people based on nationality, occupation, age, sex.
7. Suggest characteristics for leadership.
8. View an event from a variety of perspectives.
9. Conclude that history involves selection and interpretation and serves social needs.
10. Locate and organize information for a report.
11. Organize a variety of factors into plausible hypotheses about revolutions.
12. Compare the problems, values, and life-styles of the revolutionary generation with those of today.

LEARNING EXPERIENCES

Topic 1: The Idea of Revolution

1. Present and discuss the following information with students. Following instructions from the Virginia legislature, Richard Henry Lee on June 7, 1776, proposed to the Continental Congress "that these United Colonies are, and of right ought to be, free and independent States." The resolution was welcomed by most, opposed by a few, and given to a committee to prepare a statement on independence to present to the Congress for a vote. A Declaration of Independence was given to the Congress on July 2 and was readily approved by delegates from twelve colonies (New York abstaining but approving later).

   What happened to cause such a momentous decision? Some say the American Revolution began when English settlers arrived in Jamestown in 1607. Others say it occurred with a change of attitudes between 1760 and 1775. Still others point to specific events: writs of assistance, the Boston Tea Party, or most commonly the battle at Lexington on April 19, 1775. Was the Revolution planted in the nature of the people who left England for the uncertainties of the New World? Was the time and distance of geographical separation an underlying cause of the Revolution? Was it unwise governmental policies? An unhappy political accident? A conspiracy of a separatist colonial elite?

   What were the issues contributing to cause revolution? Distrust of government? Inflation? Unemployment? Taxation? Unfavorable trade practices? Rights of citizens? All of these look frighteningly contemporary.

   What makes the multitude of events and the separation of thirteen colonies from England a *revolution*? In short, simple, specific terms, a revolution is a turning around. It is profoundly wide-ranging change and, in a political sense, is normally accompanied by *illegal* and *violent* methods.

One way of looking at revolutions is presented here:

- There is a period of *conflict* and *adjustment* between the established group and the aggravated group.

- Irritations increase and each side becomes more adamant in defending its position or attacking the other regarding questions of *power* and *authority*.

- *Leadership* organizes *resources* and *public opinion* as each side sees and uses events from its special perspective.

- Incidents result in increased propaganda, *violence,* and *disregard of established laws.*

2. Check the *revolutionary spirit* of your class by using one or more of the following statements:

- There are no good reasons for the *violent* overthrow of a government.

- There are no good reasons for deliberately violating established laws.

- There will always be cases where laws are made for the good of the government that may be unfair to some people.

- America was and is controlled by a small ruling group.

- If you are dissatisfied with the laws and government of a country, you should leave.

- Poor and unhappy people cause changes; rich and powerful people are satisfied with things the way they are.

- Violence can be justified when a government refuses to change.

Have students indicate *agree* or *disagree* with these statements and explain their position. List their reasons for defending a position on the board. Apply the reasons to the time of the American Revolution; then to today's events. Does the change in time and circumstances cause students to be less certain in their opinions? Is revolution safe from a distance? Who are the revolutionaries in American society today? What are their goals? Their methods?

3. What was the Revolution about? What causes people to rebel? There is a reasonable chance that students will suggest several of the grievances listed below. Relate the grievances with some of the circumstances that exist today. Are we in the midst of a revolution today without realizing it? Is it a worldwide revolution? Are the grievances *widespread* and *intense*? Are comparisons between colonial complaints and selected bits of information about today's conditions valid? What other political, economic, social, psychological factors influence behavior toward government?

Colonial Grievance	*Conditions Today*
seek right to govern themselves	members of various minority groups, migrant workers, the poor, and students have little say about many things that affect them
military presence	military influence permeates society; defense contracts proliferate

civil rights	the high cost of lawyers; the poor, young, and minorities receive harsher penalties; racial and religious discrimination
taxation	little or no tax paid by wealthiest; business subsidies; loopholes
aristocracy	private clubs, the *Social Register*; elites based on wealth, occupation, education, etc.
government officials	conflicts of interest; favoritism; secrecy

4. James C. Davies has developed a series of diagrams useful in understanding the occurrence of revolutions. Reproduction Page 41, "The J-curve Hypothesis," can be used as a transparency or duplicated for individual student use. As a class discussion or in small groups, discuss the time span the diagram might represent, the needs and wants of the colonists, English efforts to fulfill colonial needs and wants, the idea of a tolerable gap between needs and wants, the idea of an intolerable gap, and the idea of *relative deprivation*. Is this diagram applicable to other wars, riots, and conflicts? Does it help explain why the American Revolution involved the middle and upper socioeconomic classes? Does the diagram provide an understanding of reality?

REPRODUCTION PAGE 41

THE J-CURVE HYPOTHESIS

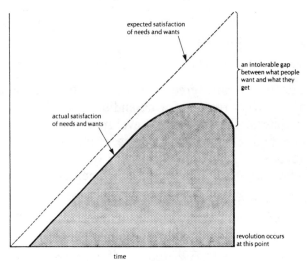

Revolutions are more likely to occur after a long period of social and economic development, followed by a sharp downturn. The people's view of conditions, their expectations, are more important than the actual conditions or state of development. The gap between reality and expectations creates a loss of confidence. When frustrations develop that are intense and widespread, they are released through violent action.

5. Reproduction Page 42, "Statements on the Revolution," begins to review some specific explanations related to the conflict. Distribute and use this page to examine the issues that led to war. Have students suggest other issues and list them on the board. You may wish to organize this activity around the concepts previously noted in the outline at the beginning of this chapter.

STATEMENTS ON THE REVOLUTION

We, his Majesty's most loyal subjects . . . affected with the deepest anxiety and most alarming apprehensions at those grievances and distresses, with which his Majesty's American subjects are oppressed, and having taken under our most serious deliberation the state of the whole continent find, that the present unhappy situation of our affairs is occasioned by a ruinous System of colony administration adopted by the British Ministry . . . evidently calculated for enslaving these colonies and with them the British Empire.—*Articles of Association, October 20, 1774, signed by delegates of twelve colonies*

Governments are instituted among Men, deriving their just powers from the consent of the governed,—That whenever any Form of Government becomes destructive of these ends, it is the Right of the People to alter or to abolish it, and to institute new Government.—*Thomas Jefferson, July 1776*

Young man, what we meant in going for those redcoats was this—we always had governed ourselves, and we always meant to. They didn't mean we should.—*Levi Preston, seventy years after he fought at the battle of Lexington*

What do we mean by the Revolution? The War? That was no part of the Revolution: it was only an effect and consequence of it. The Revolution was in the minds of the people, a change in their sentiments, their duties and obligations. . . . The real American Revolution . . . was affected from 1760 to 1775, in the course of fifteen years before a single drop of blood was shed at Lexington.—*John Adams, several years after the American Revolution*

1. According to these statements, what were key issues of the American Revolution?

2. How can the idea of *power* and *authority* be used to understand the Revolution?

3. In your opinion, which of the above statements is most helpful in understanding the Revolution? Why?

FACT OR FICTION?

	Fact	Basis for Fact	Reasons for questioning reliability
1.	triangle trade–New England–Africa–West Indies; rum-slaves-molasses	two trips made by Capt. David Lindsay, 1753–54, and magnified by nineteenth-century historians	several hundred thousand recorded voyages that did not go triangle trade route
2.	colonists rebelled because of taxes	popular interpretation of events	Navigation Acts before 1760 raised very little revenue; Stamp Act repealed; Townshend Acts repealed; Tea tax actually reduced cost of tea
3.	"no taxation without representation"	popular acceptance of slogan	misleading; colonists had strong belief in direct representation and popular consent to taxation; colonists did not want representation in Parliament but wanted to be taxed by their own representatives in their own legislatures
4.	George III was "the royal brute," as Thomas Paine called him	commonly accepted belief that he was mentally ill	new policies after 1760 were Parliament's; illness distorted perceptions, made him irritable; most trouble began in 1780s, long after the Revolution
5.	"One if by land, two if by sea"	Longfellow's poem	British actually went both ways; Revere was captured before reaching Concord

6. One-third of the people favored the Revolution, one-third opposed it, and one-third were undecided	commonly accepted paraphrase of comments made by John Adams in 1815	Adams's 1815 letter referred to American reactions to the French Revolution; in 1775 Adams estimated that 90 percent of the Americans favored the American Revolution
7. Critical period when country was governed by Continental Congress and Articles of Confederation, which was unworkable, disorganized, chaotic	based on phrase by nineteenth-century historian John Fiske	Congress fought long war to successful conclusion, established credit, made treaties, developed workable arrangement for territorial expansion

6. Many students need a frequent and healthy dose of stimulation to *question* rather than accept without questioning. Distribute Reproduction Page 43, "Fact or Fiction?," and ask why and how history is written and rewritten. What information is needed to conclusively prove or disprove these "facts"? An alternative activity is to distribute the page without the third column and have students suggest reasons for questioning factual reliability. In-depth investigations of these facts would be worthwhile for some students.

Topic 2:   Conflicts and Adjustments

1. What are sources of *authority*? What happens when a person resists authority? Ask students what happens when they resist or refuse to:

   * follow school regulations

   * give an answer to a friend during a test

   * pay rent to the landlord

   * pay taxes

   * buy products from a certain store

   * "move on" when told to do so by police

   * put postage on a letter

   * be home on time

   * dress up for a formal dinner or dance

   * pay a fine for a traffic violation

   * stand during the national anthem

   * obey laws which one has no say in making

        What compels you to obey in some cases? Are there different types of pressure that encourage you to obey? Are there circumstances in which you would resist lawful authority? When a person refuses to obey in one of these cases, there is usually a reaction. What is the next thing the person who refuses to obey does? Do some cases escalate into more serious problems?

2. Who are the radicals today? Have students suggest names or consider the groups listed below to consider the degree to which they are radical. Assign a weight of 1 to 10 based on the class's perception of the group: 1 for groups that are not radical and any other number up to 10 for groups that are most radical.

How Radical Are These Groups?

environmental action groups	black nationalists
women's liberation groups	American Indian groups
rock bands	church groups
union organizers	farmers
gay liberation groups	Democratic party
business associations	Republican party
veterans' organizations	teachers

What do the radical groups have in common? How would you describe or define a radical group? Why are they normally opposed by others in society? It may be more meaningful to substitute the names of actual groups in your area in place of the general names listed above.

3. Reproduction Page 44, "Indicators of Development," is a listing of items that help judge a country's level of development. How far had the colonies progressed by 1763? 1776? How much of an advantage do these provide in any confrontation with England?

Alternative approaches with this reproduction page include: (1) use the list and have students indicate which items are advantages for the colonies, which are advantages for England; (2) examine which factors draw the colonies and England

---

REPRODUCTION PAGE 44

INDICATORS OF DEVELOPMENT

Each of the items listed below can help or hurt a country having a conflict with another country. Decide if they helped, hurt, or didn't make any difference to the colonies before 1776. Then briefly tell how it makes a difference or why it does not.

. . . In the Colonies	helps	hurts	no difference	how it makes a difference or why it does not
1. military	___	___	___	_____
2. transportation	___	___	___	_____
3. communication	___	___	___	_____
4. education	___	___	___	_____
5. natural resources	___	___	___	_____
6. land area and features	___	___	___	_____
7. geographic location	___	___	___	_____
8. climate	___	___	___	_____
9. food supply	___	___	___	_____
10. initiative of people	___	___	___	_____
11. sense of history	___	___	___	_____
12. customs/traditions	___	___	___	_____
13. religious beliefs	___	___	___	_____
14. language	___	___	___	_____
15. government	___	___	___	_____
16. opponents of government	___	___	___	_____
17. relations with other countries	___	___	___	_____
18. population distribution, composition, and total	___	___	___	_____
19. distribution of wealth	___	___	___	_____
20. economic structure	___	___	___	_____
21. job opportunities	___	___	___	_____

together, which propel them toward separation; (3) examine items that are essential for a nation's strength or well-being by having students select the five most important, arrange in order of importance, or place into categories of importance: great, moderate, little; and (4) use the items as topics for student investigations on how it helped or hurt the colonial confrontation with England.

4. Reproduction Page 45, "Writs of Assistance," is an excerpt from James Otis's speech in Boston in 1761. Discuss individual rights and government responsibility.

REPRODUCTION PAGE 45

WRITS OF ASSISTANCE

Do government officials have the right to enter your home?

_____ yes _____ no

If a government official is looking for stolen or smuggled goods, does he have the right to enter your home?

_____ yes _____ no

The British Parliament approved a law that allowed colonial homes to be searched. James Otis, a Boston lawyer, spoke against these writs of assistance:

> Now, one of the most essential branches of English liberty is the freedom of one's house. A man's house is his castle; and while he is quiet, he is as well guarded as a prince in his castle. This writ, if it should be declared legal, would totally annihilate this privilege. Custom house officers may enter our houses when they please; we are commanded to permit their entry. Their menial servants may enter, may break locks, bars, and everything in their way; and whether they break through malice or revenge, no man, no court can inquire. Bare suspicion without oath is sufficient. This wanton exercise of this power is not a chimerical suggestion of a heated brain. The words are: "It shall be lawful for any person or persons authorized," etc. What a scene does this open! Every man prompted by revenge, ill-humor, or wantonness, to inspect the insides of his neighbor's house, may get a writ of assistance. Others will ask it from self-defence; one arbitrary exertion will provoke another, until society be involved in tumult and in blood. . . .

1. To what is Otis objecting?

2. In what situations might it be necessary or wise to allow government officials to enter a person's house?

3. Who in the colonies would the British upset with this law?

---

5. The Stamp Act required colonists to purchase and affix stamps to newspapers, pamphlets, playing cards, legal documents, and of course they affected just about everyone in the colonies. The reaction was immediate and strong. The Sons of Liberty were formed; stamp collectors were threatened or prevented from collecting the tax; merchants threatened to boycott English goods; and nine colonies met in a Stamp Act Congress in New York and prepared a declaration against the tax. The uproar, particularly the boycott of English goods, led to a repeal of the act. At the same time, Parliament passed the Declaratory Act affirming their right to legislate for the colonies.

Reproduction Page 46, "Stamp Act Congress, 1765," lists the provisions of the colonial declaration. Distribute copies to all students and have a small number represent Parliament and the king and another small group be colonial representatives delivering the document. Provide some background on the reasons for the legislation and the colonial reaction. Have students role play a scene in which each of the provisions of the declaration is being reviewed.

An alternative activity is to divide the class into small groups and have each group divide into representatives of Parliament and representatives of the Stamp Act Congress. Review the declaration to determine which provisions are agreeable to both sides. Attempt to rewrite those statements where there is a difference of opinion. If total agreement is not reached, each side should confidentially prepare a statement explaining what they will do next. These can be exchanged and read later. Would the statement of either side lead to conflict? What are the causes of disagreement? Are the differences between groups vital to their interests? Is compromise possible? Students can conclude this activity by suggesting or writing a hypothesis about conflict and compromise. If written, have several read and discussed in class.

REPRODUCTION PAGE 46

STAMP ACT CONGRESS, 1765

Representatives from the colonies met in New York in 1765 to oppose the Stamp Act. They prepared a declaration for the king which, shortened and rewritten, follows:

1. The colonists owe allegiance to the king and Parliament.

2. The colonists are entitled to all rights and privileges of British subjects.

3. It is essential to colonial freedom that no taxes be imposed on them without their consent.

4. The colonists are not and, because of distance, cannot be represented in Parliament.

5. No taxes can be imposed on the colonies except by their own legislatures.

6. It is unreasonable for Great Britain to take the property of the colonies.

7. Trial by jury is an inherent and invaluable right.

8. The acts of Parliament in taxing the colonies, and extending the admiralty courts (which conduct trials without juries), are subverting the rights and liberties of the colonists.

9. The taxes imposed by Parliament will be a burden, and the lack of coins makes payment impracticable.

10. The colonies are obligated to take manufactured goods from Great Britain, and this helps the king.

11. The restrictions imposed by the acts of Parliament will make the colonies unable to purchase manufactured goods from Britain.

12. Increases in population, prosperity, and happiness in the colonies depends on the free enjoyment of their rights and mutually advantageous trade with Britain.

13. The colonies have the right to petition the king or Parliament.

14. It is the responsibility of the colonies to be loyal to the king and Parliament in asking that these laws be repealed.

---

6. Reproduction Page 47, "Benjamin Franklin in the House of Commons, 1776," can be used independently or in conjunction with paragraph number 5, above, and Reproduction Page 46. Reproduction Page 47 is a report of the testimony that Franklin gave to Parliament about the colonial reaction to the Stamp Act. Franklin's responses to the questions from George Grenville, Frederick Lord North, Charles Townshend, Edmund Burke, and others reflect the colonial position on a number of issues. Use this material as the basis of a role play or enactment of Franklin before the House of Commons.

An alternative approach is to select a few students to assume the role of Franklin and a few to assume the role of members of Parliament, and ask the questions from this script to both. What differences develop? How do their perceptions of the situation differ? What other factors influence their judgment? For either approach, ask: Does it matter who sets the rules for regulating people's activities? Is the process of setting the rules related to their being accepted? Which of Franklin's responses were especially self-serving? How does the reliability and frequency of communication affect decision making?

REPRODUCTION PAGE 47

BENJAMIN FRANKLIN IN THE HOUSE OF COMMONS, 1766

Q. Are not the Colonies, from their circumstances, very able to pay the stamp duty?
A. In my opinion there is not gold and silver enough in the Colonies to pay the stamp duty for one year.

Q. Do you not know that the money arising from the stamps was all to be laid out in America?
A. I know it is appropriated by the Act to the American service; but it will be spent in the conquered Colonies, where the soldiers are; not in the Colonies that pay it.

Q. Do you think it right that America should be protected by this country and pay no part of the expense?
A. That is not the case. The Colonies raised, clothed, and paid, during the last war, near twenty-five thousand men, and spent many millions. . . .

Q. Do you think the people of America would submit to pay the stamp duty if it was moderated?
A. No, never, unless compelled by force of arms.

Q. What was the temper of America toward Great Britain *before the year* 1763?
A. The best in the world. They submitted willingly to the government of the Crown, and paid, in their courts, obedience to acts of Parliament. Numerous as the people are in the several old provinces they cost you nothing in forts, citadels, garrisons, or armies, to keep them in subjugation. They were governed by this country at the expense only of a little pen, ink, and paper; they were led by a thread. They had not only a respect but an affection for Great Britain; for its laws, its customs, and manners, and even a fondness for its fashions, that greatly increased the commerce. Natives of Britain were always treated with particular regard; to be an Old England-man was of itself a character of some respect, and gave a kind of rank among us.

Q. And what is their temper now?
A. Oh, very much altered. . . .

Q. And have they not still the same respect for Parliament?
A. No; it is greatly lessened.

Q. To what cause is that owing?
A. To a concurrence of causes: the restraints lately laid on their trade, by which the bringing of foreign gold and silver into the Colonies was prevented; the prohibition of making paper money among themselves; and then demanding a new and heavy tax by stamps; taking away, at the same time, trials by juries, and refusing to receive and hear their humble petitions. . . .

Q. Considering the resolutions of Parliament, as to the right; do you think if the Stamp Act is repealed that the North Americans will be satisfied?
A. I believe they will. . . .

Q. But suppose Great Britain should be engaged in a war in Europe, would North America contribute to the support of it?
A. I do think they would, as far as their circumstances would permit. They consider themselves as a part of the British Empire, and as having one common interest with it; they may be looked on here as foreigners, but they do not consider themselves as such. . . . They make no distinction of wars as to their duty of assisting in them. I know the last war is commonly spoken of here as entered into for the defense or for the sake of the people in America. I think it is quite misunderstood. It began about the limits between Canada and Nova Scotia, about territories which were not claimed by any British Colony; none of the lands had been granted to any colonist; we had, therefore, no particular interest or concern in that dispute. As to the Ohio, the contest there began about your right of trading in the Indian country, a right you had by the treaty of Utrecht, which the French infringed; they seized the traders and their goods, which were your manufactures; they took a fort which a company of your merchants and their factors and correspondents had erected there to secure that trade. Braddock was sent with an army to retake that fort and to protect your trade. It was not till after his defeat that the Colonies were attacked. They were before in perfect peace with both French and Indians; the troops were not, therefore, sent for their defense. The trade with the Indians, tho carried on in America, is not an *American interest.* The people of America are chiefly farmers and planters; scarce anything that they raise or produce is an article of commerce with the Indians. The Indian trade is a *British interest;* it is carried on with British manufacturers, for the profit of British merchants and manufacturers; therefore, the war, as it commenced for the defense of territories of the Crown (the property of no American) and for the defense of a trade purely British, was really a British war—and yet the people of America made no scruple of contributing their utmost toward carrying it on, and bringing it to a happy conclusion. . . .

Q. If the Stamp Act should be repealed, would it induce the assemblies of America to acknowledge the rights of Parliament to tax them, and would they erase their resolutions?
A. No, never!

1. What problems are discussed by Franklin?

2. What suggestions does he make for resolving them?

3. How have poor communications led to problems for the English in this case?

Q. Can anything less than a military force carry the Stamp Act into execution?
A. I do not see how a military force can be applied to that purpose.

Q. Why may it not?
A. Suppose a military force is sent into America: they will find nobody in arms; what are they then to do? They can not force a man to take stamps who chooses to do without them. They will not find a rebellion; they may, indeed, make one.

Q. If the Act is not repealed, what do you think will be the consequences?
A. A total loss of the respect and affection the people of America bear to this country, and of all the commerce that depends on that respect and affection.

Q. How can the commerce be affected?
A. You will find that if the Act is not repealed, they will take very little of your manufactures in a short time.

Q. Is it in their power to do without them?
A. I think they may very well do without them.

Q. Is it to their interest not to take them?
A. The goods they take from Britain are either necessaries, mere conveniences, or superfluities. The first, as cloth, etc., with a little industry, they can make at home; the second they can do without till they are able to provide them among themselves; and the last, which are much the greatest part, they will strike off immediately. They are mere articles of fashion, purchased and consumed because the fashion, in a respected country, but will now be detested and rejected. The people have already struck off, by general agreement, the use of all goods fashionable in mourning, and many thousand pounds' worth are sent back as unsalable.

Q. Then no regulation with a tax would be submitted to?
A. Their opinion is that when aids to the Crown are wanted they are to be asked of the several assemblies according to the old-established usage, who will, as they always have done, grant them freely, and that their money ought not to be given away without their consent, by persons at a distance, unacquainted with their circumstances and abilities . . . they think it extremely hard and unjust that a body of men in which they have no representatives should make a merit to itself of giving and granting what is not its own but theirs, and deprive them of a right they esteem of the utmost value and importance, as it is the security of all their other rights.

Q. Supposing the Stamp Act continued and enforced, do you imagine that ill humor will induce the Americans to give as much for worse manufactures of their own, and use them, preferable to better of ours?
A. Yes, I think so. People will pay as freely to gratify one passion as another—their resentment as their pride. . . .

Q. (Why did America do so little in the last war?)
A. . . . America has been greatly misrepresented and abused here, in papers and pamphlets and speeches . . . as ungrateful and unreasonable and unjust; in having put this nation to immense expense for their defense, and refusing to bear any part of that expense. The Colonies raised, paid, and clothed near twenty-five thousand men during the last war—a number equal to those sent from Britain, and far beyond their proportion; they went deeply into debt in doing this, and all their taxes and estates are mortgaged for many years to come for discharging that debt.

---

7. Reproduction Page 48, "Questions of Law," is a listing of the legal issues raised by John Adams in defending the British soldiers accused of murdering Crispus Attucks and the others in the Boston riot of 1770. Have students indicate whether they *agree* or *disagree* with each of the points. If they agree with all or most of them, they support Adams's defense and would likely acquit or find the English soldiers guilty of manslaughter.

8. Reproduction Page 49, "Citizens versus Soldiers," can be used with Reproduction Page 48 in examining the Boston Massacre. It includes John Adams's opening statement to the court and John Hancock's comments on the anniversary of the

riot. Use these, plus the materials from student texts, the famous Paul Revere engraving, and other *evidence* to conduct a trial.

Alternative activities can focus on the legal implications of this case: the right to a fair trial, a lawyer's obligation to the client, the purpose and value of judicial proceedings. Other discussions can consider the role of the propagandist in this case, the reasons for presenting controversies from one point of view, gaining and using public support, and using questionable methods to achieve objectives.

Students may wish to investigate the similarities and differences between this case and the riots and shooting at Kent State University. Other students may wish to pursue an investigation of visual propaganda through our history: Revere's engraving (taken from the original by Henry Pelham), Nast's cartoons, World War I posters, World War II films, and television coverage of the Vietnam War. And other students may want to find out more about lawyers with unpopular clients or causes in U.S. history.

REPRODUCTION PAGE 48

QUESTIONS OF LAW

Directions: Place a check mark in the space indicating that you *strongly agree, agree, disagree,* or *strongly disagree.*

	SA	A	D	SD
1. It is always safer to err on the milder side, the side of mercy. The best rule in doubtful cases is to acquit rather than convict.	___	___	___	___
2. One would rather have twenty persons escape punishment of death than have one innocent person condemned. It is better that five guilty persons escape, than one innocent person suffer.	___	___	___	___
3. A person may repel force with force in defense of person, living place, or property.	___	___	___	___
4. The killing of dangerous rioters may be justified when a person cannot otherwise suppress them, or defend himself from them.	___	___	___	___
5. In the case of an unlawful assembly, all and every one of the assembly is guilty of all and every unlawful act committed by any one of that assembly.	___	___	___	___
6. A person has a right to go to the assistance of a fellow human being in distress or danger of his life when assaulted and in danger from others.	___	___	___	___
7. If a third person accidentally happens to be killed by one engaged in a combat, or in a sudden quarrel, he who killed him is guilty of manslaughter only.	___	___	___	___
8. When a person is assaulted and kills in consequence of that assault, it is only manslaughter.	___	___	___	___

Definitions

- riot: where or when more than three persons use force or violence, for the accomplishment of any purpose whatever, all concerned are rioters; the only exception is where the law authorizes the use of force.
- assault: an attempt or actually doing a corporal hurt to another, as by striking him with or without a weapon, or by any other such act done in an angry, threatening manner, but no words can amount to an assault.

CITIZENS VERSUS SOLDIERS

John Adams's statement in defense of British soldiers accused of murdering Attucks, Gray, and others in the Boston Riot of 1770:

> You must place yourselves in the situations of [the British soldiers] Weems and Killroy—consider yourselves as knowing that the prejudice of the world about you thought you came to dragoon them into obedience, to statutes, instructions, mandates, and edicts, which they thoroughly detested—that many of these people were thoughtless and inconsiderate, old and young, sailors and landsmen, negroes and mulattoes—that they, the soldiers, had no friends about them, the rest were in opposition to them; with all the bells ringing to call the town together to assist the people in King Street, for they knew by that time that there was no fire; the people shouting, huzzahing, and making the mob whistle, as they call it, which, when a boy makes it in the street is no formidable thing, but when made by a multitude is a most hideous shriek, almost as terrible as an Indian yell; the people crying, "Kill them, kill them. Knock them over," heaving snowballs, oyster shells, clubs, white-birch sticks three inches and a half in diameter; consider yourselves in this situation, and judge whether a reasonable man in the soldiers' situation would not have concluded they were going to kill him.

John Hancock, speech delivered March 5, 1774, commemorating the anniversary of the riot:

> Tell me, ye bloody butchers! ye villains high and low! ye wretches who contrived as well as you who executed the inhuman deed! do you not feel the goads and stings of conscious guilt pierce through your savage bosoms? . . . Do not the injured shades of Maverick, Gray, Caldwell, Attucks, and Carr, attend you in your solitary walks; arrest you even in the midst of your debaucheries, and fill even your dreams with terror?
>
> Let this sad tale of death never be told without a tear: let not the heaving bosom cease to burn with a manly indignation at the barbarous story through the long tracts of future time: let every parent tell the shameful story to his listening children until tears of pity glisten in their eyes and boiling passions shake their tender frames; and whilst the anniversary of that ill-fated night is kept a jubilee in the grim court of pandemonium, let all America join in one common prayer to heaven that the inhuman, unprovoked murders of the 5th of March, 1770, planned by Hillsborough and a knot of treacherous knaves in Boston, and executed by the cruel hand of Preston and his [bloody band], may ever stand in history without parallel.

9. Reproduction Page 50, "Chronology of Events Leading to American Revolution," can be used in a variety of ways: (a) Which events were violent? Which were efforts at resolving disputes? (b) Which events can be seen as direct effects of previous events? (c) Which events were *revolutionary*? (d) After which events was war inevitable? Have students respond to these questions individually and then have small groups attempt to reach consensus and share their decisions and reasoning in a class discussion.

CHRONOLOGY OF EVENTS
LEADING TO AMERICAN REVOLUTION

1763
Feb.   French and Indian War ends
Oct.   Proclamation of 1763

1764
Apr.   Sugar Act passed
May   James Otis speaks against English taxation without colonial representation

1765
Mar.   Stamp Act passed
May   Patrick Henry proposes Virginia Resolves
Oct.   Stamp Act Congress, New York City

1766
Mar.   Parliament repeals Stamp Act
           Declaratory Act passed

1767
June   Townshend Acts passed

1768		
Oct.	British troops arrive in Boston	
1769		
May	Virginia Resolves condemn Parliament for tax	
	nonimportation agreement established	
1770		
Mar.	Boston Massacre	
Apr.	Townshend Acts repealed, except tea duty	
1772		
June	British ship *Gaspee* attacked, Providence, R.I.	
Nov	Boston forms Committee of Correspondence	
1773		
May	Tea Act passed	
Dec.	Boston Tea Party	
1774		
Mar.	Boston Port Bill closes harbor, first of Coercive Acts	
June	Quartering Act passed	
	Quebec Act extends Canadian boundary south to Ohio River	
Sep.	First Continental Congress meets in Philadelphia	
Oct.	"Declaration and Resolves" of Congress condemns most British acts since 1763	
Dec.	Fort William and Mary, Portsmouth, N.H., raided by patriots	
1775		
Mar.	Patrick Henry's "Liberty or Death" speech	
Apr.	battle at Lexington and Concord	
	siege of Boston begins	
May	Ethan Allen and Benedict Arnold capture Fort Ticonderoga	
	Second Continental Congress meets	
	Crown Point, N.Y., captured by Americans	
June	British ship *Margaretta* captured, Machias, Maine	
	Washington appointed commander in chief of Continental army	
	battle at Bunker (Breed's) Hill	
July	Washington takes command of army at Cambridge, Mass.	
Aug.	King George in proclamation declares colonies in "open and avowed rebellion"	
Sep.	Benedict Arnold begins march on Quebec	
Oct.	Continental navy and marines authorized	
Nov.	Hopkins appointed commander in chief of American naval fleet	
	U.S. Marine Corps established	
Dec.	colonial siege of Quebec	
1776		
Jan.	Norfolk, Va., burned by British	
	American forces in Quebec defeated and leave Canada	
	Thomas Paine publishes *Common Sense*	
Feb.	battle at Moores Creek, N.C.	
Mar.	British evacuate Boston	
	Rhode Island declares independence from Britain	
June	Lee introduces motion of independence to Continental Congress	
	battle of Sullivan's Island, S.C.	
July	Declaration of Independence passed by Congress; N.Y. abstains	
Aug.	battle of Long Island (Brooklyn), N.Y.	
Sep.	peace conference at Conference House, Staten Island, N.Y., fails	
	New York City occupied by British	
	battle of Harlem Heights, N.Y.	
Oct.	battle at Valcour Bay, N.Y.	
	British naval force burns Falmouth, Me.	
	battle at White Plains, N.Y.	
Nov.	British capture Fort Washington, N.Y.	
	British capture Fort Lee, N.J.	
	Washington retreats across New Jersey into Pennsylvania	
Dec.	British occupy Newport, R.I.	
	Washington crosses Delaware River and surprises British at Trenton, N.J.	

10. When is violence justified? What actions are most effective in changing government policies or practices? The actions listed below were taken by the colonists.
Have students decide under what circumstances, if any, they would be justified.
What English actions would prompt these protests? Which are peaceful? Which are
violent? Another way to use this list is to select a particular law, for instance, the
Stamp Act; have students decide what they think the colonists' objective should
be (accept, modify, eliminate); and then select those actions that would be most
likely to accomplish it.

mass meeting   write letters of protest
hang and burn effigies   riot

threaten officials	intimidate English supporters
raise liberty poles	strengthen colonial militia
refuse to buy product	gather and store weapons and ammunition
refuse to sell product	make speeches
refuse to use product	pass resolutions
destroy public property	refuse to obey law
organize groups to oppose	write newspaper articles and pamphlets opposing
send petition to king	

11. Divide the class into groups to establish the causes of the revolutionary war. Their task is to prepare and support hypotheses related to their topic, listed below. This work should be presented and discussed in class. In many cases the evidence supporting one theory will support another. Students should conclude that the use of one cause or theory to explain the American Revolution is an over-simplification.

    end of the war with France

    actions of the English government

    a struggle of oppressed people for liberty

    an economic revolution

    a conspiracy of a few radicals

    an accident

Topic 3: The Colonies State Their Case

1. The Declaration of Independence stated some basic ideals for government: equality; unalienable rights; government created by the people; the consent of the governed; the right of the people to alter, abolish, and institute a new government. Ask students if they *agree* or *disagree* with the following statements:

   • Certain things are so true that no one would deny them, for instance, that all men are created equal.

   • All people have the right to life, liberty, and the pursuit of happiness.

   • Governments derive their power to govern from those who are governed.

   • People have the right to change or abolish government.

   • People have the right to set up any kind of new government for their safety and happiness.

   • People are more likely to suffer with poor governments than to improve things by abolishing that government.

   • If there is a long time of many abuses by a government, people have a responsibility to abolish that government.

   • Information presented for world opinion can prove that a certain action is a proper one.

These, of course, are paraphrased from the Declaration of Independence. Students will probably want to attach conditions to these all-encompassing statements. Discuss the purposes of the Declaration, the importance of public opinion, the need to fight *for* as well as *against* something.

2. The following questions can be used as a study guide for reviewing specific sections of the Declaration of Independence.

    *   What are the self-evident truths noted in the Declaration?

    *   How do people secure their rights?

    *   What can people do when a government denies their rights?

    *   When is revolution a proper course of action?

    *   Why are the colonists declaring their independence?

    *   Who is responsible for the abuses to the colonists?

    *   What are some of the specific charges made against the king?

    *   What efforts have the colonists made to resolve the problems with the king and Parliament?

    *   What do the signers of the Declaration pledge to each other?

3. Review the specific grievances listed by Jefferson in the Declaration. Have students determine their validity by providing evidence indicating that the grievance is *substantiated, partly correct, exaggerated,* or *incorrect.*

4. Have students seek signatures on a petition supporting the Declaration of Independence. Working in pairs, have them explain that they are surveying general attitudes toward American ideals. One person should do the interviewing; the other should record reactions. What is the first reaction to being asked to sign? What reasons are given for signing or not signing? Are people familiar with what they are being asked to sign? What comments are made about religion, rights, revolutions? What other reactions do people have (all *women* created equal, etc.)? Use Reproduction Page 51, "A Petition," for this activity. Students should also report on the percent of people who signed or did not sign, significant differences between ages, sexes, places of residence, or any other findings.

REPRODUCTION PAGE 51

A PETITION

We hold these truths to be self-evident: That all men are created equal; that they are endowed by their Creator with certain unalienable rights; that among these are life, liberty, and the pursuit of happiness. That, to secure these rights, governments are instituted among men, deriving their just powers from the consent of the governed; that, whenever any form of government becomes destructive of these ends, it is the right of the people to alter or to abolish it, and to institute a new government, laying its foundation on such principles, and organizing its powers in such form, as to them shall seem most likely to effect their safety and happiness. . . .

I, the undersigned, support these views:

Name   *City and State*

1._____

2._____

3. _____

4. _____

5. _____

6. _____

7. _____

8. _____

9. _____

10. _____

11. _____

12. _____

13. _____

14. _____

5. Popular opinion caught up to the revolutionaries after reading Thomas Paine's "Common Sense," 1776, Reproduction Page 52. This reproduction page is an excerpt from Paine's best-seller and can be used to discuss the colonial justification for separation, the importance of public support, the value of high morale for citizens and soldiers, and the influence of this and other publications on U.S. history.

REPRODUCTION PAGE 52

COMMON SENSE

. . . I offer nothing more than simple facts, plain arguments, and common sense. . . .

Volumes have been written on the subject of the struggle between England and America. Men of all ranks have embarked in the controversy, from different motives, and with various designs; but all have been ineffectual, and the period of debate is closed. Arms as the last resource decide the contest; the appeal was the choice of the King, and the Continent has accepted the challenge. . . .

The Sun never shined on a cause of greater worth. 'Tis not the affair of a City, a Country, a Province, or a Kingdom; but of a Continent—of at least one-eighth part of the habitable Globe. 'Tis not the concern of a day, a year, or an age; posterity are virtually involved in the contest, and will be more or less affected even to the end of time, by the proceedings. Now is the seed-time of Continental union, faith and honour. The least fracture now will be like a name engraved with the point of a pin on the tender rind of a young oak; the wound would enlarge with the tree, and posterity read it in full-grown characters.

By referring the matter from argument to arms, a new era for politics is struck—a new method of thinking hath arisen. All plans, proposals, &c. prior to the nineteenth of April, i.e. to the commencement of hostilities, are like the almanacks of the last year; which tho' proper then, are superseded and useless now. . . . . .

. . . Everything that is right or reasonable pleads for separation. The blood of the slain, the weeping voice of nature cries, 'Tis time to part. . . .

1. Underline the phrases that you think are especially persuasive and supportive of the colonial position.

2. What purposes could Thomas Paine have in writing this?

3. In Paine's point of view, what is the key event that changed relations between the English and the colonies?

Topic 4:   Problems of Waging War

1. Prepare transparencies from Reproduction Page 53, "The Boston-Concord Area,"
Reproduction Page 54, "Burgoyne's March on Albany," and Reproduction Page
55, "Concentration of Forces at Yorktown," and use these to explain the military
aspects of the war, particularly the political significance of these actions.

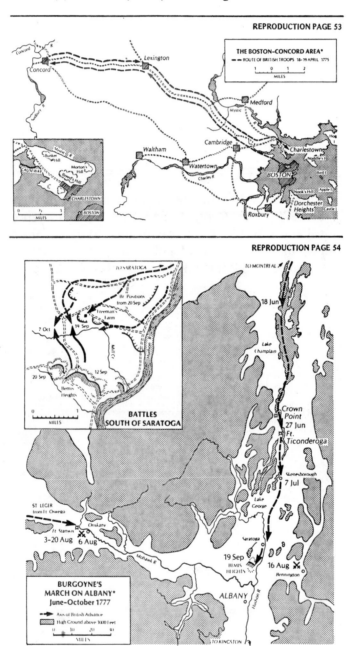

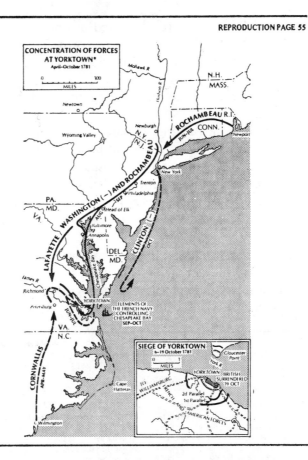

2. Present and discuss with the class: Eighteenth-century warfare was limited to territorial gain and conducted by professional armies. Most wars were fought over open,
flat land during favorable weather and in daylight. Battles were normally halted by
December, or earlier, when armies would set up winter quarters, and fighting would
not resume until spring.

   Troops marched onto the battlefield in columns and then deployed into lines,
three or four ranks deep. Loading, firing, and bayonet charging were all performed
on command. The battle would be opened by artillery fire from both sides; the
infantry would move forward; and an exchange of volleys would take place at a
range of 50 to 100 yards. This would continue until one side tried to take the field
by a bayonet or cavalry charge.

   The standard infantry weapon was a flintlock musket with bayonet. The most
famous model, the Brown Bess, had a smoothbore barrel 3 feet 8 inches long and
very inaccurately fired a smooth lead ball a distance of 150 to 200 yards.

   Cannon fired solid iron balls or, at shorter ranges, grapeshot and cannister.
Grapeshot was a cluster of small iron balls attached to a central system resembling
a bunch of grapes and dispersed by the explosion of a propellant charge. Cannister
consisted of loose pellets placed in a can and when fired were greatly dispersed.

   Military distinctions in European armies were normally based on wealth and
position and often held as a hereditary right. Nobles served as officers. The ranks
were filled by peasants and urban unemployed, paupers, and convicts.

   The colonists were in no position to form a professional army. Each state
established a militia, and citizens were to appear for training a certain number of

days a year. General officers were appointed by the legislature, and lesser officers were elected by companies in the district or town. Every individual was expected to provide his own weapon, ammunition, clothing, and food. In the early days of settlement, training was conducted once a week, and it was gradually reduced to once a year. Training consisted of learning the drill and motions required on European battlefields.

Their experience in fighting Indians led colonists to adopt many Indian methods. Scouts were used to avoid surprise. Fighting men valued individual initiative more than discipline, and the closed formation of European armies was abandoned in favor of open formation. What was seen by Europe's finest professional soldiers as inept had numerous advantages for the colonists fighting in North America.[2]

3. Reproduction Page 56, "Common Problems," has two case studies with which the Continental Congress had to contend. Distribute the page and have students recommend policies to resolve these problems. Small-group work is especially helpful in this kind of activity.

REPRODUCTION PAGE 56

COMMON PROBLEMS

The Problem of Food

The scarcity of food was extraordinary. In a country usually abounding with supplies, there was an unprecedented shortage. It's true that both the 1779 and 1780 seasons were disappointing, but there are obviously other reasons for the shortage of food.

Farmers who supported the patriots' cause were often interrupted by calls for militia duty. Those who cared for neither side, or because of religious convictions would not fight, or those who secretly aided the Loyalists, of course, supplied very little or no food.

Some say that there are not enough men to help in the fields. But the principal cause of the problem seems to be the steadily declining value of continental money the farmers receive for their crops.

The Problem of Money

Soldiers had patiently suffered for a long time. They finally pressured their officers to send a petition to the state legislature stating their complaint.

The pay received by a private was not enough to provide his family with a single bushel of wheat. The pay received by a colonel was not enough to purchase oats for his horse. Common laborers received many times as much pay as an American officer.

The petition urged that a speedy and ample remedy be provided. Without an increase in pay, the soldiers would go home.

You are a member of a committee appointed by the Continental Congress to investigate these matters. You have found that both cases are accurate descriptions of existing conditions. You must now recommend a course of action to the Congress for resolving these difficulties.

- The recommended course of action:

- A possible course of action, but less favored:

- A course of action that is possible but not recommended:

---

2. The material for this presentation is adapted from: Robert W. Coakley and Stetson Conn, *The War of the American Revolution* (Washington, D.C.: Center of Military History, U.S. Army, 1975), pp. 4–8.

4. Reproduction Page 57, "Selecting People," provides an opportunity to examine how individuals perceive others based on nationality, occupation, age, and sex. Distribute the page and inform the students that they are recruiters for the Continental army. You may wish to have half the class serve as recruiters for the king's army. After students write in the group to which they belong, review the instructions for completing the task. Have students respond to the items on the page individually and, if desired, form small groups to see if agreement can be reached on ten selections.

Discuss: On what basis were the selections made? How did the choices fulfill the needs of your group? Which were the easiest to decide? Which were left out? What characteristics did you assign to various nationalities, occupations, ages, and sexes? What attitudes, biases, and stereotypes emerged during the selection process? What criteria did you use in making decisions regarding people?

A more detailed analysis of responses and stereotyped thinking can be undertaken by concentrating on specific characteristics: What was the oldest age? Were women selected for stereotyped occupations? Are particular nationalities endowed with great wisdom, wealth, handicaps, and so on?

Responses may vary if students are assigned the task of recruiting for other special interests: Loyalists seeking supporters, Sons of Liberty seeking new members, Congress seeking military leaders or foreign representatives. Follow this activity by having students investigate the contributions of individuals from various ethnic groups to American independence. A similar, but more difficult, task can investigate the contributions of individuals based on their occupation, age, or sex.

REPRODUCTION PAGE 57

SELECTING PEOPLE

You are working for_____
and need to select 10 people from the first group. Choose a nationality and write it in front of the person you want to select; for example, *Canadian mechanic.*

You may choose the same nationality as often as you wish, but you must choose 10 different people according to their occupations. After this is completed, indicate the person's age and sex (M or F) in the space provided. Be prepared to explain the selections you have made.

Canadian	Native American	Scottish	Dutch
French	English	German	Polish
West African	Irish	Spanish	American (New
American (Middle colonies)	American (Southern colonies)	American (frontier)	England)

Section B

Nationality	Age	Sex	Nationality	Age	Sex
_____ mechanic	___	___	_____ peasant	___	___
_____ teacher	___	___	_____ student	___	___
_____ sheriff	___	___	_____ merchant	___	___
_____ apprentice	___	___	_____ banker	___	___
_____ farmer	___	___	_____ soldier	___	___
_____ doctor	___	___	_____ writer	___	___
_____ lawyer	___	___	_____ scientist	___	___
_____ dockhand	___	___	_____ blacksmith	___	___
_____ minister	___	___	_____ innkeeper	___	___
_____ government official	___	___	_____ unemployed	___	___
_____ plantation owner	___	___	_____ slave	___	___
_____ sailor	___	___	_____	___	___

5. Prepare Reproduction Page 58, "Washington as Leader," so that only the top half of the page is showing. This can be done by folding it before giving it to students or by preparing two reproduction pages. Have students describe the qualities they would seek in a leader and then read the description of Washington that follows. How closely do their accounts match that of Washington? Have students develop a revised list of leadership qualities and use it to judge other revolutionary figures and contemporary public officials.

REPRODUCTION PAGE 58

WASHINGTON AS LEADER

Directions: Without looking at the bottom half of this paper, describe your ideal political or military leader.

Physical features:

Intelligence:

Relations with others:

Beliefs and views:

Character:

How close did you come to agreeing with this view of Washington?

General Washington was a tall, well made man, rather above the common size; his frame was robust, and his constitution vigorous, and capable of enduring great fatigue. His features were manly and bold, and his eyes of a bluish tint and very lively; his hair a deep brown, his face rather . . . marked with the small-pox; his complexion sun burnt, and without much colour, and his countenance sensible, composed, and thoughtful; there was a remarkable air of dignity about him, with a striking degree of gracefulness; he had an excellent understanding without much quickness; was strictly just, vigilant, and generous; as a military man, he was brave, enterprizing, and cautious; an affectionate husband, a faithful friend, a father to the deserving; gentle in his manners, in temper rather reserved; a total stranger to religious prejudices, which have so often excited christians of one denomination to cut the throats of those of another; in his morals irreproachable; he was never known to exceed the bounds of his most rigid temperance; in a word, all his friends and acquaintants universally allow that no man ever united in his person, a more perfect alliance of the virtues of a philosopher with the talents of a statesman and a general. Candour, sincerity, affability, and simplicity, seem to have been the striking features of his character.

REPRODUCTION PAGE 59

OBITUARY OF A SOLDIER

Died, on Friday the 3d of January inst., at his residence in Upper Merion township, aged 90 years, EDWARD HECTOR, a colored man, and a veteran of the Revolution.

Obscurity in life and oblivion in death, is too often the lot of the worthy—they pass away, and no "storied stone" perpetuates the remembrance of their noble actions. The humble subject of this notice will doubtless share this common fate; he has joined the great assembly of the dead, and will soon be forgotten: and yet, many a monument has been "raised to some proud son of earth" who less deserved it than "poor old Ned." His earlier and better days were devoted to the cause of the American Revolution; in that cause he risked all he had to risk—his life, and he survived the event for a long lapse of years, to witness the prosperity of a country whose independence he had so nobly assisted to achieve, and which neglected him in his old age.

During the war of the revolution, his conduct, on one memorable occasion, exhibited an example of patriotism and bravery which deserves to be recorded. At the battle of Brandy-wine he had charge of an ammunition wagon, attached to Col. Proctor's regiment, and when the American army was obliged to retreat, an order was given by the proper officers to those having charge of the weapons, to abandon them to the enemy, and save yourselves by flight. The heroic reply of the deceased was uttered in the true spirit of the revolution: "The enemy shall not have my team," said he— "I will save my horses, or perish myself." He instantly started on his way, and as he proceeded, amid the confusion of the surrounding scene he calmly gathered up and placed in his wagon, a few stand of arms which had been left on the field by the retreating soldiers, and safely retired, with wagon, team and all, in the face of the victorious foe.

Some years ago a few benevolent individuals endeavored to procure him a pension, but without success. The Legislature of Pennsylvania, however, at the last session, granted him a donation of $40, which was all the gratuity he ever received for his revolutionary services.

It is a circumstance somewhat remarkable, that his wife, to whom he had been married up- wards of fifty years, and who attended his funeral in perfect health, suddenly expired about an hour after returning from his grave.

6. About five thousand black soldiers fought during the American Revolution. Massa- chusetts, Connecticut, and Rhode Island had some regiments composed entirely of blacks. Distribute Reproduction Page 59, "Obituary of a Soldier," and ask students why this person may have fought in the Revolution. What were his expectations? How was he rewarded? If you were a slave, would you have fought with or against the colonists? Obituaries highlight outstanding accomplishments of individuals. Find the obituaries for other revolutionary war veterans. Students living in the thirteen original colonies or in the frontier region may have cemeteries in their community for field investigations. Another follow-up activity is to prepare a biographical listing of revolutionary war soldiers from your community.

7. The contributions of black patriots go beyond that of Crispus Attucks. Have students find information about the lives and contributions of the people listed here and report to the class.

   • Peter Salem and Salem Poor at the battle of Bunker Hill

   • Black Sampson at the battle at Brandywine, Pennsylvania

   • Pompey, a spy who obtained information that led to victory at the battle at Stony Point, New York

   • James Amistead, a spy who worked with Lafayette and obtained information that led to victory at Yorktown, Virginia

   • Capt. Mark Starline, who commanded the American war vessel, *Patriot*

   • Caesar Tarrant, pilot on the war vessel, *Patriot*

REPRODUCTION PAGE 60

CANADIAN VIEW OF LOYALISTS

Perhaps 80,000 to 100,000 Loyalists left the colonies before and during the Revolution to go to Canada and other British territories. Their property and possessions were often con- fiscated or destroyed. They were often forced to flee for their lives. These new and un- expected settlers had an important impact on Canadian history. The following excerpt is from a contemporary Canadian history textbook.

The Loyalists brought with them qualities and ideas which were toughened by hard experience. No country could have asked for pioneers more likely to succeed. They had a strong loyalty to the British flag, and at the same time a determination to enjoy the liberties and rights of self- government to which they had been accustomed. The variety of people among them is one of the things which interests us most—English, Scottish, Irish, and German families, representing districts in the Thirteen Colonies all the way from New England to western Pennsylvania. Most of them were humble and obscure people, many were from well educated and prominent families. Among them were soldiers and army officers, who brought a sense of discipline and organization. Others were men and women of force and experience whose influence could be seen everywhere in the life of their pioneer communities. Many of their descendants have shown the same high qualities of leadership, and it is no wonder that the Loyalist tradition has left in Canada an indelible impression.

1. Based on this textbook excerpt, how do Canadians see Loyalists as an advantage?

2. In the long run, do you think the migration of Loyalists from the colonies was an advantage or a disadvantage to the United States? Why?

3. How were the Loyalists similar to a losing side in a civil war? Were Loyalists wrong in supporting the established government?

4. What rights should the opposition within a country have in time of war?

---

8. What was the fate of the Loyalists during the war? Many left and resettled in Canada, where they were warmly welcomed. Use Reproduction Page 60, "Canadian View of Loyalists," to explore the rights of opponents to a war, the Revolution as a civil war, and the advantages and disadvantages of Loyalists leaving the colonies.[3] Assign related student research to investigate colonial efforts to have Canada become the fourteenth colony.

9. In a war declaring that all *men* are created equal, women played an important role, especially those who maintained the family farm, kept the store operating, or handled other everyday functions that allowed their husbands to be ready to fight at a minute's notice. Their efforts were often overlooked, although New Jersey did adopt a constitution, in July 1776, that granted women the right to vote. This right was reversed in 1807. Student investigations can provide additional information about the women listed here:

   * Sybil Luddington, a sixteen-year-old girl who rode to warn colonists in Danbury, Connecticut, that the British were coming

   * Deborah Sampson Gannet, who disguised herself as a man, Robert Shurliff, and fought in several battles before being wounded near Tarrytown, New York

   * Margaret Corbin, wounded at the battle of Harlem Heights after taking the place of her husband, who had been killed

   * Lydia Darragh, reported to be a spy for Washington, also a mortician and a nurse

   * Mary Ludwig Hays, the most famous of several "Molly Pitchers" who carried drinking water to artillerymen, took the place of her husband when he was killed at the battle at Monmouth

   * Esther DeBerdt Reed, who established the Daughters of Liberty

   * Sarah Franklin Bache, who also established the Daughters of Liberty, collected money to buy supplies for soldiers

   * Mercy Otis Warren, who wrote satirical plays ridiculing the British, with brother James Otis, helped establish the Committees of Correspondence

   * Dicey Langston, who spied for colonists in South Carolina

   * Mary Katherine Goddard, Baltimore printer authorized by Congress to print the Declaration of Independence with the names of the signers

---

3. The material for this activity comes from *The American Revolution: Selections from Secondary School History Books of Other Nations* (Washington, D.C.: U.S. Department of Health, Education, and Welfare, 1976).

- Eliza Lucas Pinckney, who managed her family plantation in South Carolina and developed a new strain of indigo leading to increased trade

- Abigail Adams, advocate of women's rights

- Phillis Wheatley, famous poet and former slave

Topic 5:   Results and Retrospect

A significant treaty of commerce and military alliance was signed by the United States with France in 1778. Military supplies had been secretly provided before the battle of Saratoga, Lafayette served as a dedicated volunteer, and especially important, the French army under Comte de Rochambeau and the French navy under Admiral de Grasse contributed heavily to the defeat of the English at Yorktown—the final victory for American independence. This alliance was the only military alliance signed by the United States until World War II.

1.   Reproduction Page 61, "Treaty of Paris," includes the provisions of the peace treaty signed with Great Britain in 1783. Use these extracts to review what was settled and what was left unsettled by the treaty. What were the major concerns of both sides?

REPRODUCTION PAGE 61

TREATY OF PARIS

Treaty signed by Great Britain and the United States ending the American Revolution, 1783

1.   "His Britannic Majesty acknowledges the said United States . . . to be free, sovereign, and independent States."

2.   Boundaries shall run from Nova Scotia to and through the Great Lakes and the Lake of the Woods, "thence on a due west course to the river Mississippi, down the Mississippi to the thirty-first parallel, and then east to the Atlantic Ocean."

3.   The people of the United States shall have fishing rights in the waters of British North America.

4.   Creditors on either side "shall meet with no lawful impediments to the recovery of the full value, in sterling money, of all *bona fide* debts heretofore contracted...."

5.   Congress "shall earnestly recommend to the legislatures of the respective States" that they make restitution for confiscated Loyalist property.

6.   There shall be no future confiscations or prosecutions on account of the part anyone may have taken in the war.

7.   Hostilities shall cease, and "His Britannic Majesty shall, with all convenient speed and without causing any destruction, or carrying away any negroes or other property of the American inhabitants, withdraw all his armies, garrisons and fleets from every post, place and harbour within the same."

1.   Which provision was most important?

2.   Which provisions may cause problems later?

3.   Which provisions granted advantages to Great Britain?

4. Based on these provisions of the treaty, what were the concerns of each side?
List them here:

British concerns	American concerns

2. The meaning of an event is given to it by those who explain or interpret it. What is the meaning of the American Revolution to the students of other countries? Reproduction Pages 62a–62e, "Reflections on the American Revolution," are excerpts from textbooks of other nations. Distribute those you wish to use and discuss: (a) the different interpretations with each other and with the text your class uses; (b) what features are emphasized, omitted, or included; (c) which statements seem inaccurate, misleading, or distorted; and (d) what parts of the selection best represent the perspective of the country in which they are used.

An alternative activity is to divide the class into five or six groups and give each an excerpt from one country. Have each group respond to the same questions and then share their findings. In reproducing these pages, cover the name of the country to see if students can relate the material to what they perceive as the characteristics of other nations.

Discuss the significance of the American Revolution to others; the reasons for differing interpretations; the biases in U.S. textbooks. Ask students if they *agree* or *disagree* and discuss the following:

- We believe our thoughts are everybody's thoughts.

- We think of our country as the center of the world.

- We assume that what is good for us is good for everybody.

- What a person thinks and feels influences what he sees.

- Views of history serve special cultural needs.

- Interpretations of history change as society changes.

- We can understand ourselves better by studying others.

This activity is also useful in warning against the making of sweeping generalizations about ourselves, other people, or other countries.

REPRODUCTION PAGE 62a

REFLECTIONS ON THE AMERICAN
REVOLUTION: UNION OF SOVIET
SOCIALIST REPUBLICS

The peace was signed in 1783. The English recognized the independence of the colonies, 100,000 English aristocrats and members of their families were expelled from the United States, and their land was confiscated and put up for sale. That was the end of the war for independence that Lenin called the revolutionary war "of the American people against the plundering English, who had oppressed America and held it in colonial bondage."

Thus, during the Revolutionary War, in the course of a fierce class struggle, power in the United States passed from one class to another—from the aristocratic landowners to the commercial and industrial bourgeoisie of the North, which ruled in an alliance with the slaveowning planters of the South.

This signified that a bourgeois revolution had taken place in the United States. A republic was set up, the equality of all before the law was proclaimed, and slavery was gradually abolished in the northern States. But the capitalists and slaveowners took advantage of the people's victory to strengthen their own domination.

. . . the War for Independence did advance the development of the United States. The former English colonies became a republic. England was no longer able to hold back the development of American industry and trade. Customs were abolished among the former colonies, which now had become States, and this accelerated the development of trade relations. But since slavery had been preserved throughout the South, it subsequently, almost 100 years later, brought the United States to a new revolution, a civil war—the war between the North and the South.

REPRODUCTION PAGE 62b

REFLECTIONS ON THE AMERICAN
REVOLUTION: MEXICO

The independence of the United States had an enormous effect in America and in Europe. The road to achieving liberty and the natural rights of man had been charted. The absolute monarchies and autocracy entered a period of decline.

The colonies of Hispanic America watched with interest the separation of the English colonies from their mother country. Creoles and mestizos felt their spirit of independence strengthen, but they were aware that it was not the opportune moment to rebel.

REPRODUCTION PAGE 62c

REFLECTIONS ON THE AMERICAN
REVOLUTION: GHANA

The American colonies' successful struggle for independence was a revolution. It was the first time in modern times that a colony ruled from outside had rejected foreign rule and formed a nation of its own. Britain learned an important lesson from this. From that time onwards, Britain had a new attitude towards some of her colonies, such as Canada and, later, Australia, where her own people had settled. In their other colonies, however, the British repeated the mistake of keeping colonial rule for too long a time. This led to another revolution: the emergence of self-rule for the former Asian and African colonies.

REPRODUCTION PAGE 62d

REFLECTIONS ON THE AMERICAN
REVOLUTION: PEOPLE'S REPUBLIC
OF CHINA

The war for American independence was a bourgeois revolution against colonial oppression and feudal oppression. It was the first revolution in American history.

The victory in the War for Independence enabled the 13 States in North America to cast off the bonds of British colonialism and become an independent and self-governing bourgeois democratic republic. All the injunctions promulgated by the British Government in the past were burned to ashes in the angry fire set by the revolutionary people. The economic structure and the social complexion of the colonial period were subjected to vast changes, and certain vestiges of feudalism were swept away. The 13 States were politically united into one entity, thereby promoting the development of a national economy.

In *Das Kapital*, Marx pointed out: "The war for American independence in the 18th century sounded an alarm for the bourgeoisie of Europe." The war for American independence awakened Europe and hastened the outbreak of the French bourgeois revolution.

The war for American independence provided a successful precedent for the colonial independence and national liberation movements of the oppressed peoples. Under its impact, in the early part of the 19th century the people of Latin America successively launched revolutionary struggles against Spanish and Portuguese colonial rule and established, one after another, more than 20 independent nations. . . .

As a bourgeois revolution against colonial oppression and feudal oppression, the war for American independence had a great progressive significance in American history, but at the same time it also had the limitations of a bourgeois revolution. A bourgeois revolution is really only one exploiting group replacing another in seizing and holding power. The victory in the war for American independence only enabled the bourgeoisie and the plantation slaveowners to grasp political power, while the broad masses of the people were still relegated to an exploited and oppressed status.

The popular masses are the masters of history. During the war for American independence, workers, handicraftsmen, farmers, and Negroes made up the vast majority of the working people in the population. They not only opposed the British colonial rule, but they also wanted to push the revolution to a still higher stage.

The American people are a great people. They have a revolutionary tradition. At present, they are in a state of new awakening. We believe that the American people will make still greater contributions to the cause of human progress in the future.

REPRODUCTION PAGE 62e

REFLECTIONS ON THE AMERICAN REVOLUTION: GREAT BRITAIN

Even had the British won the war in America the political problem would have remained acute. A settlement on British terms would have left unsatisfied deep-seated American aspirations, further sharpened as these would have been by the struggle. And even if the situation could have been kept under control for the time being, for how long would this have been possible? The population of the colonies was doubling itself about every thirty years—a far higher rate of increase than that in the mother country. There were no population-statistics in the eighteenth century, but the general trend was clearly recognized. The significance of this dynamic aspect of the colonial problem appears entirely to have escaped the attention of the ministers. Time and again they said in effect: "We must assert British authority now, or it will be too late." But they failed to face the problem, how this authority was to be maintained under foreseeable future conditions. The object for which they led their country into war was, in the long run, incapable of fulfillment. Herein lay an ultimate proof of their lack of statesmanship.

ASSESSING LEARNING EXPERIENCES

The extent to which students have mastered the skills and content taught from this unit can be measured by having them submit for evaluation the final products of almost any of the activities they have completed.

1. For additional evaluation of learning experiences, have students prepare a statement suggesting hypotheses explaining the causes of the American Revolution. Each hypothesis should be a self-contained section of the paper and supported by evidence.

2. As in the previous suggestion, have students explain the factors leading to the Revolution by using the following basic ideas:

conflict and adjustment	law and order
power and authority	violence
leadership	propaganda
organization	needs and wants

3. Select any of the following statements and have students explain why they *agree* or *disagree*:

   A significant cause of the American Revolution was:

   - English decision to enforce mercantilist policies
   - development of colonial political ideas that differed from those in England
   - increased population, especially non-English-born, that felt little tie to England
   - different views of the empire, the king, Parliament, lawmaking, representation

- hostility of poor and middle class toward wealthy Loyalists

- radical propaganda

- colonial unwillingness to compromise

- mistakes of government leaders

4. Ask students to respond to any of the following questions:

   - A revolution is a complete turning around; what was revolutionary about the American experience?

   - Name five to ten basic economic, political, or social rights. Which of these did the colonists have before the Revolution? Which did they gain as a result of the Revolution? Define what you mean by *rights*.

   - Assume that the king wanted to keep control of the colonies. What policies and practices should he have followed from 1763 on?

   - A small group of radicals played a key role in bringing about the Revolution. Write ten rules for radicals for changing opinions and governments.

   - Explain how each of the following helped bring about a successful revolution: colonial complaints and English uncertainty; violence; propaganda; civil strife; unstable economy; alliances.

   - Assume that both sides wanted to win the war as quickly as possible. What steps would you suggest for one side or the other?

   - The winners of major conflicts often have the advantage of having their version of events accepted as fact. Assume the British had won the Revolution; prepare a statement explaining the causes, conflict, and consequences of the war from a Loyalist point of view.

   - The writing of history often serves the needs of society. Explain this statement by using specific examples from the American Revolution and how it is viewed by Americans as well as by people in other countries.

   - If you were to write a history of the common soldier during the American Revolution, what sources of information would you seek?

   - Name five revolutionaries (people or groups) in the United States today that are most similar to people or groups at the time of the American Revolution. Explain why you selected each one.

5. English actions and colonial reactions are listed below. These can be reproduced as a simple matching activity, or provide students with the *actions* and ask for probable *reactions,* or provide students with *reactions* and ask what could have caused them.

English action	*Colonial reactions*
Writs of assistance used to prevent colonial smuggling.	James Otis claims these violate the right to be free from unreasonable search and seizure.

Proclamation of 1763 forbids settlements beyond Appalachians.

Sugar Act raises taxes on several products and tightens enforcement.

Quartering Act requires colonists to provide living quarters for English soldiers.

Stamp Act places tax on papers, legal documents, other papers.

Townshend Acts tax glass, lead, paint, paper, tea, and use funds to pay salaries of colonial officials.

Boston Massacre indicates growing tension and friction.

Tea Act allows British East India Company to ship tea to America without paying tax.

Intolerable Acts close port of Boston, suspend Massachusetts government, extend boundary of Canada south to Ohio River.

Frontiersmen resent and ignore proclamation.

Colonists complain and defy law by continuing to smuggle.

Colonists object to England's maintaining large peacetime army in colonies.

Sons of Liberty formed to oppose; English goods boycotted; special Congress meets and declares opposition.

Colonists boycott English goods; Committees of Correspondence formed.

Citizens demand removal of English soldiers.

Merchants denounce law as unfair; tea returned to England or, in some cities, destroyed by colonists.

Colonies send food and supplies to help; meeting of all colonies called.

RESOURCES FOR TEACHING

Below is a selected list of materials and resources for teaching about the American Revolution. These materials—and those in other chapters—are meant to update and supplement the extensive bibliographies that exist in most teacher's guides. We have listed materials and resources that meet our criteria of being especially useful to the teacher, moderately priced, and thoughtfully developed. Addresses of publishers can be found in the alphabetical list on pages 191–199.

Books, Pamphlets, and Articles

American Revolution, 1775–83, an Atlas of 18th Century Maps and Charts, Theaters of Operations. Washington, D.C.: U.S. Government Printing Office, 1972.

Text of 85 pages issued in envelope with 20 maps, each 18" X 23".

American Revolution, Selections from Secondary School History Books of Other Nations, The. Washington, D.C.: U.S. Government Printing Office, 1976.

Fairly extensive selection representing the textbooks of more than a dozen other nations. Excellent materials to examine national biases, perceptions, perspectives.

American Revolution in Drawings and Prints, The. Washington, D.C.: U.S. Government Printing Office, 1975.

Portraits, maps, caricatures, and scenes of special events. Part of the collection from the Library of Congress, each graphic includes background information. Artists' while-it-was-happening view provides immediacy to the Revolution.

Atlas of the American Revolution, Skokie, Ill.: Rand McNally, 1974.

Includes 54 full-color maps, many reproduced for the first time since their original appearance more than 200 years ago. Overlays re-create the succession of events. Excellent classroom resource.

Black Presence in the Era of the American Revolution, The, 1770-1800. Washington, D.C.: U.S. Government Printing Office, 1976.

> The life and difficult times of black Americans and their contribution to independence.

Coakley, Robert W., and Conn, Stetson. *The War of the American Revolution.* Washington, D.C.: Center of Military History, U.S. Army, 1975.

> A book of essential facts written as a narrative chronology of the military history of the Revolution. Available from the U.S. Government Printing Office.

Dupuy, Trevor N., and Hammerman, Gay M., eds. *People and Events of the American Revolution.* New York: Bowker, 1974.

> Over 1,200 important events of the revolutionary war from May 17, 1733, when England enacted the Molasses Act, to January 14, 1784, when Congress ratified the peace treaty ending the war. Over 1,400 short biographical profiles of significant people.

Ferguson, Rober; Gunkel, Patricia Ann; and Truex, Donald. *The George Rogers Clark Teaching Units.* Indianapolis, Ind.: Indiana Department of Public Instruction, 1976.

> Teaching strategies and resource materials for teaching about Clark, Indiana, and the Revolution. Many good ideas and activities that are applicable to a larger setting.

Formation of the Union, The. Washington, D.C.: National Archives, 1970.

> An informative account of the events surrounding 38 documents associated with the beginnings of the United States, 1774-1790. Facsimiles of the documents are included within the book.

Gardner, William E.; Berry, Robert W.; and Olson, James. "Who Fired That First Shot?" and "Sam Adams and the Minutemen," *Selected Case Studies in American History.* Boston: Allyn and Bacon, 1975.

> Two cases that make effective use of source material, conflicting data, and logical inferences, to examine historical questions.

Garrison, Webb. *Sidelights of the American Revolution.* Nashville, Tenn.: Abingdon, 1974.

> Over 100 anecdotes about the revolutionary era— British methods of enlisting soldiers, soldier Deborah Sampson, and others. Good classroom resource.

Lyons, Nona P., ed. "Teaching About the American Revolution," *Social Education* (February 1974).

> Special issue includes activities and materials to examine colonial communities, conflicts, values.

Murfin, James V. *National Park Service Guide to the Historic Places of the American Revolution.* Washington, D.C.: U.S. Government Printing Office, 1975.

> Attractive publication describing places and listing addresses of agencies that can provide additional information about the sites.

Wills, Larry Dean, and Skaggs, David Curtis. "Using Moral Dilemmas to Study the American Revolution," *Social Education* (May 1976), pp. 307-9.

> Article includes many cases that can be used to examine conflicting values.

Other Resources

America: A Developing Democracy 1726-1776; 1776-1826; and 1826-1876. Chicago, Ill.: Denoyer-Geppert.

> Three kits of two filmstrips each on uniting the colonies, establishing a more perfect Union, and the Union in conflict. Teacher's guide with each kit.

American Heritage Series: The Revolution. New York: McGraw-Hill.

> Five color-sound filmstrips using important works of art, realistic audio, and many actual statements to examine the times that tried men's souls.

American Revolution, The: Who Was Right? Wilton, Conn.: Current Affairs.

> Six filmstrips with 12 recordings. One set of recordings discusses the topic from the English point of view; the other gives the American interpretation using the same filmstrip. The topics include economic issues, propaganda, Indians, women, Canada, and a general presentation on two sides to every issue.

American Revolutionary War, Songs to Cultivate the Sensation of Freedom. New York: Folkways Records.

> This record has "The World Turned Upside Down," "Ballad of the Tea Party," "Liberty Tree," and others. Many other records on this and other historical periods are available from this company.

Benedict Arnold: Traitor or Patriot? Wilton, Conn.: Current Affairs.

> One filmstrip with two recordings. One presents the arguments of the prosecution; the other gives the arguments for the defense. Students can decide verdict and compare their decision with the actual results.

Critical Thinking Aids. New York: Modern Learning Aids.

Short, involving filmstrips which personalize historic issues and ask students what they would do. Ten titles have been grouped into *Birth of a Nation, 1765–1790,* and are available from the publishers or from Social Studies School Service (SSSS).

Jackdaw. New York: Grossman.

These primary source collections include maps, documents, prints, diaries, letters, etc. and focus on one person or event. Those related to the Revolution include: *Women in the American Revolution, American Revolution, The Struggle for the Fourteenth Colony.*

Personal Conflicts in the Revolutionary Era. New York: Guidance Associates.

Two sound-color filmstrips with two duplicating masters and a comprehensive teacher's guide related to moral issues. One filmstrip is about John Adams's defense of British soldiers, the other about the personal conflict of "getting involved" prior to the outbreak of revolution. Background material with suggestions for teaching moral reasoning, as developed by Lawrence Kohlberg, is presented in the teacher's guide.

Soldiers of the Revolution. Washington, D.C.: U.S. Government Printing Office.

Ten color prints of scenes from the American Revolution—Bunker Hill, Saratoga, Yorktown, and others. The prints are 17" X 22" and come with a 10-page illustrated booklet.

West to Freedom. New York: Anti-Defamation League of B'nai B'rith.

Filmstrip with recording about early immigrants who came to the United States from countries other than England.

Women in the American Revolution: Legend and Reality. Stanford, Calif.: Multi-Media Productions.

Two filmstrips, one recording examine the reality of women's roles in the American Revolution—boycotts, relief movements, nursing the sick, writing propaganda, and running farms.

4

The U.S. Constitution

The Continental Congress and the Declaration of Independence provided a rationale for revolution and the destruction of British sovereignty. The Confederation period prior to the writing of the Constitution was a time of recovery and experimentation. It was an unsettled time, with major economic and other problems that the states were unable to deal with effectively. The Constitution created a new sovereignty.

Interpreting the motives of those who wrote the Constitution has long been a favorite activity for historians. George Bancroft suggested that the framers were men above men—giants gathered together through blessed historical accident. Charles Beard, on the other hand, suggested that they were hardheaded representatives of the wealthy class gathered to make political arrangement to protect and benefit their interests. Both theories have been seriously challenged.

Whatever these motivations, the Constitution has its background in the Magna Carta; the English Parliament; the experience of colonial governments; philosophers; lawyers; and the events associated with this revolutionary period. It outlines a government for people as well as an arrangement for joining separate states. Power is limited to that which is given by the people. A system of checks and balances exists between the legislative, executive, and judicial branches. A federal system divides sovereignty between the national and state governments. A republican form of government is guaranteed.

The noble purposes of the new government were to "form a more perfect union, establish justice, insure domestic Tranquility, provide for the common defence, promote the general Welfare, and secure the Blessings of Liberty."

In recent years, as in the past, the Constitution has been praised and damned in the wake of political crises or controversies. It has withstood the test of time and is an honored, although infrequently examined, document. In its entirety, it incorporates the basic values that provide the social cement for the way of life that has developed since it was written.

PERFORMANCE OBJECTIVES

As a result of working with the activities in this chapter, students will be able to:
1. Examine their own values about government and relate them to the U.S. Constitution.
2. Analyze and understand the major provisions of the Constitution.
3. Identify and explain the problems of weak governments.
4. Work in groups to develop basic statements outlining a form of government.
5. Explain the issues faced by delegates at the Constitutional Convention.
6. Experience the reality of conflict and compromise in reaching agreement on key provisions of the Constitution.
7. Consider a variety of qualifications for holding office and select and defend those that are thought to be reasonable.
8. State legal issues and offer rational arguments for contending positions.
9. Apply the Bill of Rights to contemporary cases.
10. Conduct a short research project.

LEARNING EXPERIENCES

Topic 1:   Organizing a Government

The study of the U.S. Constitution raises some fundamental issues about the way people organize to govern. The decisions they make are based on their values as human beings and views of society. The questionnaires in this chapter can be used to help students examine their own attitudes about government. Examining attitudes is a meaningful way to begin instruction and, later, to repeat when concluding this unit.

1. Use Reproduction Page 63, "Ideas about Government," as an individual or small-group activity. Some ideas that can be explored have to do with the need for government, the nature of human beings, stereotypes and generalizations, and the purpose of constitutions.

2. Reproduction Page 64, "Powers of Government," lists some of the powers that the government possesses, although students will probably not realize this while completing the questionnaire. Among the specific governmental powers referred to in this questionnaire are taxes, deceptive practices, unfair competition, public utilities and monopolies, zoning, national anthems and pledges of allegiance, national security, public health and safety, employment practices, and the general welfare.

    Discuss the purposes of government. Ask students what six purposes are noted in the Preamble to the Constitution. Each of these may be pursued at greater length as individual or group projects. Posters, scrapbooks, or similar collections can be easily compiled from newspaper and magazine articles. Students should understand that the Constitution is an important *living* influence on our lives.

REPRODUCTION PAGE 63

IDEAS ABOUT GOVERNMENT

Check the column that best expresses your opinion about each statement: *strongly agree, agree, disagree, strongly disagree.*

	Strongly Agree	Agree	Disagree	Strongly Disagree
1. Sometimes, government should be able to force people to do things that they may not want to do.	____	____	____	____
2. Government often knows what is best for people.	____	____	____	____
3. A government should never be changed by force or violence.	____	____	____	____
4. The best government is one that governs least.	____	____	____	____
5. Too much freedom is a dangerous thing.	____	____	____	____
6. Leaders of the government should be the best and the brightest people.	____	____	____	____
7. People need laws to regulate their behavior.	____	____	____	____
8. All politicians are dishonest.	____	____	____	____
9. The national government should have greater power than state governments.	____	____	____	____
10. People have some rights simply because they are human beings.	____	____	____	____

Write a statement that describes your ideas about government and what it should be.

REPRODUCTION PAGE 64

POWERS OF GOVERNMENT

Check the column that best expresses your opinion about each statement: *strongly agree, agree, disagree, strongly disagree.*

Government should be able to:

	Strongly Agree	Agree	Disagree	Strongly Disagree
1. take money from people to run the government	____	____	____	____
2. prevent businesses from buying and selling any way they want	____	____	____	____
3. regulate how people use the land	____	____	____	____
4. encourage people to have certain beliefs	____	____	____	____
5. force people to serve in the army	____	____	____	____
6. establish qualifications for doctors	____	____	____	____
7. create jobs for people out of work	____	____	____	____
8. ban books, guns, marijuana, the death penalty	____	____	____	____
9. conduct investigations by listening to telephone conversations	____	____	____	____
10. force people to attend school	____	____	____	____

Prove your point. Select three statements from the above list and find a section in the Constitution that proves that it can or cannot be done.

3. The statements in Reproduction Page 65, "Questionnaire about the Constitution and the Government," are designed to explore student values and are closely related to the actual contents of the Constitution. After this questionnaire is completed, you may want to assign two or three students to each item on the questionnaire for the purpose of proving or disproving its validity. This will provide an opportunity to become familiar with various sections of the Constitution. A brief explanation of its various sections might be undertaken at this point.

Have interested students use Reproduction Pages 63, 64, or 65 to survey the opinions of other students or adults. Whatever information is obtained this way should be compiled, interpreted, and presented to the class.

REPRODUCTION PAGE 65

**QUESTIONNAIRE ABOUT THE
CONSTITUTION AND THE GOVERNMENT**

This questionnaire is based on statements about the U.S. Constitution and government. Based on *your* opinion, check the blank space for *agree, disagree,* or *uncertain.*

Agree   Disagree   Uncertain

1. It would be illegal to make a complete, total change in our system of government.
2. The power to govern should be divided and shared among several parts of the government.
3. The government should have the power to make all laws that are needed and proper.
4. Every citizen should be guaranteed protection against unfair actions of the government.
5. Every state should have equal voting power with every other state.
6. The courts should have the final say in determining the constitutionality of laws.
7. The main job of the president should be to make new laws.
8. The president should be able to take any action he thinks best for the country.
9. Any citizen should be able to hold any government position.
10. The Constitution is the highest law in the country.
11. The president must belong to the Republican or Democratic party.
12. Supreme Court Justices should be appointed by the president.

Topic 2: The Constitutional Convention

The period after the American Revolution was one of accomplishment and growing problems. The Articles of Confederation provided for the passage of the Land Ordinance of 1785 and the Northwest Ordinance of 1787. But it was powerless to deal with the economic problems of the states. The most obvious and alarming sign of trouble was the rebellion of Daniel Shays and other debtor farmers in Massachusetts. A generally wealthy and educated group of delegates gathered in Philadelphia, supposedly to rewrite the Articles of Confederation. They lost little time in moving from that limited objective to preparing a completely new governing document outlining a federal form of government.

1. Begin an analysis of the Articles of Confederation by discussing the power of government. Consider the power to make laws, to implement them, and to interpret and determine their legality. Distribute Reproduction Page 66, "Analyzing the Articles of Confederation," and have students list what they see as problems and possible solutions. This information should be shared and a reasonable effort made to develop common agreement. At some point in this process it should become evident that there are so many problems and suggested solutions that a fresh start with a new document would be easier.

REPRODUCTION PAGE 66

ANALYZING THE ARTICLES OF CONFEDERATION

Issue	Articles of Confederation	Problems and Possible Solutions
Legislative branch	one-house (unicameral) Congress	
Voting power	one vote for each state	
Representatives	chosen by state legislatures; one-year terms, each state must send 2 or more delegates; the agreement of at least 9 states is needed to decide issues of war, peace, money	
Powers of Congress	decide war and peace appoint military officers request money and men from states send and receive ambassadors enter into treaties and alliances establish post office coin and borrow money on credit of country fix weights and measures regulate Indian affairs settle disputes between states	
Executive powers	exercised by special committees elected by Congress officials to be appointed by Congress to manage affairs	
Judicial powers	Congress shall appoint special committees to consider these	
Supremacy	each state sovereign, free, and independent	
Rights of the people	none noted	

2. What ideas are included in a constitution for a government of a country? Students should suggest several ideas, and these should be added to the appropriate sections on Reproduction Page 67, "Creating a Constitution." Divide the class into five committees and assign each the task of writing their part of a constitution. If desired, hearings could be held prior to writing to determine the opinions of others. The completed report should be presented to the class. A class arranged as a constitutional convention would stimulate political and personal interactions that often provide greater realism.

REPRODUCTION PAGE 67

CREATING A CONSTITUTION

The job of your committee is to write part of a constitution, the basic law of a country. It should be written very clearly to prevent any confusion. Each of the main sections should be numbered. Answer the questions for your committee and any others that you think are important to include.

Committee on General Government

1. Should there be both state and national governments? Laws?
2. What jobs and responsibilities should the government handle?
3. If there is a federal system, state and national government, what powers should belong to each?

Committee on the Executive

1. Who or what should be responsible for carrying out the laws of the country? Committee appointed by a Congress? Monarch? President?
2. What qualifications should the leader(s) have (sex, age, race, nationality, religion, education, experience, citizenship, etc.)?
3. What powers should the leader(s) have? How should these powers be limited?
4. How should the leader(s) get his or her position? How long should he or she hold the position?

Committee on the Legislature

1. How should the national lawmaking body be organized? Should there be one lawmaking body? Two? Should larger states have a greater say than smaller ones?
2. How should members of the lawmaking body be selected, or elected? If elected, who votes? If appointed, by whom?
3. What qualifications should members of the legislative body have? How long should their term of office last?

Committee on the Court System

1. What powers should the courts have? Should they be able to overrule government actions?
2. How should judges get their positions? How long should their term of office last? What qualifications should they have?
3. How many and what type of courts should be established?

Committee on Rights

1. What rights of the people should be protected?
2. What rights, if any, should be included in the Constitution?

---

3. There were many issues that split the Constitutional Convention. How should the power to govern be divided between the states and the national government? Should slavery be permitted? How should the governmental leaders be determined? What rights, if any, should be guaranteed to the people? Each of these and other issues can be used as individual or small-group research topics. Another related approach is to have students represent the states at the convention. After the students have researched their positions, reports should be presented to the class as a reenactment of the convention.

4. Use Reproduction Page 68, "U.S. Constitution—A Bundle of Compromises?," to have students indicate how they would have solved some of the conflicting issues. If you want to focus on economic motivations, divide the class into groups of wealthy planters or merchants, small farmers, and frontiersmen. What differences can be explained as being related to economic status? Another approach is to assign geographical areas to student groups and review these differences. It is important that you avoid oversimplification by discussing the complex nature of human beings and the multiple causes of social events.

REPRODUCTION PAGE 68

U.S. CONSTITUTION—A BUNDLE OF COMPROMISES?*

Listed below are several problems that had to be solved in writing the Constitution of the United States. Two possible solutions are given, and space is provided for you to write in any other solution. How did the members of the Constitutional Convention actually solve each of these problems? Check the correct answer or write in what the Constitution actually states.

1. How shall representatives be counted in the national legislature?

_____ one state, one vote
_____ representation based on population
_____ other:

2. How shall slaves be counted?

_____ count slaves for representation but not for taxes
_____ count slaves for taxes but not for representation
_____ other:

3. How much control over commerce (trade) shall the national government have?

_____ Congress shall regulate trade
_____ the States shall regulate trade
_____ other:

4. What kind of executive branch shall there be?

_____ many people in the executive branch
_____ one person chosen by Congress
_____ other:

5. What kind of judicial branch shall there be?

_____ no permanent federal courts
_____ strong federal courts to settle all disputes
_____ other:

5. Reproduction Page 69, "The Virginia Plan," lists several key provisions of the so-called large state plan. Divide the class into large and small states and have them develop a reasoned argument for their position. Representation for the states to the first Congress is also listed on this reproduction page, and you may wish to assign states to individual students. Discuss how people and/or states would tend to vote for their own interests. Compromising the differences is one way to resolve impasses.

REPRODUCTION PAGE 69

THE VIRGINIA PLAN

Delegates from Virginia to the Constitutional Convention introduced nineteen resolutions outlining a plan of government. Some of the important resolutions are listed below. What arguments would be offered for or against each resolution by representatives from the state of:

Representatives from states for first Congress:

New Hampshire—3	New York—6	Virginia—10
Massachusetts—8	New Jersey—4	North Carolina—5
Rhode Island—1	Pennsylvania—8	South Carolina—5
Connecticut—5	Delaware—1	Georgia—3
	Maryland—6	

Virginia Plan

1. A national government ought to be established consisting of a Supreme Legislature, Judiciary, and Executive.

2. The national Legislature ought to consist of Two Branches.

3. The Members of the first branch of the national Legislature ought to be elected by the People of the several States.

4. The Members of the second branch of the national Legislature ought to be chosen by the individual Legislatures.

5. A national Executive be instituted to consist of a Single Person.

6. A national Judiciary be established to consist of One supreme Tribunal.

7. The national Legislature be empowered to appoint inferior Tribunals.

---

6. Reproduction Page 70, "Delegates and Constitutional Issues," can be used for research or role playing by students. Distribute this page to students with or without the information provided in the columns. The names of additional delegates can be added to the chart. The class should be divided into groups based on topics of representation, slavery, rights, and federalism. Each group is to report on the major points of view and how the problem was actually resolved.

Another approach using Reproduction Page 70 is to role play the convention. Assign students to roles as delegates. Additional research is desirable to enable students to better understand each delegate's position and appreciate the complexity of some positions. Each student is to prepare a statement explaining his or her position on one or more issues. All delegates meet and present their statements. Statements could also be prepared in advance on duplicating masters and circulated to other delegates. Provide as much structure, rules of procedure, and so on as desirable and have the delegates seek to reach agreements in writing. Require a two-thirds vote for acceptance of agreements.

REPRODUCTION PAGE 70

DELEGATES AND CONSTITUTIONAL ISSUES

Delegate	Representation	Slavery	Rights	Federalism
Roger Sherman Connecticut	favors representation by population and by state	opposes but fears walkout by southern states		
Elbridge Gerry Massachusetts			fearful of democracy and common person	
Luther Martin Maryland	favors small states	opposes slave trade	favors a bill of rights	leading advocate of states' rights
William Paterson New Jersey	proposes small state plan of representation			
Alexander Hamilton New York	favors a House of Lords appointed for life and elected House of Commons		bill of rights unnecessary	abolish states; favors monarchy
Benjamin Franklin Pennsylvania	favors representation based on population			favors strong national government
James Madison Virginia		opposes slave trade		favors strong national government
George Mason Virginia		opposes slave trade	favors bill of rights	
Edmund Randolph Virginia	proposes large-state plan of representation based on population			favors strong but limited national government
George Washington Virginia				favors strong national government
John Rutledge South Carolina		defends slave trade and threatens to walk out	favors bill of rights	

7. Use Reproduction Page 71, "Biographical Outline—Constitutional Convention," to obtain information about delegates to the convention. This work is basically library research and can normally be completed in about one hour.

BIOGRAPHICAL OUTLINE—CONSTITUTIONAL CONVENTION

1. Name _____ Delegate from _____

2. Date and place of birth _____

3. Education _____

4. Occupation _____

5. Public positions _____

_____

6. Most notable comments or actions at Constitutional Convention _____

_____

_____

_____

_____

_____

7. Other interests and achievements _____

_____

_____

_____

_____

8. Date and place of death _____

Bibliography _____

_____

_____

_____

Topic 3: The Content of the Constitution

1. There are few qualifications noted in the Constitution for holding any office. But informal customs have developed over the years that indicate some qualifications are commonly accepted. Use Reproduction Page 72, "Qualifications for Being President," to have students indicate their preferences. The following examples are related to the factors listed on this reproduction page and can be used to discuss formal and informal requirements, stigmas, stereotypes, and overcoming handicaps:

   1. 18 or 90 years old
   2. divorced 4 times
   3. atheist or polytheist
   4. elementary school education
   5. transsexual or homosexual
   6. unemployed or unskilled
   7. short, fat, ugly, dirty, unkempt
   8. Alaskan tundra or New York City

9. very poor or extremely wealthy
10. argumentative, prejudiced, temperamental, paranoid
11. black, Asian, Chicano, American Indian
12. can't walk; stroke limits ability to talk; weight over 300 pounds; extremely poor sight or hearing

---

REPRODUCTION PAGE 72

QUALIFICATIONS FOR BEING PRESIDENT

Qualifications for being president. Should the following qualifications be a factor in choosing a president? In the space at the left, indicate "yes" it should be a factor, or "no" it should not be. In the space to the right, place what you think should be the requirements.

yes	no		Should this be a factor in choosing a president?
____	____	1.	age _____
____	____	2.	marital status _____
____	____	3.	religion _____
____	____	4.	education _____
____	____	5.	male/female _____
____	____	6.	occupation _____
____	____	7.	personal appearance _____
____	____	8.	residence (location) _____
____	____	9.	wealth _____
____	____	10.	personality _____
____	____	11.	race/nationality _____
____	____	12.	mental/physical fitness _____
____	____	13.	political party _____
____	____	14.	others (what?) _____

1. Which factors do you think are most important? Least important?

2. How are qualifications actually determined?

3. Which presidents do you think come closest to your qualifications?

4. Which presidents had serious handicaps to overcome?

5. Agree or disagree. Over the years, the process of determining who would be president has led to the selection of the best people for the job.

---

2. Reproduction Page 73, "Supreme Court Cases," lists several cases that have had an important impact on U.S. history. This page lists some of the notable cases and suggests an outline to follow for student research and reporting of these cases.

SUPREME COURT CASES

Supreme Court cases have important consequences. The titles of some cases are listed below. Select one and prepare a report using the following outline:

OUTLINE FOR REPORT ON COURT CASES

1. Facts
2. Issues and arguments
3. Decision and reasons
4. Importance
5. Bibliography

Powers of Government

Marbury v. *Madison*, 1803   judicial review
McCulloch v. *Maryland*, 1819   constitutionality of Bank of United States
Gibbons v. *Ogden*, 1824   federal regulation of trade
Worcester v. *Georgia*, 1832   jurisdiction over Cherokees

Citizenship

Dred Scott v. *Sanford*, 1857   slavery and property
Korematsu v. *United States*, 1944   Japanese internment

Legal Rights

Gideon v. *Wainwright*, 1963   right to counsel
Miranda v. *Arizona*, 1966   pretrial rights
In re Gault, 1967   juvenile rights

Freedom of Religion

*West Virginia State Board of
    Education* v. *Barnette*, 1943   flag salute
Abington v. *Schempp*, 1963   prayers in school
United States v. *Seeger*, 1965   conscientious objector

Freedom of Expression

Gitlow v. *New York*, 1925   anarchy law
Dennis v. *United States*, 1951   anticommunism
New York Times v. *Sullivan*, 1964   libel
Tinker v. *Des Moines School
    District*, 1969   student armband
United States v. *New York Times,
    Washington Post*, 1971   censorship and national security

Equal Opportunity

Plessy v. *Ferguson*, 1896   separate but equal
Brown v. *Board of Education*, 1954   segregation

3. The Bill of Rights holds an honored position in the ideals of the American nation. To have students understand the difficulty in writing a clear defense of human rights, assign individuals or small groups to write a new bill of rights. Have completed papers presented to other groups, or exchanged, to evaluate strengths and weaknesses. Whom does it protect? Whose actions are restricted?

4. Reproduction Page 74, "Bill of Rights Cases," provides a short and simple way to have students work with the Constitution and the Bill of Rights. Have students respond to the cases and discuss their decisions and the reasons for having these rights. The cases listed on this reproduction page can also be used individually as the basis of mock trials or student debates.

REPRODUCTION PAGE 74

BILL OF RIGHTS CASES

Read each of the following cases and decide if they violate the Bill of Rights, the first ten amendments. After each case, write the number of the amendment and the appropriate phrases that prove the case is a violation or not.

1. A man is arrested for armed robbery. He spends three years in prison waiting for his trial. He complains.

2. A man is tried and found not guilty of murder. A year later new evidence is discovered indicating the probable guilt of the man. A new trial is ordered. He objects.

3. A newspaper obtains documents that the government wants to keep secret. The newspaper plans to publish the documents, and the government demands that they do not do it. The case goes to court.

4. A well-known member of an organized crime syndicate is being tried for loan-sharking and extortion. The district attorney forces him to take the stand and testify. He refuses to answer questions.

5. It is wartime and the president fears there are spies in Washington, D.C. He orders several people arrested and placed in jail until the war is over.

6. A town needs more land around the high school. A man's property is needed, but he wants to keep it. The town forces him to sell and gives him twice the property's actual value. He sues to get his land back.

7. A man is arrested in a pool hall for stealing automobiles. He is tried and found guilty. In jail he complains that he did not have a lawyer.

8. Police agents secretly search the house of a murder suspect and find a pistol. It is used as evidence during the trial. The suspect says the police had no right to do that.

9. A man runs down and kills a person with his car. The district attorney calls it first-degree murder, and on this basis the man is brought to trial. The man's lawyer says his client is being treated unfairly.

10. A well-known movie star is accused of killing her husband. The judge is afraid she will not get a fair trial and orders the courtroom closed to the media and the public. Newspaper editorials claim this order is unconstitutional.

Use Reproduction Page 75, "Rights Guaranteed Under the Bill of Rights," as a quick and easy way of having students review and apply their own understanding of the first ten amendments. Conduct followup discussions on student-suggested reasons for each of these rights.

REPRODUCTION PAGE 75

RIGHTS GUARANTEED UNDER THE BILL OF RIGHTS

Write the number of the amendment to the Constitution that guarantees each of the rights listed below. Give at least one reason why you think the right exists.

Amendment	Right guaranteed	Reason
____	freedom of religion	_____
____	freedom of speech	_____
____	freedom of the press	_____
____	to peaceably attend meetings	_____
____	to petition the government	_____
____	to keep and bear arms	_____
____	fair treatment when accused of a crime	_____
____	privacy	_____
____	to go free on bail while waiting to be tried	_____
____	to a speedy, public trial by a fair jury	_____
____	freedom from cruel and unusual punishment	_____
____	to enjoy other rights not described in the Constitution	_____

5. Reproduction Page 76, "The Bill of Rights in School," provides an opportunity to apply student knowledge to school situations. Most students will be strong defenders of their *rights*, so it is especially important that they provide reasonable explanations. It might be advantageous to divide the class into groups representing parents, teachers, administrators, and students.

REPRODUCTION PAGE 76

THE BILL OF RIGHTS IN SCHOOL

The Constitution and especially the first ten amendments protect the rights of all Americans. But these rights are subject to many interpretations. Based on your understanding of the Constitution, check whether you *agree* or *disagree* with the following statements.

Agree Disagree

____ ____ 1. Everyone has the constitutional *right* to a free, public education.

____ ____ 2. No person should be forced to attend school against his will.

____ ____ 3. Censorship of any kind violates basic American principles of freedom of speech and press.

____ ____ 4. The school day should begin with a nondenominational prayer.

_____ _____   5. Students should be able to read anything they want in school.

_____ _____   6. Students should be able to publish anything they want in the school newspaper.

_____ _____   7. Students should be able to picket, write petitions, or demonstrate against decisions made by school teachers or principals.

_____ _____   8. Students should be able to criticize teachers or principals without fear of punishment.

_____ _____   9. No one has the right to enter a student's locker without a search warrant.

_____ _____ 10. Students should be able to hear evidence, call witnesses, and have a speedy, public trial by their peers for violating school regulations.

_____ _____ 11. The right of an individual to use a library should not be denied or limited for any reason.

_____ _____ 12. Books that contain objectionable materials should be kept out of schools or rewritten.

_____ _____ 13. School libraries should not have books that promote one religion over another, criticize race or nationality, are written by communists, or have obscene language.

_____ _____ 14. Paddling disorderly students is a fair and reasonable punishment.

_____ _____ 15. There should be no rules that discriminate between men and women.

Topic 4:   Ratification

1. Divide the class into groups representing wealthy planters, merchants and small businessmen, farmers, and frontiersmen. Have each group develop responses to the following: Does national unity help them? What do they give up under the new form of government? What do they gain? Why would they support, or oppose, the Constitution?

   The supporters and opponents of the new Constitution had strong feelings about the nature of government. Alexander Hamilton's political skill did much to bring about ratification in New York. In Virginia, Patrick Henry and George Mason strongly opposed the Constitution, and it took the efforts of George Washington, James Madison, and John Marshall to get it ratified. Students with good library skills may want to find further information about the struggle for ratification.

ASSESSING LEARNING EXPERIENCES

Several of the activities from the previous section of this chapter can be used for evaluating student achievements. The approaches suggested here can also be used as further teaching activities or for individual or group work.

1. Among the reproduction pages that can be used for evaluative purposes is Reproduction Page 65, "Questionnaire about the Constitution and the Government." Have students complete this questionnaire *before* and *after* instruction and review any changes in student opinions.

2. Student ability to locate information in the Constitution quickly can be examined by using Reproduction Page 77, "Questions from the Constitution," or Reproduction Page 78, "Constitutional Amendments."

QUESTIONS FROM THE U.S. CONSTITUTION

1. What are six reasons why the U.S. Constitution was written?
2. What part of the government makes laws?
3. What is the term of office for a member of the House of Representatives?
4. What is the age requirement for being a member of the House of Representatives?
5. How are vacancies filled in the House of Representatives?
6. What part of the government has the power of impeachment?
7. How many senators does each state have?
8. What is the term of office for a senator?
9. What is the age requirement for being a senator?
10. What other job is held by the president of the Senate?
11. What part of the government has the power to try impeachments?
12. Who conducts the impeachment trial of a president?
13. How often must Congress meet?
14. What is a quorum?
15. Who decides how to conduct the meetings in each house?
16. Can a congressman be arrested on his way to a meeting of Congress?
17. Can a senator receive a higher rate of pay if he is appointed to another government position?
18. In which house do bills to raise money start?
19. What happens to a bill that the president refuses to sign?
20. What branch of government has the power to tax?
21. What group of people within the United States can have their trade with others regulated by Congress?
22. Who decided that the United States would go on a metric system?
23. What branch of government can create more courts?
24. What branch of government can declare war?
25. Congress has the power to make all laws which shall be_____ and_____.
26. When can a write of *habeas corpus* be suspended?
27. What does the Constitution prohibit Americans from accepting?
28. What are three qualifications for being elected president?
29. Can the president's salary be changed while he is in office?
30. When he is sworn into office, what does the president promise to do?
31. In what cases can the President *not* grant reprieves and pardons?
32. What percentage of the Senate must approve treaties?
33. What are causes for impeachment and conviction of a president?
34. How long do judges hold their jobs?
35. In what cases does the Supreme Court have original jurisdiction (hear a case for the first time)?
36. What is the definition of treason against the United States?
37. What form of government is guaranteed to every state?
38. What part of government decides how new states are admitted?
39. How many members of both houses are needed to propose amendments to the Constitution?
40. What test will never be required to hold office in the United States?
41. How many states originally had to ratify the Constitution?
42. Who was the president of the Constitutional Convention?

CONSTITUTIONAL AMENDMENTS

In which amendment do you find the following information?

Amendment		Information
_____	1.	being witness against yourself
_____	2.	taking life, liberty, or property without due process of law
_____	3.	being tried twice for the same crime
_____	4.	taking private property for public use
_____	5.	right to keep weapons
_____	6.	freedom of religion
_____	7.	guarantee against unreasonable search and seizure
_____	8.	freedom of speech and press
_____	9.	cruel and unusual punishment
_____	10.	freedom to peaceably assemble and petition the government
_____	11.	right to a speedy and public trial
_____	12.	powers reserved to the states or the people
_____	13.	right to call witnesses and have an attorney
_____	14.	right of trial by jury
_____	15.	president and vice-president cannot be from the same state
_____	16.	right to vote cannot be denied because of race or color
_____	17.	power to tax money earned by people

———	18.	slavery outlawed
———	19.	senators to be directly elected by the people
———	20.	right to vote cannot be denied because of sex
———	21.	right to vote for eighteen-year-olds
———	22.	due process and equal protection of the law
———	23.	repeals another amendment
———	24.	limits president to two terms of office or ten years
———	25.	president can appoint a vice-president
———	26.	right to vote cannot be denied for failing to pay tax
———	27.	resignation of president
———	28.	prohibits making, selling, or transporting intoxicating liquors
———	29.	provides electors for the District of Columbia
———	30.	freedom of the press

3. Divide the class into six groups for the purpose of preparing a statement indicating how the Constitution fulfills the values stated in the Preamble. Assign one of the Preamble phrases to each group: (a) to form a more perfect union; (b) to establish justice; (c) to insure domestic tranquility; (d) to provide for the common defense; (e) to promote the general welfare; and (f) to secure the blessings of liberty. Have each group list those provisions of the Constitution that develop their topics.

4. Have students bring a current newspaper to class and select an article related to the Constitution. After summarizing the article have them explain its relation to one or more provisions of the Constitution.

5. Have small groups of students develop a series of key constitutional issues. Send them to an attorney or constitutional authority and invite him or her to speak about these issues to the class.

RESOURCES FOR TEACHING

Below is a selected list of materials and resources for teaching about the Constitution. These materials— and those in other chapters—are meant to update and supplement the extensive bibliographies that exist in most teachers' guides. We have listed materials and resources that meet our criteria of being especially useful to the teacher, moderately priced, and thoughtfully developed. Addresses of publishers can be found in the alphabetical list on pages 191–199.

Books, Pamphlets, and Articles

About the Constitution of the United States of America. Greenfield, Mass.: Channing L. Bete, 1976.
After a brief introduction this scriptographic booklet highlights key provisions of the Constitution. Drawings and design aid the content explanations.

Bartholomew, Paul C. *Summaries of Leading Cases on the Constitution.* Totowa, N.J.: Littlefield, Adams.
Brief concise summaries of over 500 leading Supreme Court decisions on constitutional subjects.

Borg, Kirsten E. A. *USA: Government.* Evanston, Ill.: McDougal, Littell, 1974.
Constitution forms foundation of this text with related sections on Congress, the presidency, states, cities, and elections. Examines both theory *and* practice of government.

Cutler, Charles L. *Congress in Action.* Columbus, Ohio: Xerox Education, 1973.
This booklet includes the workings of Congress and congressmen and -women.

Dort, Philip. *The Constitution of the United States, with a Clause-by-Clause Analysis.* New York: Oxford, 1976.
The first half is an explanation of the basic concepts of the Constitution, and the second half analyzes and comments on the various provisions of the document.

Kelman, Maurice. *The Supreme Court: Judicial Power and Social Change.* Columbus, Ohio: Xerox Education, 1973.

> This booklet includes chapters on judicial power, interpreting the Constitution, precedent, and so on.

Quigley, Charles. *Your Rights and Responsibilities as an American Citizen: A Civics Casebook.* Lexington, Mass.: Ginn, 1976.

> Designed to stimulate discussion and provides role-playing situations for Bill of Rights cases.

Ratcliffe, Robert, ed. *Great Cases of the Supreme Court.* Boston: Houghton Mifflin, 1975.

> Famous cases of key constitutional issues. Decisions available in a supplementary book.

_____, ed. *Vital Issues of the Constitution.* Boston: Houghton Mifflin, 1975.

> Key cases on freedom of religion, expression, equal opportunity, rights of accused persons, and others. For high school or advanced intermediate level students.

Starr, Isidore, ed. "Teaching About the U.S. Constitution," *Social Education* (May 1973).

> Insightful articles and practical teaching suggestions about the Constitution and the environment, women, the black experience, corporations, youth.

Switzer, Ellen. *How Laws Are Really Made and How They Work.* Evanston, Ill.: McDougal, Littell, 1974.

> A clear presentation of how an amendment is added to the Constitution; how bills become laws; and information on state, local, and county government.

Other Resources

Constitutional Crises and Confrontations. Mount Kisco, N.Y.: Educational Enrichment Materials.

> A multimedia kit with four filmstrips and recordings and a variety of teaching materials. Each filmstrip examines constitutional issues and events from a historical perspective. The crises of the courts, the presidency, civil liberties, and national unity come under scrutiny.

Constitutional Rights Foundation. Los Angeles, Calif.

> Promotes activities related to law and the Constitution. Sponsors conferences, publishes materials, provides consultation. Issues the *Bill of Rights in Action,* available in classroom quantities.

Crone, Tom. *For All the People . . . ?* St. Paul, Minn.: EMC.

> Multimedia kit about the realities of the legislative process. Three filmstrips and cassettes. Teacher's guide includes materials for duplication and use with students along with other involvement-type activities.

Electoral College, The Presidency, The Korematsu Trial, and others. Fresno, Calif.: Involvement.

> The titles relating to the Constitution are part of a packet of student simulations and activities. Available from the publisher or from Social Studies School Service (SSSS).

First Amendment Freedoms. Sun Valley, Calif.: Edu-Game.

> Reproducible materials for a mock trial regarding freedom of religion, speech, and assembly. Students have classroom roles and arrive at their decision by using the Constitution.

Formation of the Union, The. Washington, D.C.: National Archives, 1970.

> Facsimile packet of 38 documents written between 1774 and 1791 from Continental Congress, to Revolution, to the Constitution and the Bill of Rights. An inexpensive booklet with the same title is available.

Geltner, Michael E., and Clark, Todd. *Free Speech and Press, Search and Seizure, Fair Trial,* and *The Right to Bear Arms.* Columbus, Ohio: Xerox Education.

> Each of these four multimedia kits covers several cases and includes one filmstrip, 30 booklets, duplicating masters, and a teacher's guide.

Jackdaws. New York: Grossman.

> These collections of primary source reproductions are available on numerous topics. Two that are useful here are *The Making of the Constitution* and *The Presidency.*

Landmark Decisions of the Supreme Court. South Yarmouth, Mass.: Aids.

> The origins, personalities, conditions, and consequences of key cases are presented in this set of five filmstrips: *Baker v. Carr, Brown v. Board of Education, Dred Scott, Marbury v. Madison,* and *The Court and the New Deal.*

Law in a Free Society. Santa Monica, Calif.

> Promotes the study of law and political education. Prepares materials, provides consultation, sponsors conferences.

National Center for Law-Focused Education. Chicago, Ill.

> Prepares materials, conducts workshops and institutes, offers consulting services.

Presidents and Precedents. Mount Kisco, N.Y.: Educational Enrichment Materials.

This multimedia package has 10 filmstrips and recordings, a teacher's guide, student books, charts, posters, and duplicating masters. Each pair of filmstrips focus on presidential actions that serve as models for future actions: *A Strong Presidency* (Washington and Truman), *Masters of Politics* (Jackson and Lincoln), *Seeking Peace* (Jefferson and Wilson), *Protecting the People's Interest* (Roosevelt and Roosevelt), and *Affirming America's Strength* (Monroe and Kennedy).

Robert A. Taft Institute of Government. New York, N.Y.

Sponsors university-based seminars for teachers to gain knowledge of government and politics.

Tyler, June, and Buggey, JoAnne. *To Lead a Nation.* Minneapolis, Minn.: EMC.

Multimedia kit of four filmstrips and cassettes that examines the presidency and the men who have shaped it. The useful resource book and teacher's guide is a valuable component of this kit.

————. *With Justice for All?* Minneapolis, Minn.: EMC.

Multimedia kit of four filmstrips and cassettes that examines the federal judiciary from the perspective of history, court decisions, and the cumulative effect of justice in America. Teacher's guide with materials and activities.

U.S. Constitution Confronts the Test of Time, The. Wilton, Conn.: Current Affairs.

This filmstrip and cassette assesses the impact of the Constitution on the daily lives of Americans and asks if it is meeting the needs of today's society.

Why Do We Obey Laws? Pleasantville, N.Y.: Sunburst.

Two filmstrips and recordings look at the psychological factors that encourage obedience to laws. Case studies are used to stimulate discussion.

5

Nationalism and Sectionalism

In the first half of the nineteenth century the United States experienced the pains and pleasures of growth. The first six presidents of the country were from the revolutionary generation, and they, with some controversy and confusion, provided a reasonably solid foundation for the new government. The War of 1812 marks the beginning of a period of *nationalism.* The end of the Federalist party brought on the "Era of Good Feelings." There was confidence in the nation's future and a desire to promote national development. With varying degrees of intensity, this nationalistic feeling is found throughout our history. But in the early 1800s it was not to remain the uncontested focus of attention.

Concern with state and sectional interests—*sectionalism*—rather than concern for the entire nation, became the other dominant theme for this period. Differing economic interests led to sectional rivalry. The idea of *states' rights* was first suggested with the Virginia and Kentucky Resolutions (1798 and 1799), enlarged with a threat of secession at the Hartford Convention (1814), and defended by a determined minority for forty years before finally exploding into war.

The people of the United States during this time were beginning to exploit and control their environment. New lands became available and new technologies developed. It was also a time of developing social values. Much of the content in this unit can be considered in terms of change and social values. There are several cases where differing values shaped the behavior of individuals and groups and led to misperception and conflict. In the early 1800s these difficulties often had to do with reform, race relations, economic competition, and the use of political power—all concerns of contemporary life in America.

The activities in this chapter attempt to provide a human dimension to national issues. The material is included to provide a new or different look at old problems. Students should understand that history is a process of selection as well as of interpretation. We selected events to examine to attempt to convey the uncertainty, agony, and awe that ordinary human beings experienced as they struggled with these basic issues over a period of three generations in the nineteenth century.

PERFORMANCE OBJECTIVES

As a result of the learning experiences in this chapter, the student will be able to:

1. Recognize historical processes as requiring the selection and interpretation of data from a variety of sources.
2. Examine and explain historical issues from the perspective of different individuals, groups, sections, and interests.
3. Describe and evaluate the rights and risks of dissenters and reformers.
4. Analyze the role and purpose of myth and legend in American political life.
5. Interpret historical issues by using explanations involving multiple causation.
6. Explain historical events by formulating and defending logical hypotheses.
7. Write or ask questions to gain pertinent information.
8. Establish and apply criteria in making judgments.
9. Assume roles and respond, report, or write from a point of view not their own.
10. Analyze and provide a reasoned explanation of conflicting accounts of the same event.

LEARNING EXPERIENCES

Topic 1:   Life in the 1800s

1. Ask students to think about changes that are mentioned in history books and changes that are really important to the everyday lives of people. Use Reproduction Page 79, "A Lifetime of Change," as the basis of further discussion. What history-book-type changes were mentioned? How did they affect James? What inventions, discoveries, and practices were most important in changing James's life? In what ways did the changes make life both better and worse for James? Much of this discussion will be easily related to changes in recent years that have affected student lives. Ask students to assume that they will live to be at least seventy-six years old, James's life span, and write a brief report on the changes that have affected their lives.

REPRODUCTION PAGE 79

A LIFETIME OF CHANGE

Imagine a boy who was born in 1789 when Washington was sworn in as president, and lived to be seventy-six, when Lincoln was assassinated. Our boy, whom we shall call James, was fourteen years old when Jefferson purchased the Louisiana Territory and doubled the size of the country. James could be a blacksmith or a bootmaker. Or he could be a clerk in a village store, or studying for the ministry. But probably, like most, he was a farmer.

As a young man he is likely to marry a girl who lives nearby. They will have five or six children. If he is lucky he may have purchased land in addition to what his father gave him to get started. The temptation to move west where there is cheap and fertile soil has crossed his mind on more than one occasion.

By the time he is in his late thirties or early forties, his children begin to leave home. There are opportunities elsewhere, and they don't want the drudgery of tilling the soil. New institutions are emerging and so are new problems. Even in his own village James can see the changes taking place. The population has increased in number and variety. Jobs that his father would have done are now handled by craftsmen, who often do it better and faster than he would have done. James's wife no longer makes soap or candles but buys them at a store that has products from as far away as China. It is necessary to rely more and more on money and less and less on exchanging his goods and services for what he needs.

James's youngest son attends a public school for a good part of the year. When he's older he'll head for gold in California and never be heard from again. Textile mills have made their appearance in a nearby town. James doesn't like the mills, but two of his daughters have left home to become weavers there. He doesn't realize it, but he is witnessing the birth of what people will later call the *industrial revolution.* His youngest daughter may live until the turn of the century, by which time the United States will be producing more manufactured goods than any other country in the world.

Many other innovations occur during James's lifetime—the Erie Canal, clipper ships, steamboats, railroads, telegraph, anesthesia, a mechanical reaper, and a water supply system for the entire city of New York. He also sees the beginning of genuinely American schools of literature, art, and music. The first oil well is drilled; the Bessemer process of making steel is developed; and labor unions are formed. Before he dies, he'll see his country take land from Mexico and reach peaceful agreements with Britain. But the nation has been troubled throughout these years and cannot exist half slave and half free. After four years of bloody Civil War, the Union continues without slavery. New conflicts develop. But that's for James's children and grandchildren to worry about.

It is fashionable to think of our own era as a time of rapid change. Some say we might not be able to make appropriate adjustments to preserve our society. The dilemma of coping with rapid change has been described in recent years as "future shock." But if we consider the changes that occurred in a single lifetime, such as James's, we may gain a better perspective of our own time. Of all the traditions that have characterized American life over more than two centuries, perhaps the most important and the most enduring is the tradition of change.

2. This activity is to provide a textbook look at life in the 1800s and have students understand that history is interpretation and that it begins by making selections. Ask students to suggest topics that they would consider important if they were writing about the United States in the early nineteenth century. How does the selection of topics show what we value? Distribute Reproduction Page 80, "The United States in Mid-Nineteenth Century," and have students read these excerpts from a textbook. Ask: What topics did this author include? What does the author value? The statements seem to indicate national pride, and the author seems to value economic development. Each paragraph can be assigned as a topic for further student research about life in the 1800s or compared with today. What is important to know about a country?

REPRODUCTION PAGE 80

THE UNITED STATES IN MID-NINETEENTH CENTURY

1. The United States form one government, compromising thirty-one states, six territories, and one federal district. They occupy the most valuable and productive part of North America, and rank among the most powerful, commercial, and wealthy nations of the globe.

2. They are distinguished for the freedom and excellence of their political institutions, the rapid increase of the population, and for the intelligence, industry, and enterprise of the inhabitants.

6. Agriculture is the leading pursuit in this country. The eastern states are devoted to grazing, and the dairy; the middle and western to the raising of wheat, Indian corn, &c.; and the southern states, to cotton, tobacco, sugar, and rice. Slave labour is chiefly employed in the southern and some of the western states.

9. The commerce is, next to that of Great Britain, the largest in the world; it extends to all parts of the earth, and embraces the products and manufacture of all nations.

11. The whale fishery alone employs upwards of 600 vessels, and 16,000 men. The ships employed in this important business are absent frequently two and three years at a time.

12. No part of the world presents such an extensive inland commerce as that of the United States. Steam vessels navigate all the principal rivers, lakes, bays, &c. The Mississippi

river and its tributaries alone are traversed by near 400 steamboats, all of which make several voyages every year.

13. The employment of Steam Power is probably greater in the country than in any other part of the world, and forms one of the principal elements of American prosperity. . . .

14. The Americans have surpassed all other nations in the number and extent of their canals and rail-roads; the united length of the former is not less than 4,000 miles, the whole of which, with one or two exceptions, have been executed in less than twenty years.

15. The rail-roads, all constructed since the year 1829, amount to an aggregate of 9,000 miles, over which carriages are propelled by locomotive steam-engines at the rate of from 20 to 30 miles an hour.

16. The United States are more distinguished for the general diffusion of knowledge, than for eminence in literature and science. Common school education is more widely extended than in any other part of the world. . . .

25. The inhabitants of the United States amount to almost twenty-two millions, of which the black or coloured races form one-sixth part. The Indians number about 400,000, but are not usually considered as forming a part of the population of the union.

3. A special report prepared by *Life* Magazine for the nation's Bicentennial celebration in 1976 listed over one hundred events that shaped America.[1] Of these, nineteen took place between 1800 and 1860. You may wish to have students develop and justify their own list. Here are the selections from *Life* Magazine:

- the Louisiana Purchase, 1803

- beginnings of modern industry, 1814

- the Monroe Doctrine, 1823

- Nat Turner's slave revolt, 1831

- the balloon-frame house, 1833

- the gold rush, 1849

- discovery of oil, 1859

- the Supreme Court asserts its power, 1803

- The modern penitentiary, 1823

- the two-party political system, 1840

- Parson Weems's *Life of George Washington*, 1808

- the free public high school, 1821

- Noah Webster's American dictionary, 1828

- religious revivalism, 1835

- Walt Whitman's *Leaves of Grass*, 1855

- first use of anesthesia, 1842

- McCormick's mechanical reaper, 1848

---

1. *Life. Special Report: The 100 Events That Shaped America* (New York: Time, 1975).

- a water supply for New York, 1842

- Borden's condensed milk, 1859

4. The early clash of personalities and philosophies of Alexander Hamilton and Thomas Jefferson became institutionalized in political parties. Have students use their textbooks and explain the position of Hamilton and Jefferson on states' rights versus strong federal government, rural versus urban life, financial concerns versus human needs, farmer versus merchant, passivity versus involvement in foreign affairs, masses versus elite. Have students compare Hamilton's or Jefferson's beliefs with the actions they took. Many of the same issues remain a public concern today. You may wish to have students gather newspaper or magazine articles that are related to these issues or, perhaps, identify today's public figures as Jeffersonians or Hamiltonians. Be cautious of oversimplification and unwarranted conclusions, though.

5. On April 18, 1802, President Thomas Jefferson wrote to Robert Livingston, the U.S. minister to France, stating his position about controlling New Orleans. "There is on the globe one single spot," he wrote, "the possessor of which is our natural and habitual enemy. It is New Orleans." He further stated that Spain might have retained it quietly for years, but that would not be the case with France because of her temper, energy, and restlessness. If France takes possession of New Orleans, he held, we must join with Britain to maintain "exclusive possession of the ocean. From that moment we must marry ourselves to the British fleet and nation." This will prevent the reinforcement of French settlements in North America.

    Discuss with students the value of New Orleans as a port for American products, different characteristics of France and Spain at this time, the shifting nature of alliances, control of the oceans, Jefferson's analysis of the situation, and his recommendations. Students can be assigned to represent the United States, Britain, France, and Spain at a conference to decide the status of New Orleans.

6. U.S. history is filled with examples of people in power attempting to silence critics. John Adams's Alien and Sedition Acts provide a classic case (and a good opportunity for reviewing constitutional guarantees). Distribute Reproduction Page 81, "The Right to Disagree," and have students respond to this case study. Related discussion topics include the role of the opposition, abuse of power, other freedom of speech and press cases, and methods of combating governmental abuse.

7. The case of *McCulloch* v. *Maryland*, 1819, established the idea of judicial review, first set forth by John Marshall in *Marbury* v. *Madison*, 1803. The Supreme Court could decide if a law agreed with the U.S. Constitution. If it did not, the law was unenforceable. From this position, the Constitution increasingly came to mean what the Justices said it meant. *McCulloch* v. *Maryland* clarified and strengthened the power of the federal government at the expense of the states. Distribute Reproduction Page 82, "Can a State Tax the National Government?," and discuss the questions following the case. A more elaborate preparation of answers, including a role play of a courtroom, is a natural activity. Marshall's decision stated:

THE RIGHT TO DISAGREE

When John Adams was president, France and England were at war. The United States wanted to remain neutral and carry on trade with all foreign countries. Neither France nor England accepted this, and both attacked U.S. merchant ships.

Within the United States people took sides. Some wanted to help the British. Some wanted to help the French. President Adams and most of the Congress favored the British. Vice-President Thomas Jefferson and his followers favored the French.

Articles appeared in newspapers criticizing Adams and the government. Many articles favored Jefferson and the French. Adams was furious. In 1798 Congress passed laws which limited what people could say and write about the government. It became a crime to publish false, dishonorable, or critical comments about the President or Congress. If anyone committed this crime they could be fined $2,000 and put in jail for two years. Nothing was said about the vice-president, so the law did not apply to criticism of Jefferson.

A congressman from Vermont said President Adams had a continual grasp for power and that he was selfish and a show-off. He was fined $1,000 and imprisoned for four months. A newspaper reporter in Philadelphia criticized Adams and was fined $400 and imprisoned for six months. Two other men said they wanted Jefferson to be president and were fined and put in prison. When President Adams visited in New Jersey, cannon filled with wads of cotton instead of cannonballs were shot off in his honor and as a protest. Someone in the audience said he hoped one of the cotton wads would hit the president in the seat of his pants. He was fined $100.

1. Assume you oppose Adams. What would you say or do?

2. Knowing that the Constitution protects freedom of speech and press, what arguments could Adams and his supporters make to defend their position?

CAN A STATE TAX THE NATIONAL GOVERNMENT?

A Bank of the United States became a reality in 1791. The idea was first suggested by Alexander Hamilton, and now, several years later, even Thomas Jefferson had to admit it was a success. The United States became prosperous and gained the respect of other nations. People had faith in the money system of the country.

The Bank was also causing problems. It was making its wealthy owners even richer. Most of these men lived in the North, which was already the wealthiest area of the country. The planters and farmers of the South and West were not sharing in the success of the bank. It was seen as a *money power* and called "The Monster."

Maryland decided to take action. The state passed a law to tax the bank. A bank employee in Baltimore, James McCulloch, refused to pay the tax to the state of Maryland. The state sued McCulloch and the bank, and the case went to the Supreme Court.

How would you decide?

1. Is it constitutional for Congress to establish a bank?

2. Is it constitutional for the state to tax the bank?

3. What are the consequences of your decision?

It is entirely constitutional for Congress to charter a bank. But it is not constitutional for the state to tax the bank. It is an agent of the national government and Maryland cannot limit the nation's activity by using the taxing power since the power to tax involves the power to destroy.

Related discussion might consider the question of states determining what the Constitution means. Can each state or section determine what laws are constitutional? Have students research the Virginia and Kentucky Resolutions, 1798 and 1799; the Hartford Convention, 1814; and South Carolina's Nullification Act, 1832. The relationship of the states to the national government was eventually and decisively clarified as a result of the Civil War.

8. The election of Andrew Jackson is sometimes said to be a victory of western democracy over eastern aristocracy. Did he really represent the *common man*? Was he simply a new kind of leader? Distribute Reproduction Page 83, "Andrew Jackson Speaks Out," and have students list: (a) ideas and practices they think represent the *common man*; (b) those they think represent a *dictator*; and (c) the people or groups that would support or oppose Jackson today. Was he a defender of the common man or was he a dictator? Was he a force for better or worse in the growth of the United States?

REPRODUCTION PAGE 83

ANDREW JACKSON SPEAKS OUT

1. Jackson vetoes the bill to recharter the Bank of the United States.

 It is to be regretted that the rich and powerful too often bend the acts of government to their selfish purposes. Distinctions in society will always exist under every just government. Equality of talents, of education, or of wealth, can not be produced by human institutions. In the full enjoyment of the rights of Heaven and the fruits of superior industry, economy, and virtue, every man is equally entitled to protection by law; but when the laws undertake to add to these natural and just advantages artificial distinctions, to grant titles, gratuities, and exclusive privileges, to make the rich richer and the potent more powerful, the humble members of society—the farmers, mechanics, and laborers—who have neither the time nor the means of securing like favors to themselves, have a right to complain of the injustice. . . .

2. Accepts the idea in politics, first practiced by Thomas Jefferson, of, "To the victor belongs the spoils."

3. Statement on South Carolina's nullification ordinance: "I consider the power to annul a law of the United States, assumed by one State, incompatible with the existence of the Union, contradicted expressly by the letter of the Constitution, unauthorized by its spirit, inconsistent with every principle on which it was founded, and destructive of the great object for which it was formed."

4. Toast given to indicate views about states' rights and national government: "Our Federal union—it must and shall be preserved.

5. After Chief Justice John Marshall and the Supreme Court ruled that the relocation of Cherokee Indians from their homelands in Georgia was unconstitutional, Jackson is reported to have said: "John Marshall has made his decision; now let him enforce it."

Common Man	*Dictator*

9. The idea of the *common man* in U.S. history is part of our national heritage. What is the nature of the myth? Ask students to identify other historical figures that appealed to, or were supposed to be representatives of, the common man. Duplicate or place the following statements on the board and ask students to *agree* or *disagree*:

   • The average American is the strength of the country.

   • Anyone can get ahead by working hard.

   • A poor person can become president.

   • Wealthy people have more power than others.

   • A business executive's opinion about current events is worth more than a factory worker's.

   • The key to success in American life is to be born into a wealthy family.

   • Higher-class people have special privileges in the United States.

   • The government is run and controlled by a small group of wealthy, especially educated people who know each other.

   • Candidates for political office have to have a *common man* image to be elected, but they fool no one.

10. Another frontiersman who became a politician for a short time was Davy Crockett. The myths and legends that surround his life are, if possible, even greater than those about Andrew Jackson. Distribute Reproduction Page 84, "Davy Crockett's First Speech," and have students complete the questions following the story. Discuss their answers. Myths and legends in U.S. history would make an interesting research topic—how they start and grow, the purpose they serve, the values they reflect.

REPRODUCTION PAGE 84

DAVY CROCKETT'S FIRST SPEECH*

Davy Crockett was a member of the Tennessee legislature—a green and gawky gentleman from one of the remote counties. He tells us how he behaved to a brother member, who had alluded to the new-comer as the "gentleman from the cane." His story shows that private combat was then regarded as a thing entirely of course when men differed:

"Well," says Crockett, "I had never made a speech in my life. I didn't know whether I could speak or not; and they kept crying out to me "Crockett, answer him—Crockett, answer him:— why the deuce don't you answer him?" So up I popped. I was as mad as fury; and there I stood and not a word could I get out. Well, I bothered, and stammered, and looked foolish, and still there I stood; but after a while I began to talk. I don't know what I said about my *bill*, but I jerked it into him. I told him that he had got hold of the wrong man; that he didn't know who he was fooling with; that he reminded me of the meanest thing on God's earth, an old coon dog barking up the wrong tree.

"After the House had adjourned, seeing Mr. M— walking off alone, I followed him and proposed a walk. He consented, and we went something like a mile, when I called a halt. Said I, 'M—, do you know what I brought you here for?' 'No.' 'Well, I brought you here for the express purpose of whipping you, and I mean to do it.' But the fellow said he didn't mean anything, and kept 'pologising, till I got into a good humor. We then went back together; and I don't believe anybody ever knew anything about it."

1. Does this story accurately reflect American views of frontiersmen?

2. What purposes do such stories—true or not—serve?

3. What values are represented in this story?

4. Can you think of other stories and legends in U.S. history?

Topic 2: Territorial Expansion and Sectionalism

The territorial expansion of the United States between 1803 and 1846 was huge and rapid. And as the country grew in size, sectional interests became more pronounced. For the most part, they were economic differences and they were expressed in political ways.

1. The issue of a tariff repeatedly strained relations between sections—North, South, and West (today's Midwest). Review how a tarriff operates.

   $100 price of an imported product

   $150 price of a domestic product

   Self-interest would have people buying the imported product. As a result, manufacturing and employment in the United States—or sections of it—would suffer because they would be unable to compete in terms of price. A tariff is passed equaling 100 percent. The price structure would now be:

   $100 price of an imported product
   plus a 100% tariff, or $100
   _____
   $200 new price of an imported product
   $150 price of domestic product

   Self-interest would now have people buying the domestic product; production would be increased because of the increased demand; additional workers would be hired; and the price could even be raised to provide additional profit.
     Discuss the advantages and disadvantages of tariffs from the perspectives of producer, consumer, the North, the South, manufacturer, farmer, commercial interests, and relations between countries.

2. Should the U.S. Congress pass a protective tariff law? Assign student readings on tariff proposals made between 1800 and 1850. Divide the class into groups representing: (a) southerners, (b) westerners, (c) northerners, and (d) *nationalists.* Give each group its proper page from Reproduction Pages 85a to 85d, "The Tariff Issue," to use as a background for preparing a new tariff law for congressional debate. Have each group present its proposal. After this, call for a short recess during which informal discussion can take place regarding the legislation. Repeat this procedure until a majority accepts the wording of a new tariff proposal.

THE TARIFF ISSUE (SOUTHERN)

We are at a critical point in the competition with foreign cotton. We risk the loss of the British market if we stop taking the manufactures of Great Britain. She will certainly stop taking our cotton to the same extent. It is a settled principle of her policy to purchase from those nations who receive her manufactures. Her surplus capital and labor must be directed to manufactures, or remain idle and unproductive. A demand for her products is the primary consideration in determining her commercial relations. Britain is not blind to her own needs. She needs the foreign market for her goods. A tariff restricting the sale of her products here will be the end of our trade with her and the destruction of our commerce.

Europe will take as much cotton as we produce. They will only be limited by the amount of goods they are able to sell here. If a tariff reduces imports by 20 millions, they will buy 20 millions less of cotton. What we gain will be quickly sacrificed and the burden will be on the southern planter. He will lose his market for cotton as a consequence of unjust restrictions imposed upon lawful trade by the suicidal policy of his own government.

This law restricting the commerce of the southern states is obviously calculated and intended to promote the interest of the northern manufacturers.

THE TARIFF ISSUE (WESTERN)

The opposition to the tariff comes from the commercial interests on the seaboard and the cotton and tobacco interests in the south—one afraid that it will decrease its business and the other afraid that Europe will cease to purchase their cotton and tobacco. These two powerful interests have governed this nation and dictated its policy. The interior and the West, until lately, have had to submit. We now claim the right of full participation in our government.

Look at the effects of this policy, this system of free trade. Our government is the cheapest, freest, and best on earth; we have every advantage of climate, situation, and soil; yet we are filled with misery and wretchedness, embarrassment, bankruptcy, and ruin. Agriculture is depressed, manufactures ruined, and commerce scarcely able to keep its head above water. Why is this? It is the result of our own present ruinous policy. It is because the national industry is unprotected. Because we looked to Europe instead of our own resources to supply our needs. Because we buy from abroad almost everything we eat, drink, and wear. All the great interests of the nation are at their lowest point, struggling for life. This land of freedom, home of liberty, is cast with gloom. Could there be any doubt as to the cause?

THE TARIFF ISSUE (NORTHERN)

Are particular manufacturers protected and promoted by a tariff on foreign goods? Is it necessary? Can it be done without injustice to other types of industry?

Some say no nation has attained prosperity without encouraging manufacturing. But I ask, what nation ever reached prosperity without promoting foreign trade? These interests —manufacturing and trade—need to flourish together. The tariff will enable us to collect revenue while giving advantages to those manufacturers we may think most useful to promote at home.

And to what interests will a tariff cause distress? There will be a considerable falling off in the ships employed in foreign trade. But let it be remembered that our shipping makes its own way in competition with the whole world. It succeeds, not by aid of the government, but by patience, vigilance, toil.

Failures and bankruptcies have taken place in our large cities. A tariff will not solve all these problems but will help reduce the losses and disasters of commerce.

THE TARIFF ISSUE (NATIONALIST)

A dependence on foreign countries must lead to ruin. We need an American policy. Let us stimulate our industry. We need to protect our own interests by withdrawing support from foreign trade. This can be done by imposing a tariff on foreign goods. Even if it were true that American goods would be more expensive, it is better to have the goods being produced by American workers. Their employment will mean pay with which they will be able to make purchases. Without a job or money, cheap foreign goods are unobtainable. A government needs to remedy the evils it sees; it cannot let industry decay and people remain out of work. We need protection from the influence of foreigners by the establishment of a tariff. And what is this tariff? Nothing more than a tax on the produce of foreign industry, with a view toward promoting American industry.

3. Several attempts were made to compromise differences over slavery. This became increasingly difficult as positions hardened and new territories applied for statehood. The three giants of the Senate—Daniel Webster, Henry Clay, and John C. Calhoun—presented their last major arguments in what became known as the Compromise of 1850. Divide the class into northern and southern sections and distribute Reproduction Page 86, "Should There Be Slavery in the Territories?" Provide each side with sufficient time to agree on their position on the questions and to select a representative to speak for their side. Have each present their views and allow the debate to continue as long as it is productive. Each side should meet again to reconsider its position. The goal is to write solutions to each question to which both sides agree. The solutions provided in the Compromise of 1850 are:

   a. Admit California.

   b. California can be admitted as a free state.

   c. The inhabitants of territories would decide the slavery issue (often referred to as *popular sovereignty*).

   d. The slave *trade* in the District of Columbia would be abolished, but slavery would remain.

   e. Stricter laws were passed compelling state and local officials to return runaway slaves.

REPRODUCTION PAGE 86

SHOULD THERE BE SLAVERY IN THE TERRITORIES?

As the population of territories increased they applied for statehood. This led to difficulties between North and South over the question of admitting the territories as "free" states or "slave" states. When California applied, Congress tried to reach a compromise involving several isues. How would you resolve the following questions if you were in the U.S. Congress?

1. Should California be admitted as a state?

2. Should California be admitted as (a) slave state, (b) a free state, or (c) should the decision be left up to Californians?

3. How should Congress handle the slavery issue in the territory acquired from Mexico: (a) prohibit slavery, (b) provide for slavery, (c) leave it up to the inhabitants of the territory to decide?

4. Should slavery be allowed in the District of Columbia? Should the slave trade be allowed in the District of Columbia?

5. What should be done about the problem of slaves who run away to free states or territories?

---

4. Beginning with the uncertain purchase of Louisiana Territory by Thomas Jefferson in 1803, stimulated by nationalistic fervor after the War of 1812, and supported by growing numbers of political leaders, the United States made a deliberate effort to gain control across the entire continent—called the nation's *Manifest Destiny*. What motivations cause countries to expand and come into conflict with others? Reproduction Page 87, "Some Reasons for National Assertiveness," should be distributed for student response and discussion. After gaining some familiarity with the event, students may relate one or more items from the list to the following conflicts: (a) the subjugation of native Americans; (b) the war with the Barbary States; (c) the War of 1812; (d) the war with Mexico; (e) the Civil War. What hypotheses can be developed and supported about U.S. involvement in conflicts? Do the hypotheses hold for twentieth-century conflicts?

REPRODUCTION PAGE 87

SOME REASONS FOR NATIONAL ASSERTIVENESS

Statements about why conflicts occur between nations are listed below. Which are the most important and real reasons for conflict? Which are doubtful reasons?

	Causes of Conflict	
	Important and real	Probably doubtful
1. The spirit of the people, adventursome, belligerent, is the popular position	____	____
2. Problems over an important issue. Unwillingness to compromise, determination to maintain some position, refusal to continue past arrangements	____	____
3. Economic need for land, resources, etc.	____	____
4. Political need to solve own problems of unemployment, depression, take people's minds off other problems	____	____
5. Rivalry between nations to gain power, position, alliances, land, wealth, etc.	____	____
6. Fill a vacuum where a weak government exists to prevent other problems from occurring later	____	____
7. Miscalculation or breakdown in communications so the other's intentions are not accurately known	____	____
8. Differences over political, social, philosophical, economic, religious beliefs used as basis for protecting own ideas	____	____
9. Changes in the established order of things causes need to return to the way things were	____	____
10. An upset in the *balance of power*, alliances with other countries, treaty arrangements, etc.	____	____
11. Save face, position is important, well known, and cannot be compromised	____	____
12. Unstable, aggressive, weak, strong, leadership	____	____

5. As the United States expanded, problems developed over territories and boundary lines. Most of these were settled peacefully by treaty and to the advantage of the United States. Ask small groups of students to research one dispute and present the claim of each country, a map of the area, and any other pertinent information. For greater student involvement, divide the class to represent the interested nations and have them attempt to reach an agreement. Some of the disputed areas include:[2]

Area	Nation and year	Settlement
Great Lakes	Britain, 1817	Treaty. Naval disarmament on Great Lakes
Canadian border	Britain, 1818	Treaty. Border fixed at 49th parallel; joint occupation of Oregon
Florida	Spain, 1819	Treaty. Spain sells to U.S. for $5 million; U.S. gives up claim to Texas; border between Oregon and colony of Mexico set at 40th parallel
Southeast U.S. Georgia	Cherokee Nation, 1828	Judicial decision. Supreme Court supports Cherokee claim, but U.S. removes inhabitants and takes land
Maine	Britain, 1842	Treaty. Compromise over land area
Oregon	Britain, 1846	Treaty. Compromise divides between U.S. and Britain at 49th parallel
Mexico and Texas	Mexico, 1846	War. U.S. obtains land to Rio Grande; additional land ceded by Mexico
Southwest U.S.	Mexico, 1853	Purchase. U.S. pays $10 million to Mexico

6. Conflicts over boundaries with Mexico led to war. Did they have to? Divide the class into several small groups and have each group divide into Americans and Mexicans. Distribute Reproduction Page 88, "United States-Mexican Border: The Land Between," and have students read through the escalating incidents. At what point could this problem have been resolved? At what point, if any, had it gone too far for peaceful resolution?

REPRODUCTION PAGE 88

UNITED STATES-MEXICAN BORDER: THE LAND BETWEEN

At the invitation of the Mexican government, Americans settled in the province of Texas in the 1830s. The Americans established slavery, which was illegal under Mexican law. And they held religious views, customs, and traditions that were different from Mexico's. War broke out and the Texans eventually established an independent country. They were recognized by the United States and other countries, but Mexico considered them in rebellion and still part of Mexico. Southerners in the United States, especially, wanted to annex Texas to obtain additional lands for producing cotton and extending slavery. James K. Polk, a Democrat from Tennessee, ran for president on a platform favoring "the reoccupation of Oregon and the reannexation of Texas" and won a clear victory, indicating support for territorial expansion. Here are some of the events that took place between the United States and Mexico, as seen from each point of view.

2. Since 1607 many areas have been in dispute between settlers and the native people. In countless cases land was taken from the natives by deceptive practices, meaningless treaties, "relocation," or war. In recent years, native Americans have used the courts to regain, at least in part, some land or receive compensation for its loss. These many cases are not listed on this chart.

Mexico	United States
1. Texas is not an independent nation. To annex it is a hostile act. If the United States takes Texas it could lead to war.	1. Texas is an independent nation. No country can interfere in the affairs of the United States. People in Texas, many former Americans, have asked to be annexed.

Mexico withdraws threat of war.
The United States annexes Texas.

Mexico	United States
2. Mexican territory extends beyond the Rio Grande as far north as the Nueces River.	2. U.S. territory extends beyond the Nueces River as far south as the Rio Grande.
3. Mexican public opinion is strongly against American efforts to take over Mexican land. Most admit that Mexican government is weak and poor.	3. U.S. President Polk sends John Slidell to negotiate with Mexico for land.

The United States is prepared to pay claims made
by American citizens against Mexican government
if Mexico recognizes Rio Grande as border; the
United States would also pay $5 million for
New Mexico, $20 million for California

Mexico	United States
4. Mexico sees real purpose of the United States to get California and New Mexico; refuse to see Slidell.	4. Polk feels war is justified; orders Gen. Zachary Taylor into disputed land between the Rio Grande and the Nueces River.
5. Mexican troops attack Americans between the Rio Grande and the Nueces River.	5. Polk says: "Mexico has invaded our territory and shed American blood upon American soil."

Distribute Reproduction Page 89a and 89b, "How to Settle Boundary Disputes," and have each side within the group—Mexican and American—discuss and decide what action they will take. This information should be exchanged between sides within the group. Then each should again decide what action to take based on the latest information from the other side. Repeat these rounds three times. Does the conflict escalate further? Were any peaceful solutions suggested? Did the last round lead to war? Why?

REPRODUCTION PAGE 89a

HOW TO SETTLE BOUNDARY DISPUTES

This case involves the United States and the country of _____

The area in dispute includes _____

_____

Directions: Each of the methods of settling disputes is a realistic possibility. Your task is to explain the advantages and disadvantages from the point of view of

Be prepared to explain which method you recommend.	Map showing the claims of both sides.

| WAR. May be unavoidable. Neither side is willing to back down. Both feel they are right. Both feel they have a chance to win. Might be worth it. | ESCALATION. A buildup of power or show of force. Hope to scare or threaten other side. |

ALLIANCES. Each side lines up friends. Each tries to keep the balance of power in its favor.	NEGOTIATIONS. Discuss problem and seek solutions. What is cause? What does each side want? What will each give up?
TREATIES. Written agreements following negotiations. How is problem solved?	ARBITRATION/ADJUDICATION. Neutral, outside person decides how to settle dispute. Both sides agree in advance to accept terms.

REPRODUCTION PAGE 89b

HOW TO SETTLE BOUNDARY DISPUTES

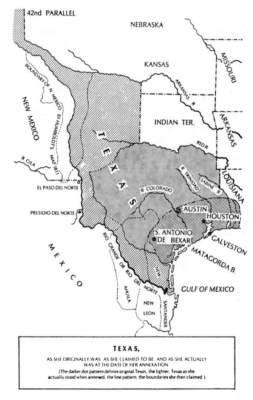

TEXAS,

AS SHE ORIGINALLY WAS AS SHE CLAIMED TO BE AND AS SHE ACTUALLY
WAS AT THE DATE OF HER ANNEXATION
(The darker dot pattern defines original Texas, the lighter, Texas as she
actually stood when annexed, the line pattern, the boundaries she then claimed.)

*Horace Greeley, *The American Conflict* (Hartford, Conn.: O.D. Case & Co., 1865), p. 161.

7. Objections to the Mexican War, slavery, and other government policies were not always based on narrow political or sectional grounds but sometimes on principle. Henry David Thoreau's "Civil Disobedience," 1849, is the classic statement for taking nonviolent action against unjust laws and government. Distribute Reproduction Page 90, "Should You Obey Unjust Laws?," and have students answer and discuss the questions. The impact of Thoreau's ideas on Martin Luther King, Jr.'s

effort against unjust laws is well known. Further student research and comparison would be worthwhile. Reproduction Page 8, "Dilemma Decision Form," is also appropriate for this activity.

SHOULD YOU OBEY UNJUST LAWS?

Henry David Thoreau states his opposition to the Mexican War and slavery in "Civil Disobedience," 1849:

> All men recognize the right of revolution; that is, the right to refuse allegiance to, and to resist, the government, when its tyranny or its inefficiency are great and unendurable. But almost all say that such is not the case now. (But a sixth of population are slaves and the country is overrunning and conquering another.)
>
> Those who, while they disapprove of the character and measure of a government, yield to it their allegiance and support are undoubtedly its most conscientious supporters, and so frequently the most serious obstacles to reform. Some are petitioning the state to dissolve the union, to disregard the requisition of the President. Why do they not dissolve it themselves,—the union between themselves and the state—and refuse to pay their quota into its treasury?
>
> Unjust laws exist: shall we be content to obey them, or shall we endeavor to amend them, and obey them until we have succeeded, or shall we transgress them at once? Men generally, under such a government as this, think that they ought to wait until they have persuaded the majority to alter them. They think that, if they should resist, the remedy would be worse than the evil. But it is the fault of the government that the remedy is worse than the evil. It makes it worse.
>
> Under a government which imprisons any unjustly, the true place for a just man is also a prison. The proper place today, the only place which Massachusetts has provided for her freer and less desponding spirits, is in her prisons, to be put out and locked out of the State by her own act, as they have already put themselves out by their principles. . . . A minority is powerless while it conforms to the majority; it is not even a minority then; but it is irresistible when it clogs by its whole weight. If the alternative is to keep all just men in prison or give up war and slavery, the State will not hesitate which to choose.

1. What is Thoreau's complaint?

2. When does the right of revolution exist?

3. What action should people take in this case?

4. Do you think Thoreau is *loyal*?

5. Where does a government get power to govern?

6. Is Thoreau suggesting a revolution?

7. Should you obey unjust laws?

Which of the following comes closest to your opinion:

_____ obey the law because you could be punished

_____ obey the law because you may be rewarded

_____ obey the law because it would please others

_____ obey the law because it is the law

_____ do what you want; individuals have rights in society

_____ do what your conscience says is right

Topic 3:   Growth of Technology and Social-Cultural Progress

1. An enormous amount of labor was required to separate cottonseed from the fiber in which it was imbedded. The separation by hand of one pound of fiber was an average day's work. This meant that extensive and profitable cultivation of cotton was unlikely. It seemed that the limit of American cotton production had been reached when Eli Whitney invented an engine in 1793 to separate fiber from seed. It revolutionized the agriculture of the slave states.

   Write the words "cotton gin" on the board and ask students to suggest what *direct and immediate* effects it had. List these around "cotton gin" and ask what further effects each of these had; continue this procedure as long as it has value. Discuss the connections between these items: land value, plantation size, production, distribution, trade, fashions, factories, the slave system, plantation society, North-South relations, international impact. Have students develop and test hypotheses about inventions; for instance, all inventions cause problems as well as bring benefits, or technological change upsets social stability.

2. Eli Whitney battled for several years to gain patent rights for his invention and was largely unsuccessful. Should an inventor have complete control over his discovery? Can he protect it if it is simple to construct and important to users? Distribute Reproduction Page 91, "Was the Cotton Gin Too Valuable?" This is Whitney's view of his problems. Discuss the relationship between an inventor and society and what each *owes* the other.

REPRODUCTION PAGE 91

WAS THE COTTON GIN TOO VALUABLE?

Eli Whitney writes a letter to Robert Fulton:

> The difficulties with which I have had to contend have originated, principally, in the want of a disposition in mankind to do justice. My invention was new and distinct from every other: it stood alone. It was not interwoven with anything before known; and it can seldom happen that an invention or improvement is so strongly marked and can be so clearly and specifically identified; and I have always believed that I should have had no difficulty in causing my rights to be respected, if it had been less valuable, and been used only by a small portion of the community. But the use of this machine being immensely profitable to almost every planter in the cotton districts, all were interested in trespassing upon the patent right.

1. Whitney thought he would have been better able to protect his patent rights if the cotton gin was less valuable and used by fewer people. Do you agree?

2. Are some inventions or discoveries so valuable or important that the inventor has an obligation to make it available?

3. Are some inventions or discoveries so dangerous that they should be kept secret or made illegal?

4. Whitney felt that his invention was "distinct from every other" and not connected with any other invention. What other inventions do you think "stand alone"?

5. The cotton gin did more harm than good. Explain why you agree or disagree.

---

3. Improvements in transportation—roads, canals, ships, railroads—aided the movement of people and products. The success of the Erie Canal began a canal-building boom. This story is most colorfully remembered today in the words of an old work song:

> I got a mule, her name is Sal,
>   Fifteen miles on the Erie Canal!
> She's a good old worker and a good old pal,
>   Fifteen miles on the Erie Canal!
> We've hauled some barges in our day,
>   Filled with lumber, coal and hay,
> And we know ev'ry inch of the way,
>   From Albany to Buffalo.
>
> Low bridge, ev'rybody down, low bridge
>   'cause we're coming to a town,
> And you'll always know your neighbor,
>   You'll always know your pal,
> If you ever navigated on the Erie Canal.

Some students may be interested in researching the lyrics of other folk songs—about work, railroads, the sea, the West, or others—to explain part of the American past. A presentation to the class is limited only by the student's musical or theatrical ability. Slides to illustrate the lyrics make an impressive and effective presentation.[3]

4. Meaningful student research can examine any number of the technological or social advances made during this period. Any change in existing arrangements has consequences, and these can be understood in terms of *costs* and *benefits*. The preparation of a *technological assessment statement* or an *environmental impact statement* will provide a way to consider long- and short-term consequences in relation to the goals or values of the society. Use Reproduction Page 92, "Impact Statement for Scientific or Social Contributions," to help students organize their work.

Some developments that might be examined include:

- Robert Fulton introduces the steamboat, 1807

- National Road, Cumberland Road, others

- Erie Canal completed, 1825

- cast-iron plow invented, 1819

- reaper invented by Cyrus McCormick, 1834

- railroads introduced by Peter Cooper, 1831

- Colt patents revolver, 1835

- John Deere introduces steel plow, 1837

- Charles Goodyear vulcanizes rubber, 1839

- photography introduced, 1839

---

3. For an authoritative and comprehensive source of folk song history, see Alan Lomas, *The Folk Songs of North America* (Garden City, N.Y.: Doubleday, 1975).

- Samuel Morse constructs telegraph line, 1844

- Elias Howe invents sewing machine, 1846

- rotary printing press invented, 1846

- transatlantic cable connects continents; Cyrus Field, 1858

- factory system introduced, 1814; Francis Cabot Lowell

- clipper ships constructed by David McKay

- Whitney develops idea of interchangeable parts

- Smithsonian Institution established, 1846

- free, public education becomes available; Horace Mann, Henry Barnard

- women's education; Emma Willard, Mary Lyon

- women's rights; Elizabeth Cady Stanton, Lucretia Mott, Susan B. Anthony

- treatment of mentally ill and prisoners; Dorothea Dix

- peace movement established; Elihu Burritt, William Ladd

- utopian communities founded

- growth of inexpensive newspapers; James Gordon Bennett, Horace Greeley

- studies in ornithology; John Audubon

- studies in geology; zoology, chemistry; Louis Agassiz, Benjamin Silliman

- use of vaccinations

- use of anesthetics

- historians; George Bancroft, Francis Parkman

- artists and musicians; George Catlin, Alfred Miller, George Innes, Thomas Cole, Stephen Foster, Dan Emmett

- writers; James Fenimore Cooper, Washington Irving, Herman Melville, Nathaniel Hawthorne, Henry Wadsworth Longfellow, Edgar Allan Poe, Henry David Thoreau, Ralph Waldo Emerson, Harriet Beecher Stowe, Walt Whitman, John Greenleaf Whittier, James Russell Lowell, William Cullen Bryant, Oliver Wendell Holmes, Emily Dickinson

---

REPRODUCTION PAGE 92

IMPACT STATEMENT FOR SCIENTIFIC
OR SOCIAL CONTRIBUTIONS

1. Inventor or contributor:_____

2. Contribution:_____

3. Year, place, or other considerations: _____

_____

Interested or affected groups	Costs (Explain how and why this is a disadvantage)	Benefits (Explain how and why this is an advantage)

Impact statement. The short- and long-term consequences of this contribution, along with my comments and recommendations, are as follows:

5. Efforts to improve conditions in the lives of women received increased attention during this period. A notable document was issued in Seneca Falls, New York, in 1848 listing women's grievances. Patterned after the Declaration of Independence, it includes descriptions of problems that many people think still exist today. To introduce this topic, ask students if they *agree* or *disagree* or are *unsure* about the following statements:

- All men and women are created equal

- the history of mankind is a history of repeated injustices on the part of man toward women.

- Men have attempted to gain absolute control over women.

These statements are from the introduction to the Seneca Falls declaration. (You may wish to put those students who *agree* with the statements in one group, those who *disagree* in another, and divide the rest.) Distribute Reproduction Page 93, "Women's Rights: Room for Reform?," and have students individually or in groups arrange the statements on the page in categories on the chart.

After completing this survey, have individuals or groups list their reasons for supporting or disapproving the need for reform today. Have conclusions presented to the class. Invite reactions and discussion. What can be done to improve the rights of women? What are the views of those who oppose expanded women's rights?

At some point in the discussion it would be worthwhile to review student comments. Or, prior to the discussion, you might wish to arrange for a student to record this information and report to the class. What goals were mentioned? What antireform views were voiced? What methods for accomplishing or thwarting goals were suggested? Conclude this activity by having students write a historical report on women's rights: "You've come a long way, baby: True? False? Or true and false?"

WOMEN'S RIGHTS: ROOM FOR REFORM?

The delegates to a convention on women's rights, held in Seneca Falls, New York, in 1848, approved a Declaration of Independence listing their grievances. Some of these are listed below. Check the appropriate column based on what you know about women's rights *today*.

	Problem today	Not a problem	Ho hum!
1. Men have not permitted women to vote.			
2. Men have not allowed women to have a say in making laws.			
3. Women have no legal rights.			
4. Women have no property rights.			
5. In marriage ceremonies, women have to promise to obey their husbands.			
6. Men have monopolized nearly all profitable employment.			
7. Women receive less wages than men.			
8. Practically no women hold positions in theology, medicine, law.			
9. Women are denied a way of getting a thorough education; many colleges are closed to them.			
10. Women are excluded from the ministry and are not allowed to participate in the affairs of some churches.			
11. Women are supposed to follow a different moral code than men.			
12. Men today try to destroy women's confidence in their own powers, lessen their self-respect, and make them dependent.			

---

6. Women who fought for women's rights, or who otherwise made important social contributions during this period, are listed here. Research or class work related to these important people would provide information about the reform movement and discrimination, neglected topics in U.S. history.

- Susan B. Anthony—women's rights, abolitionist
- Catharine Beecher—seminary to train women teachers
- Elizabeth Blackwell—medicine
- Amelia Bloomer—author, known for protest against fashions
- Prudence Crandall—courageous educator
- Dorothea Dix—crusader for mentally ill, prisoners

- Margaret Fuller—author

- Angelina Grimké—author, lecturer, abolitionist

- Sarah Grimké—author (with sister Angelina): *American Slavery as It Is: Testimony of a Thousand Witnesses*

- Sarah Josepha Hale—editor of *Godey's Lady's Book*

- Mary Lyon—founder of college for women

- Lucretia Mott—women's rights, abolitionist

- Elizabeth Ann Bayley Seton—founder of Catholic parochial school system, founder of Sisters of Charity

- Elizabeth Cady Stanton—women's rights

- Lucy Stone—women's rights, abolitionist

- Harriet Beecher Stowe—author of *Uncle Tom's Cabin*

- Sojourner Truth—abolitionist, women's rights

- Harriet Tubman—most famous conductor on the Underground Railroad

- Emma Willard—educator, women's rights

- Frances Wright—women's rights

7. During the early nineteenth century many prominent reformers were active in both the women's rights movement and abolition of slavery. Assign readings on both topics and have students develop hypotheses related to social change and conflict. How is change brought about? What are the most effective methods reformers use to accomplish change? Why do people persist in having attitudes or practices that seem wrong? What similarities are there between any and all reform movements in U.S. history?

Topic 4:   Slavery and Abolition

1. In the last half of the 1700s many states abolished slavery.

Date	State	Method
1777	Vermont	new constitution prohibits
1780	Massachusetts	interpretation of Declaration of Rights
1780	Pennsylvania	Gradual Emancipation Act; all persons born after March 1, 1780, were to be free at age 28
1783	New Hampshire	new constitution prohibits
1784	Rhode Island	all persons born in Rhode Island after March, 1784, to be free
1784	Connecticut	new law grants gradual abolition
1799	New York	new law grants gradual abolition

One of the early and important actions taken by the new government under the Articles of Confederation was the adoption of the Northwest Ordinance of 1787, which among other things prohibited slavery in the Northwest Territory. It seemed as if the slave system was slowly losing its political and economic appeal.

The one critical development that reinforced the slave system and made it attractive to southern plantation owners was the invention of the cotton gin. With cheap cotton, the worldwide demand increased spectacularly and, with it, the need for more land and more labor—slave labor. Issues associated with the slave system increasingly dominated American life until words turned to war in 1861.

2. What was the moderate view of slavery? Distribute Reproduction Page 94, "Slavery in Moderation," which notes abolitionist efforts to "stir us up." The writer, William Ellery Channing, suggests a cautious approach toward ending slavery. Have students write a letter responding to this letter as (a) an abolitionist, (b) a plantation owner, or (c) a social scientist. Is any peaceful solution possible between abolitionists and plantation owners?

REPRODUCTION PAGE 94

SLAVERY IN MODERATION?

William Ellery Channing* writes a letter to Daniel Webster:

Boston, May 14, 1848

My Dear Sir:—I wish to call your attention to a subject of general interest.

A little while ago, Mr. Lundy, of Baltimore, the editor of a paper called "The Genius of Universal Emancipation," visited this part of the country to stir us up to the work of abolishing Slavery at the South; and the intention is to organize societies for this purpose. . . .

I know that our Southern brethren interpret every word from this region on the subject of Slavery as an expression of hostility. I would ask if they cannot be brought to understand us better and if we can do any good till we remove their misapprehensions. It seems to me that, before moving in this matter, we ought to say to them distinctly: "We consider Slavery as your calamity, not your crime; and we will share with you the burden of putting an end to it. . . ."

I throw out these suggestions merely to illustrate my views. We must first let the Southern States see that we are their friends in this affair; and we sympathize with them, and, from principles of patriotism and philantrophy, are willing to share the toil and expense of abolishing Slavery; or I fear our interference will avail nothing. . . .

Assume that you are (abolitionist) (plantation owner) (social scientist today). Write a letter replying to Channing. Explain your views about: (a) abolitionists and their methods, (b) the feelings and actions of plantation owners, and (c) how the problem of slavery can best be solved.

---

3. How did plantation owners justify slavery? Some of the major arguments supporting the slave system are presented in Reproduction Page 95, "Keeping the Slave System." Divide the class into abolitionists and slaveowners. Do they agree on the order of important statements? Discuss economic motivation, social-cultural traditions, humanitarian rationalizations, comparative advantages.

REPRODUCTION PAGE 95

KEEPING THE SLAVE SYSTEM

Several statements justifying the slave system are listed below. Which do you think are most important to the *plantation owner?* Place a number 1 alongside the most important, a number 2 alongside the next most important, and so on.

Ranking		
self	group	*The plantation owner wants to keep the slave system because:*
_____	_____	There is no better alternative. Slaves are better off in the South than they would be in Africa. Sending them back would be expensive and unpopular. Freeing them would cause some to rise up against their masters. It would lead to murder or idleness.
_____	_____	The system is valuable. Slave labor gives value to the land and the economy of the South and entire country. Without it the South would be a poor wasteland and the country would lose its economic standing.
_____	_____	The slaves are valuable. The master's interest protects the slave from infancy through old age. He takes care of weaker members of his plantation society just as a parent or husband would.
_____	_____	People are happy without worries. Slaves do not have to worry about the future or having sufficient food, clothing, or shelter. It is a happy arrangement.
_____	_____	Every society has its social classes. A master-and-slave arrangement eliminates uncertainty and is part of the natural order.
_____	_____	Conditions in the South are better than those in the North. The slave system is less cruel than the factory system in the North. Wealth is more evenly distributed than in the North where a few millionaires own most of the property and many others are in jail or poorhouses.

It (was) (was not) realistic to expect the plantation owner to give up slavery because:

4. The best-known, bloodiest, and most frightening slave rebellion was led by Nat Turner in 1831. Turner went from house to house killing almost sixty white people, and it was almost two months before he was captured. Fear spread throughout the South, and more than one hundred slaves were later killed in revenge. His *Confession*, originally published in 1831 by T. R. Gray, provides information about the rebellion and insight into Turner's character. Reproduction Page 96, "The Confessions of Nat Turner," should be read and speculations made about why Turner killed the whites on the plantations. "It was not instigated by motives of revenge or sudden anger," Gray states in the *Confessions*, "but the result of long deliberation, and a settled purpose of mind—the offspring of gloomy fanaticism acting upon materials but too well prepared for such impression."

REPRODUCTION PAGE 96

THE CONFESSIONS OF NAT TURNER

The following report of the confession of Nat Turner was written shortly after he was captured:

It has been said he was ignorant and cowardly, and that his object was to murder and rob for the purpose of obtaining money to make his escape. It is notorious that he was never known to have a dollar in his life, to swear an oath, or drink a drop of spirits.

As to his ignorance, he certainly never had the advantages of education, but he can read and write (it was taught to him by his parents), and for natural intelligence and quickness of apprehension is surpassed by few men I have ever seen.

As to his being a coward, his reason as given for not resisting Mr. Phipps shows the decision of his character. When he saw Mr. Phipps present his gun, he said he knew it was impossible for him to escape, as the woods were full of men; he therefore thought it was better to surrender, and trust to fortune for his escape.

He is a complete fanatic, or plays his part most admirably. On other subjects he possesses an uncommon share of intelligence, with a mind capable of attaining anything, but warped and perverted by the influence of early impressions. He is below the ordinary stature, though strong and active, having the true negro face, every feature of which is strongly marked.

I shall not attempt to describe the effect of his narrative, as told and commented on by himself, in the condemned hole of the prison. The calm, deliberate composure with which he spoke of his late deeds and intentions; the expression of his fiendlike face when excited by enthusiasm, still bearing the stains of the blood of helpless innocence about him; clothed with rags and covered with chains, yet daring to raise his manacled hands to heaven, with a spirit soaring above the attributes of men. I looked on him, and my blood curdled in my veins.

What caused Nat Turner's rebellion?

REPRODUCTION PAGE 97

YOUR BELIEFS OR YOUR LIFE?

• What beliefs do you have that you would risk your own life to protect?
• Would you change your mind to save your life?

The night was hot in Alton, Illinois, in 1837, but no hotter than the tempers being displayed at the meeting being held by some of the town's citizens. They were upset by articles appearing in their local newspaper. They had not agreed with what the paper was printing. The paper's editor, Elijah P. Lovejoy, wrote what he believed, and he believed along with many others that slavery was wrong and his newspaper said so, day after day. The people at the meeting did not agree with Lovejoy. They told Lovejoy that he would have to stop writing his newspaper in Alton.

Lovejoy was not to be stopped. Already mobs had broken into his office and destroyed his printing presses. This had not stopped him. He now said to the people at the meeting, "Have I broken any laws? Have I committed any crime? If I have, you can convict me. But if I have not broken a law, why am I hunted and my presses broken? Tell me what I have done wrong and I will be responsible for it. If the police refuse to protect me, I will ask God's protection; and if I die, I will be buried in Alton. I have sworn to be against slavery forever and with the blessings of God, I will never stop. God can decide if I am right, but not you. I can die for my beliefs, but I will not give them up."

Four nights later Lovejoy was dead. He was killed by a mob who attacked the warehouse where his new presses were stored.

1. Why were people opposed to Lovejoy's printing his paper?
2. Was Lovejoy violating any laws or customs in Alton? Explain.
3. Why do people with unpopular ideas continue to express them when they know they are not acceptable?
4. What should Lovejoy have done in this case: moved away, changed his writing, stayed the same, or something else?
5. Would news of this event help or hurt the cause of abolition? Why?

Don Bolles, a newspaper reporter in Arizona, was investigating organized crime and finding information that was damaging and embarrassing to important political and business figures in the state. His reports grew more revealing. One day he got into his car and turned on the ignition and the car exploded. Several days later he died. You receive two telephone calls shortly after. The first mysteriously warns you to be careful. The second call is from a friend who wants to investigate Bolles's murder to find and punish those who are responsible.

Do you help investigate the murder?
You call back and say:

5. Abolitionists sharpened the slavery controversy and provided a moral fervor to the antislavery campaign. As individuals they often paid a high personal price for their strongly held convictions. Use Reproduction Page 97, "Your Beliefs or Your Life?," as a case study of Elijah Lovejoy's determination to exercise his right to express his opinion, however unpopular and dangerous.

6. Dred Scott was a slave who was taken to a free territory, back to a slave state, and then sold to a friendly antislavery owner to determine if Scott was a slave or free. The Supreme Court decision announced by Roger Taney, in the hopes of ending the slave controversy, stated that (a) slaves are property; (b) Congress cannot deprive a person of his right to take property into territories; and (c) the prohibition of slavery in the Louisiana Territory by the Missouri Compromise was unconstitutional.

    Present the facts of this case and arrange the class as a court. Assign student roles as: Supreme Court Justices (nine at that time); Dred Scott; attorney for Scott; and attorneys for Sanford, his owner. Supreme Court procedure provides for each side to make its presentation and answer any questions from the Justices. The Justices write their opinions and then meet to vote. Majority, minority, and concurring opinions are then prepared and later announced.

    This assignment should be given well before the court session, and students should research and prepare their cases. At the conclusion of this activity, discuss: the role of Supreme Court, judicial review, checks and balances, the basis for the decision, and the ramifications of this case on the slavery issue.

7. During this time, blacks began to speak and write more forcefully in defense of their own rights. The first black-owned newspaper in the United States, *Freedom's Journal*, was published March 16, 1827, and edited by John Brown Russwurm, one of the first U.S. black college graduates. "We wish to plead our own case," he said, "too long have others spoken for us." The best-known black publication was the *North Star*, begun by Frederick Douglass, November 1, 1847. "The object of the *North Star* will be to attack slavery in all its forms and aspects, advocate universal emancipation; promote the moral and intellectual improvement of the colored people; and to hasten the day of freedom to our three million enslaved fellow countrymen." Have students research and report on black efforts to plead their own case. How did slaves and former slaves communicate with each other? With the larger society? How did freed slaves help those still in slavery?

8. Reproduction Page 98, "Newspaper Reports from Harpers Ferry," presents information about John Brown's raid. Have students react in roles of: President James Buchanan, Governor Wise of Virginia, an abolitionist, a Virginia slaveowner, a Virginia slave, a resident of Harpers Ferry. This can be done quickly and easily in class by selecting willing students for each of the roles and then have them interviewed by student *reporters*. After the enactments, ask: What is happening that is important? What would each want to happen at this point in the raid? What courses of action are available to each person? Which would most likely be selected? What are the likely consequences?

NEWSPAPER REPORTS FROM HARPERS FERRY

On October 17, 1859, the country was bewildered and astounded by telegraph dispatches from Baltimore and Washington announcing the outbreak, at Harpers Ferry, of a conspiracy of abolitionists and Negroes, to destroy the South and its way of life. Here are the first reports:

Insurrection at Harpers Ferry

Associated Press, Oct. 17, 1859. A dispatch just received here . . . states that an insurrection has broken out at Harpers Ferry, where an armed band of Abolitionists have full possession of the Government Arsenal. The express train going east was twice fired into, and one of the railroad hands and a negro killed, while they were endeavoring to get the train through the town. The insurrectionists stopped and arrested two men, who had come to town with a load of wheat, and, seizing their wagon loaded it with rifles, and sent them into Maryland. The insurrectionists number about 250 whites, and are aided by a gang of negroes. At last accounts, fighting was going on.

Baltimore, 10:00 A.M.
It is apprehended that the affair at Harpers Ferry is more serious than our citizens seem willing to believe. The wires from Harpers Ferry are cut, and consequently we have no telegraphic communication with Monocacy Station. The southern train, which was due here at an early hour this morning, has not yet arrived. It is rumored that there is a stampede of negroes from this State. There are many other wild rumors, but nothing authentic as yet.

Baltimore, 2:00 P.M.
Another account, received by train, says the bridge across the Potomac was filled with insurgents, all armed. Every light in that town was extinguished and the hotels closed. All the streets were in the possession of the mob, and every road and lane leading thereto barricaded and guarded. Men were seen in every quarter with muskets and bayonets, who arrested the citizens, and impressed them into the service, including many negroes. This done, the United States Arsenal and Government Payhouse, in which was said to be a large amount of money, and all other public works, were seized by the mob. Some were of the opinion that the object was entirely plunder, and to rob the Government of the funds deposited on Saturday at the Payhouse. During the night, the mob made a demand on the Wagner Hotel for provisions, and enforced the claim by a body of armed men. The citizens were in a terrible state of alarm, and the insurgents have threatened to burn the town.

Baltimore, later
The following has just been received from Monocacy, this side of Harpers Ferry: "The Mail Agent on the western-bound train has returned, and reports that the train was unable to get through. The town is in possession of the negroes, who arrest everyone they can catch and imprison. The train due here at 3 P.M., could not get through, and the Agent came down on an empty engine.

1. What are the sources of information for these accounts?

2. What questions would you ask to get enough information to report this event accurately?

3. To whom would you want to ask your questions?

---

9. On October 17, 1859, John Brown and a small group of white and black men entered Harpers Ferry, Virginia, and took over the U.S. Arsenal Building. They held it and much of the town for two days and were finally overwhelmed by armed force. On December 2, 1859, John Brown was hanged. Was he a modern-day terrorist or a savior of oppressed people? What is his proper place in history? Divide the class into small working groups of historians. Their task is to explain the significance of John Brown and Harpers Ferry in U.S. history. Distribute Reproduction Page 99, "John Brown's Raid at Harpers Ferry," which describes the events that took place there.

10. Use Reproduction Page 99 as the basis of a trial. Assign roles for individuals named in the case—a judge, defense and prosecuting attorneys, clerk, bailiff, and jury members. Should unjust laws be violated?

JOHN BROWN'S RAID AT HARPERS FERRY

Harpers Ferry was a village of some 5,000 inhabitants lying on the Virginia side of the Potomac, 57 miles from Washington. One of its few streets was entirely occupied by the work-shops and offices of the National Armory. In the old Arsenal building, there were usually stored from 100,000 to 200,000 stand of arms.

Brown entered the town with a force of 17 white and 5 colored men without being noticed. Others cut the telegraph wires and tore up the railroad track. It was Sunday evening, October 17th.

They first extinguished the lights of the town, then took possession of the Armory buildings, which were only guarded by 3 watchmen, whom they locked up in the guard-house. At half-past ten, the watchman at the Potomac bridge was seized. At mid-night, his successor, arriving, was hailed by Brown's sentinels but ran to give the alarm. But still nothing stirred.

At a quarter past one, the western train arrived and its conductor found the bridge guarded by armed men. He and others attempted to walk across but were turned back at rifle point. The passengers took refuge in the hotel and remained there for several hours.

A little after mid-night, the house of Col. Washington was visited by 6 of Brown's men. They captured the Colonel and liberated his slaves. They then went to the house of Mr. Alstadtt, whom they captured and freed his slaves. Each male citizen as he appeared on the streets was taken to the Armory where they were confined. Brown informed his prisoners, about 40 to 50, that they could be liberated on condition of writing to their friends to send a negro apiece as ransom.

At daylight, the train proceeded. When asked the object of their captors, the uniform answer was, "To free the slave." And when one of the workmen asked by what authority they had taken possession of the public property, he was answered, "By the authority of God Almighty!"

By early Monday morning, October 17, the insurrectionists had complete military possession of Harpers Ferry.

Soon after daybreak, as Brown's guards were bringing two citizens to a halt, they were fired on by a man named Turner and, directly afterward, by a grocer named Boerly, who was instantly killed by return fire. Several Virginians took positions in a room overlooking the Armory gates and fired at the sentinels who guarded them. Two men, one of whom was Brown's son Watson, were killed.

Throughout the forenoon, the liberators remained masters of the town. There were shots fired at intervals, but no more casualties reported. The prisoners were permitted to visit their families under guard to give assurance that they were still alive and were kindly treated.

Why Brown lingered is not certain. Some have said that he had private assurances that the negroes of the surrounding country would rise at the first tidings of his movement, and come flocking to his standard, and he chose to remain where arms and ammunition for all could abundantly be had.

His doom was already sealed. Half an hour after noon, a militia force of 100 arrived and rapidly dispersed to command every available exit from the town.

The railroad bridge was re-captured. All houses around the Armory buildings were held by Virginians. Several of Brown's men, including another son Oliver, were killed by Virginians or the militia. The Armory building was attacked from the rear while another detachment attacked from the front. Brown retreated to the engine-house where he repulsed his assailants.

The militia continued to pour in. The telegraph and railroad having been repaired so that the government in Washington, Richmond and other authorities were in immediate communication with Harpers Ferry. Terror and rumor had multiplied the actual number of insurgents manyfold and troops were hurrying in from all over.

The firing ceased at nightfall. Brown offered to liberate his prisoners upon condition that his men should be permitted to cross the bridge in safety. His offer was refused.

At seven in the morning, troops broke in the door of the engine-house by using a ladder as a battering-ram. One of the defenders was shot and two marines wounded but the odds were too great. All resistance was over. Brown was struck in the face with a saber and knocked down, after which the blow was several times repeated, while a soldier ran a bayonet twice into the old man's body.

THE ENDS OF JUSTICE?

John Brown was tried and found guilty. He was asked if he had anything to say before his sentence was passed. He responded:

> In the first place, I deny everything but what I have all along admitted—the design on my part to free the slave. I intended certainly to have made a clean thing of that matter, as I did last winter, when I went into Missouri, and there took slaves without the snapping of a gun on either side, moved them through the country, and finally left them in Canada. I designed to have done the same thing again, on a larger scale. That was all I intended. I never did intend murder, or treason, or the destruction of property, or to excite or incite slaves to rebellion, or to make insurrection.
>
> I have another objection: and that is, it is unjust that I should suffer such a penalty. Had I interfered . . . in behalf of the rich, the powerful, the intelligent, the so-called great, or in behalf of any of their friends, either father, mother, brother, sister, wife, or children, or any of that class, and suffered and sacrificed what I have in this interference, it would have been all right and every man in this Court would have deemed it an act worthy of reward rather than punishment.
>
> Now, if it is deemed necessary that I should forfeit my life for the furtherance of the ends of justice, and mingle my blood further with the blood of my children and with the blood of millions in this slave country whose rights are disregarded by wicked, cruel, and unjust enactments—I submit. So let it be done.

1. What does Brown admit were his intentions?

2. Under what conditions does Brown feel his treatment would have been different?

3. What criticism does he make of the country?

4. Do you think his statement made any difference in the courtroom? Would it have made any difference if you were the judge? To whom might Brown have been addressing his comments to?

5. Several people were killed in Harpers Ferry defending U.S. government property and laws supporting slavery. Did John Brown receive a fair punishment? Explain.

6. Many stories and songs have been written about John Brown. Why do you think he has received so much attention?

11. John Brown was tried and found guilty. He was asked if he had anything to say before sentence was passed. Distribute Reproduction Page 100, "The Ends of Justice?" This is a strong defense of slaves and the poor and a defiant condemnation of "this slave country." Have students answer and discuss the questions.

12. An emotional opposition to slavery by large numbers of ordinary people was created by the book, *Uncle Tom's Cabin.* The author, Harriet Beecher Stowe, in another book described, in all its gory details, the punishment of a slave by his master. For an example of Stowe's impact, read or distribute Reproduction Page 101, "Treatment of Slaves." (This page should be used only with mature students.) Do they think it is a real account? What is their immediate reaction? How would it affect people in the 1850s? What purpose would the author have in reporting this incident? What would be the reaction of slaveowners? What are the chances for a moderate solution to the slavery problem?

REPRODUCTION PAGE 101

TREATMENT OF SLAVES

Harriet Beecher Stowe in *Dred: A Tale of the Great Dismal Swamp* describes the treatment of a slave by his master. The facts are a matter of judicial record, she reports, and the cruelty stopped only with the death of the victim.

The count charged on the 1st day of September, 1849, the prisoner tied his negro slave, Sam, with ropes about his wrists, neck, body, legs, and ankles, to a tree. That whilst so tied, the prisoner first whipped the slave with switches. That he next beat and cobbed the slave with a shingle, and compelled two of his slaves, a man and a woman, also to cob the deceased with the shingle.

That whilst the deceased was so tied to the tree, the prisoner did strike, knock, kick, stamp, and beat him upon various parts of his head, face, and body; that he applied fire to his body . . . that he then washed his body with warm water, in which pods of red pepper had been put and steeped; and he compelled his two slaves aforesaid also to wash him with this same preparation of warm water and red pepper.

That after the tying, whipping, cobbing, striking, beating, knocking, kicking, stamping, wounding, bruising, lacerating, burning, washing, and torturing, as aforesaid, the prisoner untied the deceased from the tree in such a way as to throw him with violence to the ground; and he then and there did knock, kick, stamp, and beat the deceased upon his head, temples, and various parts of his body. That the prisoner then had the deceased carried into a shed-room of his house, and there he compelled one of his slaves, in his presence, to confine the deceased's feet in stocks, by making his legs fast to a piece of timber, and to tie a rope about the neck of the deceased, and fasten it to a bed-post in the room, thereby strangling, choking, and suffocating, the deceased.

And that whilst the deceased was thus made fast in stocks, as aforesaid, the prisoner did kick, knock, stamp, and beat him upon his head, face, breast, belly, sides, back, and body; and he again compelled his two slaves to apply fire to the body of the deceased, whilst he was so made fast as aforesaid.

And the count charged that from these various modes of punishment and torture, the slave Sam then and there died. It appeared that the prisoner commenced the punishment of the deceased in the morning, and that it was continued throughout the day; and that the deceased died in the presence of the prisoner, and one of his slaves, and one of the witnesses, whilst the punishment was still progressing.

ASSESSING LEARNING EXPERIENCES

1. The following questions call for the application of knowledge and skills learned from the activities in this chapter to related situations.

   a. List the criteria you would establish for judging the most important developments in the United States from 1800 to 1860. Select three developments that took place during this time and rate their importance using your criteria.

   b. In what ways do countries obtain land from other countries? What methods exist for resolving disputes between nations over control of land? Select one nation from whom the United States obtained land between 1800 and 1860 and explain the events that took place.

   c. Technology and reform change accustomed ways of doing things. Select one scientific and one social change and explain the *costs* and *benefits* associated with it and the long-term consequences for life in the United States.

   d. What would happen if: the cotton gin had not been invented? there were no abolitionists? Africans were masters and Europeans slaves?

2. Select any of the following statements related to tariffs and sectionalism and prove or disprove them with evidence from your text or other materials:

   • It would be wise government policy to tax imports and use the money to develop domestic industries.

   • A tax on imported manufactured goods is most harmful to domestic agricultural interests.

   • One section of the country may have to be built up at the expense of another.

   • Domestic industries should be protected from foreign competition by taxes on imported products.

   • As a citizen and consumer, is it better to buy an expensive domestic product or an inexpensive foreign product?

   • The best policy is free trade among all nations.

   • Producing too much, or too little, of a product causes problems for the producers.

   • To rely on a foreign country to supply a needed product is dangerous and should be avoided.

   • Over the long run, the least expensive product will sell the best.

   • A country will buy products from whatever country buys its products in return, even if it has to pay more to get them.

   • A government is as strong and wealthy as the manufacturing interests of the country.

3. The chart below includes brief, simple statements regarding sectional interests. Present the framework of the chart and have students complete it.

	Tariff	Land	Internal Improvements	Slavery in Territories
North-east	favored high protective tariff	opposed cheap land policy	favored	opposed
West	opposed high protective tariff	favored cheap land on easy terms	favored	opposed
South	opposed high protective tarifff	favored cheap land on easy terms	opposed	favored

4. Use the chart from the previous activity and omit all statements indicating that the sections favored or opposed a particular policy. Have students simply fill in *favor* or *oppose* in each block. Then have them select one category and explain the events that took place. They should then offer one or more hypotheses regarding sectionalism and the national interest as reflected in their category.

5. Use the chart and list the sections of the country but change the categories so that other issues can be considered. Ask students to complete the chart showing the attitudes and actions of each section regarding: the *Dred Scott* decision, John Brown's raid, the Compromise of 1850, the Fugitive Slave Law, the war with Mexico, the annexation of Texas, or any other event.

RESOURCES FOR TEACHING

Below is a selected list of materials and resources for teaching about sectionalism and nationalism. These materials—and those in other chapters—are meant to update and supplement the extensive bibliographies that exist in most teacher's guides. We have listed materials and resources that meet our criteria of being especially useful to the teacher, moderately priced, and thoughtfully developed. Addresses of publishers can be found in the alphabetical list on pages 191-199.

Books, Pamphlets, and Articles

Chapbook Riddles. New York: Dover, 1974 (reprints of six titles first published between 1830 and 1870).

Day, Mahlon. *New York Street Cries in Rhyme.* New York: Dover, 1977 (first published 1825: New York, Mahlon Day, & Co.).
   These inexpensive little reproductions of popular children's books offer pleasurable reading about everyday life.

Gillon, Jr., Edmund V. *Cut and Assemble an Early New England Village*. New York: Dover, 1977.

> An inexpensive book that includes materials to construct twelve nineteenth-century New England buildings.

Hughes, Langston; Meltzer, Milton; and Lincoln, C. Eric. *A Pictorial History of Black Americans*. New York: Crown, 1973.

> Traces the history of black Americans through the use of historic documents, pictures, prose, and poetry from slave days to the modern civil rights movement.

Lester, Julius. *To Be a Slave*. New York: Laurel/Dell, 1976.

> This anthology of recollections by ex-slaves in America ranges from capture in Africa through the years after emancipation.

Parley, Peter. *The Tales of Peter Parley About America*. New York: Dover, 1974 (first published 1827: Boston, Mass., Carter, Hendee, & Co.).

Sloane, Eric. *Diary of an 1805 Boy*. New York: Ballantine, 1965.

> Everyday life with numerous drawings of common objects.

Washington: The Design for the Federal City. Washington, D.C.: National Archives.

> Illustrates the growth of the nation's capital from L'Enfant's plans to today. Includes 75 drawings and photographs.

Other Resources

America Comes of Age: A Prologue. Tarrytown, N.Y.: Prentice-Hall Media.

> Four filmstrips and recordings with a program guide trace the growth of American ideals.

American Civilization—Part I: 1783–1840 and *American Civilization—Part II: 1840–1876*. Pleasantville, N.Y.: Sunburst.

> Part I includes three filmstrips and recordings to show art, music, and literature during the period of growth. Part II includes four filmstrips and recording to show art, music, and literature during the period of change and instability.

American Experience Series, The. Englewood Cliffs, N.J.: Scholastic.

> Developed by the Smithsonian Institution, each kit has 50 11" X 14" reproductions of maps, cartoons, newspapers, posters, documents, and works of art. *The New Nation*, and *Slavery* are appropriate for this period.

Andrew Jackson: Spirit of a New Democracy. New York: Guidance Associates.

> Two filmstrips and recordings examine Jackson's career and his impact on American political life.

Critical Thinking Aids. New York: Modern Learning Aids.

> Several short, stimulating filmstrips on rebellion, the westward movement, John Marshall, Louisiana, impressment, Tecumseh, 1812, Jackson, and others. Available from Social Studies School Service (SSSS) as *The Growth of Freedom, 1790–1830*, or from the publisher.

Division: A Simulation of the Divisive Issues of the 1850's and the Crisis Election of 1860. Lakeside, Calif.: Interact.

> The class is divided into four factions each supporting one of the four candidates in the election of 1860. By examining 14 issues which divided the United States during the 1850s, students discover the role of compromise in political decision making.

Dred Scott: Black Man in a White Court. Wilton, Conn.: Current Affairs.

> One filmstrip with two cassettes, one of which gives arguments of the prosecution and the other of the defense. Students can decide the outcome and compare their findings with what actually occurred.

Federalist versus Republicans. Pleasantville, N.Y.: Educational Audio Visual.

> Multimedia kit with one filmstrip and recording, 30 duplicating masters, 28 student booklets and a 96-page teacher's guide. The self-interest, principles, and realities of representative government.

Jackdaws. New York: Grossman.

> Collections of primary source reproductions of maps, documents, engravings, prints, and letters. The following relate to the early 1800s: *War of 1812, 54–40 or Fight, The Mexican-American War, Slavery in the United States, The California Gold Rush: 1849, Nat Turner's Slave Revolt, Clipper Ships and the Cutty Sark*, and *The American China Trade*.

Jackson Years, The: The New Americans, and *Jackson Years, The: Toward Civil War*. New York: Learning Corporation of America.

> Each title includes two filmstrips and recordings. The first highlights the growth of the new nation, the second the issues that divided it.

Negro Experience in America. Mount Dora, Fla.: Documentary Photo Aids.

A packet of forty-eight 11" X 14" pictures on heavy glossy stock showing important events in black American history: slave ships, auctions, plantation life, the underground railroad, and many others.

Old Sturbridge Village. Sturbridge, Mass.: Museum Education Department.

A living museum of early-nineteenth-century life. Materials, workshops, and other services are provided to teachers. Packets of teacher-developed materials are available. Write for information and literature describing programs and services.

Pictures of United States Navy Ships, 1775–1941. Washington, D.C.: National Archives.

Package of prints and photographs of ships used by the navy.

Skins: A Simulation of the Mountain Men and the Rocky Mountain Fur Trade, 1826–1838. Lakeside, Calif.: Interact.

Students assume roles of fur traders working to accumulate the greatest number of beaver skins. Students do research on the trading life-style.

Slavery: America's Peculiar Institution. Culver City, Calif.: Zenger.

Two filmstrips and recordings showing the institution of slavery from capture in Africa, across the ocean, stopover in the West Indies, and slave life in the United States.

Steamship Historical Society of America, The. Staten Island, N.Y.

Library, photo bank, and other services are available to promote interest in history of powered ships. Publishes a quarterly journal. Write for information brochure and publications list.

War of 1812, War with Mexico, Sectionalism. Fresno, Calif.: Involvement.

Each title includes instructions and student materials for a classroom simulation. Other titles that are part of this package include *Federalist and Anti-Federalist, Immigration,* and *Reconstruction.*

6

Civil War and Reconstruction

The history of civil wars shows that they are commonly caused by competition for positions of power. The causes of the Civil War in the United States were more complicated. "Responsibility has been ascribed both to the actions of men and to forces beyond human control. Conspiracy, constitutional interpretation, human wickedness, economic interest, divine will, political ambition, climate, 'irrepressible conflict,' emotion, rival cultures, high moral principles, and chance have severally been accredited with bringing on the War."[1]

Obviously, student generalizations about the causes of the Civil War are academically hazardous. The purpose of approaching the subject in this manner is not so much to arrive at *the* answer but to go through a process of (1) selecting and examining data, (2) evaluating, and (3) forming tentative hypotheses. A review of some guidelines with students may be useful:

- Social events have *many* causes and *many* effects.

- No single satisfactory explanation is probable; *many* reasonable explanations have been developed.

- Opinions and explanations concerning the causes of the war have changed over the years.

- Causes that are fundamental should be distinguished from minor events.

- Causes of war may be different from the causes of other conflicts.

- Understand the influence of your own biases, the tendency to find what you look for.

---

1. Howard K. Beale, "What Historians Have Said About the Causes of the Civil War," *Theory and Practice in Historical Study, Social Science Research Council Bulletin,* 54 (1946), reprinted in *The Bobbs-Merrill Reprint Series in History.*

A simplified diagram may help underscore the complexity and interrelatedness of causes and effects.

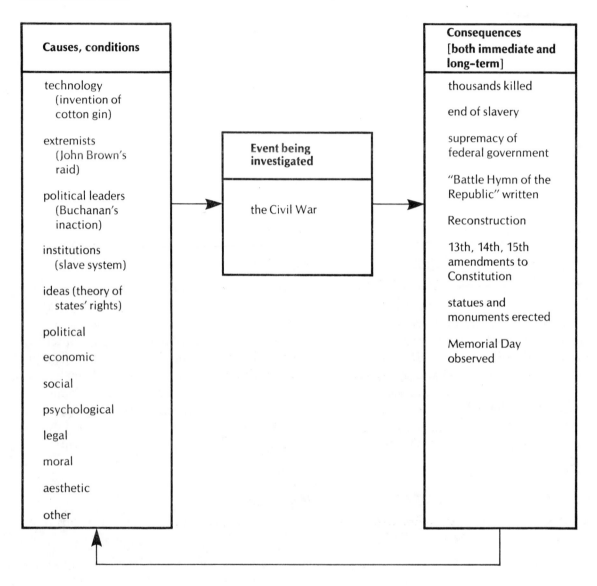

In many instances, the spark of a single immediate cause is needed to ignite the event—the firing on Fort Sumter, for instance. The activities in this chapter are organized with the above diagram in mind: the causes, the war, and the consequences.

PERFORMANCE OBJECTIVES

As a result of working with the activities in this chapter the student will be able to:
1. Select and evaluate data to form hypotheses.
2. Relate multiple causes to an event having multiple effects.
3. Share ideas with others to develop cooperatively a common response to a historical problem.
4. Generalize about the nature of civil wars.
5. Recognize and compensate for biases in historical reports.
6. Evaluate alternatives in historical situations.
7. Relate actions to objectives and values.
8. Assume a role based on geographical or political interests and develop a program to advance those interests.
9. Evaluate a risk-taking situation and predict probable outcomes for different courses of action.
10. Recognize and apply ideas of loyalty, change, control, choice, power, and social values to analyze historical situations.

LEARNING EXPERIENCES

Topic 1: The Causes of the Civil War

1. The following questions can be used to introduce the study of the Civil War and again later for evaluative purposes:

   • What evidence exists today in the actions or attitudes of people that indicate *sectional* differences?

   • What are the differences today between the North and the South?

   • Which differences are traceable to the Civil War? Which do you think existed at the time of the war? Which do you think are results of the war?

   • Do differences cause war?

2. Further question-asking and discussion activities will provide a chance for students to exchange information and ideas and also allow you to judge their level of knowledge and understanding.

   • Why did the South want to withdraw from the Union?

   • Why did the North want to prevent the South from withdrawing?

   • What do you think each side was fighting for?

   • As of today, has one side or the other been more successful in accomplishing its objectives?

3. A related approach to the above questions is to concentrate on the issue of *loyalty*—a willing devotion to a cause greater than oneself. Why do people remain

loyal to a government (state or nation)? Do people consciously decide where to place their loyalty? What criteria could you establish to help determine what a person should have done in the Civil War? When does *reform* become *rebellion* or *revolution*? Under what circumstances does a person have a responsibility to oppose, violently if necessary, his or her government?

4. After students have gained some information about the war, ask the class the questions in this activity and record their answers on the board or a transparency. Divide the class into groups of three to five students and have them write a composite answer to the questions: (a) What problems caused the Civil War? (b) What happened to these problems as a result of the war? (c) What problems related to the Civil War remain today?

    Provide each group with a spirit master to reproduce their composite answer. Distribute copies of every group's answer. Use these statements as tentative hypotheses and have students refer to them as you proceed with this unit. Students should continually refine the statements as they gain additional information and insight.

    The same questions can be used for final evaluative purposes. Group students again and provide each group with a spirit master for their statement. Reproduce copies for all groups and have students react to the statements. Guidelines for grading can be established by students prior to reading each other's papers. You may want to refer to the guidelines suggested at the beginning of this unit.

REPRODUCTION PAGE 102

EVENTS THAT HELP OR HURT THE UNION

A series of events that took place before the Civil War is listed below. Decide if they mostly *helped* or *hurt* the Union and check the appropriate place.

	Help	Hurt
• value of cotton exports increasing	___ ___ ___ ___ ___	
• canals and railroad concentrated in North	___ ___ ___ ___ ___	
• *popular sovereignty* lets people vote over slavery	___ ___ ___ ___ ___	
• *Dred Scott* decision says Congress cannot deprive people of their property (slaves)	___ ___ ___ ___ ___	
• John Brown's raid	___ ___ ___ ___ ___	
• Abraham Lincoln elected president	___ ___ ___ ___ ___	
• *Uncle Tom's Cabin* is written and widely read	___ ___ ___ ___ ___	
• abolitionists campaign against slavery	___ ___ ___ ___ ___	
• Compromise of 1850 keeps balance in Senate between slave and free states	___ ___ ___ ___ ___	
• high protective tariff	___ ___ ___ ___ ___	
• new territories apply for statehood	___ ___ ___ ___ ___	
• Fugitive Slave Law requires slaves to be returned to their master	___ ___ ___ ___ ___	
• James Buchanan's belief that he could not act against seceding states	___ ___ ___ ___ ___	
• the U.S. Constitution's sections about slavery	___ ___ ___ ___ ___	

5. Use Reproduction Page 102, "Events That Help or Hurt the Union," to have students evaluate a series of events that happened before the Civil War. That same list can be used with other headings: important or trivial, good news or bad news, for instance. Or students can be asked to prepare a time line using these events and write a statement about the events leading to war.

6. What would cause one section of the country to act against another? Which type of event would probably cause the strongest action or reaction? The following list can be used in several ways: (a) list in order of importance as a reason for war; (b) assign each a value, from 1 for unimportant to 10 for important, as a reason for war; or (c) as in the previous activity, decide if the events are important/unimportant, good/bad, helpful/hurtful, real/imagined, fundamental/trivial.

   - unfavorable laws passed by Congress
   - Supreme Court decisions
   - extremist groups
   - politicians
   - high cost of products
   - system of slavery
   - criticism of way of life
   - changing political power
   - violations of Constitution

7. Reproduction Page 103, "A Figure of the Civil War," can be used in various places during this unit. It is a set of boxes, each with two lines representing the North and the South, moving through time from an unidentified *start* to war. Most students will quickly and easily select one as representing their idea of the causes of the Civil War. Because it is an abstract diagram, however, some students will persist in having concrete details provided. You should resist doing this and encourage them to provide any needed explanations.

   After students identify a North and South line and write a title for the figure they have selected, you may wish to have them explain the reasons for their selection in more detail. Discuss the starting point; events along the way; the distance of the lines from each other; and what, if anything, could have brought lines closer together. Box G can be used for students wishing to draw any other configuration. Box H should be used to have students draw lines from "War" to "Today." Do they draw two, or more, lines? Are they heading upward or downward? Are there major shifts in direction? (This last activity can be extended into the future and used now or in later chapters to consider the United States and the Soviet Union, the People's Republic of China, the world; race relations; food and population; environment and economy; and technological developments and social progress.)

FIGURE OF THE CIVIL WAR

Each figure represents a possible explanation of the Civil War. In your opinion, which is the best explanation? Place an *N* on one line for North, an *S* for South. Write a title for the figure you select that provides an explanation for the Civil War.

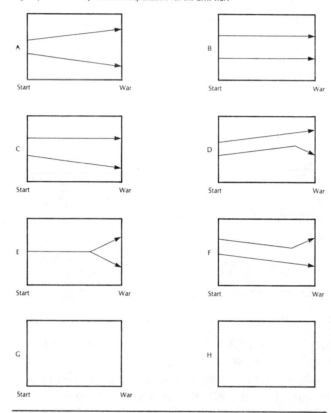

8. Reproduction Page 104, "Observations about the War," has comments made by people close to the war. Briefly stated, a northern writer, Headley, emphasizes the loss of southern political power; a southern writer, Pollard, suggests the problem was based in two hostile civilizations; a Union general, Butler, sees the conflict as rich versus poor; the Confederate vice-president, Stephens, points to constitutional differences; and the Confederate president, Jefferson Davis, states that northern discrimination against the South caused the war.

   Have students read these statements and list the reasons given for causing the war. What evidence supports each reason? What reasons might exist for the differing explanations? In your opinion, which statement offers the best explanation for the war?

   Several alternative activities are possible using these statements. After reading the statements, have students complete sentence stems:

   • The most important differences between the North and the South were . . .

   • As a cause of the war, slavery was . . .

- The Civil War was a war to . . .

- Statements about the Civil War seem to . . .

As research activities students can find additional explanations of the war. Many books of historical readings are organized to provide this information. An informative source is *The Causes of Civil War* by Kenneth Stampp.[2]

REPRODUCTION PAGE 104

OBSERVATIONS ABOUT THE WAR

. . . it sprung from a faction who sought only political power. Those make a great mistake who suppose it grew out of a desire merely to perpetuate slavery. Slavery was a means to an end—a bugbear to frighten the timid into obedience, and a rallying cry for the ignorant, deluded masses. The accursed lust of power lay at the bottom of it. The whole question may be stated thus: southern politicians saw in the rapid increase of the free states, both in number and population, and the deep hostility to the admission of any more slave states, that the power they had so long wielded in the Government would be broken.
    —J. T. Headley, 1864, 1866, *The Great Rebellion: A History of the Civil War in the United States*

. . . the slavery question was not a moral one in the North, unless, perhaps, with a few thousand persons of disordered conscience. It was significant only of a contest for political power, and afforded nothing more than a convenient ground of dispute between two parties, who represented not two moral theories, but hostile sections and opposite civilizations.
    —Edward A. Pollard, 1866, *The Lost Cause: A New Southern History of the War of the Confederates*

I saw that this Rebellion was a war of the aristocrats against the middling men—of the rich against the poor; a war of the landowner against the laborers; that it was a struggle for the retention of power in the hands of the few against the many; and I found no conclusion to it, save in the subjugation of the few and the disenthrallment of the many.
    —Gen. Benjamin Butler, Farewell Address to the People of New Orleans

The conflict in principle arose from different and opposing ideas as to the nature of what is known as the General Government. The contest was between those who held it to be strictly Federal in its character, and those who maintained that it was thoroughly National. It was a strife between the principles of Federation, on the one side, and Centralism, or Consolidation, on the other.
    —Alexander H. Stephens, 1870, *A Constitutional View of the Late War Between the States*

It was not the passage of the "personal liberty laws," it was not the circulation of incendiary documents, it was not the raid of John Brown, it was not the operation of unjust and unequal tariff laws, nor all combined, that constituted the intolerable grievance, but it was the systematic and persistent struggle to deprive the Southern States of equality in the Union—generally to discriminate in legislation against the interests of their people; culminating in . . . their exclusion from the Territories, the common property of the States. . . . The hope of our people may be stated in a sentence. It was to escape from injury and strife in the Union, to find prosperity and peace out of it.
    —Jefferson Davis, 1881, *The Rise and Fall of the Confederate Government*

9. The Civil War—a war between geographical sections or political groups within the same country—has been given many titles. Sometimes they reflect a person's point of view. A few of the more common titles are listed here with explanations. Mix and write them on the board for student matching.

war of rebellion   slavery issue, northern domination

---

2. Kenneth M. Stampp, *The Causes of the Civil War* (Englewood Cliffs, N.J.: Prentice-Hall, 1965).

second American revolution	economic issues related to the industrial revolution, or political independence from federal government
war between the states	constitutional issue, rights of states versus federal government
war for southern independence	preserve way of life

10. Reproduction Page 105, "The Differences between North and South," is a social-cultural view of antagonistic traditions. Have students read and answer the questions individually or in small groups. Discuss social values, perspective and biases of the writer, interpretations and value judgments required for writing history, awareness of unsupported generalizations, and the need for establishing criteria when attributing *superiority* or *inferiority* to a society. Have students

---

REPRODUCTION PAGE 105

THE DIFFERENCES BETWEEN NORTH AND SOUTH*

The differences between people of the North and of the South developed before the American Revolution. The Puritan exiles who settled the cold, rugged, cheerless soil of New England were never friendly with the Cavaliers who chose the brighter climate of Virginia and the South.

The intolerance of the Puritan, their painful thrift, their public display of piety, their sickly laws, their convenient morals, their lack of sentiment, and their unending search for personal wealth are traits of character which are visible in their descendants. On the other hand, the colonists of Virginia and the Carolinas were distinguished for their polite manners, their senti-ment, their attachment to a sort of feudal life, their landed gentry, their love of field sports and dangerous adventure, and the generous aristocracy that shared its wealth with frequent gatherings of hospitality and gaiety.

The civilization of the North was coarse and materialistic. That of the South was highly refined and with feeling. The South was an agricultural country. The North was thick with intricate sets of canals, railroads, and highways. The agriculture of the South fixed its features. Its people were models for the whole country and stood in striking contrast to the conceit and giddiness of the Northern people.

It was Yankee orators who established the Fourth-of-July school of rhetoric, exalted the American eagle, and spoke of the Union as the last, best gift to man. This show had little place in the South. Their civilization was a quiet one, the characteristic of the people based on a sober estimate of the value of men and things. Sensations, excitements on slight cause, fits of fickle admiration, manias in society and fashion, a high regard for exaggeration and display are indications of a superficial and restless civilization and were peculiar to the people in the North. The sobriety and reasoned judgments of the South was in striking contrast to these exhibitions of the North. In fact, it was the mark of a superior civilization.

1. Why was the South a superior civilization?

2. In your opinion, what features make up a superior civilization?

3. Select three or more features of a civilization and use them to describe the United States today. Which tend to make the United States superior? Inferior?

4. How are people influenced by their ancestors? By the society in which they live? By the occupations or economy around them? How much of these influences persist through generations?

5. Find words or statements that are the value judgments of the author. Find unsupported generalizations. What types of evidence would you need to support or disprove such generalizations?

---

attempt to restate selected sentences in neutral or pronorthern terms. List all those characteristics the author thinks are worthwhile, valuable, or better and those he thinks are inferior. To what extent do students agree with the author?

11. The emergence of Abraham Lincoln as a national figure is mostly associated with the debates against Stephen A. Douglas in 1858. Lincoln lost the Senate seat to Douglas and his statements caused fear on the part of many southerners, but it probably helped him gain the Republican nomination and eventual election as president. The "House Divided" speech made in Springfield, Illinois, outlined Lincoln's ideas about slavery and the Union. Use your imagination and tell how the country might have become "all one thing, or all the other." Use Reproduction Page 106, "A House Divided," for this activity. (On it Lincoln's speech has been divided into several brief paragraphs for ease of analysis and to focus on the clarity and strength of his words.)

REPRODUCTION PAGE 106

"A HOUSE DIVIDED"

If we could first know where we are, and whither we are tending, we could better judge what to do, and how to do it.

We are now far into the fifth year since a policy was initiated with the avowed object and confident promise of putting an end to slavery agitation.

Under the operation of that policy, that agitation has not only not ceased but has constantly augmented.

In my opinion, it will not cease, until a crisis shall have been reached and passed.

"A house divided against itself cannot stand."

I believe this government cannot endure, permanently, half slave and half free.

I do not expect the Union to be dissolved; I do not expect the house to fall; but I do expect it will cease to be divided.

It will become all one thing, or all the other.

Either the opponents of slavery will arrest the further spread of it and place it where the public mind shall rest in the belief that it is in course of ultimate extinction, or its advocates will push it forward till it shall become alike lawful in all the states, old as well as new, North as well as South.

—*Abraham Lincoln, Springfield, Illinois, 1858*

1. As a result of this speech, who would support Lincoln's election? Who would oppose it?

2. Lincoln was criticized as calling for a war between sections. Is that criticism justified?

3. With extremists in all sections of the country, how could the slavery question been solved peacefully?

4. Do you think Lincoln saw a war coming?

5. Do you think Lincoln was making a political speech with an eye on running for the presidency in 1860?

12. Lincoln was elected president with the votes of the northern states; his opponents split the remaining states. Southern states began to secede, and President James Buchanan, surrounded by southern advisers and believing he could not act, quietly completed his term. The period from November until Lincoln's inauguration on March 4, 1861, was one of uncertainty and apprehension. Most federal property in the seceding states had been taken. Ask students which, if any, of the following alternatives might have resolved the new problems of secession:

- Go along with secession movement and allow any state to leave the Union if it so desired.

- Suggest solutions to the slavery problem that would satisfy seceding states in exchange for their promise to remain and be loyal to the Union.

- Call for the seceding states to reconsider their action and offer hope of resolving difficulties between the states.

- Consider the states in rebellion and its leaders as traitors and send in troops to take control.

What are the advantages and disadvantages of each proposal?

13. Students may be able to suggest many alternatives to the Civil War. Analyze the consequences of the following as reasonable possibilities:

- Let the South go and establish a separate nation.

- Create a committee of Congress to develop a compromise.

- Call a convention of states to consider the causes of disagreement.

- Restore the Missouri Compromise.

- Submit the entire question to a vote of the people.

- Prepare amendments to the Constitution.

Each of the above alternatives was suggested and, for various reasons, unsuccessful in changing the course of events.

14. Reproduction Page 107, "Lincoln's First Inaugural Address: An Interview," can be enacted as a press conference or simply read in class. Divide the class into groups representing northern Republicans, abolitionists, and secessionists. Have each record comments with which they disagree. Which groups seem to be most upset with Lincoln's speech? What courses of action are available to them? What counterarguments can they suggest? After discussing the content of the speech and sectional reactions, ask students to review the answers from today's perspective. How would you interpret Lincoln's speech? Was it too late to save the Union?

Students can use some of the same questions and role play an interview with Jefferson Davis. Other speeches by Lincoln or other individuals can be similarly analyzed and presented. Have pairs of students undertake this activity as a research project.

LINCOLN'S FIRST INAUGURAL ADDRESS: AN INTERVIEW

Why do you think there is trouble in the South?

Apprehension seems to exist among the people of the Southern States that by the accession of a Republican Administration their property and their peace and personal security are to be endangered.

Well . . .

There has never been any reasonable cause for such apprehension. Indeed, the most ample evidence to the contrary has all the while existed and been open to their inspection. It is found in nearly all the published speeches of him who now addresses you.

What will you do about slavery?

I have no purpose, directly or indirectly, to interfere with the institution of slavery in the States where it exists. I believe I have no lawful right to do so, and I have no inclination to do so.

But what is the position of the Republican party?

Those who nominated and elected me did so with full knowledge that I had made this and many similar declarations and had never recanted them; and more than this, they placed in the platform for my acceptance, and as a law to themselves and to me, the clear and emphatic resolution which I now read:

Resolved, That the maintenance inviolate of the rights of the States, and especially the right of each State to order and control its own domestic institutions according to its own judgment exclusively, is essential to that balance of power on which the perfection and endurance of our political fabric depend; and we denounce the lawless invasion by armed force of the soil of any State or Territory, no matter what pretext, as among the gravest crimes.

What would you do about fugitive slaves?

There is much controversy about the delivering up of fugitives from service or labor. The clause I now read is as plainly written in the Constitution as any other of its provisions:

No person held to service or labor in one State, under the laws thereof, escaping into another, shall in consequence of any law or regulation therein be discharged from such service or labor, but shall be delivered up on claim of the party to whom such service or labor may be due.

Who would enforce this part of the Constitution?

There is some difference of opinion whether this clause should be enforced by national or by State authority; but surely that difference is not a very material one. If the slave is to be surrendered, it can be of but little consequence to him or to others by which authority it is done.

Do you think the Union is a temporary association of states or is it a permanent government?

I hold that in contemplation of universal law and of the Constitution the Union of these States is perpetual. Perpetuity is implied, if not expressed, in the fundamental law of all national governments. It is safe to assert that no government proper ever had a provision in its organic law for its own termination.

What do you think is the cause of disagreement?

One section of our country believes slavery is right and ought to be extended, while the other believes it is wrong and ought not to be extended. This is the only substantial dispute. The fugitive-slave cause of the Constitution and the law for the suppression of the foreign slave trade are each as well enforced, perhaps, as any law can ever be in a community where the moral sense of the people imperfectly supports the law itself.

Would secession be the solution to this problem?

Physically speaking, we can not separate. We can not remove our respective sections from each other nor build an impassable wall between them. . . . Suppose you go to war, you can not fight always; and when, after much loss on both sides and no gain on either, you cease fighting, the identical old questions, as to terms of intercourse, are again upon you.

Your election and government appointments could cause problems.

By the frame of the Government under which we live this same people have wisely given their public servants but little power for mischief, and have with equal wisdom provided for the return of that little to their own hands at very short intervals. While the people retain their virtue and vigilance no Administration by any extreme of wickedness or folly can very seriously injure the Government in the short space of four years.

Why should southerners or others wait to see what happens?

Nothing valuable can be lost by taking time. If there be an object to hurry any of you in hot haste to a step which you would never take deliberately, that object will be frustrated by taking time; but no good object can be frustrated by it. Such of you as are now dissatisfied still have the old Constitution unimpaired, and, on the sensitive point, the laws of your own framing under it; while the new Administration will have no immediate power, if it would, to change either. If it were admitted that you who are dissatisfied hold the right side in the dispute, there still is no single good reason for precipitate action. Intelligence, patriotism, Christianity, and a firm reliance on Him who has never yet forsaken this favored land are still competent to adjust in the best way all our present difficulty.

Do you think there will be war?
> In your hands, my dissatisfied fellow-countrymen, and not in mine, is the momentous issue of civil war. The Government will not assail you. You can have no conflict without being yourselves the aggressors. You have no oath registered in heaven to destroy the Government, while I shall have the most solemn one to "preserve, protect, and defend it."

What evidence supports your view?
> The Union is much older than the Constitution. It was formed, in fact, by the Articles of Association in 1774. It was matured and continued by the Declaration of Independence in 1776. It was further matured, and the faith of all the then thirteen States expressly plighted and engaged that it should be perpetual, by the Articles of Confederation in 1778. And finally, in 1787, one of the declared objects for ordaining and establishing the Constitution was "to form a more perfect Union."

What do these views have to do with recent actions by seceding southern states?
> It follows from these views that no State upon its own mere motion can lawfully get out of the Union; that resolves and ordinances to that effect are legally void, and that acts of violence within any State or States against the authority of the United States are insurrectionary or revolutionary.

What will you do about these states?
> ... to the extent of my ability, I shall take care, as the Constitution itself expressly enjoins upon me, that the laws of the Union be faithfully executed in all the States. Doing this I deem to be only a simple duty on my part, and I shall perform it so far as practicable unless my rightful masters, the American people, shall withhold the requisite means or in some authoritative manner direct the contrary. I trust this will not be regarded as a menace, but only as the declared purpose of the Union that it will constitutionally defend and maintain itself.

If necessary, will you use force?
> ... there needs to be no bloodshed or violence, and there shall be none unless it be forced upon the national authority. The power confided to me will be used to hold, occupy, and possess the property and places belonging to the Government and to collect the duties and imposts; but beyond what may be necessary for these objects, there will be no invasion, no using of force against or among the people anywhere.

What would you say to those attempting to destroy the Union?
> ... I need address no word to them. To those, however, who really love the Union may I not speak?
> Before entering upon so grave a matter as the destruction of our national fabric, with all its benefits, its memories, and its hopes, would it not be wise to ascertain precisely why we do it? Will you hazard so desperate a step while there is any possibility that any portion of the ills you fly from have no real existence? Will you, while the certain ills you fly to are greater than all the real ones you fly from, will you risk the commission of so fearful a mistake?

Don't you think parts of the Constitution have been violated?
> I think not ... Think, if you can, of a single instance in which a plainly written provision of the Constitution has ever been denied. If by the mere force of numbers a majority should deprive a minority of any clearly written constitutional right, it might in a moral point of view justify revolution; certainly would if such right were a vital one. But such is not our case. ... No foresight can anticipate nor any document of reasonable length contain express provisions for all possible questions. Shall fugitives from labor be surrendered by national or by State authority? The Constitution does not expressly say. May Congress prohibit slavery in the Territories? The Constitution does not expressly say. Must Congress protect slavery in the Territories? The Constitution does not expressly say.

Why should a minority go along with the majority?
> If a minority in such case will secede rather than acquiesce, they make a precedent which in turn will divide and ruin them, for a minority of their own will secede from them whenever a majority refuses to be controlled by such a minority. Plainly the central idea of secession is the essence of anarchy.

Plainly the central idea of secession is the essence of anarchy.

Topic 2: The War

By the time Abraham Lincoln was sworn in as sixteenth president of the United States on March 4, 1861, seven southern states had seceded. Every federal fort within their limits, except Forts Sumter and Pickens, had been taken over along with other federal property. Preparations for war were being made openly and rapidly. In early April, Confederate Gen. Pierre Beauregard was placed in command of Charleston with orders to construct fortifications to defend the harbor and take control of Fort Sumter. Having great military superiority, Beauregard asked U.S. Maj. Robert Anderson to evacuate. Anderson responded by saying he would leave if he did not receive further instructions or additional supplies. At a little past 3:00 A.M. on April 12, 1861, General Beauregard informed Major Anderson that he would open fire on Fort Sumter in one hour. And so it began.

1. Lincoln announced that he was going to supply Fort Sumter with food. Confederate soldiers were under orders to take control of the fort. It seems to have been the deliberate confrontation to test the will of opposing sides. But what of the men charged with defending the fort? Use Reproduction Page 108, "Confrontation at Fort Sumter," and have students individually or in small groups decide what should be done in this case. Should Lincoln make sure supplies arrive? Should Beauregard wait for the lack of food to force evacuation? Should Anderson destroy southern fortifications while they are being built? Was Fort Sumter a test for both sides that had to lead to fighting?

REPRODUCTION PAGE 108

CONFRONTATION AT FORT SUMTER

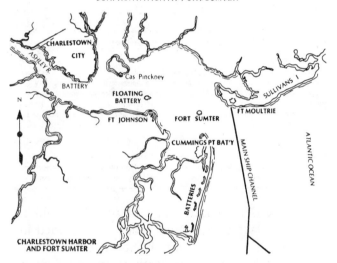

CHARLESTOWN HARBOR
AND FORT SUMTER

Inside Fort Sumter, on an island in Charleston Harbor, U.S. Maj. Robert Anderson faced a difficult choice. He knew he and his seventy-five men were surrounded by Confederate troops and fortifications. It would be impossible to win any military victories. In a few days his food supply would be exhausted. President Lincoln had announced that he would supply the fort with food but no ships had arrived yet. Confederate shore batteries would undoubtedly prevent any ships from entering the harbor.

Confederate General Beauregard had already asked Anderson when his men would evacuate. He knew the supply ship could not help. He could not stall Beauregard any longer. He had to accept the offer to evacuate without harm or follow his instructions to hold the fort and risk certain bombardment and defeat. He had less than an hour before the Confederates would open fire.

What should Anderson do? Follow orders and defend the fort or take the offer of a safe evacuation and save lives?

2. The battle at Fort Sumter had several effects. It united northern opposition to secession; it led to four more states joining the Confederacy; both Lincoln and Davis called for volunteers to serve in the army; and it ended any hope that the Union would be peacefully restored. Northern reaction was far from unanimous. Use Reproduction Page 109, "Newspapers Judge Fort Sumter," and have students select one of these editorials and complete it by suggesting what should be done.

Completed editorials should be read to the class and discussed. What reasons are used to support student opinions? Who is responsible for the battle? Would it be patriotic for the newspapers to support the president's actions?

REPRODUCTION PAGE 109

NEWSPAPERS JUDGE FORT SUMTER

New York Tribune
Ft. Sumter is lost, but freedom is saved. There is no more thought of bribing or coaxing the traitors who have dared to aim their cannon-balls at the flag of the Union, and those who gave their lives to defend it.

New York Express
The "irrepressible conflict" started by Mr. Seward and indorsed by the Republican party, has at length attained to its logical, foreseen result. That conflict, undertaken "for the sake of humanity," culminates now in inhumanity itself, and exhibits the afflicting spectacle of brother shedding brother's blood.
    Refusing the ballot before the bullet, these men, flushed with the power and patronage of the Federal Government, have madly rushed into a civil war, which will probably drive the remaining Slave States into the arms of the Southern Confederacy, and dash to pieces the last hope for a reconstruction of the Union.

Utica (New York) *Observer*
Of all the wars which have disgraced the human race, it has been reserved for our own enlightened nation to be involved in the most useless and foolish one.

Bangor (Maine) *Union*
Democrats of Maine! the loyal sons of the South have gathered around Charleston, as your fathers of old gathered about Boston, in defense of the same sacred principles of liberty— principles which you have ever upheld and defended with your vote, your voice, and your strong right arm. Your sympathies are with the defenders of the truth and the right. Those who have inaugurated this unholy and unjustifiable war are no friends of yours—no friends of Democratic Liberty.

Journal of Commerce (New York)
We will not undertake at this moment, to apportion the measure of folly and crime, on either side, which has led to the present catastrophe. . . . The Confederate authorities must, however, bear the responsibility (and it is a heavy one) of commencing the actual firing.

---

3. The creation of the Confederate States of America required a constitution. Ask students to suggest clauses they think would be included in such a constitution. What were some of the main points of contention between the southern states and the northern states? You may want to have one or more students develop a Confederate constitution in detail. Have them present it to the class and discuss it as an alternative to Union.

    Among the clauses in the Confederate Constitution were ones prohibiting taxes on imports to promote industry, protecting the right of citizens to take their slaves or any other *property* to any state of the Confederacy, returning escaped slaves to their master, and providing for slavery in any new territories that may be acquired.

4. Many southerners viewed the Republican party as being made up of abolitionists and others interested in punishing the South, a feeling that expressed itself politically for about one hundred years. Shortly after Lincoln was elected, southern representatives met in Mobile, Alabama, and issued a "Declaration of Causes" that presented a brief history of the Republican party. Use Reproduction Page 110, "Separation," with half the class responding as Republicans and half the class as secessionists.

SEPARATION

Declaration of Causes, November 15, 1860
Mobile, Alabama

The following causes summarize southern displeasure with the election of Republican candidates to office. Assume you are a Republican or a secessionist and provide additional information to disprove or prove each statement about the government.

- It has denied the extradition of murderers, marauders, and other felons.

_____

- It has concealed and shielded the murderer of masters or owners, in pursuit of fugitive slaves.

_____

- It has advocated negro equality, and made it the ground of positive legislation, hostile to the Southern States.

_____

- It has invaded Virginia, and shed the blood of her citizens on her own soil.

_____

- It has announced its purpose of total abolition [of slavery] in the States and every-where as well as in the territories, and districts, and other places ceded.

_____
_____

5. What were Lincoln's objectives in the war? In a response to newspaperman Horace Greeley, on August 22, 1862, Lincoln stated that his "paramount objective [was] to save the Union, and not either to save or destroy Slavery." Ask students which policy they think would be followed by Lincoln:

- Don't save the Union unless slavery is saved.
- Don't save the Union unless slavery is destroyed.
- Save the Union but don't save or destroy slavery.
- Save the Union without freeing slaves.
- Save the Union by freeing all of the slaves.
- Save the Union by freeing some of the slaves.

Distribute Reproduction Page 111, "Lincoln's Objective," and discuss the value of setting objectives, the importance of determining *basic* objectives, the purpose of having easily understood and supportable objectives in wartime.

LINCOLN'S OBJECTIVE

In a letter to Horace Greeley, August 22, 1862, President Lincoln explained his policy:

As to the policy I "seem to be pursuing," as you say, I have not meant to leave any one in doubt. I would save the union. I would save it in the shortest way under the Constitution.
   The sooner the national authority can be restored, the nearer the union will be to the union it was.
   If there be those who would not save the union unless they could at the same time save Slavery, I do not agree with them.

If there be those who would not save the union unless they could at the same time destroy Slavery, I do not agree with them.

My paramount object is to save the union, and not either to save or destroy Slavery.

If I could save the union without freeing any slave, I would do it—if I could save it by freeing all the slaves, I would do it—and if I could do it by freeing some and leaving others alone, I would also do that.

What I do about Slavery and the Colored Race, I do because I believe it helps to save this union; and what I forbear, I forbear because I do not believe it would help to save the union.

I shall do less whenever I shall believe what I am doing hurts the cause; and I shall do more whenever I believe doing more will help the cause.

I shall try to correct errors when shown to be errors; and I shall adopt new views so fast as they shall appear to be true views.

I have here stated my purpose according to my views of official duty; and I intend no modification of my oft-expressed personal wish that all men everywhere could be free.

Yours,

A. Lincoln

6. What were Grant's military objectives in the war? He explains them in his final report in 1865. The advantages and disadvantages of each side are stated in Reproduction Page 112, "Grant's Military Objectives." Form small groups of students and have them complete the statement by writing what they think would be worthwhile military objectives. Grant states:

REPRODUCTION PAGE 112

GRANT'S MILITARY OBJECTIVES

In his final report in 1865, Grant reviewed the strengths and weaknesses of both sides and stated his plan for defeating the enemy.

From an early period in the Rebellion, I had been impressed with the idea that active and continuous operations of all the troops that could be brought into the field, regardless of season and weather, were necessary to a speedy termination of the war. The resources of the enemy, and his numerical strength, were far inferior to ours: but, as an offset to this, we had a vast territory, with a population hostile to the Government, to garrison and long lines of river and railroad communications to protect to enable us to supply the operating armies.

The armies in the East and West acted independently and without concert, like a balky team: no two ever pulling together: enabling the enemy to use to great advantage his interior lines of communication for transporting troops from east to west, reenforcing the army most vigorously pressed, during seasons of inactivity on our part, to furlough large numbers, to go to their homes and do the work of producing, for the support of their armies. It was a question whether our numerical strength and resources were not more than balanced by these disadvantages and the enemy's superior position.

From the first, I was firm in the conviction that no peace could be had that would be stable and conducive to the happiness of the people, both North and South, until the military power of the Rebellion was entirely broken.

How would you complete Grant's statement?

Grant would do this: | *To accomplish this:*

1)_____   _____

_____   _____

_____   _____

2)_____   _____

_____   _____

_____   _____

I, therefore, determined, first, to use the greatest number of troops practicable against the armed forces of the enemy; preventing him from using the same force at different seasons against first one and then another of our armies, and the possibility of repose for refitting and producing necessary supplies for carrying on resistance. Second, to hammer continuously against the armed force of the enemy and his resources, until, by mere attrition, if in no other way, there should be nothing left to him but an equal submission with the loyal section of our common country to the Constitution and laws of the land.

7. How should civilians be treated during wartime? When Union General William Sherman was about to enter and destroy the city of Atlanta he ordered the inhabitants to leave. The mayor and two councilmen appealed to Sherman to consider the hardship his order and attack would cause. Is there any chance the general would change his mind? What would he say to the mayor? Have students write a response that Sherman could make to the mayor. Distribute Reproduction Page 113, "The General and the Mayor," and then discuss the questions that follow Sherman's response.

REPRODUCTION PAGE 113

THE GENERAL AND THE MAYOR

Gentlemen:

I have your letter of the 11th. . . . I have read it carefully, and give full credit to your statements of the distress that will be occasioned, and yet shall not revoke my orders, because they were not designed to meet the humanities of the case, but to prepare for the future struggles in which millions of good people outside of Atlanta have a deep interest. We must have peace, not only at Atlanta, but in all America. To secure this, we must stop the War that now desolates our once happy and favored country. To stop the war, we must defeat the rebel armies which are arrayed against the laws and Constitution that all must respect and obey. . . .

You cannot qualify war in harsher terms than I will. War is cruelty, and you cannot refine it; and those who brought war into our country deserve all the curses and maledictions a people can pour out. I know I had no hand in making this war, and I know I will make more sacrifices to-day than any of you to secure peace. But you cannot have peace and a division of our country. . . .

You might as well appeal against the thunderstorm as against these terrible hardships of war. They are inevitable, and the only way the people of Atlanta can hope once more to live in peace and quiet at home, is to stop the war, which can only be done by admitting that it began in error and is perpetuated in pride.

We don't want your negroes, or your horses, or your houses, or your lands, or any thing you have, but we do want and will have a just obedience to the laws of the United States. That we will have, and if it involves the destruction of your improvements, we cannot help it.

Now you must go, and take with you the old and feeble, feed and nurse them, and build for them, in more quiet places, proper habitations to shield them against the weather until the mad passions of men cool down, and allow the Union and peace once more to settle over your old homes at Atlanta. . . .

W. T. Sherman
Sept. 12, 1864

1. What is the cause of conflict between Sherman and the mayor?

2. What does Sherman value most highly? How does the forced evacuation of Atlanta serve that purpose?

3. Sherman bluntly states that "war is cruelty." Are some wars *worth it* in terms of cost, property damage, social dislocation, and loss of human life? Was the Civil War *worth it*?

4. Write a general statement explaining or listing the circumstances when a nation should go to war (even a civil war).

---

8. Present and discuss these facts for understanding the Civil War:[3]

   a. The North named its armies for large rivers; for example, the Army of the Potomac. The South named its armies for large areas of land; for example, the Army of Northern Virginia.

   b. The North referred to battles by the closest stream, river, or creek. The South referred to battles by the closest town. For example, the bloodiest one-day battle in the North is called Antietam Creek and in the South, the battle of Sharpsburg. The battle at Gettysburg is one of the few exceptions to this practice.

---

3. The following information is taken from a helpful little booklet that is recommended for students or teacher: James I. Robertson, Jr., *The Civil War* (Washington, D.C.: U.S. Government Printing Office, 1963).

c. There were two separate areas of military operations. The Appalachian Mountains extended in an almost unbroken line from Pennsylvania to Alabama, effectively preventing armies from moving across them. As a result, different armies in the East and in the West fought two practically independent wars until 1864, when they were more effectively coordinated.

d. In the 1800s an invading army did not always move directly against an enemy force. Rather, its primary target was usually an important city. Once the invading army was in motion, the defending force then tried to place itself between the invader and his target. This set the stage for battle.

e. Five Confederate cities became the principal federal targets: Richmond, New Orleans, Vicksburg, Chattanooga, and Atlanta.

f. Army organization during the Civil War is shown on the chart:

CHART OF CIVIL WAR ARMY ORGANIZATION[4]

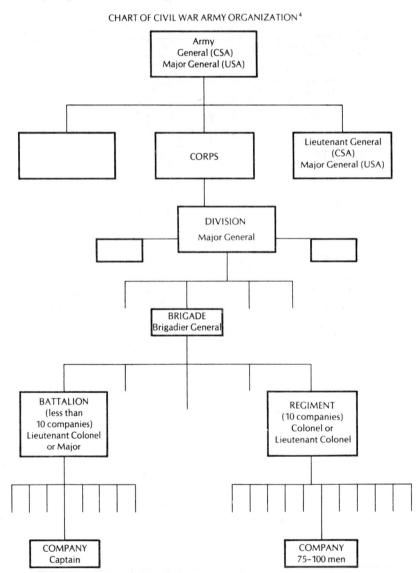

4. James I. Robertson, Jr., *The Civil War* (Washington, D.C.: U.S. Government Printing Office, 1963), p. 10.

THE CIVIL WAR[5]
1861–1865

9. Use the chart of Civil War army organization to discuss the idea of *control* in bureaucracies. Make a transparency and use it to discuss ideas of accountability, organizational politics, power, and decision making.

10. Southern sympathizers in the North—Copperheads—were numerous in New York, and newspapers vied with one another to attack federal policies. The Draft Act of 1863 became a focal point for citizens to vent their dissatisfaction. The act provided exemptions for people who could obtain a substitute or for people who would pay the government $300—a very large sum when related to an average laborer's annual pay of $500. Citizens complained that it favored the rich and that it was unconstitutional. Previously, each state would receive a quota, and it was the governor's responsibility to furnish the requested number of soldiers.

---

5. James I. Robertson, Jr., *The Civil War* (Washington, D.C.: U.S. Government Printing Office, 1963), pp. 32–33.

Many people thought Lincoln's Emancipation Proclamation changed the objective of the war from protecting the federal government to freeing the slaves. Northern laborers were opposed to fighting for that purpose and feared that freed slaves would take their jobs. Some politicians attempted to capitalize on the dissatisfaction. When riots began, New York Gov. Horatio Seymour hurried to assure workers that he was their *friend* and sent a delegation to Washington to complain about the law.

The riot in New York ended when locally stationed militia were joined by veterans returning from Pennsylvania and forcibly subdued the rioters. A bill was passed by the city council giving $300 to every man drafted to buy his way out of service, but this bill was vetoed by the mayor. The following year, a new draft bill was passed eliminating exemptions and instituting a system of bounties to entice volunteers. Incidentally, of the people drafted in New York, about seven out of ten were unfit to serve because of physical reasons, about two out of ten bought their way out, almost one out of ten furnished a substitute, and fewer than one out of ten actually served.

Distribute Reproduction Page 114, "Draft Riots in New York," which describes the riot. Discuss the causes of group violence—threat to security, frustration and aggression, hostility, fear, mob psychology. Use the multiple causation model on page 177 in this chapter to examine other causes. Should the government be able to force a person to serve in the army? If the law is unfair, as many thought the 1863 laws were, what alternatives does a citizen have? If the government owes its citizens protection, do the citizens owe it service, in return, and to the extent necessary for its self-preservation?

REPRODUCTION PAGE 114

DRAFT RIOTS IN NEW YORK

• Should the government be able to force a person to serve in the army?

• Is there some point when violent opposition to government actions is justifiable?

On a warm Saturday morning, July 11, 1863, in the northerly wards of New York City, where mostly railroad workers and other foreign-born laborers lived, the drawing of names to serve in the Union army had begun. It was called drafting and began with excited crowds and led to violence, arson, and bloodshed.

. . . Inside a large building 300 people gathered for the calling of the first names. They were quiet and orderly but not surprised when, after about one-half hour, a pistol shot from the noisy crowd outside pierced the calm atmosphere. Brickbats, stones, and other missiles were hurled at the building and the crowd rushed in to drive out the officers, tear up papers, and take complete possession. Turpentine was poured over the floor and set fire. In no time the building was in flames. Policemen and draft officers were kept away by a shower of stones.

Firemen arrived late and were cheered by the mob. No effort was made to save the building and after several more buildings were destroyed the firemen were finally able to control the flames. In the meantime, the bulk of the mob had gone elsewhere to continue the destruction.

There were reports that the outbreak had been carefully planned. Word of its early success spread through the city. The streets filled with people who dreaded the draft, hated the war, detested Abolitionists and Negroes, or had other grievances, real or imagined. The rioters added to their number by calling on railroad offices, workshops, and large manufacturing outfits demanding that all work be stopped and laborers be allowed to join them. This demand, through sympathy or cowardice, was generally granted. Of course, thieves, burglars, and other predatory types were only too happy to plunder and loot under the cloak of resisting Abolitionist rulers. The drunken, bellowing, furious mob raced through street after street, attacking peaceful citizens and destroying houses and public property.

The most revolting feature of this carnival of crime and madness were the attacks on innocent, harmless, frightened Blacks: an inoffensive Negro boy was hunted at full speed by a hundred whites intent on his murder, a poor Black woman had her small house sacked and devastated as she narrowly escaped into the street barely saving her life, and nothing else. Several Black men were killed only because they were Black. In one case, and there were others, a Black man was chased, caught, hanged, and burned. His dead and charred body remained hanging for hours, until cut down by the police. In one of the most detestable acts, the rioters attacked and burned the Colored Orphan Asylum. Its more than 200 terrified children barely escaped to safety.

The railroads were not running, vessels were stranded in port, industry was shut down, and the city was very generally paralyzed for more than three days.

1. What were the immediate cause(s) of the riot?

2. What were the underlying causes of the riot?

3. What action should the following officials have taken, and what would have been the likely result?

	should do this	*to accomplish this*
Mayor	_____	_____
	_____	_____
Governor	_____	_____
	_____	_____
Military commander	_____	_____
	_____	_____
Person just drafted	_____	_____

4. What do you think should be the (a) immediate and (b) long-term objectives of each of the above people in this case?

5. The government's right to maintain its existence is greater than individual rights. Do you agree or disagree?

Which of the following are reasonable excuses for exemption from the draft?

getting an education
being physically disabled
being mentally/emotionally unfit
getting a substitute
religious objections to war
personal objections to war
sex

unwilling to fight against family and friend
morally opposed to killing
pays the government not to serve
fears being killed
provides sole support for family
would lose farm or business

11. What were Lincoln's objectives during the Civil War? At first they were to save the Union; by late 1862 they were enlarged to include emancipation for some slaves; and by his second inaugural address in 1865 he returned to a theme of "malice toward none." Use Reproduction Page 115, "Lincoln's War Aims," and discuss Lincoln's concern for people, his political abilities, and his sense of history.

Other reproduction pages that might be useful in this activity are Reproduction Page 106, "A House Divided"; Reproduction Page 107, "Lincoln's First Inaugural Address: An Interview"; Reproduction Page 115, "Lincoln's Objectives"; and Reproduction Page 116, "Gettysburg Address."

LINCOLN'S WAR AIMS

After the attack on Fort Sumter, Lincoln issued a proclamation on April 15, 1861, calling for 75,000 volunteers. In urging support for his action, he stated in the proclamation:

> I appeal to all loyal citizens to favor, facilitate, and aid, this effort to maintain the honor, the integrity, and existence, of our national union, and the perpetuity of popular government, and to redress wrongs already long enough endured.

Careful consideration of political and military effects finally led Lincoln to issue the Emancipation Proclamation, freeing some slaves as of January 1, 1863:

> . . . all persons held as slaves within said designated States and parts of States are and henceforward shall be free; and that the executive government of the United States, including the military and naval authorities thereof, will recognize and maintain the freedom of said persons.

A hint of Lincoln's postwar objectives is contained in this well-known paragraph from his second inaugural address, March 4, 1865:

> With malice toward none; with charity for all; with firmness in the right, as God gives us to see the right, let us strive on to finish the work we are in; to bind up the nation's wounds; to care for him who shall have borne the battle, and for his widow, and his orphan—to do all which may achieve and cherish a just and lasting peace, among ourselves, and with all nations.

1. What are Lincoln's aims in each statement?

2. What effect would the Emancipation Proclamation have on each of the following: (a) northern Radicals, (b) diplomatic efforts with European countries, (c) the Union army.

3. Lincoln's opinions may have remained the same throughout the war, but his actions changed. Is it best for a person always to say and do what he thinks?

GETTYSBURG ADDRESS

12. With southern positions in the West crumbling, Lee gambled on a major attack in the North. With his army at peak strength of seventy-five thousand men, he met Union Gen. George G. Meade at Gettysburg, Pennsylvania. One attack after another failed, and Lee's battered army retreated to Virginia. Over forty thousand men were killed, wounded, or missing in action. In November, ceremonies were held dedicating a cemetery, and Lincoln was politely invited to say a few words. Use Reproduction Page 116, "Gettysburg Address," and consider the following questions with students: What ideals does Lincoln state for the country? What is "the great task remaining before us"? Is government today run *of, by,* and *for* the people? This speech used to be memorized and recited throughout the nation's schools. It has remained a much-noted statement. Ask students why they think this is so.

13. There was no shortage of cartoons and comments condemning Lincoln. He expanded the regular army, spent funds not appropriated, ordered martial law, and suspended the writ of *habeas corpus* to keep southern sympathizers in jail. He proclaimed some slaves free, he supported unpopular draft laws, and as a politician he had an abundance of personal and physical characteristics that were open to easy attack. Give students Reproduction Page 117, "A Look at Lincoln," and have students analyze the comments from the viewpoint of political supporters or opponents. Select some statements and have students reword them to favor Lincoln, or perhaps rewrite the statement. Student artists would probably have a fine time converting these words to pictures. They may find additional material in their text to develop a pictorial presentation of *the man and the myth.*

REPRODUCTION PAGE 117

A LOOK AT LINCOLN*

Mr. Lincoln was not elected President of the United States for any commanding game, or for any known merit as a statesman. . . . It was said that he was transparently honest. But this honesty was a rather facile disposition that readily took impressions from whatever was urged on it. It was said that he was excessively amiable. But his amiability was animal. It is small merit to have a Falstaffian humour in one's blood. Abraham Lincoln was neither kind nor cruel, in the proper sense of these words, simply because he was destitute of the higher order of sensibilities.

His appearance corresponded to his rough life and uncultivated mind. His figure was tall and gaunt-looking; his shoulders were inclined forward; his arms of unusual length; and his gait astride, rapid and shuffling. The savage wits in the Southern newspapers had no other name for him than "the Illinois Ape."

. . . Mr. Lincoln had formerly served, without distinction, in Congress. But among his titles to American popularity were the circumstances that in earlier life he had rowed a flat-boat down the Mississippi; afterwards been a miller; and at another period had earned his living by splitting rails in a county of Illinois.

1. What statements do you think are true? How does the author use words to place Lincoln in an unfavorable light?

---

14. Like most wars, the Civil War had its share of patriotic songs: "Dixie," "When Johnny Comes Marching Home," "The Battle Hymn of the Republic," to name a few. As its title indicates, the "Battle Hymn" is as religious as it is patriotic and is to this day sung on serious occasions and with considerable fervor—notwithstanding all the additional lyrics schoolchildren have developed over the years.

> Mine eyes have seen the glory of the coming of the Lord;
> He is trampling out the vintage where the grapes of wrath are stored;
> He hath loosed the fateful lightning of His terrible swift sword:
> His truth is marching on.
>
> I have seen Him in the watch-fires of a hundred circling camps;
> They have builded Him an altar in the evening dews and damps;
> I can read His righteous sentence by the dim and flaring lamps;
> His day is marching on.
>
> I have read a fiery gospel, writ in burnished rows of steel:
> "As ye deal with my contemners, so with you my grace shall deal;
> Let the Hero, born of woman, crush the serpent with his heel,
> Since God is marching on."
>
> In the beauty of the lilies Christ was born across the sea,
> With a glory in His bosom that transfigures you and me:
> As he died to make men holy, let us die to make men free,
> While God is marching on.

15. What role did women play in the war? As northern troops occupied more and more Confederate territory, southern women carried on their own fight against the Yankees. When New Orleans was occupied by federal troops, for instance, women displayed the Confederate flag, left church, streetcars, and other places when a Union officer arrived, defiantly hummed "The Bonnie Blue Flag" in the presence of Union soldiers, made a big display of moving into the middle of the street to avoid contact with passing officers, and through comments and gestures showed their "hatred, contempt, disgust, and loathing" of federal troops. Heading Union troops in New Orleans was a Radical politician turned incompetent general, Benjamin Butler, who seemed to be interested in power, property, and publicity and was eventually recalled by Lincoln. Butler's response to this *warfare* was the issuance of probably the most chauvinistic statement of the war, stating that his soldiers had been subjected to repeated insults and that hereafter, "when any female shall, by word, gesture, or movement, insult or show contempt for any officer or soldier of the United States, she shall be regarded and held liable to be treated as a woman of the town plying her avocation."

Denied equal rights in North and South, what role could women play in the war? How did noncombatants help the armed forces? Have students find out more about:

- Rose O'Neal Greenhow—spied for the South

- Belle Boyd—spied for the South

- Pauline Cushman—spied for the North

- Elizabeth Van Lew—spied for the North

- Clara Barton—nurse and later founder of the American Red Cross

- Mary Bickerdyke—nurse on western front

- Anna Dickinson—crusader for adopting Thirteenth Amendment

- Mary Walker—first woman to receive Congressional Medal of Honor—Civil War surgeon

16. Ulysses S. Grant has been called the first of the modern generals because of his policy of all-out war against the South. He gained a reputation early in the war when he responded to a proposal for an armistice and the appointment of commissioners to settle terms of surrender: "No terms, except unconditional and immediate surrender" can be accepted." Confederate Gen. Simon Bolivar Buckner was forced "to accept the ungenerous and unchivalrous terms which you propose."

   After an exchange of notes on April 7 and 8, Grant met Lee the following day in Wilmer McLean's house near Appomattox Courthouse, Virginia, to accept the surrender of the Army of Northern Virginia. This time the terms were generous and chivalrous:

   - Officers and men will promise not to take up arms against the United States until exchanged.

   - Arms, artillery, and public property will be turned over to the Union army.

   - Sidearms of the officers, private horses, and baggage can be retained.

   - Each officer and man will be allowed to return to his home.

   In both the "unconditional surrender" case and the surrender of Lee, Grant had sufficient power to force the other side to accept his terms. Why was he harsh in one case, lenient in the other? Should Grant have asked for stricter terms? Power might be defined as an individual or group taking action that affects the behavior of others. What power did the South lose and the North gain?

17. Robert E. Lee, sometimes called the last of the old-fashioned generals, bade farewell to his defeated army on April 10, 1865. Why did they lose? The army had been compelled to yield, he said, to "overwhelming numbers and resources." Why did he surrender? He consented because he felt that "valor and devotion could accomplish nothing that could compensate for the loss that would have attended the continuation of the contest." What will happen now? "Officers and men can return to their homes" with the satisfaction of knowing that their duty has been faithfully performed.

   When the war began Lee was offered a position in the Union army. He felt that his loyalty was owed to Virginia and joined the Confederate army. Did he do the right thing? What other conflicts in loyalty could develop during a civil war? Was he a traitor or a patriot? What difference did his decision make?

Topic 3: The Consequences of the War

1. What did the war accomplish? Have students suggest answers to this question and list responses on the board. Then ask students to consider what the war cost and

list these responses. Form small groups to work with this and additional information to prepare presentations on *The Civil War: Was It Worth It?* Some of the consequences, both short-range and long-range, include:

Union preserved	Constitution expanded
slaves emancipated	commerce and industry expanded
westward movement stimulated	cities grow
monopolized economy develops	states' rights ideas change
South devastated	Reconstruction of South
Republican political dominance	new conflicts between the races

2. With malice toward former Confederates, Congress assumed leadership in rebuilding the South. The Fourteenth Amendment to the Constitution was of lasting importance in this program. Its guarantee of equal protection of the laws and the provision that no state should deprive any person of life, liberty, or property without due process of the laws have been interpreted to expand the Bill of Rights for all citizens. To examine the other provisions of this amendment, ask students to respond to these questions and then check their answers by reading the Fourteenth Amendment. The provisions of the Amendment are indicated by check marks.

   • Should all persons born or naturalized, including former slaves, be citizens? __✓__ yes _____ no

   • Should former Confederate leaders be allowed to hold public office?   _____ yes __✓__ no

   • Should the United States or any state be allowed to pay Confederate debts? _____ yes __✓__ no

   • Should payments be made to former slaveowners for their losses from emancipation?   _____ yes __✓__ no

3. The Reconstruction Act of 1867 provided a method for the readmission of former Confederate states into the Union. Form small groups and have students decide how they would answer the issues dealt with in this act. Some questions and their answers are:

   • How should the southern states be governed? Establish five military districts and place them under the command of a military governor and federal troops.

   • Should former Confederate soldiers be allowed to vote? No.

   • How should states be readmitted? Each is required to hold convention to write a new constitution guaranteeing vote for blacks. Had to ratify the Fourteenth Amendment.

4. To review the issues involved with rebuilding the South, divide the class into five groups: (a) northern Radicals, (b) followers of Lincoln and Johnson, (c) former Confederates, (d) U.S. Army veterans, and (e) former slaves. Have each group decide what its motivations, interests, and objectives are, and outline their reconstruction proposals:

   • Who should have political rights—the right to vote, to hold office, to receive privileges or punishments?

- What should be done about former Confederate states and citizens—when and how should they be readmitted; should there be punishments; how should they be governed?

- How should the southern economy be reconstructed—who gets jobs and land; what products are bought and sold?

- How are the former slaves helped?

Inform each group that it has one vote and that the class goal is to reach agreement on a reconstruction program. After each group has developed its proposal, it should be presented to the class. After all presentations, provide a short break for informal discussions and bargaining. Additional time for revisions and rewriting may be needed. Conduct a more formal session to consider the proposals. The use of parliamentary procedures is useful for this exercise. Was there a feeling of revenge among some groups? As positions solidified, what happened to moderate proposals? Did any groups place self-interest above the supposed purpose of reconstructing the South? How did the activity relate to reality?

5. Conviction of "treason, bribery, and other high crimes and misdemeanors" is grounds for removal from office. President Andrew Johnson, attempting, as well as he could, to follow Lincoln's policy of moderation for restoring the South, collided with a Radical Congress with its own reconstruction program. Johnson was impeached and charged with violating the Tenure of Office Act; violating his powers as commander in chief; making inflammatory remarks to Congress; and, in general, being unfit for the presidency. After sufficient research, have students role play Johnson's trial in the Senate. Select defense and prosecuting attorneys, a Chief Justice to preside, witnesses, with the rest of the class serving as senators—about two-thirds Republicans, one-third Democrats. A two-thirds vote is needed for conviction.

   Several lower-court judges have resigned or been removed during impeachment proceedings. In 1804, a federal judge in New Hampshire, John Pickering, was removed as evidently senile. An attempt was made to impeach Samuel Chase, a Justice of the Supreme Court, but it was unsuccessful. Samuel Belknap, secretary of war under Grant, was removed from office for taking bribes. More recently, impeachment proceedings begun against President Richard Nixon were ended when he resigned. Have interested students investigate these cases with a view toward developing generalizations about impeachments and partisan politics. Are accusations and trials fair? Should removal of a president be possible by another election before the term is completed? Should *loss of confidence* be a reason for removal?

6. Did the North achieve its objectives? Did the South accept the results of the war? Have students consider the process of change and focus on war-related issues. Have them complete the chart presented on Reproduction Page 118, "Winning after the War?" Discuss the objectives and opinions of North and South and changes that have occurred over the years.

WINNING AFTER THE WAR?

Edward A. Pollard was the editor of the *Richmond* (Virginia) *Examiner* during the war. A year after the war was over he wrote *The Lost Cause: A New Southern History of the War of the Confederates,* in which he gave his view of what the war decided:

> The war has not swallowed up everything. There are great interests which stand out of the pale of the contest, which it is for the South still to cultivate and maintain. She must submit fairly and truthfully to *what the war has properly decided.* But the war properly decided only what was put to issue: the restoration of the Union and the excision of slavery; and to these two conditions the South submits.
> . . . the war did not decide negro equality; it did not decide negro suffrage; it did not decide State Rights . . . it did not decide the right of a people to show dignity in misfortune, and to maintain self-respect in the face of adversity. And these things which the war did not decide, the Southern people will still cling to, still claim, and still assert in them their rights and views.

Review Pollard's statement for what the war decided and what it did not decide. In the chart below, write a description of conditions in 1865, 1877, and today.

Issue	1865	1877	Today
Is the Union restored?			
Is slavery ended?			
Is there black equality?			
Is there black suffrage?			
What rights do states have?			

7. Is voting really an important power? Many students will soon be made voters, but the turnout at election time for this age group is the worst of any age group. Use Reproduction Page 119, "A Black Vote," to consider political power, the relationship between politics and economics, and the motives people have in voting the way they do. With few exceptions, the South after Reconstruction voted for Democratic candidates in national elections until the 1960s. Ask students why this *solid South* vote? Why the change in the 1960s? Are the issues of Reconstruction still important today?

A BLACK VOTE

In 1871 the U.S. Senate conducted hearings to investigate problems and progress under Reconstruction programs. This excerpt provides an idea about voting.

Q. How did he [the sharecropper's boss] tell you to vote?

A. He told me to vote the democratic ticket. I went to the election, and at night, when I came home, he said, "Cas., were you at the election today?" I said, "Yes, sir." He said, "How did you vote?" I told him I didn't know how I voted. He said, "You can't make me believe that; you are no fool." I said, "I can't read; I don't know how I voted." He said, "Who gave you the ticket you voted?" I said, "A black man gave it to me." He said, "You know how you voted; you voted the radical ticket." I said, "I don't know." He said, "I've no further use for you; I told you before this election came on that no man should live on my land who voted against my interest, and tried to give my land and property away; you can't live on it any longer; I've no further use for you." I said, "Very good; whenever you are tired of me, I am tired of you. I would like to live with you, but whenever you are tired of me, I am tired of you." It went on that way, and it didn't get any better. I was going away, but he told me that as I had started in with the next crop I had better stay there, for he would give me as good a chance as anybody else. I said, "I know that, and I would like to live with you, if we can live in peace and agreeable together; but if we don't I don't want to live with you."

1. Do you think Cas knew how he voted?

2. How did the boss try to control Cas's vote?

3. Is the boss justified in not wanting people on his land who vote against his interests?

4. Who seems to be the smarter of these two people? Why?

5. Niether man seems happy with the other but it appears that their working arrangement will continue. Why?

---

8. Would you ride with the Ku Klux Klan (KKK)? Would you risk incurring the Klan's displeasure? What social values led people to support or oppose the Klan after the Civil War? Use Reproduction Page 120, "The Klan Rides," to consider ideas of change, control, and choice. *Change:* What new ideas are forcing a modification of attitudes? Why would change be resisted? When does opposition to change turn to violence? *Control:* How does society exercise dominance over individuals to enforce conformity to norms? How are conflicts between local society and the larger, national society resolved? *Choice:* How are decisions affected by the interplay of the individual, the social environment, and standards of value?

REPRODUCTION PAGE 120

THE KLAN RIDES

A. L. Ramsour was questioned by a Senate committee:

Q. Where do you live?
A. In Catawba County, North Carolina.

Q. How long have you lived there?
A. In that county ever since I was born—fifty-two years.

Q. What is your business?
A. I was brought up a farmer, but I have worked at the mill-wright business for some ten or fifteen years.

Q. Have you been at any time visited by men in disguise, known as Ku-Klux?
A. Yes, sir.

Q. When?
A. I think it was the 7th of June, 1869.

Q. Go on and state what they did and said at the time.
A. There were some Ku-Klux in our neighborhood, as I learned from some colored people who came and told me they had been whipped by them. I asked the colored people if they could swear to any of them; they told me they thought they knew some of them, and they told me who they thought they were. I asked them why they did not tell on them; they said the Ku-Klux threatened if they did not do so and so they would get after them.

Q. Do what?
A. If they did not quit their radical principals, if they did not quit following "old Andy Ramsour." I had become a republican, or radical as they called me. I told them that they ought to hit some of these fellows, take their false-faces off, or something of that kind. They said they were afraid, that the men threatened to kill them if they said anything against the Ku-Klux. Some of my neighbors then got to talking with me about it. I told them that they ought not to go about in disguise, whipping colored people that it was just because of their politics—to intimidate them. They said I had better not talk against them, they would Ku-Klux me. I told them I did not think they would. Well, it went on for some time; some four or five colored men who had been whipped came to me about it. I told them if any of these Ku-Klux came to their house again that they should take a gun and shoot them. . . .

A few months before this time I had been attacked and knocked off my horse in the road by some of them, and beaten very badly. My son then bought a pistol and wanted me to carry it to protect myself. I told him I never intended to kill any body and I did not want to carry any arms. My son said, "Pa, if you don't shoot some of them I don't want to call you my father."

Well, so I carried the pistol two or three months. I was away from home most of the time and that was the reason, I suppose, they did not come to my house for me. One Saturday night I returned. While I was at supper my negro man came and told me that the Ku-Klux had told a man who had been whipped that week that they would be at my house one of these nights; I said I did not think they would come, but anyhow I made preparations. My son got a carbine that I had and put it in the bed behind him up stairs; I took the revolver and laid it on my bureau close by my bed; about midnight I heard the dogs rushing out on the piazza; I pulled the curtain one side and saw the yard full of Ku-Klux; they flew around the colored men's house; they were all in disguise; I called to my son saying, "They have come!" but he did not hear.

They knocked open the negro men's house, took out both the negro men, and then came into my house; I ran out of my bed-room up stairs and concealed myself in a loft, taking my pistol with me and an ax, thinking that if they came up there I could knock them down with the ax; I did not want to fight but thought I would go where I would be safe in killing them if they came up after me; I staid there a little while, and they did not come up; then I went into a concealed place with my pistol; they hunted all over the house and could not find me; at first when they came into the house they asked my wife where I was; she said she did not know. One of the men at first spoke in a disguised voice, but when he got excited I recognized his voice; he said to my wife, "I know better; you do know where he is." Then I knew who it was from the voice.

Finally they found me; they put a candle in the place where I was hid, and saw me; I snapped my pistol at the one who got just inside and told me to come out. I asked them what they wanted; they said, "Come out; we want to talk to you." Said I, "You can talk to me where you are." They said, "No; you come out!" and with that one of them jumped into the place, and as he did so I snapped the pistol at him; then they put in one of the negro boys, and I snapped at him; he says, "Andy, for God's sake, don't shoot me!" Says I, "Is that you, Rob?" Says he, "Yes; you may as well give up." "Oh," says I, "I don't intend to give up." With that they shoved the other negro man in toward me and told them to bring me out, and told me to give up my pistol; I said, "No, I do not intend to give up." "Oh yes," says one of them, "they have only threatened you and Rob, and to save my life do give up." Then they halloo out that they would burn the house.

I snapped the pistol the third time, and one of them stuck his hand in the hole and shot toward me; it missed both boys and went through the roof; with that I became alarmed. I thought I had better give up to save the house with my family, so I gave up the pistol and came out. Then they carried me down into my room; there I caught by the bedstead, but they wrenched me loose, and took me out into the yard. There they surrounded me, and, with their pistols pointed at me, told me to pull off my shirt. I had only my drawers and shirt on. There were some twenty or twenty-five around me.

Says I, "If I have got to die I will as soon die with my shirt on as off." Then one of them caught me by the shirt collar and tore it loose, and with that they pulled off my shirt; as soon as that was off three of them jumped at me, and began to cut me with hickories. They gave me some thirty-five or forty licks—I do not know how many—with long, thin hickory withes. I screamed. My daughter, twelve years old, rushed out and caught around my neck, and they stopped the whipping. One of them made a motion and they quit. One of them then whispered to me, "Just you vote the conservative ticket, and you are all right." Says I, "God only knows who I will vote for." I do not know what they were whipping me for only that I am a republican. "Yes," they said, "You have so many niggers about you; don't you know they are breaking you up?" Says I, "They are not doing me much good, but they have got to have homes." Says they, "You put away these niggers off the plantation, and quit your damned radical principles."

Then they let me go to the house, with my son and daughter, and as I went up into the house there was a crowd coming out of it. They had searched for arms in my bureaus and they took all my ammunition and some other things. An old pair of revolutionary pistols they destroyed, but they were of no account any more. They then disperesd and went away. I could not identify any one of them from sight.

1. Why did the Klan attack Ramsour? What do you think was the underlying cause for the attack?

2. Was Ramsour wise in acting the way he did? What alternatives did he have? What would you have recommended he do?

3. Why do you think many people went along with the Klan?

4. What do you think the Klan most valued about southern society? What did Ramsour most value?

5. How could this case be explained as a clash between social customs and laws?

6. Assume you were a U.S. Senator hearing this testimony. What recommendations would you make for new laws or changes in laws?

Should Ramsour change his attitudes or actions to avoid more trouble with the Klan? What risks are there if he does not change? What changes is the Klan opposing? What risks do they face? Ramsour is responding to national norms as expressed in Reconstruction laws. The Klan is responding to local norms. What values are inherent in the actions of Ramsour? The Klan?

The many issues and values in this case can be easily explored by having students propose legislation to correct what they see as wrong. Review the *objectives* of their proposals, the means by which they hope to achieve these objectives, and the underlying values that are represented.

9. A string of calamities marked presidential politics during this period: Lincoln was assassinated, Johnson impeached, Grant overwhelmed by political and financial scandals, and the election of 1876 arranged to allow Republican Rutherford B. Hayes twenty disputed electoral votes and the presidency in exchange for ending the military occupation of the South. The period of Reconstruction was over.

Hayes received 4,034,000 votes while his opponent, Samuel Tilden, received 4,289,000, with additional votes going to other candidates. This is an excellent time to review the operation of the electoral college. Was the election fair? Right? Coupled with the end of Reconstruction, was it best for the country? Who gained from the arrangement? Who lost? As a result of the Reconstruction period, is the United States today in better or worse condition?

ASSESSING LEARNING EXPERIENCES

Several activities in this chapter can be used for evaluating student achievements. Correspondingly, the following suggestions can be used as evaluative activities or as additional teaching activities.

1. Use any or all of the following statements and have students explain why they agree or disagree and support their decision with historical data:

- States that voluntarily join together should have the right to voluntarily separate.
- Extremist views and actions cause equally extreme reactions.
- Differences between ways of living lead to conflict and violence.
- It was easier for both blacks and whites to live under a slave system than it was to live during Reconstruction.
- Responsibility for the Civil War can be traced to shippers, primarily from New England, who brought slaves to America.
- Slavery should have been abolished by the U.S. Constitution, even if some states did not join the United States at that time.
- The Civil War was a war of conservatives against radicals in control of the government.

- The North violated the Fugitive Slave Law but forced the South to obey the law. The North was hypocritical.

- The South suppressed slave rebellions but rebelled when it saw no hope for itself. The South was hypocritical.

- The basic issues that led to the Civil War still exist in the United States.

2. What would you do and why? Ask students to respond to the following cases. After completing this part of the evaluation, ask students to explain when violence is justified.

    - An abolitionist sneaks onto your plantation and stirs up the slaves, but you catch him before he can get away.

    - Another slave visits your shack and tells you that he has plenty of weapons and all the slaves in the area are going to take over the plantations.

    - As a northern laborer you see the draft law as favoring the rich to force you to fight a war to free slaves who will then come to take your job. The workers around you begin throwing rocks at the building where drafting is taking place. Someone thrusts a torch into your hand, and the crowd shouts, "Burn it down!"

    - As a general in the newly formed Confederate army you have been instructed to bomb a federal fort. You know it may kill and destroy and will be the beginning of a civil war, but you have your orders.

    - Your small house is surrounded by the KKK, and you refuse their repeated demands to come out; you have a pistol and the door is being broken down.

    - A sharecropper who works for you returns to the farm and you find out he voted for candidates you oppose; you ask him why he did it and he says he doesn't know.

    - As president you are informed that several states have decided to form their own country.

3. Have students state how these topics were an advantage to the North and/or the South:

population	laborers
law and order	political leaders
fighting for a cause	military leaders
military resources	loyalty
slavery	money
European support	morale
geography	food
transportation network	army life for ordinary soldier
communication system	way of life

RESOURCES FOR TEACHING

Below is a selected list of materials and resources for teaching about the Civil War and Reconstruction. These materials—and those in other chapters—are meant to update and supplement the extensive bibliographies that exist in most teachers' guides. We have listed materials and resources that meet our criteria of being especially useful to the teacher, moderately priced, and thoughtfully developed. Addresses of publishers can be found in the alphabetical list on pages 191-199.

Books, Pamphlets, and Articles

Charleston Blockade: The Journals of John B. Marchaud, U.S. Navy, 1861-1862. Washington, D.C.: U.S. Government Printing Office, 1976.
   This journal kept by Marchaud while spending months at sea provides insight into the thankless task of blockading Confederate ports.

Civil War, The. Culver City, Calif.: Social Studies School Service (SSSS).
   This illustrated, annotated, free booklet is a valuable source of materials for teaching about the Civil War period. It is one of the specialized catalogs prepared by the Social Studies School Service (SSSS) and includes paperbacks, simulations, filmstrips, multimedia kits, records, cassettes, transparencies, and other materials for teachers. Worth writing for.

Commager, Henry Steele, ed. *The Blue and the Gray: The Story of the Civil War as Told by Participants.* 2 vols. New York: Mentor, 1950, 1973.
   The reality of war from common soldier to top command as reflected in their speeches, diaries, letters, and other primary sources.

Gardner, Alexander. *Gardner's Photographic Sketch Book of the Civil War.* New York: Dover, 1959.
   This reprint of the rare 1866 edition has over 100 dramatic views of war scenes.

Harwell, Richard, ed. *The Confederate Reader: As the South Saw the War.* New York: David McKay, 1976.
   An anthology of descriptions and opinions of southern soldiers, civilians, and foreign observers.

Miller, F. T., ed. *The Photographic History of the Civil War,* 10 vols. New York: Castle, 1974.
   Text and picture study originally published in 1911 showing military forces in all aspects of

conflict. The ten volumes make an excellent classroom resource.

Sterling, Dorothy, ed. *The Trouble They Seen: Black People Tell the Story of Reconstruction.* Garden City, N.Y.: Doubleday, 1976.
   Documentary history of the years 1865 to 1877 showing how blacks advanced in the fields of politics, education, economics, and the arts, only to be restricted by the revival of white-dominated governments.

Stowe, Harriet Beecher. *Uncle Tom's Cabin.* New York: Macmillan, 1962.
   This antislavery classic and commentary on morality includes an Afterword that places the novel in historical perspective.

Other Resources

Andrew Johnson Comes to Trial. Wilton, Conn.: Current Affairs.
   One filmstrip and two recordings analyze the impeachment. One recording presents the arguments of the prosecution; the other presents the arguments of the defense for this trial in the U.S. Senate.

Civil War. Englewood Cliffs, N.J.: Scholastic.
   This kit, developed in cooperation with the Smithsonian Institution, includes 50 11" X 14" prints of works of art and other visuals related to the war. Includes a teacher's guide and background information.

Civil War, The. New York: McGraw-Hill.
   Five filmstrips and recordings that vividly portray the disputes over slavery, growing violence, and finally the armed conflict.

Civil War in Pictures, The. Mount Dora, Fla.: Documentary Photo Aids.
   This set of photographs shows people, sites and events on 11" X 14" stock. Also available is the set *Lincoln and Related Pictures.*

Emancipation Proclamation, The. Washington, D.C.: National Archives.
   This 11" X 16½" reproduction of this five-page document is printed on one side only to facilitate exhibit.

Jackdaws. New York: Grossman.
   These packets of reproduced primary sources also include background information and suggestions for teaching. Appropriate titles include:

The Civil War, Reconstruction, and *Slavery in the United States.*

John Brown: Violence in America. Stanford, Calif.: Multi-media Productions.
One filmstrip and recording that portrays Brown's reaction to events and asks if violence is justified to deal with political problems.

Mathew Brady and the Civil War. Pleasantville, N.Y.: Imperial Educational Resources.
Four filmstrips and recordings that use Brady photographs to show the battlefield, camps, soldiers, politicians, civilians, and war.

North vs. South. Santa Clara, Calif.: History Simulations.
A classroom simulation of three northern teams versus three southern teams dealing with issues that divided the nation. Decisions must be made to secede or not, fight or not.

Personal Conflicts in a Divided Nation. New York: Guidance Associates.
Two filmstrips and recordings and a comprehensive teacher's guide relating to moral reasoning. One filmstrip involves hiding escaped slaves; the other is about brothers who fought on opposite sides during the war. Suggestions and strategies for teaching are included in the teacher's guide.

Pictures of the Civil War. Washington, D.C.: National Archives.
Photographs of all aspects of the war are available from the National Archives. Write for free descriptive pamphlet.

Preventing the Civil War. Sun Valley, Calif.: Edu-Game.
A classroom simulation of a convention held before the war. Representatives from northern, southern, and border states seek to avoid violence.

Should the Civil War Have Been Fought? Stanford, Calif.: Multi-Media Productions.
Students are asked to analyze the causes of the Civil War and then prepare an audiovisual program. Kit includes slides, background information, and a teacher's guide.

Voices of Blue and Gray: The Civil War. Guidance Associates.
Three filmstrips and recordings based on primary sources representing northern, southern, and slave viewpoints.

Years of Reconstruction: 1865–1877, The. New York: McGraw-Hill.
Two filmstrips and recordings present the impeachment trial of Johnson, radical politics, military occupation, and the end of Reconstruction.

APPENDIX A

Addresses of Producers of Resources

Abingdon Press
201 Eighth Avenue, South
Nashville, Tennessee 37202

Abt Associates
55 Wheeler Street
Cambridge, Massachusetts 02138

Addison-Wesley Publishing Company
Reading, Massachusetts 01867

Aids of Cape Cod
110 Old Town House Road
South Yarmouth, Massachusetts 02664

Akwesasni Notes
Mohawk Nation
Rooseveltown, New York 13683

Allyn and Bacon
470 Atlantic Avenue
Boston, Massachusetts 02210

American Association for State and Local History
1315 Eighth Avenue South
Nashville, Tennessee 37203

American Bibliographic Center—Clio Press
2040 Alameda Padre Serra
Santa Barbara, California 93103

American Book Company
450 West 33rd Street
New York, New York 10001

American Heritage
381 West Center Street
Marion, Ohio 43302

American Historical Association
400 A Street, SE
Washington, D.C. 20003

American Museum of Natural History
79th Street and Central Park West
New York, New York 10024

American Newspaper Publishers Association
  Foundation
P.O. Box 17407
Dulles International Airport
Washington, D.C. 20041

American Studies Association
4025 Chestnut Street
University of Pennsylvania
Philadelphia, Pennsylvania 39174

American Universities Field Staff
P.O. Box 150
Hanover, New Hampshire 03755

Amsco School Publications
315 Hudson Street
New York, New York 10013

Anti-Defamation League of B'nai B'rith
315 Lexington Avenue
New York, New York 10016

Arco Publishing Company
219 Park Avenue South
New York, New York 10003

Association for the Study of Afro-American Life
    and History
1401 14th Street, NW
Washington, D.C. 20005

The Athenaeum
East Washington Square
Philadelphia, Pennsylvania 19106

Atlas Information Services
230 Park Avenue
New York, New York 10017

AVNA
Audio Visual Narrative Arts
Box 9
Pleasantville, New York 10570

Ballantine Books
201 East 50th Street
New York, New York 10022

Bantam Books
666 Fifth Avenue
New York, New York 10019

Benziger, Bruce & Glencoe
17337 Ventura Boulevard
Encino, California 91316

Berkley Publishing Corporation
200 Madison Avenue
New York, New York 10016

Channing L. Bete Company
45 Federal Street
Greenfield, Massachusetts 01301

Bobbs-Merrill Company
4300 West 62nd Street
Indianapolis, Indiana 46206

R. R. Bowker Company
1180 Avenue of the Americas
New York, New York 10036

Caedmon Records
505 Eighth Avenue
New York, New York 10018

California Council for the Social Studies
Order through:
Social Studies School Service
10,000 Culver Boulevard
Culver City, California 90230

Castle Books
George Braziller
One Park Avenue
New York, New York 10016

Center for Cassette Studies
5316 Venice Boulevard
Los Angeles, California 90019

Center for Global Perspectives
218 East Eighteenth Street
New York, New York 10003

Center for Science in the Public Interest
1757 S Street, NW
Washington, D.C. 20009

Center for Teaching International Relations
University of Denver
Denver, Colorado 80210

Chandler & Sharp Publishing
5643 Paradise Drive
Corte Madera, California 94925

Chinese Historical Society of America
17 Adler Place
San Francisco, California 94133

Civil War Times
3300 Walnut Street
Boulder, Colorado 80302

Colonial Williamsburg
A-V Distribution Center
Box C
Williamsburg, Virginia

Columbia Records
51 West 52nd Street
New York, New York 10019

Constitutional Rights Foundation
6310 San Vicente Boulevard
Los Angeles, California 90048

Corner House
Green River Road
Williamstown, Massachusetts 01267

Coronet Instructional Media
65 East South Water Street
Chicago, Illinois 60601

Council on Interracial Books for Children
The Racism and Sexism Resource Center for
    Educators
1841 Broadway
New York, New York 10023

Thomas Y. Crowell Company
10 East 53rd Street
New York, New York 10022

Crown Publications
419 Park Avenue South
New York, New York 10016

Current Affairs Films
24 Danbury Road
Wilton, Connecticut 06897

Current History
4225 Main Street
Philadelphia, Pennsylvania 19127

Dell Publishing Company
1 Dag Hammarskjold Plaza
245 East 47th Street
New York, New York 10017

Denoyer-Geppert Company
5235 Ravenswood Avenue
Chicago, Illinois 60640

Didactic Systems
P.O. Box 457
Cranford, New Jersey 07016

Documentary Photo Aids
P.O. Box 956
Mount Dora, Florida 32757

Doubleday & Company
501 Franklin Avenue
Garden City, New York 11531

Doubleday Multimedia
1371 Reynolds Avenue
P.O. Box 11607
Santa Ana, California 92702

Dover Publications
180 Varick Street
New York, New York 10014

E. P. Dutton & Company
201 Park Avenue South
New York, New York 10003

Early American Life Society
3300 Walnut Street
Boulder, Colorado 80302

Eastman Kodak
343 State Street
Rochester, New York 14650

EAV
Educational Audio Visual
Pleasantville, New York 10570

Education Research Associates
Box 767
Amherst, Massachusetts 01002

Educational Enrichment Materials
357 Adams Street
Bedford Hills, New York 10507

Educational Masterprints Company
Box 221
Garden City, New York 11530

Educators Publishing Service
75 Moulton Street
Cambridge, Massachusetts 02138

Edu-Game
P.O. Box 1144
Sun Valley, California 91352

EMC Corporation
180 East Sixth Street
St. Paul, Minnesota 55101

Encyclopaedia Brittanica
425 N. Michigan Avenue
Chicago, Illinois 60611

ERIC Clearinghouse for Social Studies/Social
   Science Education
855 Broadway
Boulder, Colorado 80302

Everett/Edwards
P.O. Box 1060
DeLand, Florida 32720

Fawcett Publications
Fawcett Place
Greenwich, Connecticut 06830

Folkway Records
701 Seventh Street
New York, New York 10036

Follett Publishing Company
1010 West Washington Boulevard
Chicago, Illinois 60607

Foreign Policy Association
345 East 46th Street
New York, New York 10017

Genealogical Institute
10 South Main Street
Salt Lake City, Utah 84101

Ginn & Company
191 Spring Street
Lexington, Massachusetts 02173

Greenhaven Press
1611 Polk Street NE
Minneapolis, Minnesota 55413

Greenwood Press
51 Riverside Avenue
Westport, Connecticut 06880

Grossman Publishers
625 Madison Avenue
New York, New York 10022

Guidance Associates
757 Third Avenue
New York, New York 10017

Harcourt Brace Jovanovich
757 Third Avenue
New York, New York 10017

Harper & Row
School Department
2500 Crawford Avenue
Evanston, Illinois 60201

Harvard-Danforth Center for Teaching and Learning
Robinson Hall
Harvard University
Cambridge, Massachusetts 02138

Hawthorn Books
260 Madison Avenue
New York, New York 10016

Hayden Book Company
50 Essex Street
Rochelle Park, New Jersey 07662

History Simulations
P.O. Box 2775
Santa Clara, California 95051

Holt, Rinehart & Winston
383 Madison Avenue
New York, New York 10017

Houghton Mifflin Company
2 Park Street
Boston, Massachusetts 02107

Hubbard Hall
Brunswick, Maine 04011

Hubbard Scientific
1946 Raymond Drive
P.O. Box 104
Northbrook, Illinois 60062

Ideas
1785 Massachusetts Avenue
Washington, D.C. 20036

Imperial Educational Resources
19 Marble Avenue
Pleasantville, New York 10570

Indian Historian Press
1451 Masonic Avenue
San Francisco, California 94117

Indiana Department of Public Instruction
State House
Indianapolis, Indiana 46204

Institute for the Development of Indian Law
927 15th Street, NW
Suite 200
Washington, D.C. 20005

Institute of Early American History and Culture
Box 220
Williamsburg, Virginia 23185

Institute of Urban and Regional Development
Order through: Social Studies School Services
10,000 Culver Boulevard
Culver City, California 90230

Instructional Products Services
1287 Combermere
Troy, Michigan 48084

Interact
P.O. Box 262
Lakeside, California 92040

Involvement
3521 East Flint Way
Fresno, California 93720

Joint Council on Economic Education
1212 Avenue of the Americas
New York, New York 10036

Journal of the Society of Architectural Historians
1700 Walnut Street
Philadelphia, Pennsylvania 19103

Alfred A. Knopf
201 East 50th Street
New York, New York 10022

Law in a Free Society
10,680 West Pico Boulevard
Santa Monica, California 90064

Learning Corporation of America
1350 Avenue of the Americas
New York, New York 10019

Les Femmes Publications
231 Adrian Road
Millbrae, California 94030

Library of Congress
Music Division
Recorded Sound Section
Washington, D.C. 20540

The Link
855 Broadway
Boulder, Colorado 80302

J.B. Lippincott Company
East Washington Square
Philadelphia, Pennsylvania 19105

Listening Library
One Park Avenue
Old Greenwich, Connecticut 06870

Little, Brown & Company
34 Beacon Street
Boston, Massachusetts 02114

Littlefield, Adams & Company
81 Adams Drive
Totowa, New Jersey 07511

McDougal, Littell & Company
P.O. Box 1667
Evanston, Illinois 60204

McGraw-Hill Book Company
1221 Avenue of the Americas
New York, New York 10036

David McKay Company
750 Third Avenue
New York, New York 10017

Macmillan Publishing Company
866 Third Avenue
New York, New York 10022

Mentor Book Company
1301 Avenue of the Americas
New York, New York 10019

Charles E. Merrill Publishing Company
1300 Alum Creek Drive
Columbus, Ohio 43216

Microfilming Corporation of America
Oral History Program
21 Harristown Road
Glen Rock, New Jersey 07452

Midwest Publications Company
P.O. Box 129
Troy, Michigan 48099

Modern Learning Aids
1212 Avenue of the Americas
New York, New York 10036

Modern Talking Picture Service
1212 Avenue of the Americas
New York, New York 10036

William Morrow & Company
105 Madison Avenue
New York, New York 10016

Multi-Media Productions
P.O. Box 5097
Stanford, California 94305

Museum of the American Indian
Heye Foundation
Broadway at 155th Street
New York, New York 10032

National Archives & Records Service
General Services Administration
Washington, D.C. 20048

National Center for Law-Focused Education
33 North La Salle Street
Chicago, Illinois 60602

National Council for the Social Studies
2030 M Street, NW
Suite 406
Washington, D.C. 20036

National Gallery of Art
6th Street and Constitution Avenue, NW
Washington, D.C. 20565

National Geographic Society
17th and M Streets, NW
Washington, D.C. 20036

National Historical Society
206 Hanover Street
Gettysburg, Pennsylvania 17325

National Trust for Historic Preservation
740–748 Jackson Place, NW
Washington, D.C. 20006

National Urban League
55 East 62nd Street
New York, New York 10022

Navajo Times
P.O. Box 428
Window Rock, Arizona 86515

New American Library
1301 Avenue of the Americas
New York, New York 10019

Nicholas Books
Green River Road
Williamstown, Massachusetts 01267

Old Sturbridge Village
Museum Education Department
Sturbridge, Massachusetts 01566

Oral History Association
Box 24, Butler Library
Columbia University
New York, New York 10027

Organization of American Historians
112 North Bryan Street
Bloomington, Indiana 47401

Oxford Book Company
11 Park Place
New York, New York 10007

Oxford University Press
200 Madison Avenue
New York, New York 10016

Pacific Historical Review
University of California Press
Berkeley, California 94720

Pacifica Tape Library
5316 Venice Boulevard
Los Angeles, California 90019

Pantheon Books
201 East 50th Street
New York, New York 10022

Penguin Books
625 Madison Avenue
New York, New York 10022

Photo Lab
3825 Georgia Avenue, NW
Washington, D.C. 20011

Pitman Publishing Corporation
6 Davis Drive
Belmont, California 94002

Plimouth Plantation
Plymouth, Massachusetts 02360

Pocket Books
1230 Avenue of the Americas
New York, New York 10020

Population Reference Bureau
1337 Connecticut Ave., N.W.
Washington, D.C. 20036

Praeger Publishers
200 Park Avenue
New York, New York 10017

Prentice-Hall Books
Educational Division
Englewood Cliffs, New Jersey 07632

Prentice-Hall Media
150 White Plains Road
Tarrytown, New York 10591

Prime Time School TV
120 S. LaSalle Street
Chicago, Illinois 60603

Publishers Central Bureau
One Champion Avenue
Avenel, New Jersey 07131

Publishers Press
The Genealogical Institute
10 South Main Street
Salt Lake City, Utah 84101

G. P. Putnam's Sons
200 Madison Avenue
New York, New York 10016

Quadrangle/The New York Times Company
10 East 53rd Street
New York, New York 10022

R & E Research Associates
936 Industrial Avenue
Palo Alto, California 94303

Rand McNally & Company
P.O. Box 7600
Chicago, Illinois 60680

Random House
Education Division
201 East 50th Street
New York, New York 10022

Resources for Youth
33 West 44th Street
New York, New York 10036

Robert A. Taft Institute of Government
420 Lexington Avenue
New York, New York 10017

Schocken Books
200 Madison Avenue
New York, New York 10016

Scholastic Book Services
904 Sylvan Avenue
Englewood Cliffs, New Jersey 07632

Scott Education Division
104 Lower Westfield Road
Holyoke, Massachusetts 01040

Scott, Foresman & Company
Glenview, Illinois 60025

Signet Books
1301 Avenue of the Americas
New York, New York 10019

Simile II
218 Twelfth Street
P.O. Box 910
Del Mar, California 92014

Peter Smith Publisher
6 Lexington Avenue
Magnolia, Massachusetts 01930

Smithsonian Institution
Washington, D.C. 20560

Social Education
National Council for the Social Studies
2030 M Street, NW
Washington, D.C. 20036

Social Issues Resources Series
8141 Glades Road
Boca Raton, Florida 33432

Social Science Education Consortium
855 Broadway
Boulder, Colorado 80302

Social Studies Development Center
513 North Park Avenue
Bloomington, Indiana

Social Studies School Service
10,000 Culver Boulevard
Culver City, California 90230

Society for History Education
California State University
Long Beach, California 90840

Southern Historical Association
History Department
Tulane University
New Orleans, Louisiana 70118

Steamship Historical Society of America
414 Felton Avenue
Staten Island, New York 10310

Stem
Box 393
Provo, Utah

Sunburst Communications
Room 6
41 Washington Avenue
Pleasantville, New York 10570

Teachers College Press
1234 Amsterdam Avenue
New York, New York 10027

Thorne Films
Boulder, Colorado 80302

Time-Life Education
P.O. Box 834
Radio City Post Office
New York, New York 10019

Union Pacific Railroad Company
Public Relations Department
1416 Dodge Street
Omaha, Nebraska 68179

United Nations Children's Fund (UNICEF)
331 East 38th Street
New York, New York 10016

University of California Press
2223 Fulton Street
Berkeley, California 94720

University Museum
University of Pennsylvania
33rd and Spruce Streets
Philadelphia, Pennsylvania 19140

University of Nebraska Press
901 North 17th Street
Lincoln, Nebraska 68588

University of Oklahoma Press
1005 Asp Avenue
Norman, Oklahoma 73019

U.S. Department of the Interior
Bureau of Indian Affairs
1951 Constitution Avenue NW
Washington, D.C. 20242

Superintendent of Documents
U.S. Government Printing Office
Washington, D.C. 20402

Vintage Books
201 East 50th Street
New York, New York 10022

Visual Education Corporation
P.O. Box 2321A
Princeton, New Jersey 08540

Warner Books
75 Rockefeller Plaza
New York, New York 10019

Western Publications
P.O. Box 3338
1012 Edgecliff Terrace
Austin, Texas 78764

Western Publishing Company
850 Third Avenue
New York, New York 10022

Westinghouse Learning Corporation
100 Park Avenue
New York, New York 10017

World Future Society
4916 St. Elmo Avenue
Washington, D.C. 20014

Xerox Education Publications
1250 Fairwood Avenue
P.O. Box 2639
Columbus, Ohio 43216

Zenger Productions
10,000 Culver Boulevard
Culver City, California 90230

APPENDIX B

Reproduction Pages

The pages that follow have been provided to facilitate the reproducing of exercises, sample exercises, and materials needed for activities suggested in the preceding pages. Each page is perforated to make removal from this book easier. Once removed, a page can be used in several ways:

1. *For projection with an opaque projector.* No further preparation is necessary if the page is to be used with an opaque projector. Simply insert it in the projector and the page can be viewed by the entire class.

2. *For projection with an overhead projector.* The Reproduction Page must be converted to a transparency for use on an overhead projector. Overlay the Reproduction Page with a blank transparency and run both of them through a copying machine.

3. *For duplication with a spirit duplicator.* A master can be made from the Reproduction Page by overlaying it with a special heat-sensitive spirit master and running both through a copying machine. The spirit master can then be used to reproduce more than 100 copies.

MAP OF THE UNITED STATES

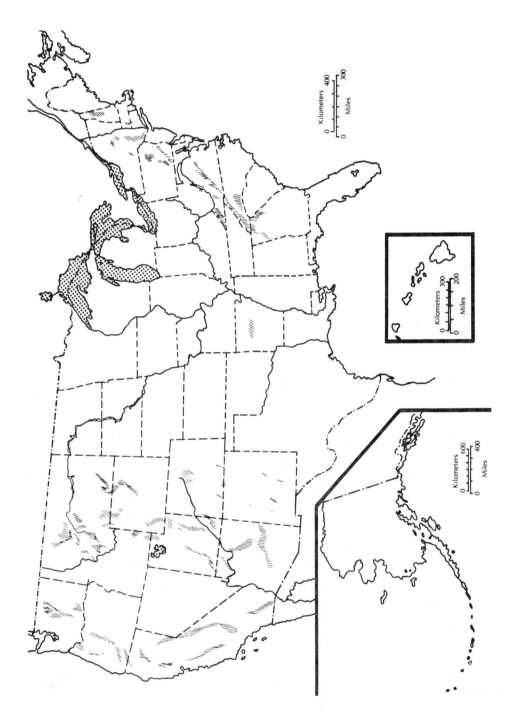

ANALYZING ARTIFACTS

One of the first tasks of a historian is to ask questions. These are often based on objects that people have had and used. From these artifacts the historian attempts to find clues to help answer his questions about people's ways of living and thinking. If your only evidence was an unfamiliar object, what questions could you ask that might provide important information?

Question	*Possible answer*	*Importance*
1. _____	1. _____	1. _____
_____	_____	_____
_____	_____	_____
2. _____	2. _____	2. _____
_____	_____	_____
_____	_____	_____
3. _____	3. _____	3. _____
_____	_____	_____
_____	_____	_____

Use the following questions as a guide for analyzing the artifact you have in class. Write a possible answer to the question and tell why it might be important for understanding the artifact and the people who created it.

1. What is the physical evidence? Size? Shape? Color? Texture? Parts? Etc.

2. What might be reasonably said about the object? Origin? Construction? Function? Etc.

3. What conclusions might be made about its meaning or value to its owner? What might be said about the society or culture?

4. What more needs to be known before making positive statements?

205

SOURCES OF INFORMATION

Listed below are sources of information that might be used by a historian. Decide which source provides the most *reliable* evidence. Place the number 1 alongside the most reliable source, number 2 alongside the next most reliable, and so on. Then note any particular *biases* or *strengths* for each item.

Reliability		*Possible biases*	*Possible strengths*
_____	newspaper report		
_____	diary of person involved		
_____	ballad about the event		
_____	photograph of the event		
_____	novel based on actual events		
_____	letter describing the event by participant		
_____	story told by someone who was there		
_____	description in a history book		

_____   television program about
             the event   _____ _____
                                          _____ _____
                                          _____ _____

_____   several tools, weapons,   _____ _____
             objects from the event   _____ _____
                                          _____ _____

1. What affects the reliability of data?

2. Does actual participation in an event provide more or less reliability? Explain.

3. This list includes both *primary* and *secondary* sources of information. Place the letter *P* alongside each primary source, the letter *S* alongside each secondary source.

SYMBOLS

There are many signs that represent commonly understood ideas in our society. Some are widely advertised trademarks that are designed to create feelings of strength, trust, speed, endurance. A skull and crossbones warns of danger, Cupid is an unmistakable sign of love, and so on. Can you think of others?

A country also has symbols that represent ideas. Write what each of the following symbols represent. In the last block list other symbols.

INCOMPLETE HISTORY

History is always incomplete. It is never set for all time. New information is discovered, new interpretations made, new theories suggested. This is true for a country or even a single event. It is true even for your own life. To see what we mean, answer the following questions.*

1. What historical evidence is available about your life (documents, diaries, people, reports, certificates, and so on)?

2. Once assembled and examined, could these sources of information be used to write the complete history of your life?

3. Could two people use the same information about your life and write different stories? Could both interpretations be different and still be valid? What is meant by interpretation?

4. One way to organize the information about you is to tell which happened first, then next, and so on. What other ways can the information be organized?

5. If someone wrote a history of your life based on the available evidence, what aspects of your life would be most emphasized? What would be left out that you think is important?

6. What conclusions can you make about the writing of history of a country or important event?

*The questions are based on Allan O. Kownslar, ed., "History as an Incomplete Story," in *Teaching American History: The Quest for Relevancy* (Washington, D.C.: National Council for the Social Studies, 1974), p. 39.

HALL OF FAME

The Hall of Fame for Great Americans is dedicated to honoring men and women who have made outstanding contributions to the advancement of human welfare. Persons eligible for election must be American citizens and have been dead for at least twenty-five years.

One person from each of the five principal fields listed below shall be elected. Subheadings are intended only to provide suggestions of categories that might be considered. The task of your group is to nominate one person for each of the five fields. Be prepared to explain why the selection was made.

Field of Endeavor   *Person Nominated*

I.   ARTS   _____
     1. musicians, composers, singers
     2. theatrical, dance, film performers
     3. producers, directors, dramatists
     4. painters, sculptors, photographers
     5. craftsmen and artisans

II. SCIENCES   _____
     1. health, biological, environmental scientists
     2. inventors
     3. physical scientists, engineers, architects
     4. land, sea, space explorers
     5. social scientists, economists, psychologists, sociologists,
        political scientists

III. HUMANITIES   _____
     1. authors, historians
     2. educators, philosophers, social welfare leaders
     3. religious leaders
     4. social, political reformers
     5. journalists, broadcasters, editors

IV. GOVERNMENT   _____
     1. statesmen
     2. lawyers, judges
     3. armed forces
     4. diplomats, ambassadors
     5. public administrators

V.   BUSINESS AND LABOR   _____
  1. business, financial leaders
  2. labor leaders
  3. farmers
  4. publishers
  5. advertising executives

VALUE ANALYSIS FORM*

This form is to help you compare the values of different people in similar situations. Write the name of the people or groups you are comparing at the top of the columns on the right side.

A statement of the question or issue: _____

_____

People or Group   1 _____ 2 _____

	1	2
1. What happened?		
2. Why did this happen?		
3. What do you think this person values?		
4. What makes you think he/she values this?		
5. What differences were there in what the people did?		
6. What similarities were there in what the people did?		
7. Why do you think people act this way in these sorts of situations?		

*Jack R. Fraenkel, "Teaching About Values," in *Values of the American Heritage: Challenges, Case Studies, and Teaching Strategies,* ed. Carl Ubbelohde and Jack R. Fraenkel (Washington, D.C.: National Council for the Social Studies, 1976), p. 179.

DILEMMA DECISION FORM

Directions: Briefly explain what the situation or event is that you are considering. Then decide what you would do in this situation. After writing what you would do, review the categories listed below and see which one comes closest to describing what you would do. Then write your reasons for making that decision in that block.

1. What the situation is: _____
    _____

2. In this case, the action I would take is: _____
    _____

3. Which of the categories below comes closest to matching what you would do? List your reasons for taking that action in that block.

1. Follow directions or be punished. _____ _____ _____ _____ _____	2. Do it because you'll get a reward or compliment. _____ _____ _____ _____ _____
3. It pleases others. _____ _____ _____ _____	4. To maintain law and order, it's your responsibility. _____ _____ _____ _____
5. Individuals have rights in a society. _____ _____ _____ _____	6. Conscience says that all human beings have rights. _____ _____ _____ _____

FAMILY CHART

Complete the information for your family. Write names in the appropriate places. Add lines for stepparents if needed. For each letter put the following information: b—born, d—died, place—place of birth.

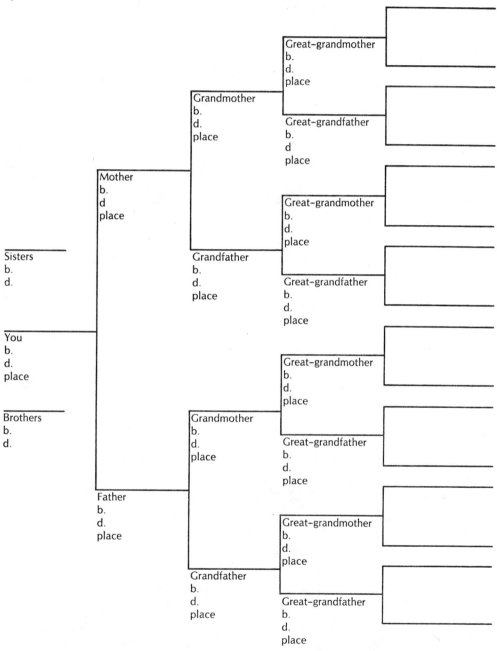

FAN OR BLOOD LINES CHART*

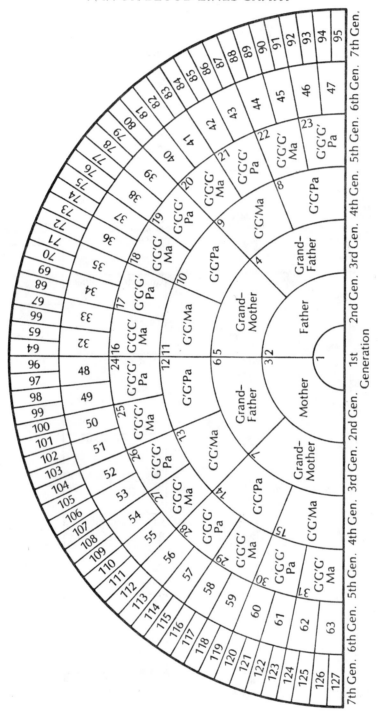

*A. Montgomery Johnston, "Genealogy: An Approach to History," *The History Teacher* (February 1978), p. 196.

FIELD STUDY: HISTORIC HOUSE*

History investigation: What was life like in this house?

Family composition: What evidence is there that shows the number, approximate ages, and sex of the residents? Servants? Hired men? Tenants? Relatives? What was the composition of this family?

Family roles and functions: What were the responsibilities of each member of the family? How did each contribute to the family economy? How did the children learn what they were supposed to do? How were they disciplined? What evidence is there of religious beliefs? Political views and participation? Education? Where was each member of the family at dawn? Midday? Early evening?

Family interaction: What evidence is there that family members were alone? Together? What situations might have caused conflicts between them? How might these have been resolved? When would children leave the family?

Economic interdependence: What things did the family produce for itself? What things could not be produced by the family? How did the family get the things that it did not produce? What exchanges were made with others? Whom did the family depend on? Who depended on the family?

Use of technology: What are the sources of heat? Light? What laborsaving devices are there? Automatic machines? Hand tools? What implements were used for cooking? For working in or around the house? Cleaning? Washing?

Communication: How did the family convey messages to others? How did news come to the house? How did the family travel?

*Based on information from Old Sturbridge Village, Teacher Education Center, Sturbridge, Mass.

Interior design: How many fireplaces are there? Windows? Doors? What does the furniture tell about its owners? How does the arrangement of the furniture tell about family members? What objects are strictly ornamental or artistic?

Land use: How large is the land area around the house? How was the land used? Garden? Farm? Landscaped yard? Animal barns? Toolsheds? Other buildings? Fruit trees? Grape arbors? Streams and ponds? Walls and fences? Paths? Cleared areas? Natural areas?

Comment on the following hypotheses:
1. Human beings have gained increasing control over their environment.
2. Family life was much more cohesive long ago than it is today.
3. Technology provides increasing benefits for human beings.

FIELD STUDY: OLD CEMETERY

Cemeteries provide an obvious source of information about the past. They can provide data about individuals and families, medical and health care, occupations, and life in the community. Here are some questions to help organize your study.

1. Who owns the larger plots? What information is provided about their background? How many generations are there? Are relatives still living in the community?

2. What names are found more commonly than others? What period of time seems to be most common? Are certain ethnic groups common?

3. What is an average or approximate size of most families? What seems to be an average life span? Do men or women seem to live longer? What are causes of death that are noted? From what wars are there soldiers?

4. What occupations seem to be most common? Do these change over a period of time? What are some possible causes for this change? What occupations are given, if any, for women?

5. What epitaphs are especially interesting? What architectural styles seem to be represented by the headstones? Are there any special markings or flags? Are foreign languages used on any headstones?

6. When are the earliest graves? Why was the cemetery located here? Who owns and maintains the cemetery today? Is it still in use? Are there restrictions on who is buried there? What was the community like at the time the cemetery began?

ORAL HISTORY

Guidelines for conducting an oral history interview.

Before the interview:

1. Decide what information you want and who might have it.

2. Contact the person and give a general idea of what you would like to ask.

3. Think of all the questions you can ask and then organize them into major categories. Research your *topic* and *person* as much as possible—the more the better—and then make an outline of the information you want.

4. Practice asking questions with another student to keep the person on the topic.

5. Obtain a tape recorder and tape that you will use and practice working it so that it can be done very easily.

Conducting the interview:

1. Spend the first few minutes in general conversation to "warm up" the person being interviewed and to check the operation of your tape recorder. Have paper and pencil for taking notes.

2. Be an active listener. Find out: Why? How? When? Where?

3. Don't interrupt a good story with questions. Instead write notes so you may ask the questions later.

4. Don't worry about silences; allow the person time to think.

5. Interview only one person at a time. If you work with another person, only one of you should be responsible for asking most of the questions.

6. Be courteous. Don't overstay your welcome. An older person may get tired. A business person may have other appointments. If needed and it is agreeable, return for a second session instead of staying too long.

7. Remember to change the tape at the proper time. Ask the person to wait a moment while you do so.

After the interview:

1. Complete the cataloging form.

2. Determine the best ways to use the information on the tape.

3. Write a thank you letter to the person interviewed.

ORAL HISTORY CATALOGING FORM

General Topic of Interview _____

Date _____ Place _____ Length _____

Person interviewed _____

Qualifications to speak on topic _____
_____

address _____

(If appropriate) Occupation _____

(If appropriate) Birthdate/place _____

Interviewer _____

Purpose of interview _____
_____

School and class _____

Sources and related information _____
_____
_____

Interview: List subjects covered in the interview in approximate order. Include brief comments about what was said and approximate time.

Approximate time   *Subject covered and comments*
____   _____
____   _____
____   _____
____   _____
____   _____

EVALUATION OF ORAL HISTORY PROJECT

Give each of the items listed below a score from 1 to 10: 1 would be very unsatisfactory, 5 is about average, 10 is outstanding.

Item	*Score*

Preinterview Preparation

1. Research of topic and background of individual to be interviewed   _____

2. Organization of questions and development of outline   _____

Quality of Interview

3. Organized and prepared   _____

4. Smooth performance (personal interaction and technical operation, question-asking style)   _____

5. Development of worthwhile information   _____

6. Alert, intelligent, courteous listener; follows up unexpected information, keeps interview on topic   _____

Postinterview Organization and Presentation

7. Key ideas identified   _____

8. Interpretations and conclusions based on evidence   _____

9. Information relates to larger issues; provides insight into human condition   _____

10. Cataloging form fully completed   _____

TOTAL SCORE   _____

Copyright © 1979 by Allyn and Bacon, Inc. Reproduction of this material is restricted to use with A Guidebook for Teaching U.S. History: Earliest Times to the Civil War and Mid-Nineteenth Century to the Present, by Tedd Levy and Donna Collins Krasnow.

GUIDELINES FOR VISUAL HISTORY PROJECT

1. Decide the question you wish to consider.

2. Conduct a preliminary search for information and opportunities for visuals.

3. Refine outline, using dialogue or descriptions for each major idea. Make notes about picture possibilities. (Divide paper into two columns: narration and visuals.)

4. Continue to refine narration and visuals, place each narration and visual combination on a single index card. Sequence cards and, if possible, tack onto a bulletin board.

5. Make arrangements to take pictures (sources might include local sites, museum pieces, students in costume, old photographs, postcards, magazines). Prepare title and credit pictures and other printed materials (these may be typed onto transparent film, cut, and placed in a holder).

6. Tape interviews, music, and other effects to be included with narration.

7. Revise and edit ideas and pictures. Retake visuals, rewrite script, rethink approach. Be critical and aim for perfection.

8. Put it all together again and preview before a small group for their *critical* reactions. Make additional changes as needed.

9. Premier presentation before class.

VISUAL ANALYSIS FORM

Pictures by artists, cartoonists, photographers, and others capture a moment and convey a message. For the historian, a picture is an important source of information. Here are some questions to help analyze visual messages.

1. What, if any, is the title of the picture?

2. Who is the artist? What do you know about his background or views?

3. What is the perspective of the artist; from what position does he view the subject(s) in the picture? How does this affect your opinion of the subject(s) in the picture?

4. Is anybody or anything being criticized or complimented? What features of the person, place, or thing attract attention?

5. What symbols or stereotypes are in the picture? Which are positive signs? Negative?

6. What parts of the picture are drawn out of proportion—either too small or too large—and why are they done that way?

7. What would be a one-sentence description of the message or point of view of this picture?

8. What facts would you need to know to support or disprove this message? What questions would you need to have answered?

9. What, if anything, do you think the artist would like to see happen about this issue?

10. Write a brief paragraph stating why you agree or disagree with the view expressed in this picture. Or find another picture or cartoon that represents another point of view on the same topic.

EVALUATION OF HISTORICAL INQUIRY

Read each question and decide how you would evaluate your historical inquiry. Place a check in the space from 1, weakness, to 5, strength.

	weakness				*strength*
	1	2	3	4	5

1. Was the question for investigation specific and achievable? Did it involve an important issue?

2. Were you able to locate the needed data?

3. Did you recognize and account for biases? Points of view?

4. Was a plausible hypothesis suggested?

5. Did you use a variety of sources? Primary? Secondary? Nonprint? Is there an indication that some were valued more than others?

6. Do you understand the process of selecting and interpreting data? Multiple causation? Fact versus opinion?

7. Were findings organized in a way that related to the hypothesis? Was the hypothesis refined as a result of research?

8. Are the findings clear to others? Were you able to express a point of view or conviction based on your research?

9. Are the findings interesting or important to others?

10. Can generalizations be made? Was your original question answered? Or was a problem solved? An action recommended? Objectives achieved?

EVALUATION OF WRITTEN
AND ORAL PRESENTATIONS

Place a checkmark on one of the five spaces between the two statements. For example, if the report was not too good but not too bad, you would place a checkmark at the middle space:

good report   ___ ___ ✓ ___ ___   poor report

well organized   ___ ___ ___ ___ ___   disorganized

important information   ___ ___ ___ ___ ___   unimportant information

thorough presentation   ___ ___ ___ ___ ___   skimpy presentation

helpful visuals, maps, etc.   ___ ___ ___ ___ ___   poor or no visuals

interesting   ___ ___ ___ ___ ___   boring

person seems to know topic   ___ ___ ___ ___ ___   person seems ill informed

person able to answer questions   ___ ___ ___ ___ ___   person unable to answer questions

audience learned many new things   ___ ___ ___ ___ ___   audience did not learn anything new

overall presentation was excellent   ___ ___ ___ ___ ___   overall presentation was poor

Total number of check marks in each column   ___ ___ ___ ___ ___

In each column, multiply check marks by   10   8   6   4   2

and place that number in this space   ___ + ___ + ___ + ___ + ___ = ___

and add the numbers from the spaces to get a total score of _____

ARCHAEOLOGICAL EVIDENCE

Archaeologists are people who study the remains of past cultures. They often face problems trying to decipher the meanings of the artifacts they find. To better understand the difficulties of their work, think about your own life. What historical evidence is available about your life? How accurate a picture would it provide 100 or 1,000 years from now? How do we know what happened before written records were kept?

Here is some evidence. Can you reconstruct the lives of the people?

Excavations at an archaeological site in central Illinois have uncovered artifacts, skeletons, plants, and animal remains of people believed to have lived there many years ago. Studies by anthropologists, archaeologists, botanists, and biologists have indicated that the people were not nomads, but lived in villages.

Historical evidence has been found in several layers, called horizons. The oldest dates from 7,000 to 8,500 years ago. In this horizon, several items have been found, including a buried dog, a buried infant, a roasting pit, a thatched house, hickory nuts, and drying deerskin.

Another horizon, from 4,500 to 7,000 years ago, contained fish on racks, a hearth lined with clay, mussel shells, a large roasting pit, and more thatched houses.

The most recent horizon, from 800 to 1,200 years ago, contains evidence of earth ovens with limestone bottoms, pots, planted crops (probably corn), and more thatched houses.

- What statements can you make for sure about these people?

- What statements can you make that are probably true about these people?

- Prepare an archaeological report explaining the questions you believe need to be answered about these people and what you would expect to discover.

Several artifacts and other remains have been discovered. What do you think is the probable meaning of each?

Artifact	*Probable Meaning*
buried human being and animals	_____
	_____
thatched houses	_____
	_____
animal skin	_____
	_____
use of clay and limestone	_____
	_____
fireplaces	_____
	_____

Based on the evidence, and the meaning you give to it, what can be said about the way people lived in this area and the changes. Use the topics below as the outline for your report.

- Why people first lived here:

- Observations about work, play, family, beliefs, relations with others:

- What eventually happened to them:

DISCOVERY QUESTIONNAIRE

Directions: Place a check in the column that best expresses your views: SD—*strongly disagree;* D—*disagree;* A—*agree;* SA—*strongly agree.*

	SD	D	A	SA
1. All important discoveries in the world have already been made.	___	___	___	___
2. Exploration of the moon today is as important as exploration of North America was in the sixteenth century.	___	___	___	___
3. Discovery of new lands has always meant progress.	___	___	___	___
4. A discovery is important only if it can be put to some use.	___	___	___	___
5. There would be fewer problems today if North America was never settled by Europeans.	___	___	___	___
6. There would have been few conflicts in North America if Indians had adopted European ways.	___	___	___	___
7. People of different backgrounds will naturally fight with each other.	___	___	___	___
8. The European settlers were more civilized than the native Americans.	___	___	___	___
9. In the long run, primitive people benefit from contact with more advanced people.	___	___	___	___
10. There was nothing unusual about the European discovery and settlement. The same things would happen today.	___	___	___	___

SETTLEMENT QUESTIONNAIRE

Directions: Place a check in the column that best expresses your views: SD—*strongly disagree;* D—*disagree;* A—*agree;* SA—*strongly agree.*

	SD	D	A	SA
1. There was nothing the Indians could have done to prevent the European settlement.	——	——	——	——
2. Indians should be given their land back.	——	——	——	——
3. Explorers have a right to claim land they settle.	——	——	——	——
4. A person who owns land can use it any way he or she pleases.	——	——	——	——
5. No one really owns land. They just use it for a period of time.	——	——	——	——
6. If a person takes your land you have the right to get it back any way you can.	——	——	——	——
7. Land should be taken from a person if it helps others.	——	——	——	——
8. People who live in any area should help new settlers get started.	——	——	——	——
9. Europeans had a right to settle in North America.	——	——	——	——
10. The Indians had (have) a right to force the Europeans from North America.	——	——	——	——

CLAIMS OF DISCOVERY

Group and discovery	Evidence	What you need to know to prove or disprove claim
Explorers from Iberian Peninsula settle in Susquehanna Valley, about 800–600 B.C.	translations from 400 stones found in area	
Norsemen settle in Newfoundland, A.D. 1000	written records, maps, artifacts	
Arab sailors in North or South America	Arabic records from Middle Ages mention plants and animals known only in America	
Chinese group reaches Mexico, about A.D. 450	legend; similarities between Aztec and Chinese language, mythology, coinage	
St. Brendan travels from Ireland to North America, about A.D. 500	archaeological findings in Newfoundland; Irish legends	
Hebrews to Tennessee-Georgia area, 1000 B.C.	similarities between Hebrew and Yuchi, an old Georgia tribe, in customs, language	

Phoenicians to North and South America	translations of inscriptions	
Romans to York, Maine, area, A.D. 200	Latin inscription in rock and discovery of Roman coin	
Welsh to Mobile, Alabama, area, A.D. 1170	Some Welsh words in Indian languages; monument erected by Daughters of American Revolution	

IDEAL SETTLEMENT

Imagine you are the leader of a group of settlers sailing from Europe to North America in 1600. You can direct your ship anywhere along the Atlantic coast. Before leaving for the journey, you need to decide on the site you will select. Your objectives are: (1) to find mineral resources; (2) to find a water route to the Pacific; and (3) to develop and control trade.

What do you select?

Land (check one)

_____ flat coastal   Further explanation:
_____ low and hilly
_____ mostly mountainous
_____ combination

Land features

_____ rivers and streams   Further explanation:
_____ rapids
_____ marsh and swamp
_____ lakes and ponds
_____ bays and inlets
_____ shoreline
_____ mountains
_____ rolling hills
_____ plains
_____ plateaus
_____ deltas
_____ peninsulas and capes
_____ islands

Elevation (check one)

_____ 0–305 meters   Further explanation:
_____ 305–610 meters
_____ 610–1525 meters
_____ 1525–3050 meters

Climate

_____ tropical rainy   Further explanation:
_____ dry steppe
_____ humid (with warm or cool summer)
_____ tundra

Temperature (check one)

_____ always cold   Fill in average temperature:
_____ cold winter, cool summer   _____ January
_____ cold winter, mild summer   _____ April
_____ cool winter, mild summer   _____ July
_____ cold winter, hot summer   _____ October
_____ cool winter, hot summer
_____ mild winter, hot summer
_____ always hot

Rainfall (check one)

_____ under 12.5 cm   Further explanation:
_____ 12.5–50 cm
_____ 50–100 cm
_____ 100–150 cm
_____ 150–200 cm
_____ over 200 cm

Natural vegetation (check one)

_____ evergreens   Further explanation:
_____ deciduous
_____ grasslands
_____ mixed
_____ shrubs and dwarf growth
_____ no vegetation

Soil (check one)

_____ alluvial   Further explanation:
_____ tundra
_____ forest
_____ prairie
_____ desert
_____ mountain

Population density (check one)

_____ under one (per square mile/km)   Further explanation:
_____ 1–10
_____ 10–25
_____ 25–50
_____ 50–100
_____ 100–1,000
_____ over 1,000

SURVIVAL AND SETTLEMENT

Imagine you are one of the first settlers in North America in 1607. Your first task is to stay alive. Place the following items in order of importance to you. In the blank space, write a 1 for the most important item, a 2 for the next most important, and so on for the rest of the list.

_____ seeds

_____ several gold coins

_____ sword

_____ shovel and hoe

_____ 50 feet of cord

_____ 5 gallons fresh water

_____ 6 blankets

_____ small rowboat

_____ compass

_____ best available map of North America

Explain the reasons for your arrangement:

PEOPLE MAKE A DIFFERENCE

You are a London merchant during the early 1600s and have invested in establishing a colony in North America. You must select people to explore and settle this new land. Since they are establishing a new colony it is very important that they be chosen with great care. Your ship is limited to exactly 100 people. You have prepared a list of possible choices and now must decide who will go. No one else can be taken. Alongside each person, place the number you will take. You may decide that some are not needed, but the entire list must total 100.

Person	Number to be taken
gentleman	_____
carpenter	_____
laborer	_____
surgeon	_____
blacksmith	_____
sailor	_____
barber	_____
mason	_____
bricklayer	_____
tailor	_____
drummer	_____
jeweler	_____
goldsmith	_____
druggist	_____
soldier	_____
	100

Why did you select the people you did?

GOVERNING A COLONY

Rules and Regulations of Virginia Company. Developed by Thomas Dale.

1. There is to be one governor with complete power.

2. Settlers are marched to church twice a day.

3. Men are to be divided into groups under the control of an officer.

4. No one can return to England without permission.

The following are punishable by serving in the ship's galleys or by death:

5. Slander against the company or its officers.

6. Unauthorized trading with the Indians.

7. Theft.

8. Killing any domestic animal without permission of the company.

9. A false accounting by any supply keeper.

10. All men must keep regular hours of work. The first offense is punishable by lying with neck and heels tied together all night, the second offense is punishable by whipping, and the third offense is punishable by serving one year in the ship's galleys.

11. All people shall have a military rank and specific responsibilities.

Your goals are to (a) increase profits, (b) obtain more workers, and (c) keep control of the colony.

1. Which regulations and/or punishments would you change or eliminate?

2. What new regulations would you develop?

3. Develop a program that would best accomplish the company's objectives.

WILL SEPARATISTS STAY TOGETHER?

You are the leader of a religious group moving across an ocean into an unknown wilderness. Your trip has been paid for by an investment company. This company asked you to take several people who were not members of your religious group. There are about twice as many nonchurch members as there are members. The company also wants you to settle on company-owned land to establish your community. Every time your group moved in the past, church members signed an agreement, or covenant, promising to help one another, follow the Bible, support the church, and obey church elders. Now you are about to land and realize that (1) you are not in the territory owned by the company, and (2) several nonchurch members are threatening to go their own way. You want to keep the group together. What kind of covenant can you write that all will sign?

We, the church and nonchurch members of this group,

Signed:

RETREAT OR REVOLT?

You and your friends live far inland at the foot of some rolling mountains. The government and wealthy people in your colony live along the fertile coast and are not concerned with the dangers you face from hostile Indians. The taxes you pay are used to pay the salaries of the governor and legislators. The right to vote is restricted to those owning houses. Every-one has to attend *Church of England* services or be fined. The members of the legislature set their own salary. No roads or other improvements have been made. You want the govern-ment to build forts and provide protection against attacks of Indians. The governor was told of Indian attacks but has done nothing. Finally, about 500 men join with you in a successful battle against some Indians. Now some of the men are urging you to march toward the capital where the governor and legislature are in session. They want to take over the govern-ment. If you return home, you disappoint your followers and perhaps lose any chance for making changes. If you go to the capital, you know it is likely to lead to armed conflict with considerable death and destruction.

In this case, here is what I would do and why I would do it:

GETTING WHAT YOU WANT

Agreement Between Adventurers and Planters

1. The adventurers (those remaining in England but venturing their money) and planters do agree that every person that goeth being aged 16 years and upward shall be given a single share of the company.

2. That he that goeth in person, and furnishes himself out in money or other provisions be given a double share of the company.

3. The persons transported, and the adventurers shall continue their partnership for _____ years during which time all profits and benefits that are not got by trade, working, fishing, or any other means shall remain in the common stock of the company until_____.

4. That a number of additional fit persons be taken to work upon the land, building houses, tilling and planting the ground, and making such commodities as shall be most useful for the colony.

5. That at the end of_____ years, the profits, houses, lands, goods be divided_____ for adventurers,_____for planters; which done, every man shall be free from other of them of any debt concerning this adventure.

6. Whosoever cometh to the colony hereafter or invest in the company shall at the end of_____years be allowed a proportionate amount of the profit.

7. He that shall take his wife and children, or servants, shall be allowed for every person now aged_____years and upward, a single share in the division of the company profits or if he provide them necessities, a double share. If they be between____years old and_____years, then two of them shall be reckoned as one person.

8. That such children under the age of_____ years have no other share in the division of company profits but shall receive _____ acres of land.

9. That such persons as die before the_____years are up, their executors shall have their share, proportionately to the time of their life in the colony.

10. That all such as are of this colony are to have (the following items)

    _____

    out of the common stock and goods of the colony.

    Additional provisions:

DISTRIBUTION OF SCARCE RESOURCES

Imagine you are with the first settlers in the New World. Your food and other resources are in short supply, and you must decide how the remaining amount will be distributed. Put the following items in order; number 1 is your first choice, number 2 your second choice, and so on. Then briefly explain the reasons for your selections.

_____ I would give food to the 10 percent of the group who worked hardest.

_____ I would get some more food and save it all until we had enough for a party.

_____ I would sell the food to the highest bidder.

_____ I would divide the food equally so that everyone would have an equal, although very small, amount.

_____ I would give the food to the three hungriest people.

_____ I would hold an election to select three people to receive the food.

_____ I would just say that it is available and let anyone who wanted it get it.

_____ I would give it to the people who have the best chance of surviving.

_____ I would give it to the weakest.

I decided this way because:

MAP OF A COLONIAL TOWN

A New England colonial town had a *village green* or *common* and a *meetinghouse* located in the center of the community. In later years there might have been a *school.*

Each family owned a *house and land* in town, and many people often had a *barn, toolshed, well, outhouse,* and *garden.* Away from the town a family might own a *field* for growing corn and grazing animals. They often shared the *woods* and *pasture.*

A *road* went through the town and was used to get to the outlying areas. Houses were close together for protection, usually along a main road. A river often provided waterpower for the *mill.*

Complete the information below. Then name your town and draw a map showing what it would look like.

Scale of kilometers: one centimeter on the map equals_____meters

The direction north is shown on the map by _____

My town will be called:_____

Draw the symbols for each of these features:

village green	meetinghouse
school	house
barn	toolshed
well	outhouse
garden	field
woods	pasture
road	mill

SLAVE SHIP

You are a sailor aboard a slave trader heading to the British North American colonies. The ship owner is a wealthy and respected member of a New England community. He, like most everyone else, thinks there is nothing wrong with enslaving non-Christians. You have heard that there have been more than 100 successful slave revolts at sea but know that most are unsuccessful. You feel that slavery is wrong and inhuman but need a job on a ship. Your task is to help sail the ship and inspect below deck each day to make sure the slaves are secured and that no pieces of iron, wood, or knives are hidden. Upon entering the hold, you surprisingly knock over an African and instinctively grab him and hold a knife to his neck. Looking up, you see that all the slaves are out of their chains. Many have knives and are momentarily stunned at what has happened. You can quickly and safely leave by locking the door and trapping everyone below. Or you can lead the revolt and hope to take over the ship. You hear another sailor coming, and the slaves are recovering from their surprise. What do you do?

RETURN THE RUNAWAY?

You have read advertisements in the paper about runaway slaves and servants. Sizable rewards are offered for their capture and return. You are having some pots and pans repaired and recently hired an itinerant tinker to do the work. He fits the description of a runaway. If you turn him in to the courthouse you will receive a reward of five pounds—a sizable amount. But you also know that he will probably be punished severely. You think people should obey the law but don't think that being a runaway is a serious crime. The tinker is bringing your pots and pans back tomorrow morning. Do you obey the law and receive a reward by turning him in, or do you warn him about the advertisement and perhaps help him escape?

WHICH WAY FOR WITCHCRAFT?

The people of your town believe that criminals have to be punished. If they are not, God will cause everyone to suffer from some natural disaster. The way to prevent everyone from being punished is to have the sinner repent—say he or she is sorry for the wrongdoing and change. And if the person does this there is really no reason for the townspeople to punish him or her. A few teenage girls claim that your image pinches them and causes them great pain. They become hysterical in your presence and say that you are a witch. You are brought to trial before the church leaders who, like yourself, believe that Satan can cause these strange happenings. You can escape punishment and probably death by confessing to being a witch, even though you know you are not. If you confess you will be expected to name other townspeople who are also witches. You can confess to something you know is not so and accuse others to save yourself, or you can tell the truth as you know it and face the consequences. The trial ends and you are asked to make a statement in your own behalf. What do you say?

DO YOU BELIEVE?

Directions: Circle the number indicating how strongly you believe in each of the statements.

DO YOU BELIEVE . . .	no				yes

- *that these things can bring good luck?*

		no				yes
1.	throwing salt over your left shoulder	1	2	3	4	5
2.	rabbit's foot	1	2	3	4	5
3.	knocking on wood	1	2	3	4	5

- *that these things can bring bad luck?*

1.	number 13	1	2	3	4	5
2.	black cat crosses your path	1	2	3	4	5
3.	walking under a ladder	1	2	3	4	5
4.	opening an umbrella indoors	1	2	3	4	5
5.	breaking a mirror	1	2	3	4	5

- *that these things are so?*

1.	that there are supernatural things that can't be scientifically explained	1	2	3	4	5
2.	that some people have extrasensory perception (can know things without seeing, hearing, feeling, touching, or smelling them)	1	2	3	4	5
3.	that some people can make others act in unusual ways or "cast a spell"	1	2	3	4	5
4.	a person's character can be read from the lines on the palm of his or her hands	1	2	3	4	5
5.	that some people today can be called witches and do have unusual powers	1	2	3	4	5

Do you think people's beliefs are: Helpful? Harmful? Dangerous? When do the beliefs of one person make a difference to another person? Are there beliefs that everyone should have? What controls, if any, should a community have on the beliefs of citizens?

PUBLISH OR PROTECT?

You have to defend the publisher of the *New York Weekly Journal* who has printed articles criticizing the governor for establishing special courts without approval from the legislature. The governor has also removed judges from the courts without any cause for doing so. The publisher you are defending wrote that the liberties of the people are in danger and they will be made slaves if the governor can do as he pleases. This angered the governor, of course, and the publisher was arrested and is being tried for libel. The judge in this case wants the jury to make its decision on whether the publisher did or did not publish the critical articles. His instructions to the jury state that no government can exist if people criticize those who are appointed to run its affairs. It is necessary for government that the people have a good opinion of it. To create distrust about the management of the government has always been a crime. No government can be safe without punishing the people who criticize it. It is now your chance to present the case for the defense to the jury. What do you say?

A COLONIAL SORT

Directions for Teacher: The items on this page are to be cut into individual statements or made into cards. Many sorts are possible. A major sort for this listing is New England (1–11), Middle Colonies (12–20), and Southern Colonies (21–30).

1. hilly and rocky land and many good harbors

2. self-sufficient family farms

3. fishing, whaling, and shipbuilding

4. triangular trade

5. strict "blue laws" forbade Sunday entertainment

6. first public school system

7. King Philip's War

8. town meeting determines local affairs

9. Williams establishes principle of separation of church and state

10. Separatists

11. Massasoit

12. coastal plains and fertile farmland

13. great wheat and corn production

14. Dutch architectural influence

15. King's College

16. Zenger trial establishes freedom of the press

17. first circulating library

18. Toleration Act provides religious freedom for Christians

19. large patroons granted to wealthy settlers

20. *Poor Richard's Almanac*

26. first representative assembly

27. plantation system of agriculture

21. fertile soil and long growing season

28. Powhatan

22. tobacco, rice, and indigo produced as "cash crops"

29. slave system

23. main house surrounded by smaller separate buildings

30. colony settled as buffer with Spanish territory

24. private tutors for wealthy children

25. Bacon's Rebellion

A PLAN OF UNION

It is during the 1750s and the colonies face increasing danger from their enemies. A meeting is called, and seven colonies send delegates to write a plan of union. They make the following decisions:

1. That there be a president general and a Grand Council

2. That the president general should be appointed by the king of England

3. That the Grand Council have representatives chosen by each colony based on population (Massachusetts and Virginia, for example, the largest, would have seven representatives; Rhode Island would have two; and so on)

4. That the Grand Council should appoint its own Speaker. The Speaker would become president general if the president general died in office

5. That the president general would approve all acts of the grand council

6. That the president general, with the advice of the Grand Council, would have the following powers:

   - make treaties and declare war with the Indian nations

   - regulate trade

   - purchase land

   - regulate new settlements

   - raise and pay for an army and navy

   - make laws

   - levy taxes

CLASH OVER COLONIAL LAND

British and Colonists

Several prominent Englishmen and Virginians have organized the Ohio Company (1748) to establish trading posts and settlements in the Ohio River Valley. A grant of 200,000 acres was obtained from the king with a promise of 300,000 more acres if 100 families settled the area within seven years. You fear encroachment by Pennsylvanians as well as French settlers and have a wagon road cut to the area and send explorers to locate favorable land for settlement.

News has reached you that the French have sent a sizable force to construct a line of forts in the area. An English trading post has been seized and occupied by the French.

You are alarmed and send a warning to the French accusing them of trespassing on English lands. The officer sent to warn the French to withdraw from the Ohio returns with the message that the French plan to stay until they are told to move by French officials.

Your objective is to gain the Ohio River Valley.

1. What courses of action are available to you?
2. What are the consequences of each?
3. Which do you select? What do you hope/ expect to happen?

—Write a letter to the French governor general regarding the presence of French soldiers in the Ohio River Valley.

New France

Last year the governor general of Canada sent about 215 French soldiers and a force of Indians to take control of the Ohio River Valley for France. The group traveled overland and by canoe posting notices on trees and burying lead plates claiming the land for the French king. Word has been received that the British are interested in the fertile lands and have been supporting colonial attempts to establish settlements in the Ohio River Valley.

You have sent an expedition of 1000 men to build a line of forts in this area to hold it for France. An English trading post was taken and now the English have sent a warning to the commander of one of the forts saying the area belongs to England. A small group of colonists delivered the message demanding that your soldiers withdraw. The soldiers informed the colonists that the Ohio River Valley would be held for France until other orders came from you, as governor general of Canada.

You are responsible for establishing French policy for North America. Your objective is to gain and hold the Ohio River Valley.

1. What courses of action are available to you?
2. What are the consequences of each?
3. Which do you select? What do you hope/ expect to happen?

—Write a letter to the colonial governor regarding the presence of English settlers in the Ohio River Valley.

STUDENT INVESTIGATIONS

Question to be investigated: _____

_____

Hypothesis (your educated guess at the answer)

Evidence (what you found to prove or disprove your hypothesis)

    Explain evidence   *Source of information*

Revised hypothesis and further explanation (based on your evidence, this is the best answer to the original question)

THE J-CURVE HYPOTHESIS*

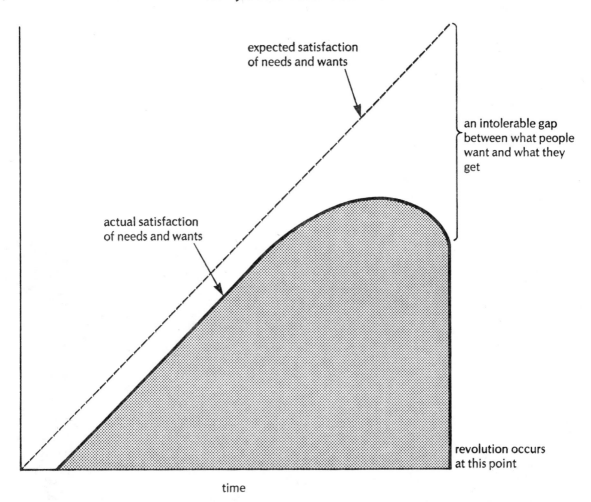

expected satisfaction
of needs and wants

an intolerable gap
between what people
want and what they
get

actual satisfaction
of needs and wants

revolution occurs
at this point

time

Revolutions are more likely to occur after a long period of social and economic development, followed by a sharp downturn. The people's view of conditions, their expectations, are more important than the actual conditions or state of development. The gap between reality and expectations creates a loss of confidence. When frustrations develop that are intense and widespread, they are released through violent action.

*James C. Davies, "The J-Curve of Rising and Declining Satsifactions as a Cause of Some Great Revolutions and a Contained Rebellion," in Hugh Davis Graham and Ted Robert Gurr, eds. *Violence in America: Historical and Comparative Perspectives.* (New York: New American Library, 1969), pp. 671–709.

STATEMENTS ON THE REVOLUTION

We, his Majesty's most loyal subjects . . . affected with the deepest anxiety and most alarming apprehensions at those grievances and distresses, with which his Majesty's American subjects are oppressed, and having taken under our most serious deliberation the state of the whole continent find, that the present unhappy situation of our affairs is occasioned by a ruinous System of colony administration adopted by the British Ministry . . . evidently calculated for enslaving these colonies and with them the British Empire.—*Articles of Association, October 20, 1774, signed by delegates of twelve colonies*

Governments are instituted among Men, deriving their just powers from the consent of the governed,—That whenever any Form of Government becomes destructive of these ends, it is the Right of the People to alter or to abolish it, and to institute new Government.—*Thomas Jefferson, July 1776*

Young man, what we meant in going for those redcoats was this—we always had governed ourselves, and we always meant to. They didn't mean we should.—*Levi Preston, seventy years after he fought at the battle of Lexington*

What do we mean by the Revolution? The War? That was no part of the Revolution: it was only an effect and consequence of it. The Revolution was in the minds of the people, a change in their sentiments, their duties and obligations. . . . The real American Revolution . . . was affected from 1760 to 1775, in the course of fifteen years before a single drop of blood was shed at Lexington.—*John Adams, several years after the American Revolution*

1. According to these statements, what were key issues of the American Revolution?

2. How can the idea of *power* and *authority* be used to understand the Revolution?

3. In your opinion, which of the above statements is most helpful in understanding the Revolution? Why?

FACT OR FICTION?*

Fact	Basis for Fact	Reasons for questioning reliability
1. triangle trade–New England–Africa–West Indies; rum-slaves-molasses	two trips made by Capt. David Lindsay, 1753–54, and magnified by nineteenth-century historians	several hundred thousand recorded voyages that did not go triangle trade route
2. colonists rebelled because of taxes	popular interpretation of events	Navigation Acts before 1760 raised very little revenue; Stamp Act repealed; Townshend Acts repealed; Tea tax actually reduced cost of tea
3. "no taxation without representation"	popular acceptance of slogan	misleading; colonists had strong belief in direct representation and popular consent to taxation; colonists did not want representation in Parliament but wanted to be taxed by their own representatives in their own legislatures
4. George III was "the royal brute," as Thomas Paine called him	commonly accepted belief that he was mentally ill	new policies after 1760 were Parliament's; illness distorted perceptions, made him irritable; most trouble began in 1780s, long after the Revolution
5. "One if by land, two if by sea"	Longfellow's poem	British actually went both ways; Revere was captured before reaching Concord
6. One-third of the people favored the Revolution, one-third opposed it, and one-third were undecided	commonly accepted paraphrase of comments made by John Adams in 1815	Adams's 1815 letter referred to American reactions to the French Revolution; in 1775 Adams estimated that 90 percent of the Americans favored the American Revolution

*The material for this activity comes from: G. B. Warden, "What NOT to Teach About the American Revolution," *The Revolution and the Bicentennial: Conference Report* (New Haven, Conn.: Yale Bicentennial Committee and the Connecticut Council for the Social Studies, 1975), pp. 1–7.

7. Critical period when country was governed by Continental Congress and Articles of Confederation, which was unworkable, disorganized, chaotic

based on phrase by nineteenth-century historian John Fiske

Congress fought long war to successful conclusion, established credit, made treaties, developed workable arrangement for territorial expansion

INDICATORS OF DEVELOPMENT

Each of the items listed below can help or hurt a country having a conflict with another country. Decide if they helped, hurt, or didn't make any difference to the colonies before 1776. Then briefly tell how it makes a difference or why it does not.

... in the Colonies	helps	hurts	no difference	how it makes a difference or why it does not
1. military	———	———	———	—————————
2. transportation	———	———	———	—————————
3. communication	———	———	———	—————————
4. education	———	———	———	—————————
5. natural resources	———	———	———	—————————
6. land area and features	———	———	———	—————————
7. geographic location	———	———	———	—————————
8. climate	———	———	———	—————————
9. food supply	———	———	———	—————————
10. initiative of people	———	———	———	—————————
11. sense of history	———	———	———	—————————
12. customs/traditions	———	———	———	—————————
13. religious beliefs	———	———	———	—————————
14. language	———	———	———	—————————
15. government	———	———	———	—————————
16. opponents of government	———	———	———	—————————
17. relations with other countries	———	———	———	—————————
18. population distribution, composition, and total	———	———	———	—————————
19. distribution of wealth	———	———	———	—————————
20. economic structure	———	———	———	—————————
21. job opportunities	———	———	———	—————————

WRITS OF ASSISTANCE

Do government officials have the right to enter your home?

_____ yes   _____ no

If a government official is looking for stolen or smuggled goods, does he have the right to enter your home?

_____ yes   _____ no

The British Parliament approved a law that allowed colonial homes to be searched. James Otis, a Boston lawyer, spoke against these writs of assistance:

> Now, one of the most essential branches of English liberty is the freedom of one's house. A man's house is his castle; and while he is quiet, he is as well guarded as a prince in his castle. This writ, if it should be declared legal, would totally annihilate this privilege. Custom house officers may enter our houses when they please; we are commanded to permit their entry. Their menial servants may enter, may break locks, bars, and everything in their way; and whether they break through malice or revenge, no man, no court can inquire. Bare suspicion without oath is sufficient. This wanton exercise of this power is not a chimerical suggestion of a heated brain. The words are: "It shall be lawful for any person or persons authorized," etc. What a scene does this open! Every man prompted by revenge, ill-humor, or wantonness, to inspect the insides of his neighbor's house, may get a writ of assistance. Others will ask it from self-defence; one arbitrary exertion will provoke another, until society be involved in tumult and in blood. . . .

1. To what is Otis objecting?

2. In what situations might it be necessary or wise to allow government officials to enter a person's house?

3. Who in the colonies would the British upset with this law?

STAMP ACT CONGRESS, 1765

Representatives from the colonies met in New York in 1765 to oppose the Stamp Act. They prepared a declaration for the king which, shortened and rewritten, follows:

1. The colonists owe allegiance to the king and Parliament.

2. The colonists are entitled to all rights and privileges of British subjects.

3. It is essential to colonial freedom that no taxes be imposed on them without their consent.

4. The colonists are not and, because of distance, cannot be represented in Parliament.

5. No taxes can be imposed on the colonies except by their own legislatures.

6. It is unreasonable for Great Britain to take the property of the colonies.

7. Trial by jury is an inherent and invaluable right.

8. The acts of Parliament in taxing the colonies, and extending the admiralty courts (which conduct trials without juries), are subverting the rights and liberties of the colonists.

9. The taxes imposed by Parliament will be a burden, and the lack of coins makes payment impracticable.

10. The colonies are obligated to take manufactured goods from Great Britain, and this helps the king.

11. The restrictions imposed by the acts of Parliament will make the colonies unable to purchase manufactured goods from Britain.

12. Increases in population, prosperity, and happiness in the colonies depends on the free enjoyment of their rights and mutually advantageous trade with Britain.

13. The colonies have the right to petition the king or Parliament.

14. It is the responsibility of the colonies to be loyal to the king and Parliament in asking that these laws be repealed.

BENJAMIN FRANKLIN IN THE HOUSE OF COMMONS, 1766*

Q. Are not the Colonies, from their circumstances, very able to pay the stamp duty?
A. In my opinion there is not gold and silver enough in the Colonies to pay the stamp duty for one year.

Q. Do you not know that the money arising from the stamps was all to be laid out in America?
A. I know it is appropriated by the Act to the American service; but it will be spent in the conquered Colonies, where the soldiers are; not in the Colonies that pay it.

Q. Do you think it right that America should be protected by this country and pay no part of the expense?
A. That is not the case. The Colonies raised, clothed, and paid, during the last war, near twenty-five thousand men, and spent many millions. . . .

Q. Do you think the people of America would submit to pay the stamp duty if it was moderated?
A. No, never, unless compelled by force of arms.

Q. What was the temper of America toward Great Britain *before the year* 1763?
A. The best in the world. They submitted willingly to the government of the Crown, and paid, in their courts, obedience to acts of Parliament. Numerous as the people are in the several old provinces they cost you nothing in forts, citadels, garrisons, or armies, to keep them in subjugation. They were governed by this country at the expense only of a little pen, ink, and paper; they were led by a thread. They had not only a respect but an affection for Great Britain; for its laws, its customs, and manners, and even a fondness for its fashions, that greatly increased the commerce. Natives of Britain were always treated with particular regard; to be an Old England-man was of itself a character of some respect, and gave a kind of rank among us.

Q. And what is their temper now?
A. Oh, very much altered. . . .

Q. And have they not still the same respect for Parliament?
A. No; it is greatly lessened.

Q. To what cause is that owing?
A. To a concurrence of causes: the restraints lately laid on their trade, by which the bringing of foreign gold and silver into the Colonies was prevented; the prohibition of making paper money among themselves, and then demanding a new and heavy tax by stamps; taking away, at the same time, trials by juries, and refusing to receive and hear their humble petitions. . . .

Q. Considering the resolutions of Parliament, as to the right; do you think if the Stamp Act is repealed that the North Americans will be satisfied?
A. I believe they will. . . .

*Information on this page is from: William Jennings Bryan, ed., *The World's Famous Orations* (New York: Funk & Wagnalls, 1906), pp. 37–52.

Q. Can anything less than a military force carry the Stamp Act into execution?
A. I do not see how a military force can be applied to that purpose.

Q. Why may it not?
A. Suppose a military force is sent into America: they will find nobody in arms; what are they then to do? They can not force a man to take stamps who chooses to do without them. They will not find a rebellion; they may, indeed, make one.

Q. If the Act is not repealed, what do you think will be the consequences?
A. A total loss of the respect and affection the people of America bear to this country, and of all the commerce that depends on that respect and affection.

Q. How can the commerce be affected?
A. You will find that if the Act is not repealed, they will take very little of your manufactures in a short time.

Q. Is it in their power to do without them?
A. I think they may very well do without them.

Q. Is it to their interest not to take them?
A. The goods they take from Britain are either necessaries, mere conveniences, or superfluities. The first, as cloth, etc., with a little industry, they can make at home; the second they can do without till they are able to provide them among themselves; and the last, which are much the greatest part, they will strike off immediately. They are mere articles of fashion, purchased and consumed because the fashion, in a respected country, but will now be detested and rejected. The people have already struck off, by general agreement, the use of all goods fashionable in mourning, and many thousand pounds' worth are sent back as unsalable.

Q. Then no regulation with a tax would be submitted to?
A. Their opinion is that when aids to the Crown are wanted they are to be asked of the several assemblies according to the old-established usage, who will, as they always have done, grant them freely, and that their money ought not to be given away without their consent, by persons at a distance, unacquainted with their circumstances and abilities . . . they think it extremely hard and unjust that a body of men in which they have no representatives should make a merit to itself of giving and granting what is not its own but theirs, and deprive them of a right they esteem of the utmost value and importance, as it is the security of all their other rights.

Q. Supposing the Stamp Act continued and enforced, do you imagine that ill humor will induce the Americans to give as much for worse manufactures of their own, and use them, preferable to better of ours?
A. Yes, I think so. People will pay as freely to gratify one passion as another—their resentment as their pride. . . .

Q. (Why did America do so little in the last war?)
A. . . . America has been greatly misrepresented and abused here, in papers and pamphlets and speeches . . . as ungrateful and unreasonable and unjust; in having put this nation to immense expense for their defense, and refusing to bear any part of that expense. The Colonies raised, paid, and clothed near twenty-

five thousand men during the last war—a number equal to those sent from Britain, and far beyond their proportion; they went deeply into debt in doing this, and all their taxes and estates are mortgaged for many years to come for discharging that debt.

Q. But suppose Great Britain should be engaged in a war in Europe, would North America contribute to the support of it?

A. I do think they would, as far as their circumstances would permit. They consider themselves as a part of the British Empire, and as having one common interest with it; they may be looked on here as foreigners, but they do not consider themselves as such. . . . They make no distinction of wars as to their duty of assisting in them. I know the last war is commonly spoken of here as entered into for the defense or for the sake of the people in America. I think it is quite misunderstood. It began about the limits between Canada and Nova Scotia, about territories which were not claimed by any British Colony; none of the lands had been granted to any colonist; we had, therefore, no particular interest or concern in that dispute. As to the Ohio, the contest there began about your right of trading in the Indian country, a right you had by the treaty of Utrecht, which the French infringed; they seized the traders and their goods, which were your manufactures; they took a fort which a company of your merchants and their factors and correspondents had erected there to secure that trade. Braddock was sent with an army to retake that fort and to protect your trade. It was not till after his defeat that the Colonies were attacked. They were before in perfect peace with both French and Indians; the troops were not, therefore, sent for their defense. The trade with the Indians, tho carried on in America, is not an *American interest*. The people of America are chiefly farmers and planters; scarce anything that they raise or produce is an article of commerce with the Indians. The Indian trade is a *British interest;* it is carried on with British manufacturers, for the profit of British merchants and manufacturers; therefore, the war, as it commenced for the defense of territories of the Crown (the property of no American) and for the defense of a trade purely British, was really a British war—and yet the people of America made no scruple of contributing their utmost toward carrying it on, and bringing it to a happy conclusion. . . .

Q. If the Stamp Act should be repealed, would it induce the assemblies of America to acknowledge the rights of Parliament to tax them, and would they erase their resolutions?

A. No, never!

1. What problems are discussed by Franklin?

2. What suggestions does he make for resolving them?

3. How have poor communications led to problems for the English in this case?

QUESTIONS OF LAW

Directions: Place a check mark in the space indicating that you *strongly agree, agree, disagree,* or *strongly disagree.*

	SA	A	D	SD
1. It is always safer to err on the milder side, the side of mercy. The best rule in doubtful cases is to acquit rather than convict.	___	___	___	___
2. One would rather have twenty persons escape punishment of death than have one innocent person condemned. It is better that five guilty persons escape, than one innocent person suffer.	___	___	___	___
3. A person may repel force with force in defense of person, living place, or property.	___	___	___	___
4. The killing of dangerous rioters may be justified when a person cannot otherwise suppress them, or defend himself from them.	___	___	___	___
5. In the case of an unlawful assembly, all and every one of the assembly is guilty of all and every unlawful act committed by any one of that assembly.	___	___	___	___
6. A person has a right to go to the assistance of a fellow human being in distress or danger of his life when assaulted and in danger from others.	___	___	___	___
7. If a third person accidentally happens to be killed by one engaged in a combat, or in a sudden quarrel, he who killed him is guilty of manslaughter only.	___	___	___	___
8. When a person is assaulted and kills in consequence of that assault, it is only manslaughter.	___	___	___	___

Definitions

- riot: where or when more than three persons use force or violence, for the accomplishment of any purpose whatever, all concerned are rioters; the only exception is where the law authorizes the use of force.

- assault: an attempt or actually doing a corporal hurt to another, as by striking him with or without a weapon, or by any other such act done in an angry, threatening manner, but no words can amount to an assault.

CITIZENS VERSUS SOLDIERS

John Adams's statement in defense of British soldiers accused of murdering Attucks, Gray, and others in the Boston Riot of 1770:

You must place yourselves in the situations of [the British soldiers] Weems and Killroy—consider yourselves as knowing that the prejudice of the world about you thought you came to dragoon them into obedience, to statutes, instructions, mandates, and edicts, which they thoroughly detested—that many of these people were thoughtless and inconsiderate, old and young, sailors and landsmen, negroes and mulattoes—that they, the soldiers, had no friends about them, the rest were in opposition to them; with all the bells ringing to call the town together to assist the people in King Street, for they knew by that time that there was no fire; the people shouting, huzzahing, and making the mob whistle, as they call it, which, when a boy makes it in the street is no formidable thing, but when made by a multitude is a most hideous shriek, almost as terrible as an Indian yell; the people crying, "Kill them, kill them. Knock them over," heaving snowballs, oyster shells, clubs, white-birch sticks three inches and a half in diameter; consider yourselves in this situation, and judge whether a reasonable man in the soldiers' situation would not have concluded they were going to kill him.

John Hancock, speech delivered March 5, 1774, commemorating the anniversary of the riot:

Tell me, ye bloody butchers! ye villains high and low! ye wretches who contrived as well as you who executed the inhuman deed! do you not feel the goads and stings of conscious guilt pierce through your savage bosoms? . . . Do not the injured shades of Maverick, Gray, Caldwell, Attucks, and Carr, attend you in your solitary walks; arrest you even in the midst of your debaucheries, and fill even your dreams with terror?

Let this sad tale of death never be told without a tear: let not the heaving bosom cease to burn with a manly indignation at the barbarous story through the long tracts of future time: let every parent tell the shameful story to his listening children until tears of pity glisten in their eyes and boiling passions shake their tender frames; and whilst the anniversary of that ill-fated night is kept a jubilee in the grim court of pandemonium, let all America join in one common prayer to heaven that the inhuman, unprovoked murders of the 5th of March, 1770, planned by Hillsborough and a knot of treacherous knaves in Boston, and executed by the cruel hand of Preston and his [bloody band], may ever stand in history without parallel.

CHRONOLOGY OF EVENTS
LEADING TO AMERICAN REVOLUTION

1763
Feb.   French and Indian War ends
Oct.   Proclamation of 1763

1764
Apr.   Sugar Act passed
May   James Otis speaks against English taxation without colonial representation

1765
Mar.   Stamp Act passed
May   Patrick Henry proposes Virginia Resolves
Oct.   Stamp Act Congress, New York City

1766
Mar.   Parliament repeals Stamp Act
            Declaratory Act passed

1767
June   Townshend Acts passed

1768
Oct.   British troops arrive in Boston

1769
May   Virginia Resolves condemn Parliament for tax
            nonimportation agreement established

1770
Mar.   Boston Massacre
Apr.   Townshend Acts repealed, except tea duty

1772
June   British ship *Gaspee* attacked, Providence, R.I.
Nov.   Boston forms Committee of Correspondence

1773
May   Tea Act passed
Dec.   Boston Tea Party

1774

Mar.	Boston Port Bill closes harbor, first of Coercive Acts
June	Quartering Act passed
	Quebec Act extends Canadian boundary south to Ohio River
Sep.	First Continental Congress meets in Philadelphia
Oct.	"Declaration and Resolves" of Congress condemns most British acts since 1763
Dec.	Fort William and Mary, Portsmouth, N.H., raided by patriots

1775

Mar.	Patrick Henry's "Liberty or Death" speech
Apr.	battle at Lexington and Concord
	siege of Boston begins
May	Ethan Allen and Benedict Arnold capture Fort Ticonderoga
	Second Continental Congress meets
	Crown Point, N.Y., captured by Americans
June	British ship *Margaretta* captured, Machias, Maine
	Washington appointed commander in chief of Continental army
	battle at Bunker (Breed's) Hill
July	Washington takes command of army at Cambridge, Mass.
Aug.	King George in proclamation declares colonies in "open and avowed rebellion"
Sep.	Benedict Arnold begins march on Quebec
Oct.	Continental navy and marines authorized
Nov.	Hopkins appointed commander in chief of American naval fleet
	U.S. Marine Corps established
Dec.	colonial siege of Quebec

1776

Jan.	Norfolk, Va., burned by British
	American forces in Quebec defeated and leave Canada
	Thomas Paine publishes *Common Sense*
Feb.	battle at Moores Creek, N.C.
Mar.	British evacuate Boston
	Rhode Island declares independence from Britain
June	Lee introduces motion of independence to Continental Congress
	battle of Sullivan's Island, S.C.
July	Declaration of Independence passed by Congress; N.Y. abstains
Aug.	battle of Long Island (Brooklyn), N.Y.
Sep.	peace conference at Conference House, Staten Island, N.Y., fails
	New York City occupied by British
	battle of Harlem Heights, N.Y.
Oct.	battle at Valcour Bay, N.Y.
	British naval force burns Falmouth, Me.
	battle at White Plains, N.Y.
Nov.	British capture Fort Washington, N.Y.
	British capture Fort Lee, N.J.
	Washington retreats across New Jersey into Pennsylvania
Dec.	British occupy Newport, R.I.
	Washington crosses Delaware River and surprises British at Trenton, N.J.

A PETITION

We hold these truths to be self-evident: That all men are created equal; that they are endowed by their Creator with certain unalienable rights; that among these are life, liberty, and the pursuit of happiness. That, to secure these rights, governments are instituted among men, deriving their just powers from the consent of the governed; that, whenever any form of government becomes destructive of these ends, it is the right of the people to alter or to abolish it, and to institute a new government, laying its foundation on such principles, and organizing its powers in such form, as to them shall seem most likely to effect their safety and happiness. . . .

I, the undersigned, support these views:

Name   *City and State*

1. _____

2. _____

3. _____

4. _____

5. _____

6. _____

7. _____

8. _____

9. _____

10. _____

11. _____

12. _____

13. _____

14. _____

COMMON SENSE

. . . I offer nothing more than simple facts, plain arguments, and common sense. . . .

Volumes have been written on the subject of the struggle between England and America. Men of all ranks have embarked in the controversy, from different motives, and with various designs; but all have been ineffectual, and the period of debate is closed. Arms as the last resource decide the contest; the appeal was the choice of the King, and the Continent has accepted the challenge. . . .

The Sun never shined on a cause of greater worth. 'Tis not the affair of a City, a Country, a Province, or a Kingdom; but of a Continent—of at least one-eighth part of the habitable Globe. 'Tis not the concern of a day, a year, or an age; posterity are virtually involved in the contest, and will be more or less affected even to the end of time, by the proceedings. Now is the seed-time of Continental union, faith and honour. The least fracture now will be like a name engraved with the point of a pin on the tender rind of a young oak; the wound would enlarge with the tree, and posterity read it in full-grown characters.

By referring the matter from argument to arms, a new era for politics is struck—a new method of thinking hath arisen. All plans, proposals, &c. prior to the nineteenth of April, i.e. to the commencement of hostilities, are like the almanacks of the last year; which tho' proper then, are superseded and useless now. . . . .

. . . Everything that is right or reasonable pleads for separation. The blood of the slain, the weeping voice of nature cries, 'Tis time to part. . . .

1. Underline the phrases that you think are especially persuasive and supportive of the colonial position.

2. What purposes could Thomas Paine have in writing this?

3. In Paine's point of view, what is the key event that changed relations between the English and the colonies?

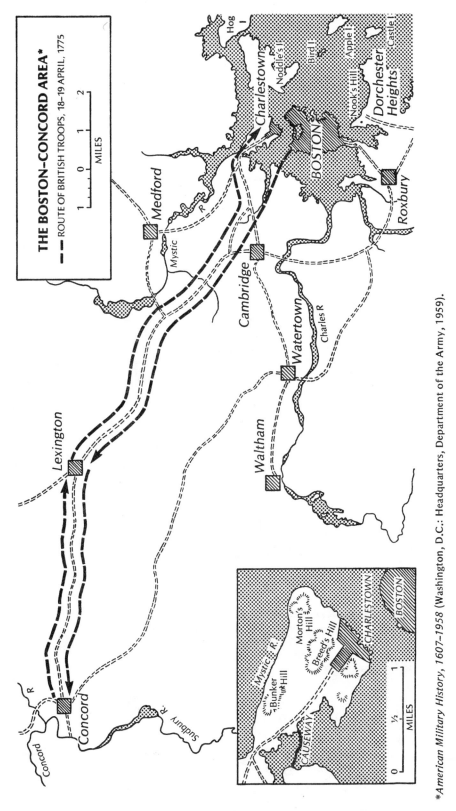

THE BOSTON-CONCORD AREA*

— — ROUTE OF BRITISH TROOPS, 18–19 APRIL, 1775

MILES

*American Military History, 1607–1958 (Washington, D.C.: Headquarters, Department of the Army, 1959).

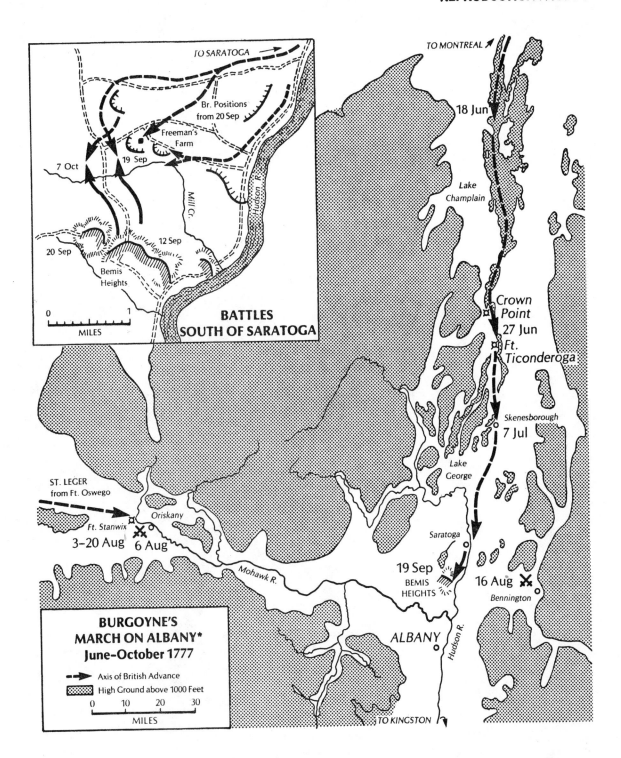

BATTLES SOUTH OF SARATOGA

TO SARATOGA

Br. Positions from 20 Sep

Freeman's Farm

7 Oct

19 Sep

Mill Cr.

Hudson R.

20 Sep

12 Sep

Bemis Heights

0   1
MILES

TO MONTREAL

18 Jun

Lake Champlain

Crown Point
27 Jun
Ft. Ticonderoga

Skenesborough
7 Jul

Lake George

Saratoga

19 Sep
BEMIS HEIGHTS

16 Aug
Bennington

ST. LEGER from Ft. Oswego

Oriskany

Ft. Stanwix
3–20 Aug   6 Aug

Mohawk R.

ALBANY

Hudson R.

TO KINGSTON

BURGOYNE'S MARCH ON ALBANY*
June–October 1777

- - -→   Axis of British Advance

▨   High Ground above 1000 Feet

0   10   20   30
MILES

American Military History, 1607–1958 (Washington, D.C.: Headquarters, Department of the Army, 1959).

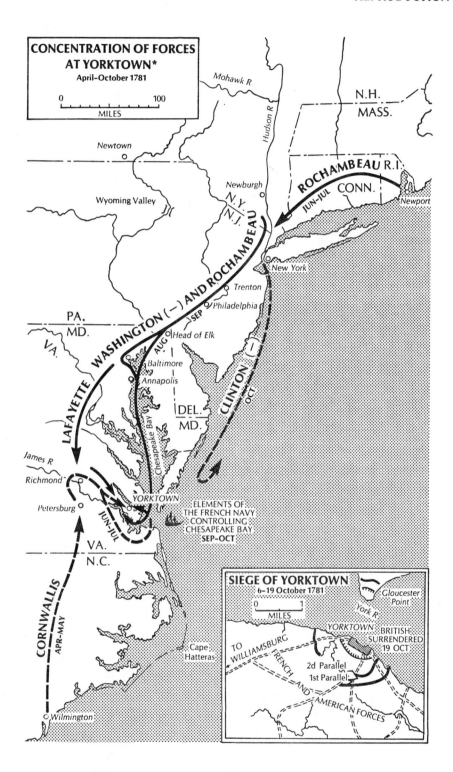

**CONCENTRATION OF FORCES
AT YORKTOWN***
April–October 1781

0   100
MILES

*American Military History, 1607–1958 (Washington, D.C.: Headquarters, Department of the Army, 1959).

COMMON PROBLEMS

The Problem of Food

The scarcity of food was extraordinary. In a country usually abounding with supplies, there was an unprecedented shortage. It's true that both the 1779 and 1780 seasons were disappointing, but there are obviously other reasons for the shortage of food.

Farmers who supported the patriots' cause were often interrupted by calls for militia duty. Those who cared for neither side, or because of religious convictions would not fight, or those who secretly aided the Loyalists, of course, supplied very little or no food.

Some say that there are not enough men to help in the fields. But the principal cause of the problem seems to be the steadily declining value of continental money the farmers receive for their crops.

The Problem of Money

Soldiers had patiently suffered for a long time. They finally pressured their officers to send a petition to the state legislature stating their complaint.

The pay received by a private was not enough to provide his family with a single bushel of wheat. The pay received by a colonel was not enough to purchase oats for his horse. Common laborers received many times as much pay as an American officer.

The petition urged that a speedy and ample remedy be provided. Without an increase in pay, the soldiers would go home.

You are a member of a committee appointed by the Continental Congress to investigate these matters. You have found that both cases are accurate descriptions of existing conditions. You must now recommend a course of action to the Congress for resolving these difficulties.

- The recommended course of action:

- A possible course of action, but less favored:

- A course of action that is possible but not recommended:

SELECTING PEOPLE*

You are working for _____
and need to select 10 people from the first group. Choose a nationality and write it in front of the person you want to select; for example, *Canadian mechanic*.

You may choose the same nationality as often as you wish, but you must choose 10 different people according to their occupations. After this is completed, indicate the person's age and sex (M or F) in the space provided. Be prepared to explain the selections you have made.

Canadian	Native American	Scottish	Dutch
French	English	German	Polish
West African	Irish	Spanish	American (New England)
American (Middle colonies)	American (Southern colonies)	American (frontier)	

Section B

Nationality	Age	Sex	Nationality	Age	Sex
_____ mechanic	____	____	_____ peasant	____	____
_____ teacher	____	____	_____ student	____	____
_____ sheriff	____	____	_____ merchant	____	____
_____ apprentice	____	____	_____ banker	____	____
_____ farmer	____	____	_____ soldier	____	____
_____ doctor	____	____	_____ writer	____	____
_____ lawyer	____	____	_____ scientist	____	____
_____ dockhand	____	____	_____ blacksmith	____	____
_____ minister	____	____	_____ innkeeper	____	____
_____ government official	____	____	_____ unemployed	____	____
_____ plantation owner	____	____	_____ slave	____	____
_____ sailor	____	____		____	____

*This activity is adapted from Thomas P. Fenton, ed., *Education for Justice* (Maryknoll, N.Y.: Orbis Books, 1975), pp. 205-7.

WASHINGTON AS LEADER

Directions: Without looking at the bottom half of this paper, describe your ideal political or military leader.

Physical features:

Intelligence:

Relations with others:

Beliefs and views:

Character:

_____

How close did you come to agreeing with this view of Washington?

> General Washington was a tall, well made man, rather above the common size; his frame was robust, and his constitution vigorous, and capable of enduring great fatigue. His features were manly and bold, and his eyes of a bluish tint and very lively; his hair a deep brown, his face rather . . . marked with the small-pox; his complexion sun burnt, and without much colour, and his countenance sensible, composed, and thoughtful; there was a remarkable air of dignity about him, with a striking degree of gracefulness; he had an excellent understanding without much quickness; was strictly just, vigilant, and generous; as a military man, he was brave, enterprizing, and cautious; an affectionate husband, a faithful friend, a father to the deserving; gentle in his manners, in temper rather reserved; a total stranger to religious prejudices, which have so often excited christians of one denomination to cut the throats of those of another; in his morals irreproachable; he was never known to exceed the bounds of his most rigid temperance; in a word, all his friends and acquaintances universally allow that no man ever united in his person, a more perfect alliance of the virtues of a philosopher with the talents of a statesman and a general. Candour, sincerity, affability, and simplicity, seem to have been the striking features of his character.*

*David Ramsay, *The History of the American Revolution* (Lexington, Ky.: Downing and Phillips, 1815), pp. 482-83.

OBITUARY OF A SOLDIER*

Died, on Friday the 3d of January inst., at his residence in Upper Merion township, aged 90 years, EDWARD HECTOR, a colored man, and a veteran of the Revolution.

Obscurity in life and oblivion in death, is too often the lot of the worthy—they pass away, and no "storied stone" perpetuates the remembrance of their noble actions. The humble subject of this notice will doubtless share this common fate; he has joined the great assembly of the dead, and will soon be forgotten: and yet, many a monument has been "raised to some proud son of earth" who less deserved it than "poor old Ned." His earlier and better days were devoted to the cause of the American Revolution; in that cause he risked all he had to risk—his life, and he survived the event for a long lapse of years, to witness the prosperity of a country whose independence he had so nobly assisted to achieve, and which neglected him in his old age.

During the war of the revolution, his conduct, on one memorable occasion, exhibited an example of patriotism and bravery which deserves to be recorded. At the battle of Brandy-wine he had charge of an ammunition wagon, attached to Col. Proctor's regiment, and when the American army was obliged to retreat, an order was given by the proper officers to those having charge of the weapons, to abandon them to the enemy, and save yourselves by flight. The heroic reply of the deceased was uttered in the true spirit of the revolution: "The enemy shall not have my team," said he— "I will save my horses, or perish myself." He instantly started on his way, and as he proceeded, amid the confusion of the surrounding scene he calmly gathered up and placed in his wagon, a few stand of arms which had been left on the field by the retreating soldiers, and safely retired, with wagon, team and all, in the face of the victorious foe.

Some years ago a few benevolent individuals endeavored to procure him a pension, but without success. The Legislature of Pennsylvania, however, at the last session, granted him a donation of $40, which was all the gratuity he ever received for his revolutionary services.

It is a circumstance somewhat remarkable, that his wife, to whom he had been married up-wards of fifty years, and who attended his funeral in perfect health, suddenly expired about an hour after returning from his grave.

---

*The Norristown Free Press, January 15, 1834.

CANADIAN VIEW OF LOYALISTS

Perhaps 80,000 to 100,000 Loyalists left the colonies before and during the Revolution to go to Canada and other British territories. Their property and possessions were often confiscated or destroyed. They were often forced to flee for their lives. These new and unexpected settlers had an important impact on Canadian history. The following excerpt is from a contemporary Canadian history textbook.

> The Loyalists brought with them qualities and ideas which were toughened by hard experience. No country could have asked for pioneers more likely to succeed. They had a strong loyalty to the British flag, and at the same time a determination to enjoy the liberties and rights of self-government to which they had been accustomed. The variety of people among them is one of the things which interests us most—English, Scottish, Irish, and German families, representing districts in the Thirteen Colonies all the way from New England to western Pennsylvania. Most of them were humble and obscure people, many were from well educated and prominent families. Among them were soldiers and army officers, who brought a sense of discipline and organization. Others were men and women of force and experience whose influence could be seen everywhere in the life of their pioneer communities. Many of their descendants have shown the same high qualities of leadership, and it is no wonder that the Loyalist tradition has left in Canada an indelible impression.*

1. Based on this textbook excerpt, how do Canadians see Loyalists as an advantage?

2. In the long run, do you think the migration of Loyalists from the colonies was an advantage or a disadvantage to the United States? Why?

3. How were the Loyalists similar to a losing side in a civil war? Were Loyalists wrong in supporting the established government?

4. What rights should the opposition within a country have in time of war?

---

*George W. Brown, *Building the Canadian Nation*, rev. ed. (Toronto: J. M. Dent & Sons, 1958). Printed in Robert D. Barendsen, et al., *The American Revolution: Selections from Secondary School History Books of Other Nations* (Washington, D.C.: U.S. Department of Health, Education, and Welfare, 1976), p. 35.

TREATY OF PARIS

Treaty signed by Great Britain and the United States ending the American Revolution, 1783

1. "His Britannic Majesty acknowledges the said United States . . . to be free, sovereign, and independent States."

2. Boundaries shall run from Nova Scotia to and through the Great Lakes and the Lake of the Woods, "thence on a due west course to the river Mississippi, down the Mississippi to the thirty-first parallel, and then east to the Atlantic Ocean."

3. The people of the United States shall have fishing rights in the waters of British North America.

4. Creditors on either side "shall meet with no lawful impediments to the recovery of the full value, in sterling money, of all *bona fide* debts heretofore contracted...."

5. Congress "shall earnestly recommend to the legislatures of the respective States" that they make restitution for confiscated Loyalist property.

6. There shall be no future confiscations or prosecutions on account of the part anyone may have taken in the war.

7. Hostilities shall cease, and "His Britannic Majesty shall, with all convenient speed and without causing any destruction, or carrying away any negroes or other property of the American inhabitants, withdraw all his armies, garrisons and fleets from every post, place and harbour within the same."

1. Which provision was most important?

2. Which provisions may cause problems later?

3. Which provisions granted advantages to Great Britain?

4. Based on these provisions of the treaty, what were the concerns of each side? List them here:

British concerns   *American concerns*

REFLECTIONS ON THE AMERICAN REVOLUTION: UNION OF SOVIET SOCIALIST REPUBLICS

The peace was signed in 1783. The English recognized the independence of the colonies, 100,000 English aristocrats and members of their families were expelled from the United States, and their land was confiscated and put up for sale. That was the end of the war for independence that Lenin called the revolutionary war "of the American people against the plundering English, who had oppressed America and held it in colonial bondage."

Thus, during the Revolutionary War, in the course of a fierce class struggle, power in the United States passed from one class to another—from the aristocratic landowners to the commercial and industrial bourgeoisie of the North, which ruled in an alliance with the slaveowning planters of the South.

This signified that a bourgeois revolution had taken place in the United States. A republic was set up, the equality of all before the law was proclaimed, and slavery was gradually abolished in the northern States. But the capitalists and slaveowners took advantage of the people's victory to strengthen their own domination.

. . . the War for Independence did advance the development of the United States. The former English colonies became a republic. England was no longer able to hold back the development of American industry and trade. Customs were abolished among the former colonies, which now had become States, and this accelerated the development of trade relations. But since slavery had been preserved throughout the South, it subsequently, almost 100 years later, brought the United States to a new revolution, a civil war—the war between the North and the South.

---

*The material for Reproduction Pages 62a–62e is from *The American Revolution: Selections from Secondary School History Books of Other Nations.*

REFLECTIONS ON THE AMERICAN
REVOLUTION: MEXICO

The independence of the United States had an enormous effect in America and in Europe. The road to achieving liberty and the natural rights of man had been charted. The absolute monarchies and autocracy entered a period of decline.

The colonies of Hispanic America watched with interest the separation of the English colonies from their mother country. Creoles and mestizos felt their spirit of independence strengthen, but they were aware that it was not the opportune moment to rebel.

---

*The material for Reproduction Pages 62a–62e is from *The American Revolution: Selections from Secondary School History Books of Other Nations.*

REFLECTIONS ON THE AMERICAN
REVOLUTION: GHANA

The American colonies' successful struggle for independence was a revolution. It was the first time in modern times that a colony ruled from outside had rejected foreign rule and formed a nation of its own. Britain learned an important lesson from this. From that time onwards, Britain had a new attitude towards some of her colonies, such as Canada and, later, Australia, where her own people had settled. In their other colonies, however, the British repeated the mistake of keeping colonial rule for too long a time. This led to another revolution: the emergence of self-rule for the former Asian and African colonies.

---

*The material for Reproduction Pages 62a–62e is from *The American Revolution: Selections from Secondary School History Books of Other Nations.*

REFLECTIONS ON THE AMERICAN
REVOLUTION: PEOPLE'S REPUBLIC
OF CHINA

The war for American independence was a bourgeois revolution against colonial oppression and feudal oppression. It was the first revolution in American history.

The victory in the War for Independence enabled the 13 States in North America to cast off the bonds of British colonialism and become an independent and self-governing bourgeois democratic republic. All the injunctions promulgated by the British Government in the past were burned to ashes in the angry fire set by the revolutionary people. The economic structure and the social complexion of the colonial period were subjected to vast changes, and certain vestiges of feudalism were swept away. The 13 States were politically united into one entity, thereby promoting the development of a national economy.

In *Das Kapital,* Marx pointed out: "The war for American independence in the 18th century sounded an alarm for the bourgeoisie of Europe." The war for American independence awakened Europe and hastened the outbreak of the French bourgeois revolution.

The war for American independence provided a successful precedent for the colonial independence and national liberation movements of the oppressed peoples. Under its impact, in the early part of the 19th century the people of Latin America successively launched revolutionary struggles against Spanish and Portuguese colonial rule and established, one after another, more than 20 independent nations. . . .

As a bourgeois revolution against colonial oppression and feudal oppression, the war for American independence had a great progressive significance in American history, but at the same time it also had the limitations of a bourgeois revolution. A bourgeois revolution is really only one exploiting group replacing another in seizing and holding power. The victory in the war for American independence only enabled the bourgeoisie and the plantation slaveowners to grasp political power, while the broad masses of the people were still relegated to an exploited and oppressed status.

The popular masses are the masters of history. During the war for American independence, workers, handicraftsmen, farmers, and Negroes made up the vast majority of the working people in the population. They not only opposed the British colonial rule, but they also wanted to push the revolution to a still higher stage.

The American people are a great people. They have a revolutionary tradition. At present, they are in a state of new awakening. We believe that the American people will make still greater contributions to the cause of human progress in the future.

---

*The material for Reproduction Pages 62a–62e is from *The American Revolution: Selections from Secondary School History Books of Other Nations.*

REFLECTIONS ON THE
AMERICAN REVOLUTION:
GREAT BRITAIN

Even had the British won the war in America the political problem would have remained acute. A settlement on British terms would have left unsatisfied deep-seated American aspirations, further sharpened as these would have been by the struggle. And even if the situation could have been kept under control for the time being, for how long would this have been possible? The population of the colonies was doubling itself about every thirty years—a far higher rate of increase than that in the mother country. There were no population-statistics in the eighteenth century, but the general trend was clearly recognized. The significance of this dynamic aspect of the colonial problem appears entirely to have escaped the attention of the ministers. Time and again they said in effect: "We must assert British authority now, or it will be too late." But they failed to face the problem, how this authority was to be maintained under foreseeable future conditions. The object for which they led their country into war was, in the long run, incapable of fulfillment. Herein lay an ultimate proof of their lack of statesmanship.

---

*The material for Reproduction Pages 62a–62e is from *The American Revolution: Selections from Secondary School History Books of Other Nations.*

IDEAS ABOUT GOVERNMENT

Check the column that best expresses your opinion about each statement: *strongly agree, agree, disagree, strongly disagree.*

	Strongly Agree	Agree	Disagree	Strongly Disagree
1. Sometimes, government should be able to force people to do things that they may not want to do.	____	____	____	____
2. Government often knows what is best for people.	____	____	____	____
3. A government should never be changed by force or violence.	____	____	____	____
4. The best government is one that governs least.	____	____	____	____
5. Too much freedom is a dangerous thing.	____	____	____	____
6. Leaders of the government should be the best and the brightest people.	____	____	____	____
7. People need laws to regulate their behavior.	____	____	____	____
8. All politicians are dishonest.	____	____	____	____
9. The national government should have greater power than state governments.	____	____	____	____
10. People have some rights simply because they are human beings.	____	____	____	____

Write a statement that describes your ideas about government and what it should be.

POWERS OF GOVERNMENT

Check the column that best expresses your opinion about each statement: *strongly agree, agree, disagree, strongly disagree.*

	Strongly Agree	Agree	Disagree	Strongly Disagree

Government should be able to:

1. take money from people to run the government

2. prevent businesses from buying and selling any way they want

3. regulate how people use the land

4. encourage people to have certain beliefs

5. force people to serve in the army

6. establish qualifications for doctors

7. create jobs for people out of work

8. ban books, guns, marijuana, the death penalty

9. conduct investigations by listening to telephone conversations

10. force people to attend school

Prove your point. Select three statements from the above list and find a section in the Constitution that proves that it can or cannot be done.

341

QUESTIONNAIRE ABOUT THE
CONSTITUTION AND THE GOVERNMENT

This questionnaire is based on statements about the U.S. Constitution and government. Based on *your* opinion, check the blank space for *agree, disagree,* or *uncertain.*

Agree	*Disagree*	*Uncertain*		
_____	_____	_____	1.	It would be illegal to make a complete, total change in our system of government.
_____	_____	_____	2.	The power to govern should be divided and shared among several parts of the government.
_____	_____	_____	3.	The government should have the power to make all laws that are needed and proper.
_____	_____	_____	4.	Every citizen should be guaranteed protection against unfair actions of the government.
_____	_____	_____	5.	Every state should have equal voting power with every other state.
_____	_____	_____	6.	The courts should have the final say in determining the constitutionality of laws.
_____	_____	_____	7.	The main job of the president should be to make new laws.
_____	_____	_____	8.	The president should be able to take any action he thinks best for the country.
_____	_____	_____	9.	Any citizen should be able to hold any government position.
_____	_____	_____	10.	The Constitution is the highest law in the country.
_____	_____	_____	11.	The president must belong to the Republican or Democratic party.
_____	_____	_____	12.	Supreme Court Justices should be appointed by the president.

ANALYZING THE ARTICLES OF CONFEDERATION

Issue	Articles of Confederation	Problems and Possible Solutions
Legislative branch	one-house (unicameral) Congress	
Voting power	one vote for each state	
Representatives	chosen by state legislatures; one-year terms, each state must send 2 or more delegates; the agreement of at least 9 states is needed to decide issues of war, peace, money	
Powers of Congress	decide war and peace appoint military officers request money and men from states send and receive ambassadors enter into treaties and alliances establish post office coin and borrow money on credit of country fix weights and measures regulate Indian affairs settle disputes between states	
Executive powers	exercised by special committees elected by Congress officials to be appointed by Congress to manage affairs	
Judicial powers	Congress shall appoint special committees to consider these	
Supremacy	each state sovereign, free, and independent	
Rights of the people	none noted	

CREATING A CONSTITUTION

The job of your committee is to write part of a constitution, the basic law of a country. It should be written very clearly to prevent any confusion. Each of the main sections should be numbered. Answer the questions for your committee and any others that you think are important to include.

Committee on General Government

1. Should there be both state and national governments? Laws?
2. What jobs and responsibilities should the government handle?
3. If there is a federal system, state and national government, what powers should belong to each?

Committee on the Executive

1. Who or what should be responsible for carrying out the laws of the country? Committee appointed by a Congress? Monarch? President?
2. What qualifications should the leader(s) have (sex, age, race, nationality, religion, education, experience, citizenship, etc.)?
3. What powers should the leader(s) have? How should these powers be limited?
4. How should the leader(s) get his or her position? How long should he or she hold the position?

Committee on the Legislature

1. How should the national lawmaking body be organized? Should there be one lawmaking body? Two? Should larger states have a greater say than smaller ones?
2. How should members of the lawmaking body be selected, or elected? If elected, who votes? If appointed, by whom?
3. What qualifications should members of the legislative body have? How long should their term of office last?

Committee on the Court System

1. What powers should the courts have? Should they be able to overrule government actions?
2. How should judges get their positions? How long should their term of office last? What qualifications should they have?
3. How many and what type of courts should be established?

Committee on Rights

1. What rights of the people should be protected?
2. What rights, if any, should be included in the Constitution?

U.S. CONSTITUTION—A BUNDLE OF COMPROMISES?*

Listed below are several problems that had to be solved in writing the Constitution of the United States. Two possible solutions are given, and space is provided for you to write in any other solution. How did the members of the Constitutional Convention actually solve each of these problems? Check the correct answer or write in what the Constitution actually states.

1. How shall representatives be counted in the national legislature?

    _____ one state, one vote
    _____ representation based on population
    _____ other:

2. How shall slaves be counted?

    _____ count slaves for representation but not for taxes
    _____ count slaves for taxes but not for representation
    _____ other:

3. How much control over commerce (trade) shall the national government have?

    _____ Congress shall regulate trade
    _____ the States shall regulate trade
    _____ other:

4. What kind of executive branch shall there be?

    _____ many people in the executive branch
    _____ one person chosen by Congress
    _____ other:

5. What kind of judicial branch shall there be?

    _____ no permanent federal courts
    _____ strong federal courts to settle all disputes
    _____ other:

---

*Based on an idea originally presented by Harry Hutson, "Smith Teaches the Constitution," *News and Notes on the Social Sciences* (Winter 1976-77), pp. 6-8.

THE VIRGINIA PLAN

Delegates from Virginia to the Constitutional Convention introduced nineteen resolutions outlining a plan of government. Some of the important resolutions are listed below. What arguments would be offered for or against each resolution by representatives from the state of:

Representatives from states for first Congress:

New Hampshire—3	New York—6	Virginia—10
Massachusetts—8	New Jersey—4	North Carolina—5
Rhode Island—1	Pennsylvania—8	South Carolina—5
Connecticut—5	Delaware—1	Georgia—3
	Maryland—6	

Virginia Plan

1. A national government ought to be established consisting of a Supreme Legislature, Judiciary, and Executive.

2. The national Legislature ought to consist of Two Branches.

3. The Members of the first branch of the national Legislature ought to be elected by the People of the several States.

4. The Members of the second branch of the national Legislature ought to be chosen by the individual Legislatures.

5. A national Executive be instituted to consist of a Single Person.

6. A national Judiciary be established to consist of One supreme Tribunal.

7. The national Legislature be empowered to appoint inferior Tribunals.

DELEGATES AND CONSTITUTIONAL ISSUES

Delegate	Representation	Slavery	Rights	Federalism
Roger Sherman Connecticut	favors representation by population and by state	opposes but fears walkout by southern states		
Elbridge Gerry Massachusetts			fearful of democracy and common person	
Luther Martin Maryland	favors small states	opposes slave trade	favors a bill of rights	leading advocate of states' rights
William Paterson New Jersey	proposes small state plan of representation			
Alexander Hamilton New York	favors a House of Lords appointed for life and elected House of Commons		bill of rights unnecessary	abolish states; favors monarchy
Benjamin Franklin Pennsylvania	favors representation based on population			favors strong national government
James Madison Virginia		opposes slave trade		favors strong national government
George Mason Virginia		opposes slave trade	favors bill of rights	

Delegate	Representation	Slavery	Rights	Federalism
Edmund Randolph Virginia	proposes large-state plan of representation based on population			favors strong but limited national government
George Washington Virginia				favors strong national government
John Rutledge South Carolina		defends slave trade and threatens to walk out	favors bill of rights	

BIOGRAPHICAL OUTLINE—CONSTITUTIONAL CONVENTION

1. Name_____ Delegate from_____

2. Date and place of birth _____

3. Education _____

4. Occupation _____

5. Public positions_____

_____

6. Most notable comments or actions at Constitutional Convention_____

_____

_____

_____

_____

7. Other interests and achievements_____

_____

_____

8. Date and place of death_____

Bibliography_____

_____

QUALIFICATIONS FOR BEING PRESIDENT

Qualifications for being president. Should the following qualifications be a factor in choosing a president? In the space at the left, indicate "yes" it should be a factor, or "no" it should not be. In the space to the right, place what you think should be the requirements.

yes	no	Should this be a factor in choosing a president?
____	____	1. age _____
____	____	2. marital status _____
____	____	3. religion _____
____	____	4. education _____
____	____	5. male/female _____
____	____	6. occupation _____
____	____	7. personal appearance _____
____	____	8. residence (location) _____
____	____	9. wealth _____
____	____	10. personality _____
____	____	11. race/nationality _____
____	____	12. mental/physical fitness _____
____	____	13. political party _____
____	____	14. others (what?) _____

1. Which factors do you think are most important? Least important?

2. How are qualifications actually determined?

3. Which presidents do you think come closest to your qualifications?

4. Which presidents had serious handicaps to overcome?

5. Agree or disagree. Over the years, the process of determining who would be president has led to the selection of the best people for the job.

SUPREME COURT CASES

Supreme Court cases have important consequences. The titles of some cases are listed below. Select one and prepare a report using the following outline:

OUTLINE FOR REPORT ON COURT CASES

1. Facts
2. Issues and arguments
3. Decision and reasons
4. Importance
5. Bibliography

Powers of Government

Marbury v. *Madison,* 1803   judicial review
McCulloch v. *Maryland,* 1819   constitutionality of Bank of United States
Gibbons v. *Ogden,* 1824   federal regulation of trade
Worcester v. *Georgia,* 1832   jurisdiction over Cherokees

Citizenship

Dred Scott v. *Sanford,* 1857   slavery and property
Korematsu v. *United States,* 1944   Japanese internment

Legal Rights

Gideon v. *Wainwright,* 1963   right to counsel
Miranda v. *Arizona,* 1966   pretrial rights
In re Gault, 1967   juvenile rights

Freedom of Religion

West Virginia State Board of Education v. *Barnette,* 1943   flag salute
Abington v. *Schempp,* 1963   prayers in school
United States v. *Seeger,* 1965   conscientious objector

Freedom of Expression

Gitlow v. *New York*, 1925	anarchy law
Dennis v. *United States*, 1951	anticommunism
New York Times v. *Sullivan*, 1964	libel
Tinker v. *Des Moines School District*, 1969	student armband
United States v. *New York Times, Washington Post*, 1971	censorship and national security

Equal Opportunity

Plessy v. *Ferguson*, 1896	separate but equal
Brown v. *Board of Education*, 1954	segregation

BILL OF RIGHTS CASES

Read each of the following cases and decide if they violate the Bill of Rights, the first ten amendments. After each case, write the number of the amendment and the appropriate phrases that prove the case is a violation or not.

1. A man is arrested for armed robbery. He spends three years in prison waiting for his trial. He complains.

2. A man is tried and found not guilty of murder. A year later new evidence is discovered indicating the probable guilt of the man. A new trial is ordered. He objects.

3. A newspaper obtains documents that the government wants to keep secret. The newspaper plans to publish the documents, and the government demands that they do not do it. The case goes to court.

4. A well-known member of an organized crime syndicate is being tried for loan-sharking and extortion. The district attorney forces him to take the stand and testify. He refuses to answer questions.

5. It is wartime and the president fears there are spies in Washington, D.C. He orders several people arrested and placed in jail until the war is over.

6. A town needs more land around the high school. A man's property is needed, but he wants to keep it. The town forces him to sell and gives him twice the property's actual value. He sues to get his land back.

7. A man is arrested in a pool hall for stealing automobiles. He is tried and found guilty. In jail he complains that he did not have a lawyer.

8. Police agents secretly search the house of a murder suspect and find a pistol. It is used as evidence during the trial. The suspect says the police had no right to do that.

9. A man runs down and kills a person with his car. The district attorney calls it first-degree murder, and on this basis the man is brought to trial. The man's lawyer says his client is being treated unfairly.

10. A well-known movie star is accused of killing her husband. The judge is afraid she will not get a fair trial and orders the courtroom closed to the media and the public. Newspaper editorials claim this order is unconstitutional.

RIGHTS GUARANTEED UNDER THE BILL OF RIGHTS

Write the number of the amendment to the Constitution that guarantees each of the rights listed below. Give at least one reason why you think the right exists.

Amendment	*Right guaranteed*	*Reason*
_____	freedom of religion	_____
_____	freedom of speech	_____
_____	freedom of the press	_____
_____	to peaceably attend meetings	_____
_____	to petition the government	_____
_____	to keep and bear arms	_____
_____	fair treatment when accused of a crime	_____
_____	privacy	_____
_____	to go free on bail while waiting to be tried	_____
_____	to a speedy, public trial by a fair jury	_____
_____	freedom from cruel and unusual punishment	_____
_____	to enjoy other rights not described in the Constitution	_____

THE BILL OF RIGHTS IN SCHOOL

The Constitution and especially the first ten amendments protect the rights of all Americans. But these rights are subject to many interpretations. Based on your understanding of the Constitution, check whether you *agree* or *disagree* with the following statements.

Agree   *Disagree*

_____   _____   1. Everyone has the constitutional *right* to a free, public education.

_____   _____   2. No person should be forced to attend school against his will.

_____   _____   3. Censorship of any kind violates basic American principles of freedom of speech and press.

_____   _____   4. The school day should begin with a nondenominational prayer.

_____   _____   5. Students should be able to read anything they want in school.

_____   _____   6. Students should be able to publish anything they want in the school newspaper.

_____   _____   7. Students should be able to picket, write petitions, or demonstrate against decisions made by school teachers or principals.

_____   _____   8. Students should be able to criticize teachers or principals without fear of punishment.

_____   _____   9. No one has the right to enter a student's locker without a search warrant.

_____   _____   10. Students should be able to hear evidence, call witnesses, and have a speedy, public trial by their peers for violating school regulations.

_____   _____   11. The right of an individual to use a library should not be denied or limited for any reason.

——— ———   12. Books that contain objectionable materials should be kept out
                  of schools or rewritten.

——— ———   13. School libraries should not have books that promote one
                  religion over another, criticize race or nationality, are written
                  by communists, or have obscene language.

——— ———   14. Paddling disorderly students is a fair and reasonable punishment.

——— ———   15. There should be no rules that discriminate between men and
                  women.

QUESTIONS FROM THE U.S. CONSTITUTION

1. What are six reasons why the U.S. Constitution was written?
2. What part of the government makes laws?
3. What is the term of office for a member of the House of Representatives?
4. What is the age requirement for being a member of the House of Representatives?
5. How are vacancies filled in the House of Representatives?
6. What part of the government has the power of impeachment?
7. How many senators does each state have?
8. What is the term of office for a senator?
9. What is the age requirement for being a senator?
10. What other job is held by the president of the Senate?
11. What part of the government has the power to try impeachments?
12. Who conducts the impeachment trial of a president?
13. How often must Congress meet?
14. What is a quorum?
15. Who decides how to conduct the meetings in each house?
16. Can a congressman be arrested on his way to a meeting of Congress?
17. Can a senator receive a higher rate of pay if he is appointed to another government position?
18. In which house do bills to raise money start?
19. What happens to a bill that the president refuses to sign?
20. What branch of government has the power to tax?
21. What group of people within the United States can have their trade with others regulated by Congress?
22. Who decided that the United States would go on a metric system?
23. What branch of government can create more courts?
24. What branch of government can declare war?
25. Congress has the power to make all laws which shall be_____ and_____.
26. When can a write of *habeas corpus* be suspended?
27. What does the Constitution prohibit Americans from accepting?
28. What are three qualifications for being elected president?
29. Can the president's salary be changed while he is in office?
30. When he is sworn into office, what does the president promise to do?
31. In what cases can the President *not* grant reprieves and pardons?
32. What percentage of the Senate must approve treaties?
33. What are causes for impeachment and conviction of a president?
34. How long do judges hold their jobs?
35. In what cases does the Supreme Court have original jurisdiction (hear a case for the first time)?
36. What is the definition of treason against the United States?
37. What form of government is guaranteed to every state?
38. What part of government decides how new states are admitted?
39. How many members of both houses are needed to propose amendments to the Constitution?
40. What test will never be required to hold office in the United States?
41. How many states originally had to ratify the Constitution?
42. Who was the president of the Constitutional Convention?

CONSTITUTIONAL AMENDMENTS

In which amendment do you find the following information?

Amendment   *Information*

_____	1. being witness against yourself
_____	2. taking life, liberty, or property without due process of law
_____	3. being tried twice for the same crime
_____	4. taking private property for public use
_____	5. right to keep weapons
_____	6. freedom of religion
_____	7. guarantee against unreasonable search and seizure
_____	8. freedom of speech and press
_____	9. cruel and unusual punishment
_____	10. freedom to peaceably assemble and petition the government
_____	11. right to a speedy and public trial
_____	12. powers reserved to the states or the people
_____	13. right to call witnesses and have an attorney
_____	14. right of trial by jury
_____	15. president and vice-president cannot be from the same state
_____	16. right to vote cannot be denied because of race or color
_____	17. power to tax money earned by people
_____	18. slavery outlawed
_____	19. senators to be directly elected by the people
_____	20. right to vote cannot be denied because of sex
_____	21. right to vote for eighteen-year-olds
_____	22. due process and equal protection of the law
_____	23. repeals another amendment
_____	24. limits president to two terms of office or ten years
_____	25. president can appoint a vice-president
_____	26. right to vote cannot be denied for failing to pay tax
_____	27. resignation of president
_____	28. prohibits making, selling, or transporting intoxicating liquors
_____	29. provides electors for the District of Columbia
_____	30. freedom of the press

A LIFETIME OF CHANGE*

Imagine a boy who was born in 1789 when Washington was sworn in as president, and lived to be seventy-six, when Lincoln was assassinated. Our boy, whom we shall call James, was fourteen years old when Jefferson purchased the Louisiana Territory and doubled the size of the country. James could be a black-smith or a bootmaker. Or he could be a clerk in a village store, or studying for the ministry. But probably, like most, he was a farmer.

As a young man he is likely to marry a girl who lives nearby. They will have five or six children. If he is lucky he may have purchased land in addition to what his father gave him to get started. The temptation to move west where there is cheap and fertile soil has crossed his mind on more than one occasion.

By the time he is in his late thirties or early forties, his children begin to leave home. There are opportunities elsewhere, and they don't want the drudgery of tilling the soil. New institutions are emerging and so are new problems. Even in his own village James can see the changes taking place. The population has increased in number and variety. Jobs that his father would have done are now handled by craftsmen, who often do it better and faster than he would have done. James's wife no longer makes soap or candles but buys them at a store that has products from as far away as China. It is necessary to rely more and more on money and less and less on exchanging his goods and services for what he needs.

James's youngest son attends a public school for a good part of the year. When he's older he'll head for gold in California and never be heard from again. Textile mills have made their appearance in a nearby town. James doesn't like the mills, but two of his daughters have left home to become weavers there. He doesn't realize it, but he is witnessing the birth of what people will later call the *industrial revolution.* His youngest daughter may live until the turn of the century, by which time the United States will be producing more manufactured goods than any other country in the world.

Many other innovations occur during James's lifetime—the Erie Canal, clipper ships, steamboats, railroads, telegraph, anesthesia, a mechanical reaper, and a water supply system for the entire city of New York. He also sees the beginning of genuinely American schools of literature, art, and music. The first oil well is drilled; the Bessemer process of making steel is developed; and labor unions are formed. Before he dies, he'll see his country take land from Mexico and reach peaceful agreements with Britain. But the nation has been troubled throughout these years and cannot exist half slave and half free. After four years of bloody Civil War, the Union continues without slavery. New conflicts develop. But that's for James's children and grandchildren to worry about.

It is fashionable to think of our own era as a time of rapid change. Some say we might not be able to make appropriate adjustments to preserve our society. The dilemma of coping with rapid change has been de-scribed in recent years as "future shock." But if we consider the changes that occurred in a single lifetime, such as James's, we may gain a better perspective of our own time. Of all the traditions that have character-ized American life over more than two centuries, perhaps the most important and the most enduring is the tradition of change.

*Adapted from Fran Pratt, "Children and Youth in Early America" (mimeo) (Old Sturbridge Village, Sturbridge, Mass.; 1975). Used with permission of the author.

THE UNITED STATES IN MID-NINETEENTH CENTURY*

1. The United States form one government, compromising thirty-one states, six territories, and one federal district. They occupy the most valuable and productive part of North America, and rank among the most powerful, commercial, and wealthy nations of the globe.

2. They are distinguished for the freedom and excellence of their political institutions, the rapid increase of the population, and for the intelligence, industry, and enterprise of the inhabitants.

6. Agriculture is the leading pursuit in this country. The eastern states are devoted to grazing, and the dairy; the middle and western to the raising of wheat, Indian corn, &c.; and the southern states, to cotton, tobacco, sugar, and rice. Slave labour is chiefly employed in the southern and some of the western states.

9. The commerce is, next to that of Great Britain, the largest in the world; it extends to all parts of the earth, and embraces the products and manufacture of all nations.

11. The whale fishery alone employs upwards of 600 vessels, and 16,000 men. The ships employed in this important business are absent frequently two and three years at a time.

12. No part of the world presents such an extensive inland commerce as that of the United States. Steam vessels navigate all the principal rivers, lakes, bays, &c. The Mississippi river and its tributaries alone are traversed by near 400 steamboats, all of which make several voyages every year.

13. The employment of Steam Power is probably greater in the country than in any other part of the world, and forms one of the principal elements of American prosperity....

14. The Americans have surpassed all other nations in the number and extent of their canals and rail-roads; the united length of the former is not less than 4,000 miles, the whole of which, with one or two exceptions, have been executed in less than twenty years.

*S. Augustus Mitchell, *A System of Modern Geography* (Philadelphia: Thomas, Cowperthwait & Co., 1852), pp. 98–103.

15. The rail-roads, all constructed since the year 1829, amount to an aggregate of 9,000 miles, over which carriages are propelled by locomotive steam-engines at the rate of from 20 to 30 miles an hour.

16. The United States are more distinguished for the general diffusion of knowledge, than for eminence in literature and science. Common school education is more widely extended than in any other part of the world. . . .

25. The inhabitants of the United States amount to almost twenty-two millions, of which the black or coloured races form one-sixth part. The Indians number about 400,000, but are not usually considered as forming a part of the population of the union.

THE RIGHT TO DISAGREE

When John Adams was president, France and England were at war. The United States wanted to remain neutral and carry on trade with all foreign countries. Neither France nor England accepted this, and both attacked U.S. merchant ships.

Within the United States people took sides. Some wanted to help the British. Some wanted to help the French. President Adams and most of the Congress favored the British. Vice-President Thomas Jefferson and his followers favored the French.

Articles appeared in newspapers criticizing Adams and the government. Many articles favored Jefferson and the French. Adams was furious. In 1798 Congress passed laws which limited what people could say and write about the government. It became a crime to publish false, dishonorable, or critical comments about the President or Congress. If anyone committed this crime they could be fined $2,000 and put in jail for two years. Nothing was said about the vice-president, so the law did not apply to criticism of Jefferson.

A congressman from Vermont said President Adams had a continual grasp for power and that he was selfish and a show-off. He was fined $1,000 and imprisoned for four months. A newspaper reporter in Philadelphia criticized Adams and was fined $400 and imprisoned for six months. Two other men said they wanted Jefferson to be president and were fined and put in prison. When President Adams visited in New Jersey, cannon filled with wads of cotton instead of cannonballs were shot off in his honor and as a protest. Someone in the audience said he hoped one of the cotton wads would hit the president in the seat of his pants. He was fined $100.

1. Assume you oppose Adams. What would you say or do?

2. Knowing that the Constitution protects freedom of speech and press, what arguments could Adams and his supporters make to defend their position?

---

*Adapted from material originally compiled by Sharon W. Lyons, Bret Harte Junior High School, Oakland, California, 1967.

CAN A STATE TAX THE NATIONAL GOVERNMENT?

A Bank of the United States became a reality in 1791. The idea was first suggested by Alexander Hamilton, and now, several years later, even Thomas Jefferson had to admit it was a success. The United States became prosperous and gained the respect of other nations. People had faith in the money system of the country.

The Bank was also causing problems. It was making its wealthy owners even richer. Most of these men lived in the North, which was already the wealthiest area of the country. The planters and farmers of the South and West were not sharing in the success of the bank. It was seen as a *money power* and called "The Monster."

Maryland decided to take action. The state passed a law to tax the bank. A bank employee in Baltimore, James McCulloch, refused to pay the tax to the state of Maryland. The state sued McCulloch and the bank, and the case went to the Supreme Court.

How would you decide?

1. Is it constitutional for Congress to establish a bank?

2. Is it constitutional for the state to tax the bank?

3. What are the consequences of your decision?

ANDREW JACKSON SPEAKS OUT

1. Jackson vetoes the bill to recharter the Bank of the United States.

> It is to be regretted that the rich and powerful too often bend the acts of government to their selfish purposes. Distinctions in society will always exist under every just government. Equality of talents, of education, or of wealth, can not be produced by human institutions. In the full enjoyment of the rights of Heaven and the fruits of superior industry, economy, and virtue, every man is equally entitled to protection by law; but when the laws undertake to add to these natural and just advantages artificial distinctions, to grant titles, gratuities, and exclusive privileges, to make the rich richer and the potent more powerful, the humble members of society—the farmers, mechanics, and laborers—who have neither the time nor the means of securing like favors to themselves, have a right to complain of the injustice. . . .

2. Accepts the idea in politics, first practiced by Thomas Jefferson, of, "To the victor belongs the spoils."

3. Statement on South Carolina's nullification ordinance: "I consider the power to annul a law of the United States, assumed by one State, incompatible with the existence of the Union, contradicted expressly by the letter of the Constitution, unauthorized by its spirit, inconsistent with every principle on which it was founded, and destructive of the great object for which it was formed."

4. Toast given to indicate views about states' rights and national government: "Our Federal union—it must and shall be preserved.

5. After Chief Justice John Marshall and the Supreme Court ruled that the relocation of Cherokee Indians from their homelands in Georgia was unconstitutional, Jackson is reported to have said: "John Marshall has made his decision; now let him enforce it."

Common Man   *Dictator*

DAVY CROCKETT'S FIRST SPEECH*

Davy Crockett was a member of the Tennessee legislature—a green and gawky gentleman from one of the remote counties. He tells us how he behaved to a brother member, who had alluded to the new-comer as the "gentleman from the cane." His story shows that private combat was then regarded as a thing entirely of course when men differed:

"Well," says Crockett, "I had never made a speech in my life. I didn't know whether I could speak or not; and they kept crying out to me "Crockett, answer him—Crockett, answer him:— why the deuce don't you answer him?" So up I popped. I was as mad as fury; and there I stood and not a word could I get out. Well, I bothered, and stammered, and looked foolish, and still there I stood; but after a while I began to talk. I don't know what I said about my *bill*, but I jerked it into him. I told him that he had got hold of the wrong man; that he didn't know who he was fooling with; that he reminded me of the meanest thing on God's earth, an old coon dog barking up the wrong tree.

"After the House had adjourned, seeing Mr. M— walking off alone, I followed him and proposed a walk. He consented, and we went something like a mile, when I called a halt. Said I, 'M—, do you know what I brought you here for?' 'No.' 'Well, I brought you here for the express purpose of whipping you, and I mean to do it.' But the fellow said he didn't mean anything, and kept 'pologising, till I got into a good humor. We then went back together; and I don't believe anybody ever knew anything about it."

1. Does this story accurately reflect American views of frontiersmen?

2. What purposes do such stories—true or not—serve?

3. What values are represented in this story?

4. Can you think of other stories and legends in U.S. history?

---

*James Parton, *Life of Andrew Jackson* (New York: Mason Brothers, 1861), p. 257.

THE TARIFF ISSUE (SOUTHERN)

We are at a critical point in the competition with foreign cotton. We risk the loss of the British market if we stop taking the manufactures of Great Britain. She will certainly stop taking our cotton to the same extent. It is a settled principle of her policy to purchase from those nations who receive her manufactures. Her surplus capital and labor must be directed to manufactures, or remain idle and unproductive. A demand for her products is the primary consideration in determining her commercial relations. Britain is not blind to her own needs. She needs the foreign market for her goods. A tariff restricting the sale of her products here will be the end of our trade with her and the destruction of our commerce.

Europe will take as much cotton as we produce. They will only be limited by the amount of goods they are able to sell here. If a tariff reduces imports by 20 millions, they will buy 20 millions less of cotton. What we gain will be quickly sacrificed and the burden will be on the southern planter. He will lose his market for cotton as a consequence of unjust restrictions imposed upon lawful trade by the suicidal policy of his own government.

This law restricting the commerce of the southern states is obviously calculated and intended to promote the interest of the northern manufacturers.

*Based on an account in J.T. Headley, *The Great Rebellion: A History of the Civil War in the United States 1864–1866* (Hartford, Conn.: Hurlbut, Scranton & Co.)

THE TARIFF ISSUE (WESTERN)

The opposition to the tariff comes from the commercial interests on the seaboard and the cotton and tobacco interests in the south—one afraid that it will decrease its business and the other afraid that Europe will cease to purchase their cotton and tobacco. These two powerful interests have governed this nation and dictated its policy. The interior and the West, until lately, have had to submit. We now claim the right of full participation in our government.

Look at the effects of this policy, this system of free trade. Our government is the cheapest, freest, and best on earth; we have every advantage of climate, situation, and soil; yet we are filled with misery and wretchedness, embarrassment, bankruptcy, and ruin. Agriculture is depressed, manufactures ruined, and commerce scarcely able to keep its head above water. Why is this? It is the result of our own present ruinous policy. It is because the national industry is unprotected. Because we looked to Europe instead of our own resources to supply our needs. Because we buy from abroad almost everything we eat, drink, and wear. All the great interests of the nation are at their lowest point, struggling for life. This land of freedom, home of liberty, is cast with gloom. Could there be any doubt as to the cause?

*Based on an account in J.T. Headley, *The Great Rebellion: A History of the Civil War in the United States 1864–1866* (Hartford, Conn.: Hurlbut, Scranton & Co.)

THE TARIFF ISSUE (NORTHERN)

Are particular manufacturers protected and promoted by a tariff on foreign goods? Is it necessary? Can it be done without injustice to other types of industry?

Some say no nation has attained prosperity without encouraging manufacturing. But I ask, what nation ever reached prosperity without promoting foreign trade? These interests —manufacturing and trade—need to flourish together. The tariff will enable us to collect revenue while giving advantages to those manufacturers we may think most useful to promote at home.

And to what interests will a tariff cause distress? There will be a considerable falling off in the ships employed in foreign trade. But let it be remembered that our shipping makes its own way in competition with the whole world. It succeeds, not by aid of the government, but by patience, vigilance, toil.

Failures and bankruptcies have taken place in our large cities. A tariff will not solve all these problems but will help reduce the losses and disasters of commerce.

---

*Based on an account in J.T. Headley, *The Great Rebellion: A History of the Civil War in the United States 1864–1866* (Hartford, Conn.: Hurlbut, Scranton & Co.)

THE TARIFF ISSUE (NATIONALIST)

A dependence on foreign countries must lead to ruin. We need an American policy. Let us stimulate our industry. We need to protect our own interests by withdrawing support from foreign trade. This can be done by imposing a tariff on foreign goods. Even if it were true that American goods would be more expensive, it is better to have the goods being produced by American workers. Their employment will mean pay with which they will be able to make purchases. Without a job or money, cheap foreign goods are unobtainable. A government needs to remedy the evils it sees; it cannot let industry decay and people remain out of work. We need protection from the influence of foreigners by the establishment of a tariff. And what is this tariff? Nothing more than a tax on the produce of foreign industry, with a view toward promoting American industry.

---

*Based on an account in J.T. Headley, *The Great Rebellion: A History of the Civil War in the United States 1864–1866* (Hartford, Conn.: Hurlbut, Scranton & Co.)

SHOULD THERE BE SLAVERY IN THE TERRITORIES?

As the population of territories increased they applied for statehood. This led to difficulties between North and South over the question of admitting the territories as "free" states or "slave" states. When California applied, Congress tried to reach a compromise involving several isues. How would you resolve the following questions if you were in the U.S. Congress?

1. Should California be admitted as a state?

2. Should California be admitted as (a) slave state, (b) a free state, or (c) should the decision be left up to Californians?

3. How should Congress handle the slavery issue in the territory acquired from Mexico: (a) prohibit slavery, (b) provide for slavery, (c) leave it up to the inhabitants of the territory to decide?

4. Should slavery be allowed in the District of Columbia? Should the slave trade be allowed in the District of Columbia?

5. What should be done about the problem of slaves who run away to free states or territories?

SOME REASONS FOR NATIONAL ASSERTIVENESS

Statements about why conflicts occur between nations are listed below. Which are the most important and real reasons for conflict? Which are doubtful reasons?

	Causes of Conflict	
	Important and real	Probably doubtful
1. The spirit of the people, adventuresome, belligerent, is the popular position	____	____
2. Problems over an important issue. Unwillingness to compromise, determination to maintain some position, refusal to continue past arrangements	____	____
3. Economic need for land, resources, etc.	____	____
4. Political need to solve own problems of unemployment, depression, take people's minds off other problems	____	____
5. Rivalry between nations to gain power, position, alliances, land, wealth, etc.	____	____
6. Fill a vacuum where a weak government exists to prevent other problems from occurring later	____	____
7. Miscalculation or breakdown in communications so the other's intentions are not accurately known	____	____
8. Differences over political, social, philosophical, economic, religious beliefs used as basis for protecting own ideas	____	____
9. Changes in the established order of things causes need to return to the way things were	____	____
10. An upset in the *balance of power*, alliances with other countries, treaty arrangements, etc.	____	____
11. Save face, position is important, well known, and cannot be compromised	____	____
12. Unstable, aggressive, weak, strong, leadership	____	____

UNITED STATES–MEXICAN BORDER: THE LAND BETWEEN

At the invitation of the Mexican government, Americans settled in the province of Texas in the 1830s. The Americans established slavery, which was illegal under Mexican law. And they held religious views, customs, and traditions that were different from Mexico's. War broke out and the Texans eventually established an independent country. They were recognized by the United States and other countries, but Mexico considered them in rebellion and still part of Mexico. Southerners in the United States, especially, wanted to annex Texas to obtain additional lands for producing cotton and extending slavery. James K. Polk, a Democrat from Tennessee, ran for president on a platform favoring "the reoccupation of Oregon and the reannexation of Texas" and won a clear victory, indicating support for territorial expansion. Here are some of the events that took place between the United States and Mexico, as seen from each point of view.

Mexico	*United States*
1. Texas is not an independent nation. To annex it is a hostile act. If the United States takes Texas it could lead to war.	1. Texas is an independent nation. No country can interfere in the affairs of the United States. People in Texas, many former Americans, have asked to be annexed.

Mexico withdraws threat of war.
The United States annexes Texas.

2. Mexican territory extends beyond the Rio Grande as far north as the Nueces River.	2. U.S. territory extends beyond the Nueces River as far south as the Rio Grande.
3. Mexican public opinion is strongly against American efforts to take over Mexican land. Most admit that Mexican government is weak and poor.	3. U.S. President Polk sends John Slidell to negotiate with Mexico for land.

The United States is prepared to pay claims made
by American citizens against Mexican government
if Mexico recognizes Rio Grande as border; the
United States would also pay $5 million for
New Mexico, $20 million for California

4. Mexico sees real purpose of the United States to get California and New Mexico; refuse to see Slidell.

4. Polk feels war is justified; orders Gen. Zachary Taylor into disputed land between the Rio Grande and the Nueces River.

5. Mexican troops attack Americans between the Rio Grande and the Nueces River.

5. Polk says: "Mexico has invaded our territory and shed American blood upon American soil."

HOW TO SETTLE BOUNDARY DISPUTES

This case involves the United States and the country of _____

The area in dispute includes _____

_____

Directions: Each of the methods of settling disputes is a realistic possibility. Your task is to explain the advantages and disadvantages from the point of view of

Be prepared to explain which method you recommend.	Map showing the claims of both sides.
WAR. May be unavoidable. Neither side is willing to back down. Both feel they are right. Both feel they have a chance to win. Might be worth it.	ESCALATION. A buildup of power or show of force. Hope to scare or threaten other side.
ALLIANCES. Each side lines up friends. Each tries to keep the balance of power in its favor.	NEGOTIATIONS. Discuss problem and seek solutions. What is cause? What does each side want? What will each give up?

TREATIES. Written agreements following negotiations. How is problem solved?	ARBITRATION/ADJUDICATION. Neutral, outside person decides how to settle dispute. Both sides agree in advance to accept terms.

HOW TO SETTLE BOUNDARY DISPUTES*

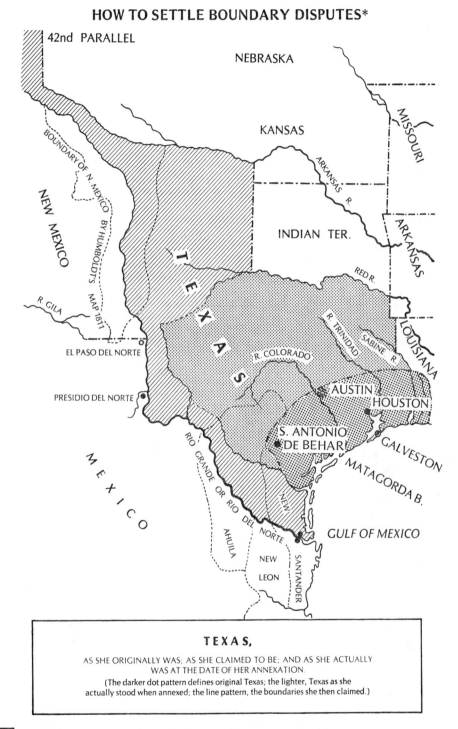

TEXAS,

AS SHE ORIGINALLY WAS; AS SHE CLAIMED TO BE; AND AS SHE ACTUALLY
WAS AT THE DATE OF HER ANNEXATION.

(The darker dot pattern defines original Texas; the lighter, Texas as she
actually stood when annexed; the line pattern, the boundaries she then claimed.)

*Horace Greeley, *The American Conflict* (Hartford, Conn.: O.D. Case & Co., 1865), p. 161.

SHOULD YOU OBEY UNJUST LAWS?

Henry David Thoreau states his opposition to the Mexican War and slavery in "Civil Disobedience," 1849:

> All men recognize the right of revolution; that is, the right to refuse allegiance to, and to resist, the government, when its tyranny or its inefficiency are great and unendurable. But almost all say that such is not the case now. (But a sixth of population are slaves and the country is overrunning and conquering another.)
>
> Those who, while they disapprove of the character and measure of a government, yield to it their allegiance and support are undoubtedly its most conscientious supporters, and so frequently the most serious obstacles to reform. Some are petitioning the state to dissolve the union, to disregard the requisition of the President. Why do they not dissolve it themselves,—the union between themselves and the state—and refuse to pay their quota into its treasury?
>
> Unjust laws exist: shall we be content to obey them, or shall we endeavor to amend them, and obey them until we have succeeded, or shall we transgress them at once? Men generally, under such a government as this, think that they ought to wait until they have persuaded the majority to alter them. They think that, if they should resist, the remedy would be worse than the evil. But it is the fault of the government that the remedy is worse than the evil. It makes it worse.
>
> Under a government which imprisons any unjustly, the true place for a just man is also a prison. The proper place today, the only place which Massachusetts has provided for her freer and less desponding spirits, is in her prisons, to be put out and locked out of the State by her own act, as they have already put themselves out by their principles. . . . A minority is powerless while it conforms to the majority; it is not even a minority then; but it is irresistible when it clogs by its whole weight. If the alternative is to keep all just men in prison or give up war and slavery, the State will not hesitate which to choose.

1. What is Thoreau's complaint?
2. When does the right of revolution exist?
3. What action should people take in this case?
4. Do you think Thoreau is *loyal*?
5. Where does a government get power to govern?
6. Is Thoreau suggesting a revolution?
7. Should you obey unjust laws?

Which of the following comes closest to your opinion:

_____ obey the law because you could be punished
_____ obey the law because you may be rewarded
_____ obey the law because it would please others
_____ obey the law because it is the law
_____ do what you want; individuals have rights in society
_____ do what your conscience says is right

WAS THE COTTON GIN TOO VALUABLE?

Eli Whitney writes a letter to Robert Fulton:

> The difficulties with which I have had to contend have originated, principally, in the want of a disposition in mankind to do justice. My invention was new and distinct from every other: it stood alone. It was not interwoven with anything before known; and it can seldom happen that an invention or improvement is so strongly marked and can be so clearly and specifically identified; and I have always believed that I should have had no difficulty in causing my rights to be respected, if it had been less valuable, and been used only by a small portion of the community. But the use of this machine being immensely profitable to almost every planter in the cotton districts, all were interested in trespassing upon the patent right.

1. Whitney thought he would have been better able to protect his patent rights if the cotton gin was less valuable and used by fewer people. Do you agree?

2. Are some inventions or discoveries so valuable or important that the inventor has an obligation to make it available?

3. Are some inventions or discoveries so dangerous that they should be kept secret or made illegal?

4. Whitney felt that his invention was "distinct from every other" and not connected with any other invention. What other inventions do you think "stand alone"?

5. The cotton gin did more harm than good. Explain why you agree or disagree.

IMPACT STATEMENT FOR SCIENTIFIC
OR SOCIAL CONTRIBUTIONS

1. Inventor or contributor:_____

2. Contribution:_____

3. Year, place, or other considerations: _____

_____

Interested or affected groups	Costs (Explain how and why this is a disadvantage)	Benefits (Explain how and why this is an advantage)

Impact statement. The short- and long-term consequences of this contribution, along with my comments and recommendations, are as follows:

WOMEN'S RIGHTS: ROOM FOR REFORM?

The delegates to a convention on women's rights, held in Seneca Falls, New York, in 1848, approved a Declaration of Independence listing their grievances. Some of these are listed below. Check the appropriate column based on what you know about women's rights *today*.

	Problem today	Not a problem	Ho hum!
1. Men have not permitted women to vote.			
2. Men have not allowed women to have a say in making laws.			
3. Women have no legal rights.			
4. Women have no property rights.			
5. In marriage ceremonies, women have to promise to obey their husbands.			
6. Men have monopolized nearly all profitable employment.			
7. Women receive less wages than men.			
8. Practically no women hold positions in theology, medicine, law.			
9. Women are denied a way of getting a thorough education; many colleges are closed to them.			

	Problem today	Not a problem	Ho hum!
10. Women are excluded from the ministry and are not allowed to participate in the affairs of some churches.			
11. Women are supposed to follow a different moral code than men.			
12. Men today try to destroy women's confidence in their own powers, lessen their self-respect, and make them dependent.			

SLAVERY IN MODERATION?

William Ellery Channing* writes a letter to Daniel Webster:

Boston, May 14, 1848

My Dear Sir:—I wish to call your attention to a subject of general interest.

A little while ago, Mr. Lundy, of Baltimore, the editor of a paper called "The Genius of Universal Emancipation," visited this part of the country to stir us up to the work of abolishing Slavery at the South; and the intention is to organize societies for this purpose. . . .

I know that our Southern brethren interpret every word from this region on the subject of Slavery as an expression of hostility. I would ask if they cannot be brought to understand us better and if we can do any good till we remove their misapprehensions. It seems to me that, before moving in this matter, we ought to say to them distinctly: "We consider Slavery as your calamity, not your crime; and we will share with you the burden of putting an end to it. . . ."

I throw out these suggestions merely to illustrate my views. We must first let the Southern States see that we are their friends in this affair; and we sympathize with them, and, from principles of patriotism and philantrophy, are willing to share the toil and expense of abolishing Slavery; or I fear our interference will avail nothing. . . .

Assume that you are (abolitionist) (plantation owner) (social scientist today). Write a letter replying to Channing. Explain your views about: (a) abolitionists and their methods, (b) the feelings and actions of plantation owners, and (c) how the problem of slavery can best be solved.

*Horace Greeley, The American Conflict (Hartford, Conn.: O.D. Case & Co., 1865), p. 353.

KEEPING THE SLAVE SYSTEM

Several statements justifying the slave system are listed below. Which do you think are most important to the *plantation owner?* Place a number 1 alongside the most important, a number 2 alongside the next most important, and so on.

Ranking		
self	*group*	*The plantation owner wants to keep the slave system because:*
_____	_____	There is no better alternative. Slaves are better off in the South than they would be in Africa. Sending them back would be expensive and unpopular. Freeing them would cause some to rise up against their masters. It would lead to murder or idleness.
_____	_____	The system is valuable. Slave labor gives value to the land and the economy of the South and entire country. Without it the South would be a poor wasteland and the country would lose its economic standing.
_____	_____	The slaves are valuable. The master's interest protects the slave from infancy through old age. He takes care of weaker members of his plantation society just as a parent or husband would.
_____	_____	People are happy without worries. Slaves do not have to worry about the future or having sufficient food, clothing, or shelter. It is a happy arrangement.
_____	_____	Every society has its social classes. A master-and-slave arrangement eliminates uncertainty and is part of the natural order.
_____	_____	Conditions in the South are better than those in the North. The slave system is less cruel than the factory system in the North. Wealth is more evenly distributed than in the North where a few millionaires own most of the property and many others are in jail or poorhouses.

It (was) (was not) realistic to expect the plantation owner to give up slavery because:

411

THE CONFESSIONS OF NAT TURNER*

The following report of the confession of Nat Turner was written shortly after he was captured:

It has been said he was ignorant and cowardly, and that his object was to murder and rob for the purpose of obtaining money to make his escape. It is notorious that he was never known to have a dollar in his life, to swear an oath, or drink a drop of spirits.

As to his ignorance, he certainly never had the advantages of education, but he can read and write (it was taught to him by his parents), and for natural intelligence and quickness of apprehension is surpassed by few men I have ever seen.

As to his being a coward, his reason as given for not resisting Mr. Phipps shows the decision of his character. When he saw Mr. Phipps present his gun, he said he knew it was impossible for him to escape, as the woods were full of men; he therefore thought it was better to surrender, and trust to fortune for his escape.

He is a complete fanatic, or plays his part most admirably. On other subjects he possesses an uncommon share of intelligence, with a mind capable of attaining anything, but warped and perverted by the influence of early impressions. He is below the ordinary stature, though strong and active, having the true negro face, every feature of which is strongly marked.

I shall not attempt to describe the effect of his narrative, as told and commented on by himself, in the condemned hole of the prison. The calm, deliberate composure with which he spoke of his late deeds and intentions; the expression of his fiendlike face when excited by enthusiasm, still bearing the stains of the blood of helpless innocence about him; clothed with rags and covered with chains, yet daring to raise his manacled hands to heaven, with a spirit soaring above the attributes of men. I looked on him, and my blood curdled in my veins.

What caused Nat Turner's rebellion?

*Adapted from material originally compiled by Sharon W. Lyons, Bret Harte Junior High School, Oakland, California, 1967.

YOUR BELIEFS OR YOUR LIFE?*

- What beliefs do you have that you would risk your own life to protect?
- Would you change your mind to save your life?

The night was hot in Alton, Illinois, in 1837, but no hotter than the tempers being displayed at the meeting being held by some of the town's citizens. They were upset by articles appearing in their local newspaper. They had not agreed with what the paper was printing. The paper's editor, Elijah P. Lovejoy, wrote what he believed, and he believed along with many others that slavery was wrong and his newspaper said so, day after day. The people at the meeting did not agree with Lovejoy. They told Lovejoy that he would have to stop writing his newspaper in Alton.

Lovejoy was not to be stopped. Already mobs had broken into his office and destroyed his printing presses. This had not stopped him. He now said to the people at the meeting, "Have I broken any laws? Have I committed any crime? If I have, you can convict me. But if I have not broken a law, why am I hunted and my presses broken? Tell me what I have done wrong and I will be responsible for it. If the police refuse to protect me, I will ask God's protection; and if I die, I will be buried in Alton. I have sworn to be against slavery forever and with the blessings of God, I will never stop. God can decide if I am right, but not you. I can die for my beliefs, but I will not give them up."

Four nights later Lovejoy was dead. He was killed by a mob who attacked the warehouse where his new presses were stored.

1. Why were people opposed to Lovejoy's printing his paper?
2. Was Lovejoy violating any laws or customs in Alton? Explain.
3. Why do people with unpopular ideas continue to express them when they know they are not acceptable?
4. What should Lovejoy have done in this case: moved away, changed his writing, stayed the same, or something else?
5. Would news of this event help or hurt the cause of abolition? Why?

Don Bolles, a newspaper reporter in Arizona, was investigating organized crime and finding information that was damaging and embarrassing to important political and business figures in the state. His reports grew more revealing. One day he got into his car and turned on the ignition and the car exploded. Several days later he died. You receive two telephone calls shortly after. The first mysteriously warns you to be careful. The second call is from a friend who wants to investigate Bolles's murder to find and punish those who are responsible.

Do you help investigate the murder?
You call back and say:

---

*Adapted from material originally compiled by Sharon W. Lyons, Bret Harte Junior High School, Oakland, California, 1967.

NEWSPAPER REPORTS FROM HARPERS FERRY

On October 17, 1859, the country was bewildered and astounded by telegraph dispatches from Baltimore and Washington announcing the outbreak, at Harpers Ferry, of a conspiracy of abolitionists and Negroes, to destroy the South and its way of life. Here are the first reports:

Insurrection at Harpers Ferry

Associated Press, Oct. 17, 1859. A dispatch just received here . . . states that an insurrection has broken out at Harpers Ferry, where an armed band of Abolitionists have full possession of the Government Arsenal. The express train going east was twice fired into, and one of the railroad hands and a negro killed, while they were endeavoring to get the train through the town. The insurrectionists stopped and arrested two men, who had come to town with a load of wheat, and, seizing their wagon loaded it with rifles, and sent them into Maryland. The insurrectionists number about 250 whites, and are aided by a gang of negroes. At last accounts, fighting was going on.

Baltimore, 10:00 A.M.
It is apprehended that the affair at Harpers Ferry is more serious than our citizens seem willing to believe. The wires from Harpers Ferry are cut, and consequently we have no telegraphic communication with Monocacy Station. The southern train, which was due here at an early hour this morning, has not yet arrived. It is rumored that there is a stampede of negroes from this State. There are many other wild rumors, but nothing authentic as yet.

Baltimore, 2:00 P.M.
Another account, received by train, says the bridge across the Potomac was filled with insurgents, all armed. Every light in that town was extinguished and the hotels closed. All the streets were in the possession of the mob, and every road and lane leading thereto barricaded and guarded. Men were seen in every quarter with muskets and bayonets, who arrested the citizens, and impressed them into the service, including many negroes. This done, the United States Arsenal and Government Payhouse, in which was said to be a large amount of money, and all other public works, were seized by the mob. Some were of the opinion that the object was entirely plunder, and to rob the Government of the funds deposited on Saturday at the Payhouse. During the night, the mob made a demand on the Wagner Hotel for provisions, and enforced the claim by a body of armed men. The citizens were in a terrible state of alarm, and the insurgents have threatened to burn the town.

Baltimore, later
The following has just been received from Monocacy, this side of Harpers Ferry: "The Mail Agent on the western-bound train has returned, and reports that the train was unable to get through. The town is in possession of the negroes, who arrest everyone they can catch and imprison. The train due here at 3 P.M., could not get through, and the Agent came down on an empty engine.

1. What are the sources of information for these accounts?

2. What questions would you ask to get enough information to report this event accurately?

3. To whom would you want to ask your questions?

JOHN BROWN'S RAID AT HARPERS FERRY

Harpers Ferry was a village of some 5,000 inhabitants lying on the Virginia side of the Potomac, 57 miles from Washington. One of its few streets was entirely occupied by the work-shops and offices of the National Armory. In the old Arsenal building, there were usually stored from 100,000 to 200,000 stand of arms.

Brown entered the town with a force of 17 white and 5 colored men without being noticed. Others cut the telegraph wires and tore up the railroad track. It was Sunday evening, October 17th.

They first extinguished the lights of the town, then took possession of the Armory buildings, which were only guarded by 3 watchmen, whom they locked up in the guard-house. At half-past ten, the watchman at the Potomac bridge was seized. At mid-night, his successor, arriving, was hailed by Brown's sentinels but ran to give the alarm. But still nothing stirred.

At a quarter past one, the western train arrived and its conductor found the bridge guarded by armed men. He and others attempted to walk across but were turned back at rifle point. The passengers took refuge in the hotel and remained there for several hours.

A little after mid-night, the house of Col. Washington was visited by 6 of Brown's men. They captured the Colonel and liberated his slaves. They then went to the house of Mr. Alstadtt, whom they captured and freed his slaves. Each male citizen as he appeared on the streets was taken to the Armory where they were confined. Brown informed his prisoners, about 40 to 50, that they could be liberated on condition of writing to their friends to send a negro apiece as ransom.

At daylight, the train proceeded. When asked the object of their captors, the uniform answer was, "To free the slave." And when one of the workmen asked by what authority they had taken possession of the public property, he was answered, "By the authority of God Almighty!"

By early Monday morning, October 17, the insurrectionists had complete military possession of Harpers Ferry.

Soon after daybreak, as Brown's guards were bringing two citizens to a halt, they were fired on by a man named Turner and, directly afterward, by a grocer named Boerly, who was instantly killed by return fire. Several Virginians took positions in a room overlooking the Armory gates and fired at the sentinels who guarded them. Two men, one of whom was Brown's son Watson, were killed.

Throughout the forenoon, the liberators remained masters of the town. There were shots fired at intervals, but no more casualties reported. The prisoners were permitted to visit their families under guard to give assurance that they were still alive and were kindly treated.

Why Brown lingered is not certain. Some have said that he had private assurances that the negroes of the surrounding country would rise at the first tidings of his movement, and come flocking to his standard, and he chose to remain where arms and ammunition for all could abundantly be had.

His doom was already sealed. Half an hour after noon, a militia force of 100 arrived and rapidly dispersed to command every available exit from the town.

The railroad bridge was re-captured. All houses around the Armory buildings were held by Virginians. Several of Brown's men, including another son Oliver, were killed by Virginians or the militia. The Armory building was attacked from the rear while another detachment attacked from the front. Brown retreated to the engine-house where he repulsed his assailants.

The militia continued to pour in. The telegraph and railroad having been repaired so that the government in Washington, Richmond and other authorities were in immediate communication with Harpers Ferry. Terror and rumor had multiplied the actual number of insurgents manyfold and troops were hurrying in from all over.

The firing ceased at nightfall. Brown offered to liberate his prisoners upon condition that his men should be permitted to cross the bridge in safety. His offer was refused.

At seven in the morning, troops broke in the door of the engine-house by using a ladder as a battering-ram. One of the defenders was shot and two marines wounded but the odds were too great. All resistance was over. Brown was struck in the face with a saber and knocked down, after which the blow was several times repeated, while a soldier ran a bayonet twice into the old man's body.

THE ENDS OF JUSTICE?

John Brown was tried and found guilty. He was asked if he had anything to say before his sentence was passed. He responded:

> In the first place, I deny everything but what I have all along admitted—the design on my part to free the slave. I intended certainly to have made a clean thing of that matter, as I did last winter, when I went into Missouri, and there took slaves without the snapping of a gun on either side, moved them through the country, and finally left them in Canada. I designed to have done the same thing again, on a larger scale. That was all I intended. I never did intend murder, or treason, or the destruction of property, or to excite or incite slaves to rebellion, or to make insurrection.
>
> I have another objection: and that is, it is unjust that I should suffer such a penalty. Had I interfered . . . in behalf of the rich, the powerful, the intelligent, the so-called great, or in behalf of any of their friends, either father, mother, brother, sister, wife, or children, or any of that class, and suffered and sacrificed what I have in this interference, it would have been all right and every man in this Court would have deemed it an act worthy of reward rather than punishment.
>
> Now, if it is deemed necessary that I should forfeit my life for the furtherance of the ends of justice, and mingle my blood further with the blood of my children and with the blood of millions in this slave country whose rights are disregarded by wicked, cruel, and unjust enactments—I submit. So let it be done.

1. What does Brown admit were his intentions?

2. Under what conditions does Brown feel his treatment would have been different?

3. What criticism does he make of the country?

4. Do you think his statement made any difference in the courtroom? Would it have made any difference if you were the judge? To whom might Brown have been addressing his comments to?

5. Several people were killed in Harpers Ferry defending U.S. government property and laws supporting slavery. Did John Brown receive a fair punishment? Explain.

6. Many stories and songs have been written about John Brown. Why do you think he has received so much attention?

TREATMENT OF SLAVES

Harriet Beecher Stowe in *Dred: A Tale of the Great Dismal Swamp* describes the treatment of a slave by his master. The facts are a matter of judicial record, she reports, and the cruelty stopped only with the death of the victim.

The count charged on the 1st day of September, 1849, the prisoner tied his negro slave, Sam, with ropes about his wrists, neck, body, legs, and ankles, to a tree. That whilst so tied, the prisoner first whipped the slave with switches. That he next beat and cobbed the slave with a shingle, and compelled two of his slaves, a man and a woman, also to cob the deceased with the shingle.

That whilst the deceased was so tied to the tree, the prisoner did strike, knock, kick, stamp, and beat him upon various parts of his head, face, and body; that he applied fire to his body ... that he then washed his body with warm water, in which pods of red pepper had been put and steepted; and he compelled his two slaves aforesaid also to wash him with this same preparation of warm water and red pepper.

That after the tying, whipping, cobbing, striking, beating, knocking, kicking, stamping, wounding, bruising, lacerating, burning, washing, and torturing, as aforesaid, the prisoner untied the deceased from the tree in such a way as to throw him with violence to the ground; and he then and there did knock, kick, stamp, and beat the deceased upon his head, temples, and various parts of his body. That the prisoner then had the deceased carried into a shed-room of his house, and there he compelled one of his slaves, in his presence, to confine the deceased's feet in stocks, by making his legs fast to a piece of timber, and to tie a rope about the neck of the deceased, and fasten it to a bed-post in the room, thereby strangling, choking, and suffocating, the deceased.

And that whilst the deceased was thus made fast in stocks, as aforesaid, the prisoner did kick, knock, stamp, and beat him upon his head, face, breast, belly, sides, back, and body; and he again compelled his two slaves to apply fire to the body of the deceased, whilst he was so made fast as aforesaid.

And the count charged that from these various modes of punishment and torture, the slave Sam then and there died. It appeared that the prisoner commenced the punishment of the deceased in the morning, and that it was continued throughout the day; and that the deceased died in the presence of the prisoner, and one of his slaves, and one of the witnesses, whilst the punishment was still progressing.

EVENTS THAT HELP OR HURT THE UNION

A series of events that took place before the Civil War is listed below. Decide if they mostly *helped* or *hurt* the Union and check the appropriate place.

	Help				Hurt
• value of cotton exports increasing	___	___	___	___	___
• canals and railroad concentrated in North	___	___	___	___	___
• *popular sovereignty* lets people vote over slavery	___	___	___	___	___
• *Dred Scott* decision says Congress cannot deprive people of their property (slaves)	___	___	___	___	___
• John Brown's raid	___	___	___	___	___
• Abraham Lincoln elected president	___	___	___	___	___
• *Uncle Tom's Cabin* is written and widely read	___	___	___	___	___
• abolitionists campaign against slavery	___	___	___	___	___
• Compromise of 1850 keeps balance in Senate between slave and free states	___	___	___	___	___
• high protective tariff	___	___	___	___	___
• new territories apply for statehood	___	___	___	___	___
• Fugitive Slave Law requires slaves to be returned to their master	___	___	___	___	___
• James Buchanan's belief that he could not act against seceding states	___	___	___	___	___
• the U.S. Constitution's sections about slavery	___	___	___	___	___

FIGURE OF THE CIVIL WAR

Each figure represents a possible explanation of the Civil War. In your opinion, which is the best explanation? Place an *N* on one line for North, an *S* for South. Write a title for the figure you select that provides an explanation for the Civil War.

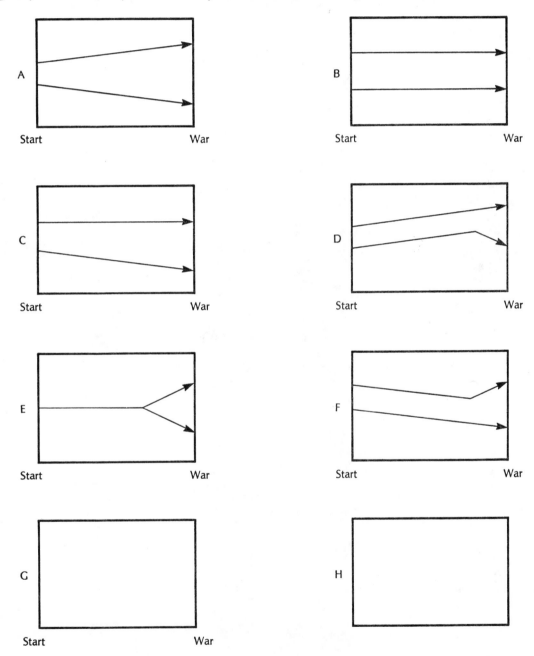

OBSERVATIONS ABOUT THE WAR

. . . it sprung from a faction who sought only political power. Those make a great mistake who suppose it grew out of a desire merely to perpetuate slavery. Slavery was a means to an end—a bugbear to frighten the timid into obedience, and a rallying cry for the ignorant, deluded masses. The accursed lust of power lay at the bottom of it. The whole question may be stated thus: southern politicians saw in the rapid increase of the free states, both in number and population, and the deep hostility to the admission of any more slave states, that the power they had so long wielded in the Government would be broken.

> —J. T. Headley, 1864, 1866, *The Great Rebellion: A History of the Civil War in the United States*

. . . the slavery question was not a moral one in the North, unless, perhaps, with a few thousand persons of disordered conscience. It was significant only of a contest for political power, and afforded nothing more than a convenient ground of dispute between two parties, who represented not two moral theories, but hostile sections and opposite civilizations.

> —Edward A. Pollard, 1866, *The Lost Cause: A New Southern History of the War of the Confederates*

I saw that this Rebellion was a war of the aristocrats against the middling men—of the rich against the poor; a war of the landowner against the laborers; that it was a struggle for the retention of power in the hands of the few against the many; and I found no conclusion to it, save in the subjugation of the few and the disenthrallment of the many.

> —Gen. Benjamin Butler, Farewell Address to the People of New Orleans

The conflict in principle arose from different and opposing ideas as to the nature of what is known as the General Government. The contest was between those who held it to be strictly Federal in its character, and those who maintained that it was thoroughly National. It was a strife between the principles of Federation, on the one side, and Centralism, or Consolidation, on the other.

> —Alexander H. Stephens, 1870, *A Constitutional View of the Late War Between the States*

It was not the passage of the "personal liberty laws," it was not the circulation of incendiary documents, it was not the raid of John Brown, it was not the operation of unjust and unequal tariff laws, nor all combined, that constituted the intolerable grievance, but it was the systematic and persistent struggle to deprive the Southern States of equality in the Union— generally to discriminate in legislation against the interests of their people; culminating in . . . their exclusion from the Territories, the common property of the States. . . . The hope of our people may be stated in a sentence. It was to escape from injury and strife in the Union, to find prosperity and peace out of it.

    —Jefferson Davis, 1881, *The Rise and Fall of the Confederate Government*

THE DIFFERENCES BETWEEN NORTH AND SOUTH*

The differences between people of the North and of the South developed before the American Revolution. The Puritan exiles who settled the cold, rugged, cheerless soil of New England were never friendly with the Cavaliers who chose the brighter climate of Virginia and the South.

The intolerance of the Puritan, their painful thrift, their public display of piety, their sickly laws, their convenient morals, their lack of sentiment, and their unending search for personal wealth are traits of character which are visible in their descendants. On the other hand, the colonists of Virginia and the Carolinas were distinguished for their polite manners, their sentiment, their attachment to a sort of feudal life, their landed gentry, their love of field sports and dangerous adventure, and the generous aristocracy that shared its wealth with frequent gatherings of hospitality and gaiety.

The civilization of the North was coarse and materialistic. That of the South was highly refined and with feeling. The South was an agricultural country. The North was thick with intricate sets of canals, railroads, and highways. The agriculture of the South fixed its features. Its people were models for the whole country and stood in striking contrast to the conceit and giddiness of the Northern people.

It was Yankee orators who established the Fourth-of-July school of rhetoric, exalted the American eagle, and spoke of the Union as the last, best gift to man. This show had little place in the South. Their civilization was a quiet one, the characteristic of the people based on a sober estimate of the value of men and things. Sensations, excitements on slight cause, fits of fickle admiration, manias in society and fashion, a high regard for exaggeration and display are indications of a superficial and restless civilization and were peculiar to the people in the North. The sobriety and reasoned judgments of the South was in striking contrast to these exhibitions of the North. In fact, it was the mark of a superior civilization.

1. Why was the South a superior civilization?

2. In your opinion, what features make up a superior civilization?

3. Select three or more features of a civilization and use them to describe the United States today. Which tend to make the United States superior? Inferior?

4. How are people influenced by their ancestors? By the society in which they live? By the occupations or economy around them? How much of these influences persist through generations?

5. Find words or statements that are the value judgments of the author. Find unsupported generalizations. What types of evidence would you need to support or disprove such generalizations?

*Adapted from: Edward A. Pollard, *The Lost Cause: A New Southern History of the War of the Confederates* (New York: E. B. Treat & Co., 1866).

"A HOUSE DIVIDED"

If we could first know where we are, and whither we are tending, we could better judge what to do, and how to do it.

We are now far into the fifth year since a policy was initiated with the avowed object and confident promise of putting an end to slavery agitation.

Under the operation of that policy, that agitation has not only not ceased but has constantly augmented.

In my opinion, it will not cease, until a crisis shall have been reached and passed.

"A house divided against itself cannot stand."

I believe this government cannot endure, permanently, half slave and half free.

I do not expect the Union to be dissolved; I do not expect the house to fall; but I do expect it will cease to be divided.

It will become all one thing, or all the other.

Either the opponents of slavery will arrest the further spread of it and place it where the public mind shall rest in the belief that it is in course of ultimate extinction, or its advocates will push it forward till it shall become alike lawful in all the states, old as well as new, North as well as South.

—Abraham Lincoln, Springfield, Illinois, 1858

1. As a result of this speech, who would support Lincoln's election? Who would oppose it?
2. Lincoln was criticized as calling for a war between sections. Is that criticism justified?
3. With extremists in all sections of the country, how could the slavery question been solved peacefully?
4. Do you think Lincoln saw a war coming?
5. Do you think Lincoln was making a political speech with an eye on running for the presidency in 1860?

LINCOLN'S FIRST INAUGURAL ADDRESS: AN INTERVIEW

Why do you think there is trouble in the South?

Apprehension seems to exist among the people of the Southern States that by the accession of a Republican Administration their property and their peace and personal security are to be endangered.

Well . . .

There has never been any reasonable cause for such apprehension. Indeed, the most ample evidence to the contrary has all the while existed and been open to their inspection. It is found in nearly all the published speeches of him who now addresses you.

What will you do about slavery?

I have no purpose, directly or indirectly, to interfere with the institution of slavery in the States where it exists. I believe I have no lawful right to do so, and I have no inclination to do so.

But what is the position of the Republican party?

Those who nominated and elected me did so with full knowledge that I had made this and many similar declarations and had never recanted them; and more than this, they placed in the platform for my acceptance, and as a law to themselves and to me, the clear and emphatic resolution which I now read:

Resolved, That the maintenance inviolate of the rights of the States, and especially the right of each State to order and control its own domestic institutions according to its own judgment exclusively, is essential to that balance of power on which the perfection and endurance of our political fabric depend; and we denounce the lawless invasion by armed force of the soil of any State or Territory, no matter what pretext, as among the gravest crimes.

What would you do about fugitive slaves?

There is much controversy about the delivering up of fugitives from service or labor. The clause I now read is as plainly written in the Constitution as any other of its provisions:

No person held to service or labor in one State, under the laws thereof, escaping into another, shall in consequence of any law or regulation therein be discharged from such service or labor, but shall be delivered up on claim of the party to whom such service or labor may be due.

Who would enforce this part of the Constitution?

There is some difference of opinion whether this clause should be enforced by national or by State authority; but surely that difference is not a very material one. If the slave is to be surrendered, it can be of but little consequence to him or to others by which authority it is done.

435

Do you think the Union is a temporary association of states or is it a permanent government?

> I hold that in contemplation of universal law and of the Constitution the Union of these States is perpetual. Perpetuity is implied, if not expressed, in the fundamental law of all national governments. It is safe to assert that no government proper ever had a provision in its organic law for its own termination.

What evidence supports your view?

> The Union is much older than the Constitution. It was formed, in fact, by the Articles of Association in 1774. It was matured and continued by the Declaration of Independence in 1776. It was further matured, and the faith of all the then thirteen States expressly plighted and engaged that it should be perpetual, by the Articles of Confederation in 1778. And finally, in 1787, one of the declared objects for ordaining and establishing the Constitution was "to form a more perfect Union."

What do these views have to do with recent actions by seceding southern states?

> It follows from these views that no State upon its own mere motion can lawfully get out of the Union; that resolves and ordinances to that effect are legally void, and that acts of violence within any State or States against the authority of the United States are insurrectionary or revolutionary.

What will you do about these states?

> . . . to the extent of my ability, I shall take care, as the Constitution itself expressly enjoins upon me, that the laws of the Union be faithfully executed in all the States. Doing this I deem to be only a simple duty on my part, and I shall perform it so far as practicable unless my rightful masters, the American people, shall withhold the requisite means or in some authoritative manner direct the contrary. I trust this will not be regarded as a menace, but only as the declared purpose of the Union that it will constitutionally defend and maintain itself.

If necessary, will you use force?

> . . . there needs to be no bloodshed or violence, and there shall be none unless it be forced upon the national authority. The power confided to me will be used to hold, occupy, and possess the property and places belonging to the Government and to collect the duties and imposts; but beyond what may be necessary for these objects, there will be no invasion, no using of force against or among the people anywhere.

What would you say to those attempting to destroy the Union?

> . . . I need address no word to them. To those, however, who really love the Union may I not speak?
> Before entering upon so grave a matter as the destruction of our national fabric, with all its benefits, its memories, and its hopes, would it not be wise to ascertain precisely why we do it? Will you hazard so desperate a step while there is any possibility that any portion of the ills you fly from have no real existence? Will you, while the certain ills you fly to are greater than all the real ones you fly from, will you risk the commission of so fearful a mistake?

Don't you think parts of the Constitution have been violated?

I think not . . . Think, if you can, of a single instance in which a plainly written provision of the Constitution has ever been denied. If by the mere force of numbers a majority should deprive a minority of any clearly written constitutional right, it might in a moral point of view justify revolution; certainly would if such right were a vital one. But such is not our case. . . . No foresight can anticipate nor any document of reasonable length contain express provisions for all possible questions. Shall fugitives from labor be surrendered by national or by State authority? The Constitution does not expressly say. May Congress prohibit slavery in the Territories? The Constitution does not expressly say. Must Congress protect slavery in the Territories? The Constitution does not expressly say.

Why should a minority go along with the majority?

If a minority in such case will secede rather than acquiesce, they make a precedent which in turn will divide and ruin them, for a minority of their own will secede from them whenever a majority refuses to be controlled by such a minority. Plainly the central idea of secession is the essence of anarchy.

What do you think is the cause of disagreement?

One section of our country believes slavery is right and ought to be extended, while the other believes it is wrong and ought not to be extended. This is the only substantial dispute. The fugitive-slave cause of the Constitution and the law for the suppression of the foreign slave trade are each as well enforced, perhaps, as any law can ever be in a community where the moral sense of the people imperfectly supports the law itself.

Would secession be the solution to this problem?

Physically speaking, we can not separate. We can not remove our respective sections from each other nor build an impassable wall between them. . . . Suppose you go to war, you can not fight always; and when, after much loss on both sides and no gain on either, you cease fighting, the identical old questions, as to terms of intercourse, are again upon you.

Your election and government appointments could cause problems.

By the frame of the Government under which we live this same people have wisely given their public servants but little power for mischief, and have with equal wisdom provided for the return of that little to their own hands at very short intervals. While the people retain their virtue and vigilance no Administration by any extreme of wickedness or folly can very seriously injure the Government in the short space of four years.

Why should southerners or others wait to see what happens?

Nothing valuable can be lost by taking time. If there be an object to hurry any of you in hot haste to a step which you would never take deliberately, that object will be frustrated by taking time; but no good object can be frustrated by it. Such of you as are now dissatisfied still have the old Constitution unimpaired, and, on the sensitive point, the laws of your own framing under it; while the new Administration will have no immediate power, if it would, to change either. If it were admitted that you who are dissatisfied hold the right side in the dispute, there still is no single good reason for precipitate action. Intelligence, patriotism, Christianity, and a firm reliance on Him who has never yet forsaken this favored land are still competent to adjust in the best way all our present difficulty.

Do you think there will be war?

In your hands, my dissatisfied fellow-countrymen, and not in mine, is the momentous issue of civil war. The Government will not assail you. You can have no conflict without being yourselves the aggressors. You have no oath registered in heaven to destroy the Government, while I shall have the most solemn one to "preserve, protect, and defend it."

CONFRONTATION AT FORT SUMTER

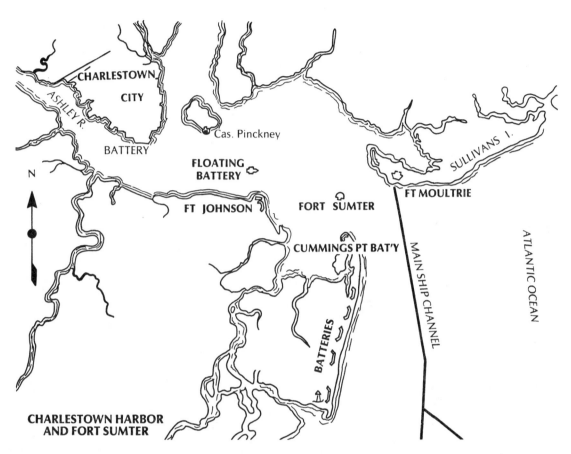

**CHARLESTOWN HARBOR
AND FORT SUMTER**

Inside Fort Sumter, on an island in Charleston Harbor, U.S. Maj. Robert Anderson faced a difficult choice. He knew he and his seventy-five men were surrounded by Confederate troops and fortifications. It would be impossible to win any military victories. In a few days his food supply would be exhausted. President Lincoln had announced that he would supply the fort with food but no ships had arrived yet. Confederate shore batteries would undoubtedly prevent any ships from entering the harbor.

Confederate General Beauregard had already asked Anderson when his men would evacuate. He knew the supply ship could not help. He could not stall Beauregard any longer. He had to accept the offer to evacuate without harm or follow his instructions to hold the fort and risk certain bombardment and defeat. He had less than an hour before the Confederates would open fire.

What should Anderson do? Follow orders and defend the fort or take the offer of a safe evacuation and save lives?

NEWSPAPERS JUDGE FORT SUMTER

New York Tribune
Ft. Sumter is lost, but freedom is saved. There is no more thought of bribing or coaxing the traitors who have dared to aim their cannon-balls at the flag of the Union, and those who gave their lives to defend it.

New York Express
The "irrepressible conflict" started by Mr. Seward and indorsed by the Republican party, has at length attained to its logical, foreseen result. That conflict, undertaken "for the sake of humanity," culminates now in inhumanity itself, and exhibits the afflicting spectacle of brother shedding brother's blood.

Refusing the ballot before the bullet, these men, flushed with the power and patronage of the Federal Government, have madly rushed into a civil war, which will probably drive the remaining Slave States into the arms of the Southern Confederacy, and dash to pieces the last hope for a reconstruction of the Union.

Utica (New York) *Observer*
Of all the wars which have disgraced the human race, it has been reserved for our own enlightened nation to be involved in the most useless and foolish one.

Bangor (Maine) *Union*
Democrats of Maine! the loyal sons of the South have gathered around Charleston, as your fathers of old gathered about Boston, in defense of the same sacred principles of liberty— principles which you have ever upheld and defended with your vote, your voice, and your strong right arm. Your sympathies are with the defenders of the truth and the right. Those who have inaugurated this unholy and unjustifiable war are no friends of yours—no friends of Democratic Liberty.

Journal of Commerce (New York)
We will not undertake at this moment, to apportion the measure of folly and crime, on either side, which has led to the present catastrophe. . . . The Confederate authorities must, however, bear the responsibility (and it is a heavy one) of commencing the actual firing.

SEPARATION

Declaration of Causes, November 15, 1860
Mobile, Alabama

The following causes summarize southern displeasure with the election of Republican candidates to office. Assume you are a Republican or a secessionist and provide additional information to disprove or prove each statement about the government.

- It has denied the extradition of murderers, marauders, and other felons.

_____

_____

- It has concealed and shielded the murderer of masters or owners, in pursuit of fugitive slaves.

_____

- It has advocated negro equality, and made it the ground of positive legislation, hostile to the Southern States.

_____

_____

- It has invaded Virginia, and shed the blood of her citizens on her own soil.

_____

_____

- It has announced its purpose of total abolition [of slavery] in the States and everywhere as well as in the territories, and districts, and other places ceded.

_____

_____

LINCOLN'S OBJECTIVE

In a letter to Horace Greeley, August 22, 1862, President Lincoln explained his policy:

As to the policy I "seem to be pursuing," as you say, I have not meant to leave any one in doubt. I would save the union. I would save it in the shortest way under the Constitution.

The sooner the national authority can be restored, the nearer the union will be to the union it was.

If there be those who would not save the union unless they could at the same time save Slavery, I do not agree with them.

If there be those who would not save the union unless they could at the same time destroy Slavery, I do not agree with them.

My paramount object is to save the union, and not either to save or destroy Slavery.

If I could save the union without freeing any slave, I would do it—if I could save it by freeing all the slaves, I would do it—and if I could do it by freeing some and leaving others alone, I would also do that.

What I do about Slavery and the Colored Race, I do because I believe it helps to save this union; and what I forbear, I forbear because I do not believe it would help to save the union.

I shall do less whenever I shall believe what I am doing hurts the cause; and I shall do more whenever I believe doing more will help the cause.

I shall try to correct errors when shown to be errors; and I shall adopt new views so fast as they shall appear to be true views.

I have here stated my purpose according to my views of official duty; and I intend no modification of my oft-expressed personal wish that all men everywhere could be free.

Yours,

A. Lincoln

GRANT'S MILITARY OBJECTIVES

In his final report in 1865, Grant reviewed the strengths and weaknesses of both sides and stated his plan for defeating the enemy.

> From an early period in the Rebellion, I had been impressed with the idea that active and continuous operations of all the troops that could be brought into the field, regardless of season and weather, were necessary to a speedy termination of the war. The resources of the enemy, and his numerical strength, were far inferior to ours: but, as an offset to this, we had a vast territory, with a population hostile to the Government, to garrison and long lines of river and railroad communications to protect to enable us to supply the operating armies.
>
> The armies in the East and West acted independently and without concert, like a balky team: no two ever pulling together: enabling the enemy to use to great advantage his interior lines of communication for transporting troops from east to west, reenforcing the army most vigorously pressed, and to furlough large numbers, during seasons of inactivity on our part, to go to their homes and do the work of producing, for the support of their armies. It was a question whether our numerical strength and resources were not more than balanced by these disadvantages and the enemy's superior position.
>
> From the first, I was firm in the conviction that no peace could be had that would be stable and conducive to the happiness of the people, both North and South, until the military power of the Rebellion was entirely broken.

How would you complete Grant's statement?

Grant would do this: *To accomplish this:*

1) _____   _____

   _____   _____

   _____   _____

2) _____   _____

   _____   _____

   _____   _____

THE GENERAL AND THE MAYOR

Gentlemen:

I have your letter of the 11th. . . . I have read it carefully, and give full credit to your statements of the distress that will be occasioned, and yet shall not revoke my orders, because they were not designed to meet the humanities of the case, but to prepare for the future struggles in which millions of good people outside of Atlanta have a deep interest. We must have peace, not only at Atlanta, but in all America. To secure this, we must stop the War that now desolates our once happy and favored country. To stop the war, we must defeat the rebel armies which are arrayed against the laws and Constitution that all must respect and obey. . . .

You cannot qualify war in harsher terms than I will. War is cruelty, and you cannot refine it; and those who brought war into our country deserve all the curses and maledictions a people can pour out. I know I had no hand in making this war, and I know I will make more sacrifices to-day than any of you to secure peace. But you cannot have peace and a division of our country. . . .

You might as well appeal against the thunderstorm as against these terrible hardships of war. They are inevitable, and the only way the people of Atlanta can hope once more to live in peace and quiet at home, is to stop the war, which can only be done by admitting that it began in error and is perpetuated in pride.

We don't want your negroes, or your horses, or your houses, or your lands, or any thing you have, but we do want and will have a just obedience to the laws of the United States. That we will have, and if it involves the destruction of your improvements, we cannot help it.

Now you must go, and take with you the old and feeble, feed and nurse them, and build for them, in more quiet places, proper habitations to shield them against the weather until the mad passions of men cool down, and allow the Union and peace once more to settle over your old homes at Atlanta. . . .

W. T. Sherman
Sept. 12, 1864

1. What is the cause of conflict between Sherman and the mayor?

2. What does Sherman value most highly? How does the forced evacuation of Atlanta serve that purpose?

3. Sherman bluntly states that "war is cruelty." Are some wars *worth it* in terms of cost, property damage, social dislocation, and loss of human life? Was the Civil War *worth it*?

4. Write a general statement explaining or listing the circumstances when a nation should go to war (even a civil war).

DRAFT RIOTS IN NEW YORK

- Should the government be able to force a person to serve in the army?

- Is there some point when violent opposition to government actions is justifiable?

On a warm Saturday morning, July 11, 1863, in the northerly wards of New York City, where mostly railroad workers and other foreign-born laborers lived, the drawing of names to serve in the Union army had begun. It was called drafting and began with excited crowds and led to violence, arson, and bloodshed.

. . . Inside a large building 300 people gathered for the calling of the first names. They were quiet and orderly but not surprised when, after about one-half hour, a pistol shot from the noisy crowd outside pierced the calm atmosphere. Brickbats, stones, and other missiles were hurled at the building and the crowd rushed in to drive out the officers, tear up papers, and take complete possession. Turpentine was poured over the floor and set fire. In no time the building was in flames. Policemen and draft officers were kept away by a shower of stones.

Firemen arrived late and were cheered by the mob. No effort was made to save the building and after several more buildings were destroyed the firemen were finally able to control the flames. In the meantime, the bulk of the mob had gone elsewhere to continue the destruction.

There were reports that the outbreak had been carefully planned. Word of its early success spread through the city. The streets filled with people who dreaded the draft, hated the war, detested Abolitionists and Negroes, or had other grievances, real or imagined. The rioters added to their number by calling on railroad offices, workshops, and large manufacturing outfits demanding that all work be stopped and laborers be allowed to join them. This demand, through sympathy or cowardice, was generally granted. Of course, thieves, burglars, and other predatory types were only too happy to plunder and loot under the cloak of resisting Abolitionist rulers. The drunken, bellowing, furious mob raced through street after street, attacking peaceful citizens and destroying houses and public property.

The most revolting feature of this carnival of crime and madness were the attacks on innocent, harmless, frightened Blacks: an inoffensive Negro boy was hunted at full speed by a hundred whites intent on his murder, a poor Black woman had her small house sacked and devastated as she narrowly escaped into the street—barely saving her life, and nothing else. Several Black men were killed only because they were Black. In one case, and there were others, a Black man was chased, caught, hanged, and burned. His dead and charred body remained hanging for hours, until cut down by the police. In one of the most detestable acts, the rioters attacked and burned the Colored Orphan Asylum. Its more than 200 terrified children barely escaped to safety.

The railroads were not running, vessels were stranded in port, industry was shut down, and the city was very generally paralyzed for more than three days.

1. What were the immediate cause(s) of the riot?

2. What were the underlying causes of the riot?

3. What action should the following officials have taken, and what would have been the likely result?

	should do this	*to accomplish this*
Mayor	_____	_____
	_____	_____
Governor	_____	_____
	_____	_____
Military commander	_____	_____
	_____	_____
Person just drafted	_____	_____

4. What do you think should be the (a) immediate and (b) long-term objectives of each of the above people in this case?

5. The government's right to maintain its existence is greater than individual rights. Do you agree or disagree?

LINCOLN'S WAR AIMS

After the attack on Fort Sumter, Lincoln issued a proclamation on April 15, 1861, calling for 75,000 volunteers. In urging support for his action, he stated in the proclamation:

> I appeal to all loyal citizens to favor, facilitate, and aid, this effort to maintain the honor, the integrity, and existence, of our national union, and the perpetuity of popular government, and to redress wrongs already long enough endured.

Careful consideration of political and military effects finally led Lincoln to issue the Emancipation Proclamation, freeing some slaves as of January 1, 1863:

> ... all persons held as slaves within said designated States and parts of States are and henceforward shall be free; and that the executive government of the United States, including the military and naval authorities thereof, will recognize and maintain the freedom of said persons.

A hint of Lincoln's postwar objectives is contained in this well-known paragraph from his second inaugural address, March 4, 1865:

> With malice toward none; with charity for all; with firmness in the right, as God gives us to see the right, let us strive on to finish the work we are in; to bind up the nation's wounds; to care for him who shall have borne the battle, and for his widow, and his orphan—to do all which may achieve and cherish a just and lasting peace, among ourselves, and with all nations.

1. What are Lincoln's aims in each statement?

2. What effect would the Emancipation Proclamation have on each of the following: (a) northern Radicals, (b) diplomatic efforts with European countries, (c) the Union army.

3. Lincoln's opinions may have remained the same throughout the war, but his actions changed. Is it best for a person always to say and do what he thinks?

GETTYSBURG ADDRESS

Four score and seven years ago our fathers brought forth upon this continent, a new nation, conceived in Liberty, and dedicated to the proposition that all men are created equal.

Now we are engaged in a great civil war, testing whether that nation, or any nation so conceived, and so dedicated, can long endure. We are met on a great battle field of that war. We have come to dedicate a portion of that field, as a final resting place for those who here gave their lives, that that nation might live. It is altogether fitting and proper that we should do this.

But, in a larger sense, we can not dedicate— we can not consecrate— we can not hallow— this ground. The brave men, living and dead, who struggled here, have consecrated it, far above our poor power to add or detract. The world will little note, nor long remember, what we say here, but it can never forget what they did here. It is for us, the living, rather, to be dedicated here to the unfinished work which they who fought here have, thus far, so nobly advanced. It is rather for us to be here dedicated to the great task remaining before us— that from these honored dead we take increased devotion to that cause for which they here gave the last full measure of devotion— that we here highly resolve that these dead shall not have died in vain— that this nation, under God, shall have a new birth of freedom— and that government of the people, by the people, for the people, shall not perish from the earth.

A LOOK AT LINCOLN*

Mr. Lincoln was not elected President of the United States for any commanding game, or for any known merit as a statesman. . . . It was said that he was transparently honest. But this honesty was a rather facile disposition that readily took impressions from whatever was urged on it. It was said that he was excessively amiable. But his amiability was animal. It is small merit to have a Falstaffian humour in one's blood. Abraham Lincoln was neither kind nor cruel, in the proper sense of these words, simply because he was destitute of the higher order of sensibilities.

His appearance corresponded to his rough life and uncultivated mind. His figure was tall and gaunt-looking; his shoulders were inclined forward; his arms of unusual length; and his gait astride, rapid and shuffling. The savage wits in the Southern newspapers had no other name for him than "the Illinois Ape."

. . . Mr. Lincoln had formerly served, without distinction, in Congress. But among his titles to American popularity were the circumstances that in earlier life he had rowed a flat-boat down the Mississippi; afterwards been a miller; and at another period had earned his living by splitting rails in a county of Illinois.

1. What statements do you think are true? How does the author use words to place Lincoln in an unfavorable light?

---

*Edward A. Pollard, *The Lost Cause: A New Southern History of the War of the Confederates* (New York: E. B. Treat & Co., 1866), p. 100.

WINNING AFTER THE WAR?

Edward A. Pollard was the editor of the *Richmond* (Virginia) *Examiner* during the war. A year after the war was over he wrote *The Lost Cause: A New Southern History of the War of the Confederates,* in which he gave his view of what the war decided:

> The war has not swallowed up everything. There are great interests which stand out of the pale of the contest, which it is for the South still to cultivate and maintain. She must submit fairly and truthfully to *what the war has properly decided.* But the war properly decided only what was put to issue: the restoration of the Union and the excision of slavery; and to these two conditions the South submits.
>
> . . . the war did not decide negro equality; it did not decide negro suffrage; it did not decide State Rights . . . it did not decide the right of a people to show dignity in misfortune, and to maintain self-respect in the face of adversity. And these things which the war did not decide, the Southern people will still cling to, still claim, and still assert in them their rights and views.

Review Pollard's statement for what the war decided and what it did not decide. In the chart below, write a description of conditions in 1865, 1877, and today.

Issue	1865	1877	Today
Is the Union restored?			
Is slavery ended?			
Is there black equality?			
Is there black suffrage?			
What rights do states have?			

A BLACK VOTE*

In 1871 the U.S. Senate conducted hearings to investigate problems and progress under Reconstruction programs. This excerpt provides an idea about voting.

Q. How did he [the sharecropper's boss] tell you to vote?

A. He told me to vote the democratic ticket. I went to the election, and at night, when I came home, he said, "Cas., were you at the election today?" I said, "Yes, sir." He said, "How did you vote?" I told him I didn't know how I voted. He said, "You can't make me believe that; you are no fool." I said, "I can't read; I don't know how I voted." He said, "Who gave you the ticket you voted?" I said, "A black man gave it to me." He said, "You know how you voted; you voted the radical ticket." I said, "I don't know." He said, "I've no further use for you; I told you before this election came on that no man should live on my land who voted against my interest, and tried to give my land and property away; you can't live on it any longer; I've no further use for you." I said, "Very good; whenever you are tired of me, I am tired of you. I would like to live with you, but whenever you are tired of me, I am tired of you." It went on that way, and it didn't get any better. I was going away, but he told me that as I had started in with the next crop I had better stay there, for he would give me as good a chance as anybody else. I said, "I know that, and I would like to live with you, if we can live in peace and agreeable together; but if we don't I don't want to live with you."

1. Do you think Cas knew how he voted?

2. How did the boss try to control Cas's vote?

3. Is the boss justified in not wanting people on his land who vote against his interests?

4. Who seems to be the smarter of these two people? Why?

5. Niether man seems happy with the other but it appears that their working arrangement will continue. Why?

---

*Report on the Alleged Outrages in the Southern States, By the Select Committee of the Senate (Washington, D.C.: Government Printing Office, 1871), pp. 343-44.

THE KLAN RIDES*

A. L. Ramsour was questioned by a Senate committee:

Q. Where do you live?
A. In Catawba County, North Carolina.

Q. How long have you lived there?
A. In that county ever since I was born—fifty-two years.

Q. What is your business?
A. I was brought up a farmer, but I have worked at the mill-wright business for some ten or fifteen years.

Q. Have you been at any time visited by men in disguise, known as Ku-Klux?
A. Yes, sir.

Q. When?
A. I think it was the 7th of June, 1869.

Q. Go on and state what they did and said at the time.
A. There were some Ku-Klux in our neighborhood, as I learned from some colored people who came and told me they had been whipped by them. I asked the colored people if they could swear to any of them; they told me they thought they knew some of them, and they told me who they thought they were. I asked them why they did not tell on them; they said the Ku-Klux threatened if they did not do so and so they would get after them.

Q. Do what?
A. If they did not quit their radical principals, if they did not quit following "old Andy Ramsour." I had become a republican, or radical as they called me. I told them that they ought to hit some of these fellows, take their false-faces off, or something of that kind. They said they were afraid, that the men threatened to kill them if they said anything against the Ku-Klux. Some of my neighbors then got to talking with me about it. I told them that they ought not to go about in disguise, whipping colored people—that it was just because of their politics—to intimidate them. They said I had better not talk against them, they would Ku-Klux me. I told them I did not think they would. Well, it went on for some time; some four or five colored men who had been whipped came to me about it. I told them if any of these Ku-Klux came to their house again that they should take a gun and shoot them. . . .

Report on the Alleged Outrages in the Southern States, By the Select Committee of the Senate (Washington, D.C.: Government Printing Office, 1871), pp. 415–416.

A few months before this time I had been attacked and knocked off my horse in the road by some of them, and beaten very badly. My son then bought a pistol and wanted me to carry it to protect myself. I told him I never intended to kill any body and I did not want to carry any arms. My son said, "Pa, if you don't shoot some of them I don't want to call you my father."

Well, so I carried the pistol two or three months. I was away from home most of the time and that was the reason, I suppose, they did not come to my house for me. One Saturday night I returned. While I was at supper my negro man came and told me that the Ku-Klux had told a man who had been whipped that week that they would be at my house one of these nights; I said I did not think they would come, but anyhow I made preparations. My son got a carbine that I had and put it in the bed behind him up stairs; I took the revolver and laid it on my bureau close by my bed; about midnight I heard the dogs rushing out on the piazza; I pulled the curtain one side and saw the yard full of Ku-Klux; they flew around the colored men's house; they were all in disguise; I called to my son saying, "They have come!" but he did not hear.

They knocked open the negro men's house, took out both the negro men, and then came into my house; I ran out of my bed-room up stairs and concealed myself in a loft, taking my pistol with me and an ax, thinking that if they came up there I could knock them down with the ax; I did not want to fight but thought I would go where I would be safe in killing them if they came up after me; I staid there a little while, and they did not come up; then I went into a concealed place with my pistol; they hunted all over the house and could not find me; at first when they came into the house they asked my wife where I was; she said she did not know. One of the men at first spoke in a disguised voice, but when he got excited I recognized his voice; he said to my wife, "I know better; you do know where he is." Then I knew who it was from the voice.

Finally they found me; they put a candle in the place where I was hid, and saw me; I snapped my pistol at the one who got just inside and told me to come out. I asked them what they wanted; they said, "Come out; we want to talk to you." Said I, "You can talk to me where you are." They said, "No; you come out!" and with that one of them jumped into the place, and as he did so I snapped the pistol at him; then they put in one of the negro boys, and I snapped at him; he says, "Andy, for God's sake, don't shoot me!" Says I, "Is that you, Rob?" Says he, "Yes; you may as well give up." "Oh," says I, "I don't intend to give up." With that they shoved the other negro man in toward me and told them to bring me out, and told me to give up my pistol; I said, "No, I do not intend to give up." "Oh yes," says one of them, "they have only threatened you and Rob, and to save my life do give up." Then they hallood out that they would burn the house.

I snapped the pistol the third time, and one of them stuck his hand in the hole and shot toward me; it missed both boys and went through the roof; with that I became alarmed. I thought I had better give up to save the house with my family, so I gave up the pistol and came out. Then they carried me down into my room; there I caught by the bedstead, but they wrenched me loose, and took me out into the yard. There they surrounded me, and, with their pistols pointed at me, told me to pull off my shirt. I had only my drawers and shirt on. There were some twenty or twenty-five around me.

Says I, "If I have got to die I will as soon die with my shirt on as off." Then one of them caught me by the shirt collar and tore it loose, and with that they pulled off my shirt; as soon as that was off three of them jumped at me, and began to cut me with hickories. They gave me some thirty-five or forty licks—I do not know how many—with long, thin hickory withes. I screamed. My daughter, twelve years old, rushed out and caught around my neck, and they stopped the whipping. One of them made a motion and they quit. One of them then whispered to me, "Just you vote the conservative ticket, and you are all right." Says I,

"God only knows who I will vote for." I do not know what they were whipping me for only that I am a republican. "Yes," they said, "You have so many niggers about you; don't you know they are breaking you up?" Says I, "They are not doing me much good, but they have got to have homes." Says they, "You put away these niggers off the plantation, and quit your damned radical principles."

Then they let me go to the house, with my son and daughter, and as I went up into the house there was a crowd coming out of it. They had searched for arms in my bureaus and they took all my ammunition and some other things. An old pair of revolutionary pistols they destroyed, but they were of no account any more. They then disperesd and went away. I could not identify any one of them from sight.

1. Why did the Klan attack Ramsour? What do you think was the underlying cause for the attack?

2. Was Ramsour wise in acting the way he did? What alternatives did he have? What would you have recommended he do?

3. Why do you think many people went along with the Klan?

4. What do you think the Klan most valued about southern society? What did Ramsour most value?

5. How could this case be explained as a clash between social customs and laws?

6. Assume you were a U.S. Senator hearing this testimony. What recommendations would you make for new laws or changes in laws?

APPENDIX **C**

Feedback Form

Your comments about this book will be very helpful to us in planning other books in the Guidebook for Teaching Series and in making revisions in *A Guidebook for Teaching U.S. History: Earliest Times to the Civil War*. Please tear out the form that appears on the following page and use it to let us know your reactions to *A Guidebook for Teaching U.S. History: Earliest Times to the Civil War*. Mail the form to:

Mr. Tedd Levy and Ms. Donna Collins Krasnow
c/o Longwood Division
Allyn and Bacon, Inc.
470 Atlantic Avenue
Boston, Massachusetts 02210

Your school:

Address:

City and state:

Date:

Mr. Tedd Levy and
Ms. Donna Collins Krasnow
c/o Longwood Division
Allyn and Bacon, Inc.
470 Atlantic Avenue
Boston, Massachusetts 02210

Dear Tedd and Donna:

My name is   and I wanted to
tell you what I thought of your book *A Guidebook for Teaching U.S. History: Earliest Times to the Civil War.* I liked certain things about the book, including:

I do, however, feel that the book could be improved in the following ways:

There were some other things that I wish the book had included, such as:

Here is something that happened in my class when I used an idea from your book:

Sincerely,